The Italian Boy

The Italian Boy

A TALE *of* MURDER

and BODY SNATCHING

in 1830s LONDON

Sarah Wise

Metropolitan Books

Henry Holt and Company, New York

Metropolitan Books
Henry Holt and Company, LLC
Publishers since 1866
115 West 18th Street
New York, New York 10011

Metropolitan Books™ is a registered
trademark of Henry Holt and Company, LLC.

Library of Congress Cataloging-in-Publication Data

Wise, Sarah.
  The Italian boy : a tale of murder and body snatching in 1830s London / Sarah
Wise.—1st ed.
    p.   cm.
  Includes bibliographical references and index.
  ISBN 0-8050-7537-2
    1. Murder—England—London—Case studies. 2. Poor—England—London—
History—19th century. 3. Body snatching—England—London—History—19th
century. 4. London (England)—Social conditions—19th century. I. Title.
HV6535.G6L6595 2004
364.152'3'09421—dc22   2003068559

First Edition 2004
Printed in the United States of America

1   3   5   7   9   10   8   6   4   2

For Peter

Of the common folk that is merely bundled up in turf and brambles, the less said, the better. A poor lot, soon forgot.

—Stony Durdles,
funerary stonemason, in Charles Dickens's
The Mystery of Edwin Drood (1870)

Contents

Preface

Toward the end of 1831, London's Metropolitan Police were alerted to a ghastly series of crimes. They appeared to be imitations of the notorious Burke and Hare killings in Edinburgh three years earlier, in which at least sixteen people were murdered and their bodies sold for medical dissection. I first came across the London killings—or the "Italian Boy" case, as it was known—in the course of writing a newspaper article about an East End council housing estate in Bethnal Green that had been built on the site of one of the nineteenth century's most notorious slums. It was said that the surrounding district had been tainted for decades by the grisly crimes committed in Nova Scotia Gardens, a neighborhood of tiny, odd-looking cottages that had probably been built as homes-cum-workshops for weavers, of whom there were some fifteen thousand in the area at the start of the nineteenth century. And indeed, on investigation I learned that in the late autumn of 1831, No. 3 Nova Scotia Gardens had had infamy thrust upon it by its residents, John Bishop and Thomas Williams, and an associate, James May—all of them body snatchers, or "resurrection men," who were charged with murdering a vagrant child.

The "London Burkers" have been eclipsed by their Edinburgh counterparts, whose story has inspired many retellings and film and stage interpretations; but in fact it was the London case, not Burke and Hare, that sped the passage of controversial legislation to make the unclaimed bodies of paupers legally available to surgeons for dissection. The Anatomy Act was passed by Parliament within ten months of the investigation into the events at Nova Scotia Gardens, heralding the beginning of the end of body snatching in Britain. But the case also revealed some extremely unpleasant aspects of life in London—a city that had increased by one-third between 1801 and 1831 to over one and a half million inhabitants, the most diverse population anywhere on earth.

The Italian Boy case occurred on one of recent history's fault lines: the Regency was over—those years of roistering dandies and beaux, of newly gaslit streets and shopping arcades, and the heroics of the Napoleonic Wars, but also of political oppression and economic collapse, of sclerotic institutions unable to adapt to the new industrial age, of the Bloody Code and its vicious punishments for petty crimes, and of a rigid governing elite determined to avoid the violent fate of France's ancien régime. Victoria was yet to ascend the throne, and her new age of moral certainty and love of order—the era when statistics, bureaucracy, a highly professionalized civil service, and legal and medical elites came to dominate—was not in place. Not yet. Not quite. William IV ruled from 1830 to 1837—a short reign, but a mighty turbulent one for all that. There is no mistaking the flavor, the mood, of the late 1820s and early 1830s in the writings that have survived. Everywhere is heard an insistent call for more fundamental and faster change in every aspect of British life: Parliament, the judiciary, the church, medicine, jails, schools, public and private manners and mores, architecture, city planning—all were loudly condemned as outmoded, inefficient, unworkable, "old." Britain was seen as tottering on the edge of collapse because it could not embrace and implement change.

In this Era without a Name, the Reform Act of 1832 would see the middle classes begin to wrest power from the aristocracy and the church, and the newly enfranchised tradesmen, industrialists, and administrators strive to separate themselves from the poor. But if the common man—laborer, artisan, or pauper—had expected to benefit from the advance of democracy, he was to be badly disappointed. The 1832 act gave the vote to just one-seventh of the adult male population; the Poor Law Amendment Act of 1834 would see those who sought parish relief incarcerated in institutions that were prisons in all but name, while the living conditions of "the submerged tenth" (the phrase belongs to William Booth, founder of the Salvation Army, writing in 1890) were to remain a source of shame and disgrace to the richest nation on earth for the rest of the century.

Following the Italian Boy case in the newspapers of the day, I became curious about the type of people who had fallen into the path of the accused on their nightly prowls around the metropolis. What sort of city was London in 1831—what sort of country was England?— that children and young adults could seemingly be picked off by anyone who chose to prey on their fellow man: burkers, brothel keepers, Fagin-style procurers of pickpockets, sex offenders, press-gangs. What sort of people could simply disappear unnoticed from the city's streets? Why, even in death, did their identities remain mysterious? How much of the history of the very poor—the destitute—has come down to us? What sorts of evidence could be trusted to give a reliable picture of their lives? What did they think of themselves?

The Italian Boy case also seemed to provide a rich archival source for learning how *non*destitute, ordinary lower-class Londoners perceived themselves, as well as those both poorer and wealthier than them, and for examining their notions of community and criminality in this strange new society that was forming in their city. The story appeared to me to be a window on the lives of the poor at a period of great change: a window that is badly damaged—opaque in places, blacked out or shattered in others—but offers a rare glimpse of those who have left little authentic trace of themselves.

Before the advent of oral history, the poor were able to tell us little about themselves directly; the very poor could tell us even less. The material remnants of their lives have largely disintegrated— the coarse paper of the broadsheets they read, the hovels they lived in—while most of their songs, stories, and sayings have passed unrecorded. The very poor are persons unknown—an enigma for the social historian, a deafening silence that roars down the centuries. Those working-class people in the 1820s and 1830s who were literate (around half of poor Londoners were) had, ordinarily, scant access to writing materials and publishers or printers, still less time to write. Committing thoughts and feelings to paper—making oneself the object of investigation and discussion—is a strange act for anyone to undertake, all the more bizarre if you have little time and money. And while a number of British working-class autobiographies have been discovered by historians, these were almost all written in later years by people who had been able to change their social status or who had become part of a larger force—labor unions or religious societies—with which their sense of self and personal history had merged.

What we know of the lives of the very poor in the first half of the nineteenth century is thus mediated by those outside their culture; we hear their stories filtered through people who, with the most sympathetic of hearts and imaginative of minds, were nevertheless strangers traveling in a strange land—even William Cobbett, even Thomas De Quincey, even Henry Mayhew. I have had to rely on such sources far more than I would have liked. The journalist, the magistrate, the prison official, the Parliamentary Select Committee member, the charity official all allow us to see the very poor over their shoulders; but they edit, paraphrase, pass comment on, and even overtly criticize the object of their interest. Despite these reservations, I still believe the greatest commentator on the London very poor remains Charles Dickens, who was able to draw on personal experience when he wrote *Oliver Twist* in 1837–38. As a twelve-year-old left to fend for himself in central London, he had felt himself in danger of falling into destitution; he had observed the vagrant young of Covent Garden at first hand, and with his creation of Jo, the street-crossing sweeper in *Bleak House* (1852–53), he managed to climb inside the mind of one of the hordes of urban outcast children. For this reason, Dickens weaves in and out of the following pages.

Researching this book took me down many blind alleys as I tried to piece together the criminal careers of John Bishop, Thomas Williams, James May, and other London body snatchers. Official records were not obliged to be kept of cases heard in magistrates' courts (which is where anyone arrested for possession of an illegally disinterred body would be examined), and justices of the peace habitually failed to supply the higher courts with written details of those they had convicted—an oversight that was as infuriating to the Home Office of the day as it is to the modern historian. Body-snatching cases did make it into the national newspapers, but the coverage of the hearings is uneven at best; worse still, most snatchers had aliases—some of them had several—and it was not always clear who, exactly, was on trial. (To compound the researcher's problem, the 1820s and 1830s registers of the London jails where snatchers were confined if convicted—primarily Coldbath Fields Prison and Clerkenwell New Prison—have not, for the most part, survived.) In an age when guilt was often established by eyewitness evidence, and sentences decided on the notion of good or bad repute, it was in the criminal's interest to keep his or her identity as fluid as possible. As one penal reform campaigner wrote in despair: "No man goes into Newgate twice with the same name, trade, or place of nativity." So Bishop, Williams, and May may well be lurking in the records under assumed names.

Several other things spoke out from the archive sources: the deference shown by many in the case toward the judiciary and other authority figures; the central role of drink in the lives of the protagonists; the increasing tendency in the city toward the identification of its citizens—badges and uniforms, registers, licenses, and permits were all coming into place or were expected soon; allied to this, the growing urge to tie things down, to lash people to their "proper" place and put a stop to urban nomadism; and finally, the sense that, in these years before the laying of London's great drains, people were living in a giant cesspit—picking their way between fecal matter and pools of urine. Physically this was a city quite different from today's capital; many of the most famous structures and the broadest, most traveled roads had yet to be constructed; populous, densely built areas were yet to be razed. To those in authority in 1831, London's topography—its sinuous streets and unlit warrens—connived at criminality: there were frequent calls for the lanes and alleys to be illuminated, straightened out, or flattened altogether. Nova Scotia Gardens itself was so obscure a destination its name never appeared on any map. The Italian Boy case reminded city dwellers, rich and poor, that at the heart of London—a city that felt itself to be on the brink of reform and "modernization"—lay unknown, unknowable mysteries.

Notes for Non-Londoners

The action in this book took place in a number of central London districts, all within a radius of two miles of the area known as the City. Also known as the Square Mile, the City was and remains an administrative enclave within Greater London. It abuts the poor East End district of Whitechapel; to the west it is bordered by Holborn, to the north by St. Luke's, Old Street, and to the south by the river Thames.

Covent Garden, lying west of the City, was a half-poor, half-prosperous area between the Strand and the dreadful slum area of St. Giles.

Just to the northeast of Covent Garden, Holborn was an area of similarly mixed levels of prosperity, and parts of it were called "Little Italy" because of the many Italian immigrants who settled there.

Although both Covent Garden and Holborn are to the west of the City, neither counts as the West End, which is the term applied to the wealthier areas slightly farther west, such as Regent Street, Oxford Street, Hanover Square, and Mayfair.

Smithfield is just inside the City border, at its western edge; it was notorious for the filth, noise, and commotion caused by its famous live-meat market.

Bethnal Green in 1831 was a desperately poor working-class area to the northeast of the City.

Spitalfields, Whitechapel, and Shoreditch, which were once equally poor eastern districts, lie to the south of Bethnal Green.

The Elephant and Castle, another area that, like Covent Garden, contained a population with mixed fortunes, is one mile south of the Thames.

The Borough—site of the United Hospitals of St. Thomas's and Guy's, plus the Webb Street private anatomical school—is just over London Bridge on the south bank of the Thames.

Currency Conversion

One guinea	=21 shillings	=252 pennies (d)
One pound	=20 shillings	=240d
One crown	=5 shillings	=60d
Half a crown	=2 shillings and 6d	=30d
One florin/guilder	=2 shillings	=24d
One shilling (bob)		=12d
One farthing		=¼d

London Prices, Early 1830s

Hackney cab fare, Old Bailey to Shoreditch Church (1½ miles)	2 shillings
Glass/pint of Blue Ruin gin	3d/1 shilling
Glass/pint of cheap gin	2d/10d
A quarter loaf of bread	9d
A pint of porter	2d
10 lbs. potatoes	4d
Charles Dickens's weekly factory wage as a twelve-year-old in 1824	6–7 shillings (15–16 guineas/year)
Weekly wage of an East End silk weaver in 1831 (twelve-hour day)	5–7 shillings (12–16 guineas/year)
A well-paid workingman's yearly salary	75–80 guineas
A well-paid manservant's weekly salary	1 guinea (50–55 guineas/year)
Starting weekly salary for New Police constables	1 guinea (50–55 guineas/year)
Average cost of an Old Bailey prosecution	£3 10s
Average cost of a fresh corpse in 1831	8–12 guineas

The Italian Boy

Suspiciously Fresh

George Beaman, surgeon to the parish of St. Paul's, Covent Garden, turned back the scalp of the corpse lying before him. Beneath the skin he observed coagulated blood, and, peeling away the flesh along the length of the neck, he saw similar minor hemorrhages at the top of the spinal column. He concluded that death had been caused by a sharp blow to the back of the neck.

The body was that of a boy of around fourteen years of age, four feet six inches in height, with fair hair and gray eyes that were blood-shot and bulging. Blood oozed from an inch-long wound on his left temple, and his toothless gums were dripping blood. At the time of his killing, a meal—which had included potatoes and a quantity of rum—was being digested. A large, powerful hand had grasped the boy on his left forearm—black bruises from the finger marks were plainly visible—and earth or clay had been smeared across the torso and thighs. The chest appeared to have caved in slightly, as though someone had knelt on it. The heart contained scarcely any blood, which Beaman took to indicate a very sudden death, but all the other organs were found to have been unremarkable and perfectly healthy.

The most perplexing thing about the corpse was its freshness: it had
been alive three days earlier, Beaman felt sure; and it was also clear to
the surgeon that despite the bits of earth and clay, this body had never
been buried, had never even been laid out in preparation for burial—
and yet it had been delivered to King's College's anatomy department
as a Subject for medical students to dissect.

It was late evening, Sunday, 6 November 1831, and Beaman was
anatomizing the corpse in the tiny watch house in the graveyard of St.
Paul's Church, Covent Garden, at the request of local magistrates.
He and a number of fellow surgeons had been probing and exploring
the body in the first-floor room since early afternoon. A sunny winter's
day had turned into a chilly evening by the time the medical men had
made up their mind about the cause of death. As Beaman and his colleagues left, two young trainees, by now feeling faint with tiredness
and nausea, stayed in the cold, stuffy room to sew up the corpse.
Working alongside Beaman had been Herbert Mayo and Richard Partridge, respectively professor and "demonstrator," or lecturer, of
anatomy at King's College, just a few streets away in the Strand. The
day before, Partridge had sent for the police when one of the body-
snatching gangs that supplied disinterred corpses to medical schools
had tipped this body out of a sack and onto the stone floor of the dissecting room at King's. It had looked suspiciously fresh. Partridge
tricked the body snatchers into waiting at King's while police officers
were summoned, and at three o'clock in the afternoon, John Bishop,
James May, and Thomas Williams were arrested on suspicion of murder, along with Michael Shields, a porter who had carried the body.

Earlier that day, worried parents of missing sons had been admitted
to the watch house to view the body, having read a description of the
boy circulated in police handbills and notices posted on walls, doors,
and windows throughout the parish. Among the visitors had been several Italians. Signor Francis Bernasconi of Great Russell Street,
Covent Garden, "plasterer to His Majesty," had wondered whether
the deceased was a boy from Genoa who had made his living as an
"image boy"—hawking wax or plaster busts of the great and the good,
past and present, about the streets of London. Bernasconi was a plas-

ter figurine maker, or *figurinaio,* and he employed a number of Italian child immigrants to advertise and sell his wares in this way. Another figurinaio said that the dead boy had sometimes helped paint the plaster figures and that his "master" had left England at the end of September. The minister at the Italian Chapel in Oxenden Street, off the Haymarket, claimed that the boy had been a member of his congregation but was unable to name him. Two more Italians identified the dead boy as an Italian beggar who walked the streets carrying a tortoise that he exhibited in the hope of receiving a few pennies, while Joseph and Mary Paragalli of Parker Street, Covent Garden, said the boy was an Italian who wandered the West End exhibiting white mice in a cage suspended around his neck. (Joseph was a street musician, playing barrel organ and panpipes.) The Paragallis had known the child for about a year, they said, but neither of them suggested a name for him. Mary Paragalli claimed she had last seen him alive shortly after noon on Tuesday, 1 November, in Oxford Street, near Hanover Square.

Charles Starbuck, a stockbroker, came forward to tell the Bow Street police officers that he believed the boy was an Italian beggar who was often to be seen near the Bank of England exhibiting white mice in a cage; Starbuck had viewed the body and was in "no doubt" about its being the same child. He had seen the boy looking tired and ill, sitting with his head sunk almost to his lap, on the evening of Thursday, 3 November, between half past six and eight o'clock. Starbuck was walking with his brother near the Bank and said, "I think he is unwell," but his brother replied, "I think he's a humbug. I've often seen him in that position." A crowd gathered round, concerned at the boy's condition, and one youth told the boy he ought to move on as police officers were heading that way. The Starbucks walked on. But on Wednesday the ninth, three days after viewing the body, Charles Starbuck wrote to the coroner to say that he had subsequently seen this boy near the Bank, and retracted his identification.

The newspapers seized on the possible Italian connection remarkably swiftly. As the coroner's hearing began on 8 November, the *Times* referred to the proceedings as "The Inquest on the Italian Boy," when no such identity had been confirmed. In fact, the *Times* reporter seems to have been quite carried away with emotion by the death of

VERY FINE VERY CHEAP

London Published as the Act directs December 31 1815
by John Thomas Smith, N 4 Chandos Street Covent Garden.

An Italian boy, or image boy, from J. T. Smith's Etchings of
Remarkable Beggars, *1815*

"the poor little fellow who used to go about the streets hugging a live
tortoise, and soliciting, with a smiling countenance, in broken English
and Italian, a few coppers for the use of himself and his dumb friend."
The report continued: "We saw the body last night, and were struck
with its fine healthy appearance. . . . The countenance of the boy does
not exhibit the least contortion, but, on the contrary, wears the repose

of sleep, and the same open and good-humoured expression which marked the features in life is still discernible."[1] This was a fantastical statement, since only someone able to give a positive identification could possibly know how the child had looked when alive. The following day, the *Times* thundered, in an extraordinary editorial: "If it shall be proved that he was murdered, for the purpose of deriving a horrible livelihood from the disposal of his body—if wretches have picked up from our streets an unprotected foreign child, and prepared him for the dissecting knife by assassination—if they have prowled about in order to obtain Subjects for a dissecting-room—then we may be assured that this is not a solitary crime of its kind."

In such a way, rumor was being reported as fact—a matter that was not lost on the coroner's jury. "We are proceeding in the dark," complained a member of the jury. The hearing was under way at the Unicorn, a public house in Covent Garden that backed onto St. Paul's watch house. It appeared to the jury that no one in authority was able to rebut or confirm the various speculations about the identity of the dead boy. How, the jury asked, can we be expected to arrive at a verdict when we don't even know who has died? And to make matters worse, as soon as any goings-on at hospitals were mentioned or any surgeon looked likely to be named, the coroner and the parish clerk of St. Paul's would go into a huddle to discuss whether the inquest should continue or be adjourned.

The jury's exasperation compelled vestry clerk James Corder, who was overseeing the proceedings, to state that he understood "from inquiries he had made" that the dead boy was called Giacomo Montero, a beggar who had been brought to London a year earlier by an Italian named Pietro Massa, who lived in Liquorpond Street, in the area of Holborn known colloquially as Little Italy.[2] But here Joseph Paragalli spoke up to say that he himself had made his own inquiries at the Home Office's "Alien Office," near Whitehall, and that the description held there of Montero did not fit the dead boy in the least. Perhaps then, said Corder, the boy had been Giovanni Balavez-zolo, another Italian vagrant boy who was said to be missing from his usual haunts. To solve the problem, Corder suggested the jury simply return a verdict of willful murder against some person or persons unknown. The jury remained unconvinced.

The Watch House, Covent Garden, circa 1830; St. Paul's Church is to the right in the picture, the Unicorn tavern to the left, and an Italian boy can be seen just to the right of the arch.

It was only at this awkward point for Corder that the prisoners were summoned from their underground cells in the St. Paul's, Covent Garden watch house (the building was at that time being used as a temporary jail/police office; it was originally built as a place of surveillance, from which the graveyard could be guarded against snatchers and other trespassers) to give their account of how they had come into possession of the boy's body. They entered the crowded room at the Unicorn to be viewed by a fascinated public; the memory of the crimes committed by William Burke and William Hare in Edinburgh just three years earlier was fresh. Had similar events been occurring in the English capital? And what would these monsters look like? The answer: very ordinary indeed, your common or garden Londoner. John Bishop was thirty-three, stocky, slightly sullen-looking, but with a mild enough expression; he had a long, slender, pointed nose, high cheekbones, large, slightly protruding gray-green eyes, and thick, dark hair that continued down into bushy muttonchop sideburns that covered a good deal of his cheeks. James May, thirty, was tall and handsome, with a mop of unruly fair hair and dark, glittering eyes; he looked pleasant enough. Like Bishop, he was still wearing his smock frock—the typical garment of a rural laborer—in which he had been arrested, which perhaps made him seem even more guileless; his left hand was bandaged. Thomas Williams, in his late twenties, was shorter than the other two, with deep-set hazel eyes and narrow lips that gave him a slightly cunning appearance, but mischievous rather than malevolent; his hair was mousy, his face pale, and he could have passed for someone much younger. Michael Shields just looked like a frightened old man.

The accounts of Bishop, May, and Williams of the events of Friday, 4 November, and Saturday, 5 November, given at the coroner's inquest and at hearings yet to come, differed remarkably little from those offered by the various eyewitnesses also called to testify. There were a few discrepancies, but these would appear small and insignificant. The following train of events, at least, was not in dispute.

John Bishop and Thomas Williams awoke in No. 3 Nova Scotia Gardens, the cottage they shared in Bethnal Green, at about ten o'clock on Friday morning, breakfasted with their wives and the Bishops' three children, and set off for the Fortune of War pub in Giltspur Street, Smithfield—opposite St. Bartholomew's Hospital, and a regular meeting place for London's resurrection men. Here, they began their day's drinking and met up with James May. May had known Bishop for four or five years and was introduced to Williams, whom May knew only by sight, having seen him in the various pubs around the Old Bailey and Smithfield. The three men drank rum together

and ate some lunch. May admired a smock frock that Bishop was
wearing and asked him where he could buy a similar one. Bishop
took May a few streets away, to Field Lane, one of the districts given
over to London's secondhand clothes trade. Field Lane was also
known colloquially as Food and Raiment Alley, Thieving Lane, and
Sheeps' Head Alley, and Charles Dickens was to add to its notoriety
six years later by siting one of Fagin's dens there, in *Oliver Twist*. A
steep, narrow passage, Field Lane comprised Jacobean, Stuart, and
early Georgian tenements that were largely forbidding, rotting hovels; those on its east side backed on the Fleet River—often called
the Fleet Ditch, since it was by 1831 almost motionless with solidi-
fying filth, though when it flooded, its level could rise by six or seven
feet, deluging the surrounding area with its detritus. By weird contrast, the windows in Field Lane were a dazzling display of brightly
colored silk handkerchiefs ("wipes"); if the commentators of the day
are to be believed, the vast majority of these were stolen by gangs of
young—often extremely young—"snotter-haulers," who would soon
be incarnated in the popular imagination as the Artful Dodger
(though Dickens used the more polite slang term, "fogle-hunters").
Here, in Field Lane, James May bought a smock frock from a clothes
dealer, then decided he wanted a pair of trousers, too, and turned
the corner into West Street, where he attempted to bargain with the
female owner of another castoffs shop.[3] Already pretty drunk, May
was unable to agree on a price with the woman but, feeling guilty at
having wasted her time, insisted on buying her some rum, which the
three enjoyed together in the shop. May and Bishop then went back
to the Fortune of War to have more drink with Williams, before
Bishop and Williams set off for the West End, to try to sell the
corpse of an adolescent boy lying trussed up in a trunk in the wash-
house of 3 Nova Scotia Gardens.

Their first call was made at Edward Tuson's private medical
school in Little Windmill Street, off Tottenham Court Road, where
Tuson said he had waited so long for Bishop to come up with a
"Thing" that he had bought one from another resurrection gang the
day before. So they walked a few streets south to Joseph Carpue's
school on Dean Street in Soho. Carpue spoke to the pair in his lecture theater with several students present who wanted to know how

BISHOP.   WILLIAMS.   MAY.

THE MURDERERS OF THE ITALIAN BOY.

London : Published by SEARS, Charterhouse Square.

John Bishop, James May, and Thomas Williams as they appeared to two court sketch artists. While Bishop's appearance changes comparatively little from sketch to sketch, depictions of May and Williams vary dramatically and in fact the sketch above has mislabeled May and Williams in its caption.

*Field Lane, one of the districts of London where secondhand clothing
was bought and sold*

fresh the Thing was. Carpue offered to pay eight guineas and Bishop
agreed to this price, promising to deliver the boy the next morning at
ten o'clock.

Bishop and Williams got back to the Fortune of War at a quarter
to four and shared some more drink there with May. Bishop now

began to wonder whether he could get more than the eight guineas Carpue had offered—the boy was extremely fresh, after all. Bishop called May out onto the street to ask him—away from the ears of other resurrectionists—what sort of money he was achieving for Things. May told Bishop that he had sold two corpses at Guy's Hospital for ten guineas each just the day before and that he would never accept as little as eight guineas for a young, healthy male. Bishop told May that if he were able to help sell the body for a higher price, May could keep anything they earned over nine guineas. They went back into the Fortune of War for a round to seal the bargain and then, leaving Williams drinking, set off to procure a coach and driver in order to collect the body.

This was not easy. At around a quarter past five, as dusk was falling, they approached hackney-coach-driver Henry Mann in New Bridge Street, but Mann refused to take them because, as he later said, "I knew what May was"; he hadn't spotted Bishop, who was standing behind his cab in the increasing gloom.

They next tried James Seagrave, who, having given his horse a nose bag of corn, was taking tea in the King of Denmark, just south of the Fortune of War. Bishop and May asked Thomas Tavernor, who helped out at the nearby cabstand, to call Seagrave out to the street. Seagrave came out, and May, leaning against the wheel of a nearby cart, asked if he would be willing to do a job for them. Seagrave, suspicious, replied that there were a great many jobs, long ones and short ones—what kind did they mean? May said it was to be "a long job" carrying "a stiff 'un," for which trip they would "stand" one guinea. The driver was intrigued and allowed May to buy him tea in the King of Denmark to discuss the journey but also to find out more about the resurrection world. Seagrave had no intention of letting them hire him, intending to "do them," as he later told the coroner's court.

The King of Denmark combined the operations of inn, teahouse for cab and coach drivers, and booking office for errand carts. (It was also the best spot in London for watching public hangings, since it stood immediately opposite Newgate's Debtors Door, where the scaffold was erected on execution days.) Inside, closely observed by a barman, May, Bishop, and Seagrave sat down

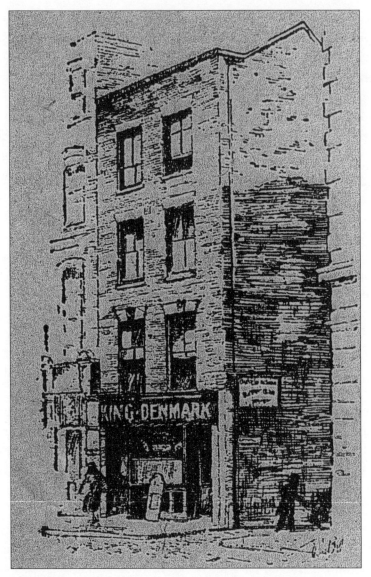

The King of Denmark pub in the Old Bailey, opposite Newgate's Debtors Door

to talk. During their discussion, May poured gin into Bishop's tea from a pint bottle and Bishop protested, laughing, "Do you mean to hocus or burke me?" Seagrave did not know what this meant.[4] A man sitting close by nudged Seagrave and muttered to him that Bishop and May were well-known snatchers. His curiosity about them satisfied, Seagrave went out into the street while Bishop and May's attention was distracted and drove off. "It won't do," he muttered to Tavernor on his way out. "They want me to carry a stiff 'un." As he pulled away, he looked back and spotted Bishop and May walking up and down the Old Bailey cab rank, trying to hire a driver. No one would take them.

They had better luck in nearby Farringdon Street, where they found someone willing to drive them to Bethnal Green and then south of the river to the Borough for ten shillings—more than double the going rate for such a journey. But there was yet more drinking to fit in first, and Bishop and May took the driver to the George pub in the Old Bailey (where Williams had arranged to meet them) and then on to the Fortune of War for another round, before the trip to Nova Scotia Gardens.

They arrived at the Gardens at around half past six, observed by several neighbors: the doors of their hired vehicle were bright yellow, and it was a "chariot"—a grander version of the hackney coach. Bishop and May jumped out and went up the path that led to No. 3, leaving Williams chatting with the driver; the chariot door was left wide open. They were watched by George Gissing, the twelve-year-old son of the owner of the Birdcage pub, which stood opposite the Gardens (and still does). Gissing, from the doorway of the Birdcage, had a good view of the men. He recognized both Bishop and Williams, though not May; he saw that Bishop and May were in smock frocks and that May was smoking a pipe. Another youth, Thomas Trader, observed the three men too, recognizing Bishop and Williams, as did a local girl, Ann Cannell. Cannell's mother passed by and started to watch as well, saying to Trader, "This looks strange. See where they are going so quick." But Trader replied, "I'm sure I won't go after them. If I did, they wouldn't mind giving me a topper" (boxing slang for a violent punch).[5] But the boy did try to note the license number of the chariot, though it was obscured by the open door and he gave up when he saw the driver staring at him. After ten minutes or so, Williams went down the path to the cottage and shortly afterward returned with Bishop and May. May was carrying a sack and Bishop was helping to hold it up. They placed it in the chariot, all three men got in, and they drove off.

At seven o'clock, the chariot arrived at the main gate at Guy's Hospital, where Bishop and May were allowed in by the porter of the main gate, John Chapman, Williams staying outside in the chariot. Chapman noticed that the sack—carried by Bishop—appeared to contain something heavy. He showed Bishop and May through to James Davis, the porter of the medical school's dissecting room. Davis noted that a human foot was protruding from the sack and concluded from its size that the corpse of a woman or boy was inside; but Davis was in no need of a Subject since he had bought two corpses from May just the day before. Bishop asked if he could leave the Thing there until the next morning and Davis agreed, locking it in a small chamber off the dissecting room. Bishop took Davis's assistant, James Weeks, aside to tell him not to allow the body to be removed unless he, Bishop, was present; overhearing him, May took James Davis aside to say that, although the Thing belonged to Bishop, it should not be handed over to him without May's being present, otherwise May would end up out of pocket. May had bought all the drinks that day, including James Seagrave's in the King of Denmark, and he had also agreed to pay the cab fares.

Before discharging their driver, May and Bishop dashed to Richard Grainger's private anatomical school in nearby Webb Street and tried to make a sale of the Thing—telling the porter there that it was "a rare fresh Subject"—but without success. Then they rejoined Williams, May paid the driver his ten shillings, and the three went to a nearby pub before hiring another coach to take them back to the Fortune of War for more drink.

Thomas Wigley, a porter at the Cross Keys Inn in Cheapside, was a regular drinker at the Fortune of War. He watched as Bishop entered the pub at about half past seven, followed a short while later by May. Wigley had been at the pub since about half past six, sitting in a corner of the taproom drinking beer. He knew both Bishop and May by sight, but not to speak to. Bishop came and sat down next to Wigley, and May sat opposite Bishop—both with a glass of "rum-hot."[6] Wigley heard Bishop say to May, "What do you think of our new one? Didn't he go up to him well? I told you he was a stanch one—don't you think he's a stanch one now? Do you stick by me and

I will stick to you. I know the other one is all right, he's nothing but a good one."*

About an hour later, Williams came into the pub. As he entered, Bishop said to May, "There he is. I knew he would come. I knew he was a game one," to which May replied, "I don't know what you mean." Bishop said, "That's all right then."[7] Bishop, who appeared to Wigley to be more drunk than either May or Williams, then said, "You know what I mean," and May replied, "I am going home." Bishop said, "We are all going the same road," to which May said, "I shall stop a bit," and picked up a newspaper and began to read as Bishop and Williams walked out. It's likely that Bishop and Williams did not leave the Fortune of War at this point but simply left the taproom of the pub, which appears to have been a separate area, since May did share part of the journey home with Bishop and Williams.

Later in the evening, shortly before nine o'clock, May went up to the bar of the Fortune of War, poured some water over something he was holding in a handkerchief, and began rubbing it. Henry Lock, the barman, took a look and saw that May was cleaning blood and flesh from a set of human teeth. Lock remarked to May that they looked like the teeth of a young person and would no doubt be worth something, and May boasted that he expected to get two pounds for the set.

Bishop, May, and Williams left the Fortune of War together sometime after nine, stopping off for another drink in Golden Lane, May treating the coachman to a drink too. Farther east, in Old Street, May got out of the coach and said he was going home—home was south of the river—handing over a loan of three shillings to Bishop and three to Williams. The men agreed to meet up the next morning at Guy's Hospital and parted ways. Bishop and Williams took the coach on to the corner of Union Street and Kingsland Road in Bethnal Green, paid the driver, and walked the rest of the way home—not a great distance, but it is possible Bishop and Williams did not want

---

* "Stanch" or "staunch" meant trustworthy, loyal. It had a secondary meaning: close, private, tight-lipped, and it could be that Bishop was indicating Williams's ability to be discreet—essential for successful body snatching.

their address to be known to the coachman, who may well have deduced how they made their living. There's another, more mundane explanation: they may have been attempting to save a few pennies; while the fare from Old Bailey to Kingsland Road was two shillings, to proceed any farther east would have pushed it up to three.[8]

James May, meanwhile, was meeting up with one of several sweethearts, Mary Ann Hall, joining her outside the Alfred's Head pub—a large inn that faced the Elephant and Castle—at around half past eleven, before going back to the lodgings they shared nearby.

At around nine o'clock the next morning, James May entered the shop of dentist Thomas Mills in Bridge House Place, not far from May's rooming house. He showed Mills a set of twelve teeth that still had portions of gum attached; a small piece of jawbone clung to the lower set. Mills pointed out that one of the front teeth had a chip in it and did not look as though it belonged with the others, but May swore that all the teeth had been taken from the same mouth and that, furthermore, the body had never been buried. Mills thought they looked like a woman's teeth but May replied, "The fact is, they belonged to a lad about fourteen or fifteen years of age. Upon my soul to God, they all belonged to one head not long since." May said he was looking to receive a guinea, but Mills—though he considered them a fine and fresh set—would pay only twelve shillings.

At around the same hour, Bishop and Williams were at the Fortune of War, hiring Michael Shields, over pints of beer, to carry a heavy load between various hospitals for a fee of half a crown. Shields had known Bishop for eight or nine months; he did not know Williams. Bishop asked Shields to get hold of a hamper, but Shields refused, so Bishop went across the street himself to take a hamper from just inside the gates of St. Bartholomew's Hospital. This was not an act of theft; one of several matters that were to embarrass the medical profession during the hearings was the fact that hospitals would "leave" hampers lying around their precincts where resurrection men could easily pick them up in order to deliver their produce.

Bishop, Williams, and Shields set off for Guy's Hospital—crossing the brand-new London Bridge—where they met May, as arranged. Williams and Shields went to a pub while Bishop and May again unsuccessfully tried to persuade the dissecting-room porters at Guy's and then at Grainger's school to buy the boy. Bishop and May joined Williams and Shields for more drink (May having stopped a passerby and asked, politely, for money for drink, whereupon the stranger handed him six pennies from his purse); then the pair set off to try to strike a bargain at King's College, crossing the Thames by ferry to the imposing new building at the eastern end of Somerset House in the Strand—so new a bricklayer was still at work as they rang the bell of dissecting-room porter William Hill shortly before noon. Hill knew Bishop and May well; they had been among his most prolific suppliers in one of his earlier jobs, at George Dermott's private anatomy school in the West End. They asked Hill whether King's professors and students needed a body. Hill replied, "Not particularly," but asked, "What have you got?" and, on hearing the reply, went to fetch anatomist Richard Partridge to double-check on the medical school's supply. Hill told Bishop and May that there was a good fire blazing in the grate downstairs, why didn't they come down and warm themselves? Richard Partridge entered the room where Bishop and May were warming up and said he didn't need a Thing; but then he took Hill aside and told him to offer nine guineas for the body, which he did. May, visibly drunk, shouted at Hill, "I'll be damned if it should go under ten guineas!" But when May stepped outside to urinate, Bishop murmured to Hill that he would be able to persuade May to accept nine guineas. "He is tipsy," explained Bishop. "I'll bring it in for nine." Then Bishop and May left by cab for the pub near London Bridge where Williams and Shields were still drinking, and the four men had lunches of steaks and beer.

There was a kind of desperation about Bishop's attempts to sell the corpse—this relentless traipsing from school to school and from one side of the river to another as the produce became less and less desirable. He was about to earn only one more guinea than Joseph Carpue had offered the day before, and from that additional guinea, deductions for fares and drink would leave him worse off than if he had delivered to Carpue as arranged. Back at Guy's once more, the four men packed the sacked-up body into the hamper and placed it on the porter's knot on Shields's head. Bishop warned Shields to be

King's College/Somerset House seen from the river; the building, across from the industrial south bank, was accessible by boat.

careful not to stumble and fall; like the others, Shields had been drinking since nine o'clock in the morning. Williams and Shields walked together, Bishop and May following in a cab, though sometimes edging slightly ahead. They reached King's at around a quarter past two. Shields carried the hamper into an anteroom to the anatomy theater and was greeted as an old acquaintance by William Hill, who even mentioned that it had been a while since the two men had met. May clumsily tipped the body out of the sack and onto the floor. While Shields and Williams loitered outside in the courtyard, Bishop and May asked Hill to make out to Williams that just eight guineas was being paid for the body—Bishop and May would split the remaining guinea between them, giving Hill half a crown as reward for his part in the deceit.

Hill noted that the body appeared to be that of a boy between fourteen and sixteen years of age, and unusually fresh; its left arm was awkwardly twisted above its head and the left hand was clenched. Bishop and May told Hill this body was "a good 'un," and Hill agreed that it was. He asked what the child had died of, and May replied,

"I neither know nor care," and Bishop added, "It is quite indifferent what he died of, for here he is, stiff enough."[9] Pointing out a cut on the boy's forehead, Hill was told by Bishop that the wound had just occurred as the body was tipped from the sack. Hill was not convinced, nor did he believe the body had ever been buried, despite the marks of clay on its thighs and torso, which would indicate resurrection.

Hill revealed his suspicions about the state of the body to Richard Partridge, who came downstairs to inspect it. Some of Partridge's pupils came down as well, having read a notice about a London youth of around fourteen who had recently gone missing from his home in Oxford Street. Alarmed by what he saw, Partridge told the resurrectionists that as he had only a fifty-pound note, they should wait at King's while he went to get change with which to pay them. Bishop said he would take what change Partridge had and collect the rest on Monday; May said he would take the fifty-pound note and get it changed himself, at which Partridge smiled strangely and said, "Oh no," and left the room. Twenty minutes later he returned with Police Superintendent Joseph Sadler Thomas and several officers from Division F, Covent Garden's branch of the Metropolitan Police, and the four men were taken into custody, May putting up a violent struggle when one of the constables refused to allow him to speak to Bishop. It took a number of officers to restrain May, and he entered the station house on all fours, with his smock frock over his head.

Superintendent Thomas told May that he was being charged on suspicion of "improper" possession of a Subject. May replied, "The Subject is the property of that gentleman," pointing at Bishop. "I only came with him to get the money." Turning to Bishop, Superintendent Thomas asked how he had come by the body, and Bishop sneered: "If you want to know how I got it, you may find it out, if you can." He also claimed that he was simply moving it from Guy's to King's. When asked whose body it was, Bishop replied, "It's mine." Asked what his trade was, Bishop told Thomas, "I'm a bloody body snatcher."

Only Michael Shields's testimony was at odds with this narrative, especially as concerned his role in the story, but he crumbled easily each time he was pressed on various points. He told the coroner's court, "If I was to speak my last words, I did not know what the hamper contained. . . . I don't know how Bishop got his livelihood. I don't know as he dealt in dead bodies before this." Shields even claimed to be unaware that the Fortune of War was a house of call for resurrectionists. In fact, Shields had carried bodies for Bishop on at least one other occasion and was deeply involved in the resurrection trade. After being dismissed from his position as watchman-caretaker at Moorfields Roman Catholic chapel for stealing silverware, Shields worked partly as a porter at Covent Garden market, partly as a gravedigger at St. Giles-in-the-Fields' churchyard, and partly as a sack or hamper carrier for resurrectionists.[10] He knew very well what sort of pub the Fortune of War was.

He told the coroner's court that he had accidentally met Bishop in Covent Garden on the Saturday morning, and he denied being in the Fortune of War altogether. Warned by vestry clerk James Corder, "Take care—the pot-boy is present. Don't you recollect having any egg-hot at the Fortune of War that morning?" Shields immediately admitted that the meeting in Covent Garden on the Saturday was a lie—at which a murmur of astonishment passed around the upstairs room at the Unicorn pub. Shields claimed that when they reached King's College, he had stood outside while Bishop, May, and Williams took the hamper into the dissecting room; but Hill had already told the coroner's court of the friendly conversation he had had with Shields. When asked if he knew anything about the death of the boy, Shields replied, "Bishop said that the body was got from the ground, and that he knew where it was got from. He smiled as he said so, saying that if he were brought before the jury, he would give them ease about it."

After Shields stepped down, Bishop was brought forward and, with James Corder recording every word, said: "I cannot account for the death of the deceased. I dug the body out of the grave. The reason why I decline to say the grave I took it out of is that there were two watchmen in the ground, and they intrusted me, and being men of family, I don't want to deceive them. I don't think I can say any more. I took it for sale to Guy's Hospital, and as they did not want it, I left it there all night and part of the next day. And then I removed it to the King's College. That is all I can say about it. I mean to say that this is

Stallholders selling fruit and vegetables as Covent Garden's new market build-ing approaches completion, in 1829, sketched by artist George Scharf

the truth. I shall certainly keep it a secret where I got the body. I know nothing as to how it died." The coroner was not impressed by Bishop's explanation and warned him that a higher court was likely to interrogate him far more closely. The coroner said it was impossible for someone to be in possession of a body that was almost warm with-out knowing what had happened to it. Facetious in the face of pom-posity, Bishop replied that it was impossible for it to have been warm—it had passed a night at Guy's Hospital. Bishop offered to sign his statement, though in law he was not obliged to sign; by withhold-ing his signature, he would have been able to make subtle alterations to his version of events, to counteract any new information that might come to light during the investigation. But he chose to sign; it looked more honest. He had not created a good impression in court. A series of mocking, sardonic interjections had backfired on him. When William Hill had been giving evidence, Hill had been asked by the magistrate, "Is it customary for persons in your station to receive such presents?" with regard to the tip that Bishop had promised him. Bishop had called out, "He gets many a guinea in that way!" And Bishop had laughed when Hill told the court of his worries about the body's freshness; the body snatcher had sneered across the court-room, "The fact is, you are not in the habit of seeing fresh Subjects and you don't know anything about it!"

Next, it was James May's turn to speak. He confidently explained that he wished to tell the court everything he knew—he would speak only the truth. "I live at 4 Dorset Street, Newington. I went into the country last Sunday week and returned on the following Wednesday evening. I brought home a couple of Subjects with me. I took them to Mr Grainger's in Webb Street the same evening, and on the following morning, which was Thursday, I removed them to Mr Davis at Guy's and after receiving the money, went away. I went to the Fortune of War in Smithfield and I stayed there, I dare say, for two or three hours. Between four and five o'clock, to the best of my recollection, I went to Nag's Head Court, Golden Lane, and there I stopped with a female till eleven or twelve the next day, Friday. From Golden Lane I went to the Fortune of War again, and there I stopped drinking till six o'clock, or half past. Williams and Bishop both came in there. They asked me if I would stand any thing to drink, which I did. Bishop then called me out and asked me where I could get the best price for Things. I told him where I had sold two at Guy's and he told me he had got a good Subject, and he had been offered eight guineas for it. I told him I could get more for it. He said all I could get over nine guineas I might have for myself, and I agreed to it. We went from there to the Old Bailey and we had some tea at the watering house in the Old Bailey, leaving Williams at the Fortune of War. After we had tea we called a chariot off the stand and drove to Bishop's house. When we came there, Bishop showed me the lad in a box or trunk. I then put it into a sack and took it to the chariot myself, and took it from thence to Mr Davis at Guy's. Mr Davis said, 'You know, James, I cannot take it, because I took two off you yesterday, and I have not got [student] names enough down for one, or else I would.' I asked him if I might leave it there that night and he said, 'Certainly.' Bishop then desired Mr Davis not to let any person have it but himself, for it was his own Subject, which Mr Davis said he would not, and told his man James not to let any person have it besides himself. I told Mr Davis not to let it go until I came as well, for I should be money out of pocket if it went before I came. I went home that evening, where I slept, and in the morning I went to Mr Davis and had not been there many minutes before Bishop came in, and Shields with a hamper, and took it from thence to King's College, and there I was taken into custody." May was happy to sign his statement. There was no mention of the clothes buying and rum drinking in Field Lane and West Street. But he did own up to the selling of the teeth: "I admit all that, and what does it amount to? I did use the brad awl to extract the teeth from the boy, and that was in the regular way of business, and in doing so, I wounded my hand slightly—there is nothing very wonderful in that."

For his part, Thomas Williams claimed that he had gone along to King's only to see what the new building was like—perhaps not such an unreasonable claim: the Robert Smirke–designed college was considered a glorious new addition to the capital. "I live at Number 3 Nova Scotia Gardens and am a glass-blower. In the first place, I met with Bishop last Saturday morning in Long Lane, Smithfield. I asked him where he was going. He said he was going to King's College. We then went to the Fortune of War public house. Instead of going to King's College, we went to Guy's Hospital and he came out of there and went to the King's College. Then May and the porter met us against the gate, then Bishop went in, and I asked him to let me go in with him. A porter took a basket from the Fortune of War to Guy's Hospital, and I helped him part of the way with it. That is all I have got to say." Williams declined to sign this slightly different version of events.

Richard Partridge and George Beaman explained to the coroner and his jury their findings at the postmortem. Although they disagreed on the details, both men found that death had been caused by a blow to the back of the neck, probably with a stick or some other implement. The wound on the boy's temple was superficial, they agreed.

At *half past ten* on the evening of Thursday, 10 November, the foreman of the coroner's jury returned the verdict: "We find a verdict of wilful murder against some person or persons unknown, and the jury beg to add to the above verdict that the evidence produced before them has excited very strong suspicion in their minds against the prisoners Bishop and Williams, and that they trust that a strict inquiry

will be made into the case by the police magistrates." No mention
was made of May.

A juror stood up to praise Superintendent Thomas; the jury foreman added his praise for the policeman and also praised vestry clerk
James Corder; the coroner praised Corder, and Corder thanked the
jury and praised the coroner.

The apparent similarities to the Burke and Hare murders, and the
deep embarrassment that case had caused the medical and legal pro-
fessions, had prompted Home Secretary Viscount Melbourne to
request James Corder to forward the verdict and a report of the coroner's hearing to him as quickly as possible. This Corder did, at eleven
o'clock at night in a hand-delivered letter, apologizing for disturbing
his lordship at such a late hour but saying that his urgency was due to
the fact that "the enquiry into the present case has been the means of
eliciting the fact that several boys of a similar age to the deceased
have recently been missed by their friends, and there is too much
ground for justifying the conclusion that they have, with him, been
the victims of a horrid system carried on for some time past by
wretches whose business it is to supply the hospitals."[11] Outside
Corder's office, in the dark and the freezing fog of November,
beneath the stalls and in among the fruit and vegetable baskets of
Covent Garden's market building, some hundred or so destitute boys
and girls were bedding down for the night.

Persons Unknown

John Bishop had been a resurrection man for twelve years; James May had started to disturb the dead in 1825, acquiring the nickname Jack Stirabout (slang for "prison," after the maize and oatmeal staple jail diet) and a string of convictions for grave robbery; Thomas Williams was new to the trade, having recently emerged from a prison sentence for theft; Michael Shields was a familiar face around the graveyards of central London. Resurrection was a revolting but potentially highly lucrative trade, with earnings way beyond those of even the most highly skilled worker. In 1831, a silk weaver in the East End of London could earn as little as five shillings a week working a twelve-hour day, six days a week.[1] A well-paid manservant to a wealthy London household could expect to earn a guinea a week, which was also the starting wage for the first constables recruited to the Metropolitan "New" Police force in 1829. By contrast, a disinterred body could bring in between eight and twenty guineas, depending on its freshness and on how many Things were being hawked around London's four hospital medical schools and seventeen private anatomy schools in any given week.[2] It was a speculative trade, and John Bishop himself missed out on more than one occasion by failing to procure promptly a corpse for a surgeon who went ahead and bought one from a rival who had delivered more quickly. There were periodic gluts as well as lulls: the work was largely seasonal, since the hospital schools ran courses from October to April, though many private lecturers held summer classes.

Male corpses were more highly prized than female because they offered greater scope for the study of musculature, while a fresh, well-developed limb could be worth more than a whole body that was on the verge of putrefaction. Other "offcuts"—a woman's scalp with long, thick hair attached; unchipped teeth ("grinders"), either singly or as whole sets—were profitable sidelines for the resurrectionist as the living paid well to patch themselves up from parts of the dead. High infant mortality resulted in a brisk trade in children, either as "big smalls," "smalls," or fetuses. Specialty corpses achieved higher-than-average prices: in the autumn of 1827, when a young female inmate of an insane asylum succumbed at last to a long illness, William Davis, a member of the notorious Spitalfields Gang of snatchers, was offered twenty guineas by surgeons keen to anatomize her brain; but Davis was arrested by a parish watchman as he was digging up the corpse in a private burial ground in Golden Lane.[3]

There were around eight hundred medical students in London in 1831, of whom five hundred dissected corpses as part of their anatomical education; each student was said to require three bodies during his sixteen-month training—two for learning anatomy, one for learning operating techniques.[4] The only legal supply of flesh came from the gallows, with the corpses of those executed for murder being made available to the nation's surgeons. But the number of murderers being executed was far too low to meet the needs of an expanding, research-hungry medical profession. Death sentences for any crime were increasingly unlikely to be carried out as the Bloody Code of the eighteenth century—a series of legal enactments that introduced capital punishment for a wide range of petty theft and antisocial acts—was diminished by wave upon wave of legislation.[5] However, the concurrent rise in arrests and convictions guaranteed that the number of those executed held steady. Thus, while 350 death sentences were passed in England and Wales in 1805, only 68 people were executed (10 for murder); in 1831, 1,601 people were condemned to death, yet only 52 were executed (12 for murder).[6] And so the anatomists and their students relied on the "snatchers," "grabs," "lifters," "exhumators," or "resurgam homos" to make up the numbers.

Digging up the dead in overcrowded city graveyards was physically arduous, but an exhumation could be completed in as little as half an hour by the well-practiced. Resurrection men would also travel to outlying villages to retrieve corpses. Just as livestock, vegetables, herbs, and milk were imported daily into the capital and touted around the streets by itinerant sellers, the country dead were regularly ferried into town on covered "go-carts." A network of informers passed details to the London gangs of an impending death or recent burial in villages and hamlets, with corrupt sextons, gravediggers, undertakers, and local officials taking a cut of the sale price. The Wednesday before his arrest, James May had just got back from the country, where he had been disinterring the rural dead; on the Thursday, he had failed to make a sale of his two dead rustics at Grainger's, but Guy's took them off his hands for ten guineas each.

Another, increasingly popular method of obtaining Things—and one that could involve the womenfolk of resurrectionists—was to pose as the friend or relative of a dying pauper, one who was too ill to alert workhouse or hospital staff to the imposture; the corpse would then be signed over for private burial (the institution being glad to be free of the cost of interment). This grotesque vigil might last for days, but after the pauper's death, the resurrectionist could take possession of the body with every appearance of respectability and peddle it to a surgeon for dissection. A variation on this theme was demonstrated in March 1830 in Walworth, then a village in south London. One Miss Christy had been unwell for some time and her health was deteriorating rapidly. As she lay in her sickbed, a gang of known resurrectionists could be spotted lurking near her home. When she died, Miss Christy was buried in the graveyard of St. John's chapel, West Lane, Walworth. But a day later, a police officer stopped a man carrying a sack in a street near the chapel, and it was found to contain Miss Christy. An inquest was held at a local inn, and here another pair of resurrectionists sat at the back of the room, trying to pass themselves off as relatives waiting to claim Miss Christy's body when the coroner

The Bodysnatcher *by Morris Meredith Williams, 1913; in fact, disinterment was just one of several ways in which resurrectionists obtained corpses.*

had finished with her remains. Enraged locals had them ejected from the hearing, and when Miss Christy was again laid to rest, her friends pledged to keep watch at the grave until such time as she would be too putrid to be saleable.[7]

Even more opportunistic, or impatient, snatchers would simply steal a corpse that was known to be in a family home awaiting burial. On Saturday, 15 October 1831, Thomas Williams used a crowbar to open the door of a house very near to his Nova Scotia Gardens home and made off with the body of fourteen-year-old William Sullivan, who had died, after a long illness, a day or two before. The boy's mother, a widow, had gone out on an errand, leaving him lying in his coffin on the kitchen table. Neighbors saw a man passing by carrying a large, stinking basket; because of the smell, they took particular care to note the man's face (though it is interesting that none had the temerity to challenge him). When Mrs. Sullivan returned and raised the alarm, the neighbors' description was so precise that a police officer arrested Williams the next day. He was identified by the witnesses, but since the boy's body could not be found and no other evidence was offered, the local magistrate dismissed the charge.[8] Dissection disfigured and eventually destroyed corpses, a process that provided resurrectionists with their best chance of avoiding prosecution. No body, no evidence; no evidence, no case.

Some snatchers were so confident that they felt no need to be circumspect. At the funeral of a dustman at St. Andrew's Church in Holborn, on 29 December 1828, snatchers mingled with the huge crowd of white-jacketed fellow dustmen. The deceased, who had died in an accident, had been a very popular man; the white jackets were a sign of respect. His widow had already been approached by resurrectionists offering to buy the body from her; since she had refused to sell, they determined to "izzey" (steal) it in a stunningly brazen manner. They staggered drunkenly into the church and swore and blasphemed throughout the service; they then hovered by the graveside as the coffin was lowered. None of the crowd remonstrated with or attacked the resurrectionists, but one friend of the dead man jumped down onto the coffin, calling to another, "Come, Bill, let's squeeze the bugger down tight, and then he von't be fit for the knife." Another declared, "Ve'd better stop up at night and votch," since they did not trust St. Andrew's "votchman."[9]

At once close-knit and highly volatile, the resurrection trade had a tight network of meeting places. Certain pubs and inns operated as unofficial guild halls, where bodies could be stored and tips and warnings exchanged, and as houses of call for those indirectly involved in the trade (such as Michael Shields and, possibly, Thomas Wigley, the porter at the Cross Keys Inn). The hub of London resurrection culture north of the river was the Old Bailey, the thoroughfare that gave its name to the famous courthouse and that was just a few yards south of the Fortune of War and St. Bartholomew's Hospital and medical school, which faced the pub. South of the river, the Bricklayer's Arms and the Rockingham Arms were both handily situated for south London's two large hospital medical schools—Guy's and St. Thomas's—and their private competitor, Grainger's school in Webb Street. Such pubs were comparatively safe places for resurrection men to gather; here, they would not be subjected to the scorn of other working people. (When John Bishop and James May took tea in the King of Denmark, a nonresurrection pub, their presence caused something of a frisson.)

No pub was more associated with the resurrectionists than the Fortune of War. It had originally been called the Naked Boy; in the seventeenth century, a tailor had run the pub, and his shop sign was a lad with no clothes on, with the inscription: "So fickle is our English nation / I would be clothed if I knew the fashion." But the Naked Boy himself was inherited from an earlier age: shortly after the Fire of London in 1666, the Golden Boy of Pye Corner, a gilded wooden statue of a corpulent cherub, was "in Memmory Put up for the late Fire of London Occasion'd by the Sin of Gluttony." In 1721, the Naked Boy was bought by a man who had lost both legs and one arm in a sea battle: the "fortune of war" was mutilation.[10] How the pub fell into its role in the resurrection community is not known, though its proximity to St. Bartholomew's Hospital is likely to have played a role in its transformation.

In its day, the pub, which stood until 1910 at the northwest corner of the junction of Giltspur Street and Cock Lane, was said to have been so welcoming to snatchers that they would stash their stolen corpses, with tickets of ownership attached, on or under the pub's benches while they went off to strike a bargain. But by 1828, it is likely that the trade had become so shameful, so vulnerable to public distaste and police action, that no produce was kept on site; certainly, John Bishop made no attempt to bring his wares to the pub.

Outside such places, the resurrection man could expect to be reviled and ostracized by those he lived among and shunned, too, by strangers—shopkeepers, publicans, coachmen—who suspected his profession. Knowing this, resurrectionists wishing to take revenge on a rival would leave disfigured corpses or body parts festooned around the rival's home to arouse the fury of the neighbors and possibly the attention of the police.[11] From the mid-1820s, the work itself became more dangerous, with armed guards posted at many London graveyards as popular revulsion at the increasing incidence of body snatching grew. In the eyes of the law, however, resurrection was only a misdemeanor, not a felony. What was considered by the public one of the worst of crimes was, to lawmakers, comparatively trivial. The misdemeanor was

The Fortune of War resurrectionist pub shortly before demolition; the Golden Boy cherub commemorated the Great Fire of London.

"unlawful disinterment," an act that breached "common decency," according to a legal judgment of 1788, and was punishable by a fine, or up to six months in jail. The human body was deemed to belong to no one and therefore did not constitute property. For this reason, resurrection men were scrupulous about replacing shrouds and coffin lids, in order to avoid the more serious charge of theft.

Magistrates—or "justices of the peace"—in some parts of London were said to be more inclined to convict and imprison resurrectionists toward the end of the 1820s, though there was a wide range of attitudes among even senior, long-serving JPs. Records of cases are rare for this period, just before the boom years of bureaucracy; newspaper reports and anecdotal evidence of magistrates' hearings give a colorful though incomplete picture, so it is difficult to ascertain whether there really was a crackdown. In 1828, the Parliamentary Select Committee on Anatomy, convened to consider and instruct Parliament on the problems experienced by surgeons in obtaining corpses to dissect, reported that London magistrates had been coming down harder on the resurrection community. However, none of the justices of the peace who gave evidence to the committee corroborated this statement: Thomas Halls said he could remember presiding at only two resurrection cases in the previous seven years; Samuel Twyford was able to recall six in as many years, while the representative of the Thames police office claimed that he had never had a resurrectionist up before him.

Several contemporary newspaper reports suggest that the newly formed Metropolitan Police were responsible for an increasing number of arrests—many of which, nevertheless, did not end in conviction.[12] But if there really was an increase in police vigilance and a rise in the number of detentions, this may have reflected the taking into custody of part-time resurrectionists for perfectly ordinary thieving. Dr. James Somerville stated to the Select Committee on Anatomy that the majority of "resurrection" carts that were stopped by police were found to be carrying not exhumed corpses but the proceeds of housebreaking.[13] Increasingly, resurrection was becoming a specialist's field, where only the best-informed, most fearless, physically strong, discreet, and levelheaded men were able to farm the city's dead on a full-time basis. The aging, the drunk, the boastful, and the careless were better advised to look elsewhere for a living.

Resurrection was one of the most covert underworld activities of the day, and tantalizingly little about it has ever come to light: the researcher continually hits a wall. A handwritten index card in the

St. Bartholomew's Hospital archives states baldly that "since obtaining bodies from resurrectionists was surreptitious, there are no written records of this process"; the minutes of meetings of senior staff at King's College refer to various sums granted to the medical school, including fifty pounds to Richard Partridge on 31 October 1831 "received on account of the anatomical department"—its purpose not specified, unlike all the other sums of money mentioned in the minutes; and a biography of surgeon Sir Charles Bell contains a typical admission: "That Bell did business with these blackguards may be accepted, but with regard to that side of his affairs, information is scanty."[14] The Select Committee on Anatomy conducted interviews with three resurrection men—identified as "AB," "CD," and "FG"—and a number of the surgeons they supplied, and the committee's report and evidence form a major part of what is known of the trade.[15] Other glimpses of resurrection culture appear in the recollections, reminiscences, and memoirs of various medical men of the day—though such references are always hostile, with little interest shown in the everyday working lives of "the most iniquitous set of villains who ever lived."[16] It is not even clear how many resurrection men were at work in London in 1831. There may have been as many as seven London gangs, but with infighting a common feature of resurrection life, gangs were likely to have been constantly breaking up, reforming, and disintegrating again—so a "gang" could at any point have comprised two men or as many as fifteen. The Select Committee believed that while there were around two hundred London resurrectionists, the vast majority of these were part-timers, making most of their living through more orthodox theft and dealing in bodies only if these came their way with ease. "They get a Subject or two and call themselves resurrectionists," complained AB to the Select Committee, bitterly regretting the influx of "petty common thieves" who were ruining the business. The specialists—the men that a number of anatomists grudgingly admitted they could trust not to overcharge, cheat, blackmail, fail to deliver, or turn informer to magistrates—were thought to number around ten. It is quite possible, though unprovable, that John Bishop and James May were among this elite.

It is also possible, and equally unprovable, that AB was Bishop himself: there is a similarity between AB's intelligent, sardonic, and saturnine replies to committee questions and the syntax and flavor of Bishop's answers in his court hearings. The committee report reveals that AB started snatching at roughly the same time that Bishop is thought to have become a full-time resurrectionist. AB worked with one partner; Bishop worked with just one accomplice for seven years, between 1821 and 1828, the date of the Select Committee's hearings. AB claimed to know the Spitalfields Gang; Spitalfields is just south of Bethnal Green. AB had been shot at by a graveyard guard from two yards' distance; Bishop had scars on his chin and had broken both legs at some point. AB had served a six-month sentence in jail; so had Bishop. AB had in his best year lifted a hundred corpses; Bishop had lifted five hundred to a thousand by 1831.

The committee's hearings were described years later in *All the Year Round*, the journal that Charles Dickens "conducted" and wrote for: "For several days in the summer of 1829, a certain committee room of the House of Commons, as well as all the passages leading to it, were thronged by some of the vilest beings that have perhaps ever visited such respectable places. Sallow, cadaverous, gaunt men, dressed in greasy moleskin or rusty black, and wearing wisps of dirty white handkerchiefs round their wizen necks. They had the air of wicked sextons, or thievish gravediggers; there was a suspicion of degraded clergymen about them, mingled with a dash of Whitechapel costermonger. Their ghoulish faces were rendered horrible by smirks of self-satisfied cunning, and their eyes squinted with sidelong suspicion, fear and distrust. They had been raked together from their favourite house of call, the Fortune of War in Smithfield. There were terrible rumours that when 'subjects' ran short, they had a way of *making* dead bodies."[17] This has the smack of eyewitness remembrance, and it is possible that Dickens himself had a hand in the piece (though no Dickens authority has made such an attribution). However, the Select Committee on Anatomy sat in the summer of 1828, not 1829 (which would have been an unusual error for Dickens to have made), and there is something rather fanciful about the notion of a "throng" of London resurrectionists coming to Parliament by invitation. Whatever the truth, only three men's evidence has entered the record.

....

If information on the resurrection trade is hard to come by, the life of John Bishop is—happily—better documented. He was born in Highgate in 1797, the son of a hardworking, locally respected, "plain, plodding man" also called John, who ran a successful carting business from the family home on North Hill, Highgate, transporting goods to and from the city 350 feet below and four miles to the south.[18] Transportation was one of Highgate's biggest trades; some eighty coaches a day stopped at the village's Red Lion inn on the route to and from the north. Highgate also had a formidable drinking culture, with around twenty licensed taverns within its parish boundaries.[19]

John Bishop the son, the second of five children, lost his mother when he was eight years old. His father remarried and had more children, including a daughter, Rhoda, born in 1813; when the second wife died, Bishop married for a third time. In November 1816, John Bishop the father was run over by a van and both his legs had to be amputated at the hip; he died two weeks after the operation. The people of Highgate collected the considerable sum of three hundred pounds for his widow, Sarah, who was eight months pregnant. But within weeks it became apparent that John Bishop the son and Sarah were living as man and wife. The locals tried to recoup their money, but most of it had already been spent—on what, it is not known.

John Bishop took over his father's carting business and added three other moneymaking activities: informing on local criminals to the parish constables to secure reward money (his favorite drinking den was the Green Dragon, where informers congregated), hiring himself out as a witness/alibi man in court cases—committing perjury for a fee, and ferrying bodies around in his cart for a resurrection gang. The Old Bailey—as well as being a gathering place for resurrectionists—was the center of London's carting trade, and the Bailey's dual role is likely to have played a part in drawing Bishop further and further into resurrection and away from legitimate carting. (Many, perhaps most, resurrectionists had a prior and/or simultaneous connection with conveying goods, as carters or as porters.) Bishop teamed up with a noted resurrectionist—identity unknown—and between them they were reputed to have emptied the churchyard at the nearby village of Holloway. Sometime before 1820, Bishop sold his father's business to a rival firm and disposed of a small piece of Highgate

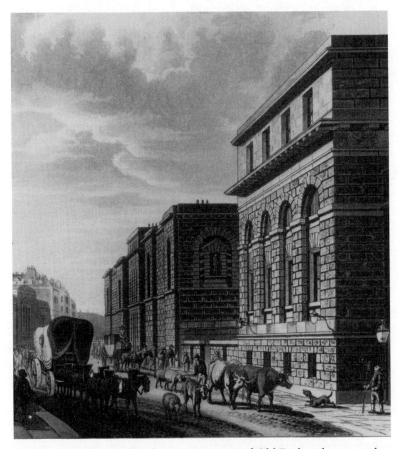

Thomas Hosmer Shepherd's 1814 aquatint of Old Bailey, the street that gave its name to the Sessions House (seen on the right). Newgate Prison is the building to the left of the courthouse; out of view on the far left is the King of Denmark, and hidden by the covered wagon is the Fortune of War. The cattle, sheep, and drovers have walked down from Smithfield, which lies beyond.

Common owned by his father, raising eighty pounds—more than a year's wages for an averagely successful workingman. Sarah, for her part, had been given a charitable allowance of fifteen shillings a week, paid out by the duchess of St. Albans (Highgate's own local aristocrat, who had taken pity on Sarah's plight and had been unable or unwilling to stop the payments on hearing the scandalous talk of the widow's relationship with her stepson). Whatever else they were, John Bishop and his stepmother-wife did not start their life together poor. They married on 2 August 1818, and it is likely that Highgate residents' disapproval of their liaison contributed to their decision to abandon the north London village for the east of London; in the mid-1820s, the family was living in Pitfield Street, Hoxton, a poor but relatively "respectable" eastern area.[20]

By 1831, according to his own estimate, Bishop had sold between five hundred and a thousand bodies to the surgeons of London. He had always been confident of his talents; on one occasion, after being released from Bow Street magistrates court when a charge against him was dropped, he passed the courthouse the next day, pulled a handful of sovereigns from his pocket, and called across to one of the police officers standing outside, "You see! You cannot keep me from it. I got another stiff 'un last night and had nine guineas for it."[21] According to a report in the *Morning Advertiser*, Bishop's success as a snatcher was the result of his patience and stealth rather than of any feats involving daring or physical strength; the newspaper claimed that among resurrectionists, he was considered something of a coward. As graveyard security tightened, Bishop became a prolific stealer of corpses from coroners' and undertakers' premises and from parish "bone houses" after bribing the watchman or splitting his fees with him. He was also said to be adept at playing the relative of a vagrant dying in a workhouse, often accompanied, the same report claimed, by Sarah or "a friend." He must have operated on tip-offs, for it is said that he occasionally took lodgings, posing as a traveling carpenter and carrying a large basket, in a house where a corpse was lying in wake, absconding on his first night and taking the body with him. Bishop was once double-crossed by a watchman at a workhouse in Shoreditch—not far from his Hoxton home—who had promised to sell him six pauper bodies; the watchman alerted the authorities but Bishop and his accomplices spotted the trap and ran off. He would not always be so lucky and spent several stretches in jail.

In 1825, he served two months in Clerkenwell New Prison for having possession of an illegally disinterred corpse.[22] As a result of a later stretch, in Coldbath Fields Prison, he makes an appearance in Captain George Laval Chesterton's *Revelations of Prison Life*. Chesterton was the governor of Coldbath Fields from 1829 (later becoming a friend of Charles Dickens's), and Bishop passed through Chesterton's jail sometime in 1829, 1830, or 1831. Writing in 1856, Chesterton recalled Bishop as "without exception, the most finished ruffian within my memory," with a "powerful frame, of repulsive countenance, and of brutal address and manners. . . . He entered the prison uttering oaths and execrations, and indulging in the grossest language, while he assailed the subordinates, and even myself, with menace and defiance. He had received no provocation, but gave vent to the irrepressible brutality of his nature." However, fourteen days of solitary confinement (a treatment being pioneered by Chesterton) wrought an extraordinary change in the man: "That iron-souled miscreant became so meek and subdued, so prone to tears, so tremulous and agitated . . . he could hardly be recognised as the same coarse and blustering bully." Nevertheless, claimed Chesterton, when Bishop passed from Coldbath Fields to Newgate Prison, where he was free to mingle with other prisoners, "I found, on inquiry, that renewed association with lawless men had revived the brutality so inseparable from his nature."[23]

Bishop narrowly escaped being transported for perjury in December 1827, when, for a fee of three pounds, he gave a false alibi for two horse thieves, Thomas Chapman and William Johnson. The jury at Chapman and Johnson's trial did not accept Bishop's story that the pair had been drinking with him in the Plough Inn, Smithfield (directly opposite the Fortune of War), on the afternoon of 5 October, believing instead that they had been stealing two mares 120 miles away in Gloucestershire. Bishop was hopelessly evasive in the witness box and attempted to pass himself off as a general carrier ("I move any goods—it does not make much odds to me"), refusing to name the crime for which he had twice been arrested.[24] Instead of being transported, Bishop was jailed for a brief time for lying to the court; Chapman and Johnson were executed.

In April 1831, he was involved in a perplexing case, which was heard at Guildhall magistrates court. Bishop and codefendant Joseph Taylor were accused of stealing the body of an elderly man called Gardner from St. Bartholomew's Hospital. Gardner's daughter-in-law deposed that she had given Gardner, who had been suffering with "a spinal complaint," a meal on the evening of Friday, 18 March, and

Coldbath Fields Prison stood on the site of today's Mount Pleasant Royal Mail depot, London's main post office. John Bishop served more than one sentence here for body snatching.

sent him off with a shilling to find a bed for the night in a lodging house. The next day, Taylor and Bishop called at Mrs. Gardner's house and said that they had met the old man in the street, that he had been feeling very ill, and that if Mrs. Gardner would give them a shilling, they would see that he gained free admittance to the casual ward at St. Bartholomew's; they would swear to the medical staff that Gardner had no friends within a hundred miles of London, which would, they said, guarantee him free treatment. Mrs. Gardner agreed to this, and on Sunday the twentieth Taylor came to her to say that he had indeed had the old man admitted as a charity patient but that she should not go to see him in the hospital as her visit might jeopardize his free treatment. One week later, however, Taylor turned up again to tell her that Gardner had died in the hospital on the twenty-fourth and had been quickly interred within St. Bartholomew's own burial ground. When Mrs. Gardner checked with the hospital, she was told that Bishop and Taylor had called for and removed the corpse themselves, saying that they would pay for a private burial outside the hospital's grounds.

Though several details are troubling—Did Bishop and Taylor hasten the old man's death somehow, before his admission to St. Bartholomew's? And why would Mrs. Gardner give money to a stranger to assist her frail father-in-law?—there is no suggestion that anything other than body snatching was suspected by the Guildhall magistrates, and indeed all charges against Bishop and Taylor were eventually dropped.[25]

In July 1830, Bishop and his family moved to a rented cottage in a semirural, semislum part of Bethnal Green—a neighborhood more impoverished than nearby Hoxton. Their landlady was Sarah Trueby, who lived nearby with her husband and grown-up son. The relocation suggests that the Bishops had come down in the world—for reasons unknown, though the proportion of his income that Bishop was spending on drink is likely to have been a factor. Despite a generous inheritance, the duchess's allowance, the funds raised locally, the earnings from resurrection and from Sarah's work as a seamstress and laundress, the Bishops and their children were reduced to living in one of the most squalid areas of east London.

Right on the border of Bethnal Green and Shoreditch, Nova Scotia Gardens was a stretch of land just north of St. Leonard's Church. Its level was slightly below that of the surrounding streets, and some referred to it as the Hackney Road Hollow. John Stow's *Survey of London* (1603) mentions some houses recently built in the vicinity upon "the common soil—for it was a leystall" (dunghill). By 1750, according to contemporary maps, the area consisted largely of fields on the fringes of the Huguenot settlements of Spitalfields, to the south.

It is possible that these fields were at some point ploughed up for clay and mud to be made into bricks, which were baked in kilns built on the field itself; this had been the fate of many of the meadows of Bethnal Green during the eighteenth-century building boom.[26] By the 1820s, the older horticultural and food-related names of surrounding streets (Crabtree Row, Birdcage Walk, Orange Street, Cock Lane, Bacon Street) were being joined by the martial, naval, and colonial designations of the rows of two-story, brick terraced housing springing up in the environs. The Gardens had become Nova Scotia Gardens and nearby were Virginia Row, Nelson Street, Gibraltar Walk, and Wellington Street.

The Gardens comprised a number of cottages that by 1831 were noticeably quaint; they were interconnected by narrow, zigzagging pathways. Nos. 2 and 3, both of which were owned by the Trueby family, formed a semidetached unit and were not inside the labyrinth of Nova Scotia Gardens but near Crabtree Row and the main entrance into the Gardens. Bishop's house, No. 3, had a side gate, opening onto a path known locally as the Private Way, and the house was entered by a back door, close to a coal cellar. No. 2 opened directly onto the largest path, connecting the Gardens to Crabtree Row. A four-inch-thick brick wall separated the dwellings. Each cottage consisted of two upstairs rooms, a downstairs parlor, eight feet by seven, a smaller room housing the staircase, and a washhouse extension. The downstairs window overlooked the back garden. The roof of Nos. 2 and 3 was unusual in sloping sharply down from the front of

Nova Scotia Gardens in 1831. John Bishop's cottage, No. 3, is on the right, abutting No. 2, where Thomas Williams lived for a few weeks.

the building to the back, and this may indicate that the cottages were built—like so much housing in Bethnal Green and Spitalfields—as homes for weavers: the lack of an overhanging front gable would allow light to pour into the upper rooms, which may once have contained looms. Each cottage had a thirty-foot-long, ten-foot-wide garden, divided from its neighbor by three-foot-high wooden palings, in which was a small gate. The generous size of these back gardens may reflect an earlier use as tenter grounds, to stretch and dry silk; a second theory is that the Gardens had once been allotments and that the cottages had developed from a colony of gardeners' huts or summer houses.[27]

At the end of each garden was a privy. The garden of No. 3 also contained a well to be shared with Nos. 1 and 2, though in fact the residents of many of the cottages could have reached it easily; it was halfway down the garden and consisted of a wooden barrel, one and a half feet in diameter, sunk into the soil.

The former dunghill and its surrounds had, during the 1664–65 plague, seen some of the highest mortality figures in the capital. In 1831, the area's old reputation for poverty and despair was returning. The 1825 collapse of the English silk trade—the result of a surge in cheaper textile imports from France—proved calamitous, since weaving and cloth working had provided thousands of households in Bethnal Green and Spitalfields with an income. By 1829, wages among skilled workers in the silk trade, which employed an estimated fifteen thousand people, were half what they had been between 1815 and 1825. The governor of the Bethnal Green workhouse revealed that admissions had risen from 498 in 1821 to 1,160 in 1831.[28] One eyewitness wrote of "the dwarfish and dwindled weavers of Spitalfields"; any man over five feet two inches was not a native of Spitalfields, he claimed. These men rarely made it to the age of sixty and proved too weak and broken by their fourteen-to-sixteen-hour workdays to say more than a few sentences at a public meeting convened to discuss the issue of free trade, which had opened English markets to foreign imports. At twenty, the commentator noted, Spitalfields men looked thirty; at forty, they looked sixty, with "squalor and misery etched into their faces."[29] Letters from Londoners concerned about conditions in this part of the East End—unpaved, undrained, unlit—were starting to appear in the newspapers. The *Morning Advertiser* printed a complaint about the filth outside the violin-string factory in Princes Street, just south of Nova Scotia Gardens—a mess (mainly consisting of cat offal) that was five feet wide and one foot deep—while "An Observer" wrote to the same paper to report the level of filth in Castle Street, two hundred yards from the Gardens and home to the Feathers, one of the local beerhouses patronized by John Bishop.[30]

In July 1831, one year after the Bishops arrived, the house adjoining theirs was leased by the Truebys to Thomas Williams. Williams was born Thomas Head in Bridgnorth, Shropshire, on 28 February 1803. Although Bridgnorth was a thriving town at the start of its long and lucrative association with the carpet-weaving industry, George and Mary Head, his parents, moved with their children to London, to Highgate, at some point in the second decade of the century, and from there to the less salubrious Smithfield district. Thomas tried and failed at more than one trade, having been apprenticed to a bricklayer, then taking up carpentry before turning to working as a porter for local glass manufacturers. As an adolescent, he had started to drink heavily and steal, despite coming from what appears to have been a comparatively stable and loving family. His mother was reportedly devoted to her son and watched with dismay his decline into crime.

He went by at least four different though similar names: his own, Thomas Williams, William Jones, and John Head—the name of a younger brother of his, born in 1805, who died in 1807. He also tampered with his date of birth, perhaps to take advantage of looking younger than his years in order to receive more lenient treatment from magistrates and constables. He gave his age as twenty in 1827—shaving off four years.[31] It was a well-known ruse for those who were under arrest or in prison to adopt combinations of common Christian and surnames; one lawyer counted fifteen prisoners at Newgate who were using the same combination of aliases. In this way, it was harder for police, magistrates, and judges to identify "known criminals" with any certainty, and a case could be lost if a jury felt that the accused had not been securely identified.[32]

Head/Williams was in and out of court from an early age. His luck finally ran out in February 1827, when he was found guilty at the Old Bailey court of the theft of a twenty-shilling copper bathtub from the kitchen of his parents' landlord. He had attempted to sell the vessel at Pontifex's copper and brass foundry in Shoe Lane and was convicted on the eyewitness evidence of a chimney sweep (who saw him leaving the house at the time of the theft) and of Henry Pontifex. He was sentenced to seven years' transportation to Australia, though in the event he served four years in Millbank Penitentiary—the controversial "Panopticon" prison on the banks of the Thames.[33]

Head passed through Newgate on his way to Millbank, and the ledger book noting the physical description, "character," and conviction of each prisoner shows that, as prisoner 489, he again gave his age as twenty, as he had at the Old Bailey. His trade was noted as bricklayer, his religion Church of England, and he was found to have two intertwined love hearts shot through with arrows tattooed on his right forearm and the characters T.H.N.A on his left forearm—"N.A." presumably being his sweetheart. He was five feet four inches tall, had hazel eyes, was in good health ("stoutish" with a "fresh" complexion), and had a "good" character—which in prison parlance tended to mean tractable.[34]

Received at Millbank in the same month was one Thomas Williams of Eaton in Buckinghamshire, a twenty-two-year-old who had been sentenced to seven years for the theft of a looking glass. It is possible that Head borrowed the name and date of birth of this fellow convict, but Thomas Williams was also the name of a prolific East End body snatcher—he lived just off the Commercial Road—and in choosing to give this name upon his arrest at King's College, Head may have been trying to fool the authorities into thinking that he was nothing more sinister than a regular resurrectionist.

Millbank Penitentiary had opened in 1816 but soon closed down and did not reopen until 1824: not only had its buildings proved substandard, sinking into the marshy site, but in 1823 there had been outbreaks of scurvy and dysentery that had affected almost every inmate. The rehabilitation of the prisoner was to be paramount at Millbank. It was intended that both male and female inmates would be taught a skill (this may be where Williams learned the glass trade) and subjected to an aggressively proselytizing form of religious instruction. There was also a new emphasis on seclusion, in order to bring the prisoner to a closer relationship with God and to minimize the chances of moral "contamination" from other villains; under "the separate system," Millbank prisoners were allowed no contact with one another—a treatment that was said to result in soaring rates of insanity. Millbank pioneered the use of surveillance, and the building (the Panopticon comprised six pentagons abutting a central hexagon containing a chapel) was designed so that prisoners would be visible at all times. This failed to prevent outbreaks of rioting in 1826 and 1827 by a group of inmates who called themselves the Friends of the Oppressed. In March 1827, they hanged a warder's pet cat as part of their campaign to get themselves transferred to the "hulks"—decommissioned warships moored in British waters as floating prisons and normally the most dreaded of all penal institutions—which may reflect how appalling conditions were felt to be at Millbank.[35]

In 1831, upon his early release from Millbank, Williams rented No. 2 Nova Scotia Gardens, which had a large fireplace that he intended to adapt as a furnace, in order to manufacture glass. But his new start lasted just a month. Williams failed to register his trade with Customs and Excise (under an act of 1825, glass manufacture required an annual license, costing twenty pounds; there had been a recent clampdown on unlicensed traders), who raided his home on 6 August, confiscated his equipment and large quantities of glass, cullet, and iron, and mounted a prosecution, which was still unheard at the time of his arrest for murder. Williams had walked in and found the confiscation in progress and called the excise officer "an opprobrious name."[36] Now without an income, he began to join his next-door neighbor, John Bishop, in supplying Subjects to the private anatomy schools. The new term was about to start at the hospital medical schools, and Bishop seems to have been happy to take on an apprentice. If Bishop had indeed been attached to the Spitalfields Gang, who were infamous for their feuds and fallings out, it could be that he had suddenly found himself without a partner; if there really had been some sort of crackdown on snatchers, many potential accomplices may have been in prison. Perhaps Bishop felt he could trust this new neighbor who was so down on his luck yet so enterprising, with new ideas on how to obtain bodies; perhaps the friendship was helped along by their both having grown up in Highgate. Whatever the case, Williams had so smitten Rhoda, Bishop's seventeen-year-old

Millbank Penitentiary sketched in 1828 and photographed shortly before demolition in 1903. Thomas Williams served four years here for theft.

half sister/stepdaughter, that on 26 September Williams married her at St. Leonard's Church, Shoreditch.[37] After the service, celebratory beers were drunk at the Birdcage pub, then there was a small family celebration in the back garden of No. 2, and Williams moved into No. 3 with his bride, John and Sarah Bishop, and their children. No. 2 would remain empty for three more weeks.

James May was also a married man, and a father too, though he never let that stop him. He shared lodgings at 4 Dorset Street with Mary Ann Hall ("We do not live together exactly, but I think he is more with me than with anybody else")—a woman so devoted she once stayed up until three in the morning trying to dry his soaking-wet jacket as he slept.[38]

Like both Bishop and Williams, May had tried and found wanting more than one trade before becoming a resurrectionist. He was the illegitimate son of a barrister at New Inn—one of London's smaller inns of court, just north of Fleet Street—and the inn's laundress. May's mother doted on her only child, to the extent that he was known locally as something of a mama's boy. He was educated at a boarding school, had fine handwriting, and his father found him a position as a lawyer's clerk at New Inn. But he quickly became bored, preferring to work as a butcher's assistant in Clare Market, the tiny seventeenth-century market square that was just around the corner from the inn.[39] But before long he was finding this dull too, and, despite the concerns of his parents and friends, he began to mix with thieves and resurrectionists and bought himself a horse and cart with which he helped them transport corpses. Then he became a grave robber himself.

May took lodgings in Clement's Lane, just south of Clare Market, overlooking the burial ground of St. Clement Danes Church. This cemetery, known as the Green Ground, was also the graveyard of the local workhouse in Portugal Street and was notoriously overcrowded, with new burials often lying just a foot beneath the surface. The walls of the Clement's Lane houses backing on the Green Ground ran with stinking slime, and the stench from the graveyard was so bad that windows were kept shut year-round. The children who attended Sunday school just across the lane in the Enon Chapel learned their lessons as "body bugs" (mayflies) buzzed around them, while during services parishioners often passed out because of the smell emanating from the chapel's crypt, where some twelve thousand bodies lay packed one on top of the other (the coffins having been broken up for firewood) in a space just sixty feet by twenty-nine by six.[40] From his Clement's Lane room, May kept watch for imminent and recent interments in the Green Ground: at last he had found a trade to which he could stick, although when asked by the authorities he would continue to give his trade as "butcher." But he couldn't keep quiet about the excitement and high earnings of his new job and would brag around the streets of Clare Market. He soon found himself shunned in the district in which he had grown up, so he moved south of the Thames, to Elephant and Castle.

He was accustomed to the attention of the police, having been arrested on a number of occasions for being in possession of an illegally disinterred body. In April 1825, he and fellow snatcher John Jerrome were caught by two watchmen, accompanied by a number of local residents, in the graveyard of St. Leonard's, Shoreditch, with a body in a sack, a spade, and a pickaxe close to a newly refilled—and empty—grave. In court, May and Jerrome's attorney attempted the audacious defense that the pair had simply been two among the concerned crowd of locals trying to apprehend those who had robbed the grave and fled. This defense caused much laughter in court, but astonishingly, the jury acquitted May and Jerrome.

So despite putting the arresting officers to great trouble on the afternoon of 5 November 1831, May was not taking this latest run-in very seriously. He felt sure the New Police's mistake would soon be cleared up.

THREE

The Thickest Part

On Friday, 18 November, eight days after the verdict of the coroner's jury, Bishop, Williams, May, and Shields were brought to the bar at the Bow Street magistrates office for the first of a series of hearings. The office was packed with spectators; the bench where the magistrates sat facing the accused across the room was crowded with "gentlemen," many of them London surgeons, whose presence suggested that they, too, had some authority over the prisoners and were on the side of right. George Rowland Minshull, magistrate, was in charge of the proceedings; James Corder would present the evidence against the prisoners, which had been collected by Superintendent Joseph Sadler Thomas.

It was a small room, formerly the parlor of what had once been a private house, and Charles Dickens was shortly to describe it thus: "The room smelt close and unwholesome; the walls were dirt discoloured; and the ceiling blackened. . . . [There was] a thick greasy scum on every inanimate object."[1] Minshull himself had written to the commissioners of the New Police protesting that the cesspools in the adjoining lockup rooms were in urgent need of emptying, since the "soil" was oozing through the cell walls.[2] Moreover, wrote Minshull, "The water closet is so situated as to open immediately upon the entry appropriated to the whole public, including prisoners and paupers, and we can only reach it by passing through the crowd. This has always been a source of inconvenience and discomfort and in some respects endangers the health of the magistrates, and we are now more than ever desirous of having a water closet placed in an accessible and safe position." He went on to point out that the magistrates were obliged to sit in front of the fireplace, a damp and gusty spot that "attracts the smell of the whole room."[3]

Into this fetid environment walked witness Margaret King, heavily pregnant and described in reports of the hearings as "a decent-looking woman." She told the court that at about one o'clock in the afternoon of "the Thursday before Guy Fawkes Night" she was walking with her children near Nova Scotia Gardens when she saw what she described to the magistrate as "an Italian boy" standing about thirty yards from her, with a small box or cage slung around his neck and resting on his chest.[4] He had his back to her. King lived with her husband, son, and daughter at 3 Crabtree Row, near the Birdcage pub, and she claimed that she had often seen the boy in the area. On that day she had refused to let her children go across to him to see what was in his box. No, she had not seen his face. She went on to say that the following week, "I heard some gentlemen speaking about the awful murder that had been committed on the body of a poor Italian boy, and I immediately said, 'Dear me! I saw a boy such as is described standing at the end of Nova Scotia Gardens a short time ago.'" On that day, she said, the boy had been standing with his back to her, but nevertheless she was sure it was "the poor Italian" she had seen so often. And she had not seen him since that Thursday.

Before Margaret King spoke, John Bishop had been smiling and James May appeared nonchalant; when King mentioned the cage, both sat up, leaned forward, stared, and began to listen carefully.

Mary Paragalli now repeated the evidence she had given to the coroner—that the dead boy was the Italian she used to see displaying a cage of white mice, that she had last seen him just after noon in Oxford Street, near Hanover Square, on Tuesday, 1 November, and that she had seen his corpse on Sunday the sixth at the watch house.

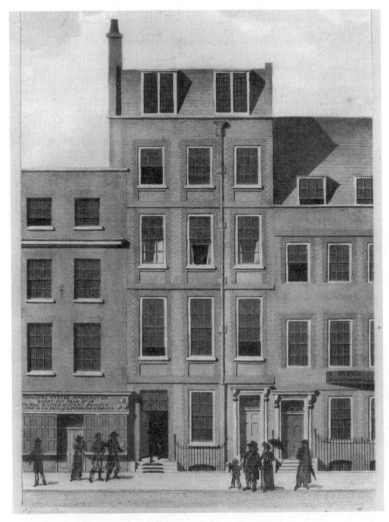

The Bow Street police office/magistrates court

From across the room, John Bishop asked her: "Are you quite certain that the boy you saw in Oxford Street was the same boy whose body lay at the station?"

"I have no doubt of it," she replied, adding, "and at a distance, the cage might appear like a box," as though to explain away Margaret King's confusion about the contraption in which the boy had kept his mice. Quite how Mrs. King could have seen it at all when the boy had his back to her was a matter the magistrate did not pursue.

Minshull appears to have been generous in exercising his discretion to allow Bishop, Williams, May, and Shields to ask questions and call out contradictions. But Minshull's courtesy in allowing them to speak so freely could also invite the men to incriminate themselves, and it is possible the magistrate was stretching the rules in order to pick up anything at all that would assist the inquiry.

James Corder announced to the court that its task—and the task of the New Police—was "to fill up the links in the chain of evidence already brought forward."[5] Corder had given his private opinion to Home Secretary Lord Melbourne that Shields and May were probably only accessories after the fact and might therefore be persuaded to turn king's evidence.[6] But none of the prisoners had offered to assist the prosecution in return for immunity. Turning king's evidence had been the only way in which any sort of justice had been achieved in the Burke and Hare case; if Hare had not complied, it is quite pos-

Another representation of May, Williams, and Bishop, in the Bow Street dock

sible that a jury would have acquitted both the Edinburgh killers or brought in the unique Scottish verdict "not proven." It was at Hare's lodging house that an aged Highlander, Donald, had died in his bed, owing three pounds in back rent; and it was Hare, who, like Burke, had never been a resurrectionist, who struck upon the idea of imitating the body snatchers. Donald was sold to Dr. Knox for seven pounds, ten shillings. When another old and feeble lodging-house inmate, a miller called Joseph, was taking too long to die of a fever, he was suffocated by Burke and Hare and sold to Knox for ten pounds. With the next murder, probably of elderly street peddler Abigail Simpson (the precise order of the killings is unknown), Burke and Hare perfected their modus operandi of holding shut the victim's nose and mouth. This method was to be used on prostitutes Mary Paterson and Mary Haldane (and Mary Haldane's retarded daughter); eighteen-year-old "Daft Jamie" Wilson; Burke's cousin by (common-law) marriage Ann M'Dougal; an unnamed Englishman suffering from jaundice; and a number of beggars and peddlers whose names never came to light. Hare is also alleged to have dispatched at least one victim by himself. The killers were arrested on 1 November 1828, when guests at the lodging house discovered the body of beggar Mary Docherty in bedding straw. One month later, Hare betrayed Burke and escaped the gallows, laughing openly in court at finding himself a witness for the prosecution in the trial of his colleague.

This was the sort of treachery that James Corder was hoping for from Bishop, Williams, May, or Shields. The investigation would be easier if somebody snitched: if they didn't, establishing the order of events that converted an unidentified boy into the Subject that was tipped onto the floor at King's College would require the tracking down and bringing together of witnesses and physical evidence in order to create a plausible narrative for an Old Bailey jury to consider. But the concept of objects being able to tell tales and supply solutions to mysteries was in its infancy; observation, deduction, analysis, and "scientific" forensics were only on the verge of replacing traditional approaches to criminal cases. In the 1830s, guilt was still established by eyewitness accounts, being caught in the act, having a bad reputation, or simply looking and sounding the part of a criminal. But the eyes not just of the capital but of the whole nation were

William Burke and William Hare as they appeared in court in Edinburgh in December 1828

focused on these proceedings. Melbourne himself had told Superintendent Joseph Sadler Thomas "to employ his men without reserve as to labour or expense" and had offered a king's pardon "under the usual limitations" to any accomplice, and a two-hundred-pound reward for anyone who came forward with evidence that would secure the conviction of the suspects in the case of the Poor Italian Boy—for even Whitehall had taken to referring to the victim in this way.[7] This, Thomas's first murder case, shows the fumbling beginnings of a methodical analysis of a crime scene and possible weapons, the checking of alibis and the testing of eyewitness evidence. As with any new science, the experiments, to later ages, can appear ludicrous.

Item No. 1 was a tortoise. Following newspaper reports that the dead boy was being tentatively identified as an Italian beggar who exhibited white mice and/or a tortoise, an anonymous letter was received at Bow Street claiming a "similar-looking" tortoise was for sale in a shop in Middle Row, Holborn.[8] Superintendent Thomas had wasted no time in going to the shop, where the owner's wife had told him that her husband had purchased the creature in Leadenhall Market. Nevertheless, Thomas took the tortoise into custody, and when he shortly afterward showed it to Joseph Paragalli, the

Italian claimed that, yes, it certainly looked like the dead boy's tortoise.

In court on Friday the eighteenth, Thomas flourished before Minshull the hamper and bloodstained sack that had been used to transport the body to King's College and presented in a small box the teeth that May had sold to the dentist, Mills. At this point in the hearing, James May dropped his usual facetiousness; he was perhaps realizing how a jury might interpret the fact that he had told Mills that all the teeth had come from the same body and that the body had never been buried. The *Times* reporter noted that May now began to stare wildly, compressing his lips tightly as he took in every word the dentist said: "May appeared for the first time to lose that hardness of nerve that distinguished him."[9] Then May self-consciously attempted to compose his features and laughed a rather hollow laugh, before starting and staring again, muttering, "You bloody rascal," at Mills.

May was also alarmed to learn that his lodgings had been searched by Thomas's men and a number of items retrieved. The officers had found a waistcoat with marks of clay on it, some metal implements, and a pair of bloodstained trousers; there was also blood on the floor near where the trousers had lain. May protested, telling the court that after his arrest, a jackdaw had hopped onto his trousers after injuring its leg; he knew, because one of the other tenants had visited him in prison and told him so. Superintendent Thomas said that he was inclined to believe this story, since the search had taken place a full week after May's arrest and the bloodstains were "entirely too fresh and glutinous" to have had any connection with the murder, though Constable Joseph Higgins pointed out that a rain shower that came down as the clothing was being carried back to the police station may have made the blood look fresh. In his evidence, Higgins made no mention of the jackdaw story, and May picked up on this attempt to implicate him, saying, "Now Mr Policeman, do you remember the jackdaw having hurt his leg? You did not state that to the worthy justice when you ought to have done." The bloodied jackdaw was no bizarre invention; Charlotte Berry, one of the residents at the lodging house, admitted that she had been playing with the bird—which was kept as a pet by the landlady, Mrs. Carroll—on the first-floor landing at 4 Dorset Street and had accidentally injured it by pinching its foot in the door; the bird had then hopped into May's room, which was next to Berry's.

In investigating May's alibi, the police had examined Rosina Carpenter, "a young woman with whom one of the prisoners had occasionally co-habited." May claimed that he had spent the night of Thursday, 3 November, with Carpenter, from late in the afternoon. Carpenter was a childhood friend of May's with whom he was now intimate; whatever she had told the authorities was withheld from the press, however, on the grounds that "it would be very imprudent to publish at present."[10]

Superintendent Thomas's energetic police work did not always achieve results. He had received an unsigned letter stating that John Appleton, the dissecting-room porter at Grainger's medical school, had told a postman that the body offered to him by Bishop and May on Friday, 4 November, was still warm. But when Thomas brought Appleton before Minshull, the porter indignantly denied having said any such thing to anyone and insisted he had never even seen the body.

As interesting as the evidence brought to court is the evidence the authorities decided not to pursue. A Jewish clothes dealer who lived in Saffron Hill had come forward to claim that four men came into his shop in West Street, Smithfield, at half past two on the afternoon of Friday, 4 November, to exchange a pair of bloodstained corduroy breeches and a waistcoat for clean versions of the same and bought a smock frock with unusual stitching; two of the four men were already wearing smock frocks. The clothes dealer was escorted to see the prisoners in Clerkenwell New Prison, where they were being held on remand, on Saturday, 12 November, in an attempt to identify the four men he had served; he was able to pick out May and Bishop, though not Williams or Shields.[11] If indeed two other men came to his shop, their identities would never be established: Bishop and May had made no mention of them in their statements about their movements that Friday. For reasons that are not clear, James Corder told Minshull that the prosecution did not intend to investigate further the clothes-exchanging episode, despite the identification that had been made. Perhaps Corder decided to abandon this promising line of inquiry in order to protect the clothes dealer from possible attacks from the accused if they were acquitted or from their associates in the event of their conviction. Or perhaps with two unknown men entering the story, the case was becoming too convoluted to be put convincingly before a jury. The plot was thickening, or as Minshull put it: "We are now in the thickest part of the horrid affair." Yes, "the facts certainly thickened upon them," replied Superintendent Thomas.[12]

With reference to the cause of death, Thomas announced to Minshull that he believed the cut on the forehead of the dead boy was probably the fatal blow; in saying this, he was contradicting the unanimous evidence of the anatomists who had studied the corpse. Thomas also saw significance in the fact that James May's left hand was poulticed and bandaged, and he asked Richard Partridge to step across the court to examine the wound. This Partridge did, announcing that there was an injury to the top of the forefinger that had probably occurred just before the arrest. May said he had received the

Clerkenwell New Prison, where Bishop, Williams, and May were detained during the police investigation

wound as he punched out the dead boy's teeth with a brad awl at 3 Nova Scotia Gardens.

Every comment made by the accused was seized upon by Superintendent Thomas. Bishop had said shortly after his arrest that the body had come from Guy's Hospital. (This wasn't strictly a lie, since Bishop and May had collected it from there on the morning of Saturday the fifth.) Thomas immediately sent a message to Guy's with a request to know whether any boy had died there lately. Guy's sent back a slip of paper stating that since 28 October three people had died at the hospital—a woman and two males, aged thirty-three and thirty-seven.

Thomas was also proud to reveal that while the four men were waiting to be taken to the coroner's hearing at the Unicorn pub, Bishop had leaned over Williams and muttered to May that it had been the blood dripping from the boy's forehead injury that had given them away: "It was the blood that sold us," Bishop said. The men were sitting beneath a police notice about the murder for which they were being held. Bishop stood up and read the notice, gave a forced laugh, and told his colleagues, "This states that there were 'marks of violence.' The marks of violence were only breakings-out on the skin." He sat down smiling. These comments were overheard and written down by a plainclothes officer sitting nearby. Before Minshull, Bishop denied having made them, but his protestations carried little weight: things were not looking good for the accused.

Minshull was profoundly impressed by the energy and diligence with which Thomas was amassing clues and memorizing possibly telling exchanges. And it is striking how at every crucial point of the proceedings, Thomas pops up like a deus ex machina, revealing his latest "information received," producing tantalizing physical evidence, conjuring up new witnesses. However, just in case his confidence was misplaced, Minshull also called on one of the oldest of the Bow Street Runners, Samuel Taunton, to make inquiries around Bethnal Green and Shoreditch, a move not calculated to please Thomas. London's New Police were not supposed to be a detective force, after all: they had been created to prevent crime from happening. Such clearing up of mysteries that did take place was still the work of the Bow Street Runners—the small plainclothes force set up by Henry Fielding in 1749 that would work alongside the New Police until being disbanded in August 1839. The Runners received a retaining fee from the authorities but relied on rewards for their real earnings. While idolized by many, they depended heavily on informants to solve crimes and achieved their success by mixing with the very thieves, fences, and procurers they were supposed to be thwarting; pure analysis had little to do with it. Later in the century, Dickens would puncture their reputation, claiming they were "far too much in the habit of consorting with thieves and the like. . . . They never lost a public occasion of jobbing and trading in mystery and making the most of themselves. . . . As a detective police they were very loose in their operations."[13]

The coexistence of the Runners and the New Police was an oddity peculiar to London. Before 1829, London was policed by a ramshackle medley of parish constables, the Bow Street Night Patrol, the Bow Street Day Patrol, the Horse Patrol (to protect the highways), the Thames River Police, and the Runners, as well as the much-mocked Charleys—widely reputed to be elderly men who dozed the night away in their sentry boxes while stealing and brawling went on all around.[14] That there had been popular dissatisfaction with the officers of the Bow Street Day Patrol is suggested by a report of an angry meeting of the parishioners of St. Paul's, Covent Garden, in September 1828, who alleged that the patrol officers had been too drunk to be of any assistance when two houses fell down in Exeter Street, off the Strand, killing a woman and a child. According to those trying to free the injured from the debris, only the St. Paul's parish constables—quite probably including Thomas—were sober and came immediately to help.[15]

Not every metropolitan parish was as fortunate in its constables, however. In St. Pancras, eighteen rival watch trusts divided up the policing of the parish without any common system; Lambeth, Fulham, and Wandsworth were said to have no night watchmen at all, while at one point Kensington was said to have had just three parish constables. If a parish constable saw a crime taking place on the other side of the street and that other side was in another parish, he was unable to intervene.

A Charley is removed far from his place of watch as he dozes, in this unsigned engraving of 1825.

This "old" system of policing—much of it dating back to Tudor times—was generally perceived as inadequate to the needs of modern society, as well as inherently corruptible: in 1816, six Runners had been transported after having been found guilty of setting up robberies. It was to change this system that Robert Peel, home secretary in Wellington's premiership, devised his Metropolitan Police Act in 1829. The act proposed a single, unified police force for London that would be uniformed (a controversial innovation) and under the command of two government-appointed commissioners: this, too, was inflammatory, because it made central government—rather than the London parishes and the local magistrates at London's nine police offices—responsible and answerable for policing. Hostility was also expressed toward attempts to put any Englishman under state surveillance—a distinctly foreign concept, it was believed, that would imperil the freedom of the individual. There were fears that Peel's New Police would be a

militaristic body, placing the country at the mercy of thousands of uniformed petty despots, acting as they wished with full governmental
backing.

Faced with such strong opposition, Wellington's government
passed a watered-down version of Peel's bill, excluding the City of
London; the City (the "Square Mile" enclave within Greater London
bordered by Whitechapel to the east, Holborn to the west, the rundown district of St. Luke's, Old Street, to the north, and the river
Thames to the south) was permitted to continue with its own ancient
method of policing. This meant that areas within the City boundary,
such as Smithfield, the Bank of England, St. Paul's, Fleet Street, and
Barbican, retained their chaotic Charleys-plus-parish-watchmen sys-
tem, overseen by the similarly antiquated government of the City—
the court of aldermen and the Corporation of London. The rest of
London, lying outside the City, was divided by the first Metropolitan
Police commissioners into seventeen divisions, covering an area of
about twelve miles radiating from Charing Cross: Whitehall was A
Division, Westminster was B, St. James's C, Marylebone D, Holborn
E, and so on. Each division was headed by a superintendent (Joseph
Sadler Thomas was the superintendent of F Division—Covent Garden) and comprised eight sections, each section consisting of eight
"beats" worked by ten men (one sergeant and nine constables). A beat
was one to one and a half miles long—an officer was to be able to see
each part of his beat every quarter of an hour or so, walking at around
two and a half miles an hour. This pattern was superimposed on the
parochial geography of London, cutting right across old parish boundaries.

On the morning of Saturday, 26 September 1829, almost one
thousand men (some two thousand had applied for the positions)
lined up on the grounds of the Foundling Hospital, near Gray's Inn
Road, to be sworn in as London's first New Police officers and were
issued their blue uniforms and equipment—their only weaponry was
a short wooden stave, or baton. From the moment of their formation
the Metropolitan Police encountered tremendous resistance. Contempt for Peel's Bloody Gang, Peel's Private Army, the Blue Devils, the
Plague of Blue Locusts permeated the whole of London society. The
antipathy was as deeply felt in the drawing rooms of the West End as

it was in the capital's "flash houses"—pubs and taverns where stolen goods were fenced and new robberies plotted. Many among the middle classes wondered whether the arrival of the New Police was simply the first in a line of measures to restrict an Englishman's liberty; even an Englishwoman's liberty was at risk. This letter to the *Times* was a characteristic response:

> Sir, I see by your paper that a few days since [magistrate] Mr Roe, of Great Marlborough Street, committed some dozen women of the town for not obeying the policemen when desired to leave the [Regent Street] Quadrant. I have observed lately various instances of the same illegal and arbitrary conduct. I am no patroniser of disorderly persons of any class or description, but if our personal liberty is of any value, and is not to be at the mercy of every insolent policeman, I should wish to know by what legal authority this very constitutional force assumes to itself the power of seizing and imprisoning any woman, disorderly or not, who does not choose to leave the streets at their command. I should also wish to be informed under what authority that excellent magistrate Mr Roe commits women of the town by wholesale upon the bare assertion (not oath) of the constable that the said women were disorderly, when it is well known that punishment is not inflicted for any act of disorder but for presuming to remain in the streets contrary to the prohibition of the policeman.
>
> Let a law be passed that these unfortunate persons are not to be permitted to walk the streets at all and then they will at least be acquainted with the laws to which they are subject; but at present the law stands thus, "that any prostitute being found in the streets in a state of drunkenness, or acting otherwise in a disorderly manner, may be committed" &c. It is, therefore, clearly contrary to law to seize or imprison them for any thing short of this.[16]

Many property owners and tradesmen were angered by the imposition of a centralized body over a set of local men—no matter how corruptly these may have been elected. On a more mundane level, parish authorities resented the new police levy that was imposed in place of the old watch rate, or tax, which had brought the additional benefit of keeping old men in employment and thus off the parish poor rate; some London parishes withheld their police-rate payments for as long as possible. Even Whitehall proved obstructive: when Melbourne took over from Robert Peel as home secretary in the new government of Earl Grey in November 1830, he tended to side with chief London magistrate Sir Richard Birnie (who once stated, "I never saw a constable who was perfectly competent") in his relentless criticisms of the Metropolitan Police's first joint commissioners, Charles Rowan and Richard Mayne. Rowan and Mayne, meanwhile, spilt a great deal of ink mollifying newspaper editors, refuting the notion that there was to be any increase in the numbers of Metropolitan Police officers.[17] George IV himself made a point of very loudly praising the manager of the Drury Lane Theatre in Covent Garden after a performance for refusing to allow any New Police into the building. The Runners were to retain their exclusive role of keeping an eye on pickpockets within the theater for ten more years.[18]

The New Police were supposed to differ from their precedessors in practice as well as in structure. Members of the new force were to be drawn from the "respectable" sections of the working class: an ingenious stroke—using the poor to police the poor. Rowan and Mayne explicitly advised recruits to the New Police against cultivating informers and mixing with villains, and officers were expressly forbidden to enter the pubs and lodging houses in which thieves were said to meet. So the Runners were kept on in their capacity of infiltrating the underworld of thieves and receivers. In a sense, they were containing crime, by keeping a close eye on the most likely offenders and the premises where such people congregated. However, the much-loathed figure of the "common informer" continued to play a significant part in policing and securing convictions in the 1830s; indeed, this role had broadened during the eighteenth century to become crucial to the detection and prosecution of criminals. Every trial had to have a prosecutor. In trials for murder and manslaughter, rex or regina played the part—these crimes were deemed to have been committed against the Crown of England; but property crimes required a private prosecutor, and the real victim of the loss was often unable (through poverty or lack of free time) or unwilling to institute proceedings. In those instances, the informer would mount the case against a suspected thief and fill the role of prosecutor in the courts; upon a conviction, a portion of the value of the goods stolen was passed to the informer as a reward. In addition, an informer who brought to the attention of the authorities any citizen who committed a broad range of nuisances—shortchanging, food adulteration, the dumping of refuse in the highway, Customs and Excise abuses, for example—received cash payments. So unpopular was this role that an act of Parliament was passed specifically to outlaw physical attacks on informers. (An informer did not have to be a professional snitch, though. Not only were members of the public entitled to tell tales but they were often paid when they did—just one way in which the community was deemed capable of policing itself. However, juries were known to take into consideration the fact that "information received" had often been paid for and could choose to treat such evidence with skepticism.)

By contrast, there were to be no rewards for a Metropolitan Police officer who solved a crime or returned stolen goods to their rightful owner, and no justice-evading out-of-court deals were to be done by the new force. But if an officer was not close to the source of the criminality—mingling with thieves, fences, procurers, swindlers, and forgers; keeping the channels open between himself and the common informers—how could he realistically find out what he needed to know? If, as it seemed at the time, criminals were becoming increasingly well organized, what strategies could be put in place to discover their networks and thwart their plots?

The age of the detective as hero was imminent; in 1841 Edgar Allan Poe would introduce the sleuth to English-language fiction with Auguste Dupin in *The Murders in the Rue Morgue*. But in 1831, detection was a phenomenon as new and experimental as railway travel, gallstone removal, the omnibus, phrenology, Catholics in Parliament, the concept of votes for all. The notion of one man exploring the mechanisms and milieu of urban crime had been introduced to London in 1828 with the publication of the English translation of the memoirs of Eugène-François Vidocq (1775–1857), a criminal turned informer who went on to head Napoleon's police department. Ghost-written and unreliable, Vidocq's *Mémoires* nevertheless enjoyed huge success in Britain and reached poorer homes through stage adaptations and plagiarisms. Vidocq's appeal was that he could penetrate seemingly alien strata of urban society, bring back tales of the habits of these worlds, and provide solutions to crimes and mysteries.[19] That was the sort of man it would take to crack the Italian Boy case, since none of those in the know was talking.

Joseph Sadler Thomas was, in many ways, the model of the new type of policeman—but could he also be a London Vidocq? Although the New Police were a nondetective force, Thomas seems to have been keen to act the sleuth. Known for his zeal, he was already something of a local legend when he became the first superintendent of Covent Garden's Division F at its formation in September 1829. But if "zealous" could have been his middle name, so too could histrionic, lachrymose, prudish, self-pitying, and outspoken. Since October 1827, Thomas had been the parish constable (that is, one of the "old" police) of St. Paul's, Covent Garden—an unpaid post that he combined with his paid job as cashier at the box office of Covent Garden Theatre. Thomas's aim, he told the Parliamentary Select Committee convened in 1828 to explore the parlous state of the police in London, was "to correct the many evils with which my neighbourhood abounds. . . . In consequence of my interference, I have reason to believe that a very great change has taken place for the better."[20]

Thomas's opinions ("I perceived, as anybody else does, a wonderful apathy in the police officers")[21] and activities (applying to magistrates to have cab stands removed, coffee stalls shut down, pub-license applications denied) had made him many enemies. His high arrest rate, which cast doubt on the competence of other officers, infuriated his Bow Street rivals. Thomas received threats of harm to his wife and three children, and once he was physically assaulted and dragged through the streets by two Runners and two officers of the Bow Street Day Patrol who, tired of his criticism of their indolence, decided to arrest him for loitering outside Drury Lane Theatre. "I was struck and dragged through the streets like a felon . . . past an exulting set of blackguards," he told the 1828 Police Select Committee. Magistrate Sir Richard Birnie dismissed the charge of loitering that the Runners and Day Patrol had brought against Thomas; but many other London magistrates had little patience with him.

Those in even higher positions of authority frequently belittled Thomas and lost no opportunity to trip him up—a task he made much easier for them by his habit of speaking before thinking. The 1828 Select Committee had quite a bit of fun questioning him, playing on his moral certainty, which combined rather disastrously with his lack of knowledge of basic law. Thus Thomas asserted to the committee that it was well known that the two pubs that stood opposite the Bow Street police office—the Brown Bear and the Marquis of Anglesey—were flash houses. When pressed, he backed down, saying that they probably weren't flash houses after all but that they certainly didn't keep to their licensing hours.[22] At a later Select Committee hearing, Thomas was accused of relying on "defective evidence," showing "weak and childish conduct," and being "weak and pusillanimous and childish. . . . For in fact, he shed tears," sneered Middlesex magistrate Sir John Scott Lillie.[23] Even Commissioners Rowan and Mayne wrote him frequent reprimands when he failed to adhere to the new, post-1829 way of doing things: "The Commissioners of Police notice in *The Times* of this morning that Mr Thomas asked advice from the magistrates at Bow Street, respecting the state of dogs in the street. The Commissioners have more than once had occasion to notice the irregularity of such a course, and acquainted Mr Thomas that he was to apply to them in all cases when he required any advice for the guidance of the police. The Commissioners now desire Mr Thomas to understand that if they find him again repeating this practice they will consider it a wilful disobedience of their orders."[24] And so on.

But Thomas had two well-placed allies: the first, George Rowland Minshull, seems to have been cut from similar cloth. The magistrate was often derided for being unworldly, and the phrase he frequently let slip when hearing evidence—"Oh! How shocking!"—was a source of fun to his detractors.[25] He was one of the few London magistrates who wanted the New Police to succeed, and he saw that Thomas was, apart from anything else, an effective officer. Shortly after the New Police were formed, the new superintendent had marshaled forty Division F officers and broken up a mass brawl in the Seven Dials district of Covent Garden, arresting thirty drunken, fighting men.[26] Then, on Wednesday, 27 April 1831, in the Strand, Thomas had walked into the middle of a crowd of two to three thousand angry Londoners— including many women and children—who were protesting the defeat of the Reform Bill and persuaded them not to riot as they marched through the West End. The bill was intended to widen male suffrage by lowering the property-value threshold, thereby enfranchising certain sections of the merchant class for the first time; many (perhaps most) workingmen believed this step would bring them the vote too. The bill was also intended to put an end to the phenomenon of "rotten," or "pocket," boroughs—districts with few constituents, which were under the control of wealthy landowners and enjoyed a representation in Parliament that was disproportionate to their small populations. The bill had been defeated on the twentieth, and on the twenty-second Parliament had been "prorogued" (suspended), which meant the measure would not be debated again for months. In response, Wednesday, 27 April, was designated the night of the General Illumination, on which Londoners were to light lamps or candles and place them in their windows to show their support for parliamentary reform. The instructions to carry out this dramatic but nonviolent form of civil protest had been spread by street criers, by handbills, and in the Radical press. In addition to homes, shops, and pubs, the boats and barges on the Thames, theaters, banks, and newspaper offices were all ablaze with light. Many protesters had also decided to march through town, and, although most were peaceful (some even sang "God Save the King"), a number had stoned darkened windows, and missiles were thrown at Thomas and his men in the Strand. He was struck twice by wooden staves, but he stood his ground, and some in the crowd even shouted, "Bravo, Police!" By the end of the protest, at four o'clock in the morning, 168 stone throwers had been arrested; almost all were later acquitted, released on bail, or lightly fined, which seems to indicate either the lack of seriousness of the offenses or the tacit sympathy of the magistrates.[27]

Thomas also had the support of influential London Radical and political reformer Francis Place (1771–1854), who often consulted the superintendent on policing matters. Place thought Thomas "very useful and intelligent," and the two men together worked out a theory of crowd control—the baton charge—to deal with the frequent expressions of popular unrest. Eager to stop the government from finding excuses to deploy troops on the streets, Place and Thomas decided that if an unruly mob should assemble in London and appear intent on looting and damage to property, sound thrashings would be meted out, but not until the police were certain that they were about to be attacked. Only "sufficient" violence, as Place termed it, was to be used—just enough to disperse the large groups that Place believed had no interest in political or social issues, merely "a vague hope of plunder." These London mobs, he wrote, had no genuine "bond of union" and "were composed of idle and miscreant people" and were "remarkably cowardly."[28]

The baton-charge theory was put into practice on 9 November 1830. Reform Bill unrest had been fomenting for some time; the Radical, pro-Reform press were accused of stirring it up and of encouraging anti–New Police sentiment. But the behavior of King William IV, his courtiers, and other aristocratic Londoners—apparently flaunting their wealth by riding through town, gorgeously dressed, in fine carriages—was also cited as incendiary. A magnificent procession, with the king riding in state to a fete hosted by the lord mayor, was due to take place on 9 November; it was postponed amid fears that it would provoke popular unrest and result in "mobbing." Despite the cancelation, a crowd—an unknown contingent of which had apparently been taking part in a march in the East End in support of the unemployed Spitalfields weavers—came across the City boundary at Temple Bar in Fleet Street, armed with staves (in fact, pieces of wood stolen from a building site in Chancery Lane) and shouting "Down with the police." Thomas and a large body of policemen were waiting in Catherine Street, close to Drury Lane, and fanned out across the Strand to block the crowd's progress. The police, brandishing their batons, rushed toward the crowd, who scattered instantly. Place claimed that this rout marked the end of that particular type of mobbing in London.

Thrashings and military-style maneuvers aside, Superintendent Thomas was also capable of kindness and empathy. He often returned runaway children to their parents when he came across them sleeping in Covent Garden market. One of these was the son of

a surveyor from Marylebone whom Thomas had found at three
o'clock in the morning asleep under a market stall; the child had taken
his father's watch and said he was planning to stow away on board
a ship when dawn came.[29] Although Thomas was compelled under
threat of a fine to arrest anyone sleeping in the open air, he had admitted to the 1828 Police Select Committee that he never arrested the
dozen or so paupers who bedded down every night at the king's
entrance to the Drury Lane Theatre when the actors and audience
had departed. As he put it, "in many of those instances, they are very
unfortunate people who have seen better days."

FOUR

Houseless Wretches

The number of anxious parents who had come to see the young boy's body in the Covent Garden watch house, and the tales of loss they told, had amazed the coroner, his jury, the magistrates, and the parish authorities of St. Paul's. It had also surprised the home secretary; Lord Melbourne was indolent and indecisive, where his predecessor, Robert Peel, had had a horrified curiosity about the new urban society that was emerging and had effected measures to confront it. (Typical of Melbourne's effete manner was his response on being offered the role of prime minister, later, in 1834: "He thought it was a damned bore and he was half inclined to turn it down.")[1] But James Corder's letter accompanying the report of the coroner's findings had elicited an uncharacteristically vigorous reply from Melbourne in which he asked Corder to see if he could find out why it was that so many young people appeared to have gone missing in the city.[2]

In addition to the various Italians who had come forward, eight sets of parents had notified the Bow Street magistrates of their sons' disappearance and had asked to see the dead child. The mother and father of a deaf-mute boy told Bow Street magistrate George Rowland

Minshull that they feared their child had been abducted, killed, and sold to surgeons for dissection, since they had heard that the men being held in custody were known resurrectionists. A Mr. Hart, the owner of a linen shop in Oxford Street, "a most respectable trades-man, in affluent circumstances," according to the *Morning Advertiser,* wept as he told Minshull that his fourteen-year-old son had gone missing on Tuesday, 1 November, and that he had placed a notice, with a full description of the boy, in the newspapers; it may have been this advertisement that Richard Partridge's pupils had read when their suspicions were aroused about the corpse delivered to King's. According to local solicitor James Isaacs, Hart's son "was well-educated, of moral pursuits, and could not be suspected of a roving inclination, and yet he had disappeared all at once, and no trace could be obtained of him."[3] (The body of Hart's son was pulled from the Regent's Canal at Lisson Grove one week later, fully clothed and decomposing. The cause of his death was never to be established, but the newspapers nevertheless decided that it was likely he had been "burked.")

Perhaps most startling was the nature of the families reporting lost children—ordinary working people, many of them in trade, whose predicament presented an unsettling glimpse of the fragility of family life in the world's largest, wealthiest city. If children from set-tled, reasonably well-off families could simply disappear, what chance the orphans or the offspring of the desperately poor or impris-oned? "I know that I have lounged about the streets insufficiently and unsatisfactorily fed. I know that, but for the mercy of God, I might easily have been, for any care that was taken of me, a little robber or a little vagabond. . . . It is wonderful to me how I could have been so easily cast away at such an age": this was Charles Dickens, toward the end of his life. At twelve years old, Dickens had found himself living alone in a boardinghouse in Camden Town and working in a small factory just off the Strand when the rest of his family moved into the debtors' prison, the Marshalsea, following his father's bankruptcy. Dickens earned six or seven shillings a week, but he felt that shock-ingly little separated him from the fate of the vagrant children he saw all about him in the streets around Covent Garden; and he never forgot the vulnerable condition into which he had been plunged.[4] Dickens's parents teetered in and out of genteelly distressed circumstances; the step into destitution was a short one. Only the intervention of family connections, who gave Dickens's father the chance to make a living as a journalist, rescued them. In households less blessed with skills and contacts, even contentedly married couples could find themselves with little time to devote to their children, since many families were able to subsist only if both parents worked virtually every hour they were awake. Other parents, though, may have been too attentive: the governor of Newgate Prison claimed that many of the child thieves in his care were the children of "decent working tradesmen" but had fled their homes because parental discipline was too harsh.[5]

A thirteen-year-old boy called Williams was found starving, diseased, and fast asleep in a doorway in Bedford Street, Covent Garden, by a parish constable in March 1826. Though he claimed he was an orphan from Devizes in Wiltshire, come to town to seek his fortune, it transpired that Williams's parents lived just a mile away, in a street off Fitzroy Square, and that the boy had run away from them at least twenty times. The magistrates ordered Williams to be looked after at the St. Martin's-in-the-Fields watch house until an apprenticeship could be arranged for him.[6]

The ten-year-old son of an army surgeon named Macher was inveigled away from the family home in Knightsbridge in 1824 by a former shoemaker turned vagrant variously known as Thomas Wood, Thomas Buxton, or Thomas Cox, whose speciality was to chalk poems on the pavement and await contributions from passersby. Seven months after the boy's disappearance, constables spotted Wood/Buxton/Cox sitting begging in Keppel Street, off Gower Street in Bloomsbury, with an "attractive little boy" alongside him—this was Master Macher. The boy "strenuously denied" that he was Macher and was seen waiting patiently for hours for his abductor to be released from police questioning; however, he eventually and reluctantly admitted his identity "and he was, to the utmost joy of his disconsolate parents, delivered over to them." It's not quite the picture of happy family life that this newspaper report wished to convey.[7]

Police and magistrates also heard many stories of parents who would send their children into the streets, telling them not to come home until they had earned a certain sum, through either begging or theft; those children who were too afraid to return empty-handed were frequently reported to be among those found sleeping in London's more secluded spots—under the stalls of the various markets, in the shrubs of Hyde Park, in the shells of houses under construction, curled up in the haystacks of Marylebone, in the coopers' barrels of Whitechapel, among the warm kilns of East End brickyards.[8] Some vagrant children took it upon themselves to live entirely outside the realm of adult supervision. One gang of Covent Garden vagabond boys formed the Forty Thieves, and its members identified themselves by a primitive form of tattoo: a needle dipped in gunpowder pricked the gang-membership number into the skin of the palm. In September 1828, Nos. 5 and 8, both around the age of twelve, were arrested by the parish constable, possibly Joseph Sadler Thomas, and brought to trial on theft charges.[9]

Children under the age of seven were not criminally liable, since they were not deemed to be capable of crime. Yet London's prisons had plenty of slightly older children serving sentences for begging. In 1827, according to the 1828 *Police Select Committee Report,* seventeen boys and twenty-seven girls under the age of twelve served sentences in the Bridewell prison. (Newgate Prison even had a schoolmaster to teach the inmates under fourteen.) And Elizabeth Butler, imprisoned in a small jail in Westminster on a charge of vagrancy in January 1828, was, in fact, seven years old, as the Select Committee's own tables showed.[10]

Several factors contributed to the heightened vulnerability of young people in British cities, and one of the biggest of these was the strain placed on the traditional family. While divorce would not be available to anyone outside the aristocracy until 1857, common-law marriages increased in number from the end of the eighteenth century, with stepparents becoming more notable in descriptions of the makeup of urban families. Abandoned wives figure large in any data, descriptive or numerical, on the urban poor of these times, and while many women were widowed by the Napoleonic Wars (1799–1815) or saw their husbands rendered unfit for work through injury, some men had found conscription a handy exit from family life. Other men decamped for the cities to find work and never called for their wives and children to join them. Absconding fathers could be arrested and jailed for failing to maintain their dependents, and advertisements about them often appeared in the London publication *Hue and Cry* (renamed the *Police Gazette* in 1828), a twice-weekly compendium of recent court hearings and notices of stolen property, escaped prisoners, deserting soldiers, wanted criminals, and, from time to time, missing children.

Another destabilizing factor for young people was the end of "living-in" apprenticeships. Traditionally, young males who were apprenticed to learn a trade moved in with the "master's" family and received board and lodging as well as training. A formal apprenticeship lasted seven years—the years of adolescence and early manhood. The master took over the role of paterfamilias as long as the apprenticeship lasted, and many contracts stipulated that the apprentice was to abstain from drink and fornication. The signings of these "indentures" were witnessed by a senior figure in the parish, or even by a magistrate. (Their importance in a young man's life is indicated by the fact that John Bishop's own signed indenture had his birth caul attached to it.) In 1814, the Statute of Apprentices was repealed by Parliament in a move to free up the labor market and enlarge the pool of semiskilled workers who could take jobs without needing highly specialized training. The practice of shorter "out-apprenticeships" began, removing the board, lodging, and moral-supervision elements; when the day's training was over, young men had more time on their hands, unsupervised by either family or master. Some police officers and magistrates claimed this rise in the amount of leisure hours brought greater opportunities for youths to be led into "juvenile depravity," as it was coming to be termed. Only about one in eight cases heard at the Old Bailey involved any kind of violence (although this figure is unlikely to reflect the true level of violence—particularly in the home), and, in fact, London was a safer place for the person (though not for property) in the early decades of the nineteenth century than it had been in the eighteenth. But it didn't seem so. Though the highwaymen and "footpads" (muggers) of the Hanoverian age had been largely eradicated, vaguer, less easily located anxieties about urban evil remained. There began to be voiced, from the early 1820s, a suspicion that an organized, systematic layer, or web, of criminality existed that was becoming harder and harder for the authorities to penetrate. Such matters did not appear to be measurable, quantifiable, governable; and the aspects of city life that were evading the tables and lists began to prey on official minds precisely because of their unknowability.

London's rapidly swelling population further exacerbated the already precarious situation of the poor. Some thirty thousand babies were born in London each year in the first decades of the nineteenth century; yet the rising ranks of Londoners were not merely the result of the city's birth rate but reflected the phenomenon of urbanization. In 1801, the year of the first English census, just over one-third of the population lived in rural areas; by 1831, this proportion had dropped to just below one-quarter. In 1801, London's population had passed the one million mark; in 1831, it had risen to 1,646,288, representing almost one-eighth of the population of England and Wales. But people were coming to towns and cities from the country not so much to seek their fortune as to subsist. Internal migration had swelled from a steady stream to a torrent after 1815—an increase that was, arguably (and many historians have argued about it), accelerated by the process of "enclosure." Some 740,000 acres of farmland were amalgamated into large agricultural estates by 1815, while five million acres of common had also been enclosed, depriving of a livelihood those who made a humble living from grazing on commons and "waste" land. (These livings were a long-held custom, not a legal right.) The flight to the cities was the only reasonable prospect for the landless, propertyless, and unskilled; but it coincided with an economic collapse following the end of the Napoleonic Wars, which had demobilized half a million men home to a contracted employment market and a land where food prices fluctuated wildly and bread prices were kept artificially high to protect the incomes of landowners and owners of large farms.[11] Then, in 1825, came another, sudden economic depression.

Edward Pelham Brenton, a retired naval captain and philanthropist, noticed the saddest results of the mass migration on the streets of London every day. In addition to setting up refuges for the destitute, Brenton urged the wealthy, in a series of open letters, to remember their traditional, paternalistic duties to the poor in this rapacious new age of industrial and agrarian capitalism: "There are in the streets of this great Metropolis about 15,000 poor boys who gain their bread by lying, cheating, thieving, sweeping the streets and holding gentlemen's horses, and they are all perishing for want of our care. . . . We found them in the streets without food and clothes, or house, or friend, the objects of persecution and punishment, alternately the inmates of workhouses, of prisons, of dark cells, of tread mills, pursuing an uninterrupted course through all the gradations of misery and infamy, to the hulks and the gibbet."[12]

But destitution, like crime, was proving hard to catalog. London's transient population fell outside the scope of the census, and London's 153 parish vestries were under no obligation to collect such information.[13] The various charities, the police, and a number of Parliamentary Select Committees attempted head counts that were heavily reliant on anecdotal evidence. The London Society for the Suppression of Mendicity reported that over 40,000 people had come to its office in 1828; Edward Pelham Brenton, as noted, put the figure for vagrant boys in London at 15,000; the Society for Relieving the Houseless Poor admitted more than 6,500 different individuals to its three London refuges in the bitter winter of 1830–31 (providing bread, water, and clean straw to sleep on), with a total of 55,000 visits recorded. Police and judicial statistics are difficult to interpret, since magistrates habitually—either through carelessness or for reasons of humanity—failed to supply the sessions courts with details of convictions for vagrancy, as they were legally obliged to do.[14] One glimpse of such humanitarian feeling is caught in a report in the *Morning Post* in which Bow Street magistrate Thomas Halls lamented having to jail twelve vagrant men who had been found asleep in a prison van that was stored at nighttime in the vaults under the Adelphi Terrace, between the Strand and the Thames. Halls handed out one-month sentences to the reoffenders among the group and seven-day sentences to the first-time offenders, saying that he disliked having to imprison men "without their committing any other crime than that of having no place to go."[15]

Removing, or at least hiding, the poor was becoming an increasingly urgent task. The Vagrancy Act had become law in 1824: properly entitled An Act for the Punishment of Idle and Disorderly Persons, and Rogues and Vagabonds, in That Part of Great Britain Called England, the legislation was intended to tighten up outmoded, unworkable statutes and to form the bedrock of policing the public activities of the poor; instead, it was a ramshackle collection of prohibitions of various open-air "misdeeds." In its strictest application, anyone who looked out of place and failed to give a plausible account of him- or herself could be imprisoned. The following were deemed to be criminal and subject to one month's hard labor if the 1824 act was followed to the letter: anyone who could work but willfully refused or neglected to do so and applied for parish relief, anyone applying for relief in a parish where he or she had no settlement, any unlicensed itinerant peddler, and any prostitute wandering in the public streets behaving in an indecent manner. Moreover, "every person wandering abroad . . . in any public Place, Street, Highway, Court or Passage, to beg or gather alms, or causing or procuring or encouraging any Child or Children so to do, shall be deemed an idle and disorderly person within the true intent and meaning of this act."

Three months' hard labor was the punishment for anyone found sleeping in the open air with no visible means of subsistence and unable to give a good account of him- or herself, anyone asking for charity under false pretenses or showing wounds or deformities to gain alms, itinerant fortune-tellers and palmists, anyone betting or gambling in a public place, anyone selling or exposing to view an obscene picture or exhibition, any man found indecently exposing himself "with the intent to insult any female," any man who deserted his wife and/or family, leaving them dependent on parish relief, anyone carrying implements that could be used for burglary, and "every suspected person or reputed thief, frequenting any River, Canal, or navigable Stream, Dock or Basin, or any Quay, Wharf or Warehouse near to or adjoining thereto, or any Street, Highway or Avenue . . . with intent to commit Felony."[16]

Demobbed soldiers and sailors and discharged prisoners were entitled to permits to gather alms on their journey back to their home parishes, as were certain seasonal workers, such as harvesters. Aside from these exceptions, the act, far from settling once and for all the definition of "beggar," or of "loiterer with intent," or of "suspicious character," left vast leeway for police and magistrates to decide who was, and who was not, legally entitled to occupy public space. It conflated the concepts of idle and of disorderly, eliding unemployment with criminality; and it had the potential to circumscribe the activities of street entertainers and the sort of peripatetic sellers who provided a useful, less expensive alternative to fixed-location retailers. When the Parliamentary Select Committee on the Police of the Metropolis gathered its evidence in 1828, Joseph Sadler Thomas admitted to being unsure whether simply sleeping out in the open constituted an offense under the act.[17] (It did, and was punishable by three months' hard labor.)

But stints of jail and hard labor could hardly solve the problem. The question of what should be done with the vagrant poor, especially children, preoccupied numerous organizations. Parliamentary Select Committees convened to discuss the destitute in 1816, 1821, and 1828. There was a lively pamphlet debate about the best way to rescue street children and train them for "useful" lives. A variety of philanthropic societies—some harshly disciplinarian, others humane in intention—sprang up, supported by contributions from the wealthy. The London Society for the Suppression of Mendicity (colloquially known among the poor as the Dicity) was founded in 1818; the Children's Friend Society and the Society for the Suppression of Juvenile Vagrancy were founded in 1830; and the Nightly Shelter for the Houseless opened in 1822, with asylums in Playhouse Yard, off Golden Lane, and in London Wall. There were specialist charities too, such as the Society for Foreigners in Distress, the Marine Society for destitute former sailors, and the National Guardian Society for those who had formerly been employed as servants. Other bodies named themselves after the specific kind of help given, and in the East End, the Soup Society, the Blanket Association, even a City of London Truss Society attempted to alleviate the suffering of the very poor.

This piecemeal, haphazard charitable giving had two motives: humanity and the need to head off the threat of revolution. What had happened in Paris in 1789 informed much of the activity and behavior of the powerful and the wealthy. The year 1831 saw the formation of the National Union of the Working Classes, a coalition of London workingmen, mainly artisans in the furniture-making and weaving trades, who sought universal male suffrage, the reform of the House of Commons, and the passage of laws to protect the British working-man from exploitation. A number of independent political unions were springing up all over Britain in manufacturing towns and cities. With the shocking news in October 1831 that the House of Lords had thrown out the second attempt to pass the Reform Bill, there was nationwide civil unrest, with three days of rioting in Bristol (the town hall and bishop's palace were torched) and severe disturbances in Nottingham (the castle was razed), while in the capital the houses of prominent anti–Reform Bill figures were stoned. The newspapers of Monday, 7 November 1831, carried two major domestic stories: the discovery of a possible Burke and Hare case in Bethnal Green; and the suppression of a meeting of a body calling itself the Eastern Division of the Political Union of the Working Classes of the Metropolis— described by the *Times* as "The Mob." This rally, which the union itself billed as a "Monster Meeting," had caused so much alarm that the New Police posted public notices declaring it illegal—many of which were flamboyantly torn down by Londoners supportive of the Radical, pro-Reform cause; however, the union leaders called off the rally late in the day, their obedience confounding those who painted them as irrational, bloodthirsty Jacobins.

Meanwhile, in the countryside, protest against the enclosure of farmland, against low wages, unemployment, and the corruption of many rural parochial authorities—in particular, those who adminis-tered relief for the poor—gave rise to widespread civil unrest. The Captain Swing riots—fourteen hundred incidents of arson, livestock-maiming, and damage to farm property—lasted throughout the sum-mer and autumn of 1831, spreading across the whole of southern England, from Kent to Cornwall.[18]

However, the lower classes contained elements within their own ranks that proved the most effective means of quashing unrest and maintaining the status quo. Before the 1824 Vagrancy Act, anyone— including a parish constable—apprehending a beggar had been enti-tled to a financial reward. One of the most despised figures was the local "vagrant collector," such as John Conway of Highgate, who turned to the trade when his stay-making business collapsed. Conway was a prolific professional vagrant collector, receiving ten shillings from the parish upon the conviction of every beggar he apprehended and delivered to the magistrates.[19] The new act abolished these rewards—though many people were to remain unaware of this change in the law—but introduced fines of up to five pounds for any parish constable who failed to arrest a beggar. The belief that an apprehender of beggars was paid for turning in vagrants meant that there were plenty of dangers in undertaking such an arrest. The London Society for the Suppression of Mendicity employed a number of plainclothes officers, recruited from the lower-middle classes, to go into the streets to arrest suspected vagrants and bring them to the society's offices, at 13 Red Lion Square, Holborn. (Residents of the square protested at the "numerous and tumultuous assemblage" that gathered outside the Dicity upon the sudden arrival of the very cold winter of 1830–31.)[20] Once there, the vagrant would be either handed over to the authorities (to magistrates for trial on vagrancy charges or to the appropriate parish for relief) or supplied with vouchers for cheese, potatoes, rice, bread, and soup—or, for a skilled worker, a loan with which to buy the tools of his trade. If a vagrant proved up to stone breaking or oakum picking when put to the test in the Dicity's yard, he or she could be admitted to its very own poorhouse, whence around one in seven absconded. To qualify for relief, the claimant had to give a full account of his or her life—in effect, had to agree to be surveyed. This type of punitive snooping activity was loathed by the London poor, and Dicity officers were often attacked as they attempted to make arrests. One day in 1829, several hundred bystanders took the side of "MD," a forty-two-year-old Irish woman who had traveled almost two hundred miles to London from Macclesfield with her four children, all of whom were visibly feverish. The Dicity had given her financial aid in the past and its officers attempted to arrest her when they spotted her begging once more, but they were prevented from taking her into custody by the crowd that gathered round.[21] (Even authority figures faced such hostility: one evening in 1829 a number of police officers attempted to rescue a senior London magistrate, Allan Laing, who had had to barricade himself inside a shop in Lambs Conduit Street, Holborn, when a

crowd attacked him for attempting to make a citizen's arrest on an itinerant match seller who had asked him "for a penny or two." "Bonnet
[punch] him! Bring him out!" shouted the crowd, after they had freed
the beggar from Laing's clutches, to loud cheers.[22])

The Dicity produced annual reports praising its deeds of the past
year and providing a statistical breakdown and anecdotal evidence of
the "Objects" it had processed. Thus, the 1830 report gives the following picture of the 671 people detained by Dicity constables: 21
claimed to be impoverished because of old age, 6 cited business failure, 4 claimed to be foreigners who could not afford their fare home,
64 (mainly women) were destitute through loss—by death, desertion,
or imprisonment—of a husband or close relative, 1 had lost everything
in a fire, 1 had been shipwrecked, 61 had met with an accident or had
suffered a serious illness, 4 had had their pay or pension suspended, 2
were ex-convicts who could not find anyone to vouch for their good
name when seeking employment, 7 had no clothes in which they could
decently seek work, another 7 had no tools with which to carry out
their trade, 493 described themselves simply as "in want of employment." Of the 671, only 156 described themselves as native Londoners; some 285 had come up to London from the English countryside in
search of work; 127 were from Ireland; 28 were described as coming
"from Europe," regions unspecified; 28 were Scottish; 10 were Welsh;
7 were American; 5 were West Indian; 2 were from the East Indies; 2
were African; and a disproportionate 21 were Italian. The London
parish most likely to be named as place of abode was St. Giles, the rotting slum—in the process of becoming a national embarrassment—
just north of Covent Garden. Twice as many impoverished Londoners
came from St. Giles as from the next two parishes on the list—St.
Mary's, Whitechapel, and St. Andrew's, Holborn.

Since this data appeared in what was essentially a booklet appeal-
ing for funds, the attempt at categorization and quantification was no
doubt supposed to impress potential sponsors. After the report's figures come some brief notes on certain of the Dicity Objects of 1830:

> "JT," wife, four children, no job, good character, had sold
> all belongings and was begging;

"WR," 38, a failed Oxford Street linen-draper with debts, friends helped but they were in trouble too, on the streets;

"MD"'s husband a long-term hospital patient, he had been a manservant, Irish, good character;

"WS," 39, discharged lieutenant and now a failed artist, a wife, four children, starving in an empty garret with not even a bed;

"JG," 39, a Manchester manufactory lad, induced to seek fortune in London, abandoned by his pals, he was returned to his grateful parents in Salford;

a failed umbrella maker, 31, of Liverpool, came to London but he and his wife and two children were begging in Covent Garden, could only get casual shifts at the dock;

"JH," 27, of Birmingham, was found with a placard "Obligation! Myself, my wife and two children are nearly starving in a land of plenty! My wife wants bread, my children pine and cry, Kind reader, pray a mite impart as you pass by."[23]

The Dicity was a tantalizing mixture of narrow-minded judgmentalism punctuated by outbursts of compassion and even sentimentality; in its publications, skeptical comments about beggars' claims of unemployment do battle with exclamations on how dreadful the state of the labor market had been of late. In 1830, one-third of vagrancy cases brought before London magistrates were the result of arrests made by Dicity workers.[24]

The London Society for the Suppression of Mendicity had come into being not to help the poor but to ensure that as many vagrants were apprehended and prosecuted as the law allowed. The term used in its literature for the activities of its constables is "clearing the streets"—that is, seeing to it that public places were free from the sights, sounds, and smells of extreme poverty.

Many vagrants did nevertheless go to Red Lion Square of their own accord, to seek shelter, food, or safety. One such was a twelve-year-old native of Parma, in northern Italy, who had been seen around the streets of central London carrying a wax doll in a wooden box. He was in dreadful physical condition; his skin was covered in scabs, his eyes were infected—probably a result of scurvy—and his face was bruised. In April 1834 he went to the Dicity and told its officers that he was too frightened to go back to his lodgings in Vine Street, off Saffron Hill, in Little Italy. He said that he had been beaten by the man he worked for, Alexander Ronchatti, because he had failed to bring back enough money from his begging; Ronchatti also "employed" two other boys to go out into the street to beg, said the boy. When questioned through an interpreter, Ronchatti denied the boy's story, saying that the child had absconded from his lodgings with the doll, which belonged to Ronchatti. The Dicity officer on duty claimed to have witnessed such a scene before, where an Italian running a troupe of beggar boys had used an interpreter to lie and cover up for him. However, Ronchatti was discharged, after being admonished via the interpreter. The boy was given into the care of the Italian ambassador's staff. Only the doll was arrested—it was impounded by the Dicity, being worth three pounds.[25]

It was a telling incident. By the 1830s, a separate group of vagrant children had emerged, combining the role of entertainer and outcast and catering to that hunger for spectacle that saw people flock to the flimsiest, makeshift, unlicensed theatrical performances ("penny gaffs") and to horse-drawn caravan shows featuring midgets, bizarre animals, waxworks, and people with unusual deformities—even to gawk at the oranges and pineapples and other exotic fruit when their season arrived at Covent Garden market.[26] To a population with little access to books or periodicals, and no access to parks, zoos, galleries, or museums—forbidden to them by price and by social exclusivity—Italian boys brought music, pathos, intriguing objects, and strange animals, plus, in many cases, their own physical beauty, to some of London's grimmest streets. The imaginative life of the poor was kept from starvation by such humble food.

The economies of the Italian states had been devastated by the Napoleonic Wars; some northern regions experienced famine in 1816

Caravan shows and puppet booths attracted adults as well as children, despite a crackdown on street noise and "nuisance" in London.

and 1817, while political repression was common in the disputed areas of Piedmont and Savoy, which bordered France. (Savoy would be ceded to France in 1860; Piedmont to Italy.) There was large-scale migration throughout the 1820s, with many Italian artisans moving to northern European cities to pursue their trades. In London, Italians were renowned for their skill in manufacturing optical devices—spectacles, telescopes, barometers—musical instruments, puppets, and waxworks. They introduced to Britain *fantoccini,* grotesque puppets in elaborate costume; grown men were observed to collapse into giggles at fantoccini performances in booths at street corners.[27] The wax and plaster artists, the *figurinai,* came mainly from Lucca in Tuscany and settled in Holborn and Covent Garden. While later in the century Italian street children would be known for playing instruments and dancing, until the mid-1830s their principal source of income was exhibiting small animals as well as wax and plaster figures. There was a good trade in silk or paper flowers to which wax birds were attached; busts of literary and theatrical greats, as well as military and naval heroes, would be transported on large trays carried on an image boy's head, as a walking advertisement for the *figurinaio* who had created them, while an image boy's *boîtes à curiosité* included anatomical wax models, notably a copy of a sketch of recently stillborn Siamese twins who had been dissected by anatomists. Let the rhymester responsible for "The Image Boy," in the January 1829 issue of the *New Monthly Magazine,* explain:

Who'er has trudged, on frequent feet,
From Charing Cross to Ludgate Street,
That haunt of noise and wrangle,
Has seen on journeying through the Strand,
A foreign Image-vendor stand
Near Somerset's quadrangle.

His coal-black eye, his balanced walk,
His sable apron, white with chalk,
His listless meditation,
His curly locks, his sallow cheeks,
His board of celebrated Greeks,
Proclaim his trade and nation.

Not on that board, as erst, are seen
A tawdry troop; our gracious Queen
With tresses like a carrot,
A milk-maid with a pea-green pail,
A poodle with a golden tail,
John Wesley, and a parrot.

No, far more classic is his stock;
With ducal Arthur, Milton, Locke,
He bears, unconscious roamer,
Alcmena's Jove-begotten Son,
Cold Abelard's too tepid Nun,
And pass-supported Homer.

....

Poor vagrant child of want and toil!
The sun that warms thy native soil
Has ripen'd not thy knowledge;
'Tis obvious, from that vacant air,
Though Padua gave thee birth, thou ne'er
Didst graduate in her College.

'Tis true thou nam'st thy motley freight;
But from what source their birth they date,
Mythology or history,
Old records, or the dreams of youth,
Dark fable, or transparent truth,
Is all to thee a mystery.

But it wasn't all poets and philosophers. Exhibiting creatures that were highly unusual to London eyes could prove lucrative too, and one Italian boy, "PG," arrested by the Dicity in 1826 while entertaining a passerby with his dancing monkey, was found to be carrying £21 7s and 6d.[28] Beasts for display included white mice, guinea pigs, monkeys (uniformed or "naked"), tortoises, porcupines—even a marmot, a groundhog native to the mountains of the Savoy region. The objects and creatures were rented out to the boys each morning by the men who ran the trade, at these daily rates:

Box of wax Siamese twins	2s
Organ with waltzing figures	3s 6d
Porcupine	2s 6d
Organ	1s 6d
Organ plus porcupine	4s
Monkey in a uniform	3s
Monkey without uniform	2s
Box of white mice	1s 6d
Tortoise	1s 6d
Monkey on a dog's back	3s
Four dancing dogs, in costume, with pipe and tabor	5s[29]

It was said that one happy outcome of the 1824 Vagrancy Act was a reduction in the practice of beggars waving their deformities in the face of the public; what had arisen in its place was an appeal to sympathy, with plaintive looks and an air of patient submission becoming more prevalent among those with a regular pitch. Italian boys were indeed pitiful—victims of organized child-trafficking by their fellow countrymen. The so-called *padroni* ("masters," "owners," or "employers," also called *proveditori,* "providers") paid a sum of money to impoverished peasants in rural, mainly northern Italy in return for the services of their son—a sort of beggars' apprentice-ship.[30] The parents were told that their child was being taken abroad to learn a trick or skill, usually theatrical in nature, which would earn him a living. The parents' (dialect) term for their son's fate was *"È peo mondo co a commedia,"* which translated as "He is wandering the world with a theater company"; in reality, once the child had been walked through France to England, he would find himself a virtual slave to his padrone.

The Italian boy trade stretched across Britain: Bristol, Birming-ham, Liverpool, Manchester, Sheffield, Bradford, Glasgow, Brighton, and Worthing were all home to padroni. In London, whole houses in the Holborn area—in Saffron Hill, Vine Street, Eyre Street, Greville Street, Bleeding Heart Yard—as well as the streets around the south-ern end of Drury Lane were taken over by padroni, and boys were packed into dormitories, for which they were charged four pence a night. The animals belonged to the padroni, who joined into syndi-

Some Italian boys exhibited exotic animals.

cates, owning *una zampa per uno*—"a paw apiece." The boys, who often learned little English during their stay, were instructed to tell anyone who asked that the padrone was their uncle or much older brother and to provide false names for themselves and the padrone. Procuring a child to solicit alms was a breach of the Vagrancy Act, after all, but little action appears to have been taken against the padroni until certain notorious assaults and deaths later in the century.[31]

Londoners appear to have felt sentimental about Italian boys/image boys/white mice boys, with their dark, imploring eyes, sweet, melancholy expressions, and picturesque destitution. In a curious case in 1834, Lord Dudley Coutts Stuart, Whig member of Parliament and "champion of the oppressed" (according to his obituarists), announced that he would personally request the home secretary to secure the release of two Italian boys sentenced to two weeks in prison by magistrates White and Burrell at the Queen Square magistrates office, Holborn. Metropolitan Police constables Simpson and Brockway of B Division (Westminster) had arrested Antonio Loniski and Barnard Malvarham, both aged about fourteen, for begging in Wilton Street, Pimlico—close to Stuart's residence—at three o'clock in the afternoon of Easter Monday; one boy had a monkey, the other a cage of white mice. The magistrates had jailed them for committing an offense under the Vagrancy Act, and the court sold off the animals to help pay the boys' prison costs. On hearing the news, Stuart went straight to the Queen Square justices to explain that the boys had been two of a party of nine Italian entertainers invited by him to an Easter feast at his London home and that they had simply been waiting outside his house for the door to be answered. Stuart's footman had told the constables this, he said, but they had still taken the boys into custody. Stuart failed to free the boys, and he left the court declaring his intention to petition Lord Melbourne for their release.[32]

It is possible that Loniski and Malvarham were arrested, while the other seven Italians were not, because they were not playing instruments; if playing could be defined as "skilful," the Vagrancy Act did not apply—or rather, it might have made a police officer unsure of his grounds for arrest. Displaying animals involved very little skill and left the child more vulnerable to arrest, which may be why from the 1840s on it was more common for Italian street children to play music and dance for money than exhibit animals. "If they are considered vagrants, they are the most inoffensive and amusing vagrants," declared journalist Charles MacFarlane of Italian boys. "No offences or crimes are committed, despite their poverty and youth." In any

Many Italian immigrants made a living as itinerant musicians.

case, MacFarlane added, such entertainments were probably good for the lower orders, being instructive and educational: "They propagate a taste for the fine arts . . . and [their] animals may awaken an interest in natural history." Fellow journalist Charles Knight agreed, writing in 1841, "We have some fears that the immigration of Italian boys is declining. We do not see the monkey and the white mice so often as we could wish to do. . . . What if he be but the commonest of monkeys? Is he not amusing? Does he not come with a new idea into our crowded thoroughfares, of distant lands where all is not labor and traffic? These Italian boys, with their olive cheeks and white teeth— they are something different from your true London boy of the streets, with his mingled look of cunning and insolence."[33]

All in all, Italy was providing London with a better class of vagrant. The pathos an Italian boy evoked could earn his master six or seven shillings a day. Dead—and apparently murdered to supply the surgeons—his appeal seemed only to increase.

FIVE

Systematic Slaughter

At daybreak on Saturday, 19 November, the body of the dead boy was exhumed. He had been buried (described in the register of burials as "A Boy Unknown") on the eleventh in the graveyard of St. Pancras workhouse, which served as the spillover burial ground for St. Paul's, Covent Garden, and was where the poorest of the parish were destined.[1] (Later, there would be criticism that the subject of an ongoing criminal case had been buried so swiftly, the *Lancet* medical journal pointing to the decision as one more example of the incompetence of coroners.) Augustine Brun, an elderly Birmingham-based padrone named by Joseph Paragalli as the dead boy's master, had been brought to London to view the corpse. This, along with other new evidence that had come to light, so excited George Rowland Minshull that he convened a special hearing for the Italian Boy case at Bow Street, on Monday, 21 November. Joseph Paragalli acted as Brun's interpreter to the magistrates.

Brun revealed that he had brought a boy called Carlo Ferrari to England from northern Italy in the late autumn of 1829; though from Piedmont, Carlo was a Savoyard, said Brun. His father, Joseph, had signed Carlo over to Brun for a fee. Brun had had charge of the boy for his first nine months in England, though Carlo had lodged at the house of another man, called Elliott, at 2 Charles Street, just south of Bow Street.

In the summer of 1830, Brun had bound Carlo over to a new master, an Italian called Charles Henoge who played the hurdy-gurdy and exhibited monkeys, for a period of two years and one month, and, as far as Brun knew, the new master had taken Carlo to Bristol. Carlo would now be about fifteen years old, Brun believed. (The *Globe and Traveller* newspaper report has Brun additionally claiming, "The poor boy ran away from his master about a year ago," and that Carlo made sure that he left London whenever this particular padrone—presumably Henoge, though the newspaper does not make this clear—was rumored to be coming to the capital.)[2]

As soon as the coffin lid came off at the St. Pancras workhouse, Brun was reported to have exclaimed, *"Mon pauvre garçon, pauvre Carlo, mon pauvre garçon."* This seems odd: if Brun had spoken French, Paragalli would not have been the only person who could have acted as his translator. Even odder was Brun's subsequent statement to the magistrates that he had been unable to identify the dead boy because of the extent to which the body had decomposed. The child was green, and the facial features were disfigured; the attentions of the surgeons at the postmortem had not helped matters either. Brun said he believed the hair color and stature of the dead boy were similar to Carlo's. He added that Carlo had been a well-known figure in the squares of the West End of London and that his customary phrase—in French, though he was an Italian boy—was *"Donnez un louis, signor."* (Short for *un louis d'or,* a gold coin with a value of twenty francs. Presumably the word was used figuratively—twenty gold sovereigns was a steep price to pay for a look at white mice.) Superintendent Joseph Sadler Thomas now revealed that the corpse had a number of warts on its left hand, and he asked Brun whether Carlo Ferrari had had such blemishes. Brun replied that the hand had been too green for him to tell if there were any warts on it—not the question he had been asked.

Vestry clerk James Corder, however, was quite satisfied with Brun's evidence, telling the magistrates court that it was clear to him that Brun had identified the boy as his former charge, Carlo Ferrari, since Brun had been unable to stop crying since viewing the corpse— itself a rather extraordinary claim. Corder added that Margaret King had also been taken to see the exhumed corpse—a pointlessly distressing exercise, since King had admitted that she had not seen the boy's face on the day he appeared in Nova Scotia Gardens; King, sure enough, was unable to identify the dead boy.

Next, Joseph Paragalli explained that he was now able to recall that a boy called Carlo Ferrari had been living at 2 Charles Street eighteen months ago. He stated that when he had first seen the body, he had thought that it was Carlo, whom he had last seen alive standing outside the County Fire Office at the southern end of Regent Street ("the Quadrant") in early October. It had been raining hard that day, and the child had looked cold and unhappy. Paragalli said that he had not noticed what the boy was wearing but he had seen that the mice were kept in a box that was divided in two; one half was a cage with a wheel for the mice to run round in; the other half was wooden and

One sketch artist's concept of Carlo Ferrari, named as the victim two weeks after the discovery of the corpse

enclosed, and this was where the animals slept. Paragalli said he often visited Elliott's house in Charles Street and had seen Carlo there on a number of occasions, and was even present when Brun had bound Carlo over to Charles Henoge. One week before seeing him in the Quadrant, Paragalli claimed, he had spoken to Carlo in Portland Place, just north of Oxford Circus.

Proceedings in the magistrates court were about to finish for the day when Superintendent Thomas stepped forward and asked if he could—in his capacity as a public officer—make a further charge against Bishop and Williams only. May and Shields having been escorted from the dock, Thomas charged Bishop and Williams with "the murder of another boy, whose name for the present is unknown." He expected to be able to present evidence in this second case before long. Minshull told Thomas that he had acted very properly in bringing the new charge. The case could not be in better hands, said the magistrate, deeply impressed.

On Superintendent Thomas's orders, Sarah Bishop and Rhoda Head had been taken into custody on Wednesday, 11 November, and had been remanded. Thomas had told Minshull that he would soon prove that the women had known about the killing of the Italian boy. There was no suspicion that they had taken an active role, but Thomas was convinced that anyone living in a house as small as 3 Nova Scotia Gardens must have been aware of everything that had gone on there.

Sarah and Rhoda had been arrested by Constable Higgins at the Fortune of War at four o'clock in the afternoon. Higgins went with them to Nova Scotia Gardens, accepting that Sarah had to make provision for her children—two boys, aged twelve and seven, and a two-year-old girl. While there, Higgins searched the cottage and took away with him what he believed to be significant objects: two chisel-like iron implements, each with one end bent into a hook; a brad awl with dried blood on it; a thick metal file; and a rope tied into a noose.

Later, before the magistrates, Richard Partridge examined these tools and gave his opinion that one of the bent chisels could have been used to inflict the wound on the dead boy's forehead and that

The Quadrant at the southern end of Regent Street, under construction in 1813; the County Fire Office is to the far right in the picture.

the heavy file could have dealt the blow to the back of the neck. Partridge told Minshull that he and George Beaman were certain that death had been caused by a blow to the back of the neck, repeating the evidence they had given to the coroner's court. The two surgeons differed, said Partridge, only in one respect: Beaman believed death had been caused by blood entering the spinal column as a result of the blow, while Partridge thought death had occurred as a result of concussion of the spinal marrow. George Douchez, another local surgeon who had been present at the postmortem, was called and gave his opinion that the boy had been stunned by a blow to the head and then killed by having his neck wrung "like a duck's." At this, a thrill of horror—gasps and murmurs—ran around the Bow Street courtroom.

Forensic medicine was a young discipline. While celebrated surgeon and anatomist William Hunter had written his *Signs of Murder* treatise in 1783, the first coroners' guides were not published until thirty-five years later. The courtroom discussion of the Italian boy's cause of death reflected the limits of knowledge. So

Partridge confidently announced: "Blood never coagulates after death," in reply to a query about whether the injury to the back of the neck would have had the same appearance if it had been inflicted after death. In fact, some of his contemporaries had begun to suspect the truth—that such congealing could in fact take place in a still-warm corpse.

"Could the deceased have committed suicide?" wondered Minshull.

"It is just barely possible that a person might inflict a blow on the back of his own neck which would cause death," replied Partridge. "It is, however, exceedingly improbable and almost impossible."

And Beaman added, "There was nothing to show that he died of indigestion."

As to whether the blood-clotted brad awl could have been the murder weapon, James May didn't wait for the medical men's opinion, calling out to the magistrates, "I took the teeth out with that."

In fact, all the implements found at No. 3 were the paraphernalia used to haul bodies up out of graves. A resurrection man's work required a wooden spade—wood making less noise than metal—to dig down to the head of the coffin; two large iron hooks attached to ropes were inserted under the lid of the coffin at the head to snap the upper part off, and the corpse was then pulled up through the hole.[3] (It was not unlike fishing—which is the term Dickens's fictional body snatcher Jerry Cruncher uses to describe his work in *A Tale of Two Cities*.) These were the very objects likely to be found in the home of a body snatcher, and Constable Higgins recognized them as such. (Higgins had challenged Sarah about the tools in the cottage, saying, "I know what these are for." "I dare say you do," she replied, "but do not speak before the children." She then claimed that the brad awl was used by Bishop for mending shoes.) But Partridge and Beaman did not appear to realize the implements' functions and decided that the collection had a more sinister purpose.

Higgins had also found Sarah to be in possession of a document that read: "The humble petition of John Bishop, and three others, most humbly showeth that your petitioners have supplied many Subjects on various occasions to the several hospitals, and being now in custody, they are conscious in their own minds that they have done nothing more than they have been in the constant habit of doing as resurrectionists, but being unable to prove their innocence without professional assistance, they humbly crave the commiseration of gentlemen who may feel inclined to give some trifling assistance in order to afford them the opportunity of clearing away the imputation alleged against them. The most trifling sum will be gratefully acknowledged, and your petitioners, as in duty bound, will ever pray. . . ." It was unsigned.

Petitions such as these were also part of a resurrectionist's kit. They were a reasonably gentle form of blackmail, letting the surgeon(s) know that it might be in the interest of the good name of the medical profession to come up with bail money, to arrange and pay for the advice of an attorney, or perhaps—using connections, nods, winks—to get the misdemeanor charges dropped altogether. At worst, the resurrection man's family could be given financial help until the breadwinner was out of jail. Surgeon Sir Astley Cooper, created a baronet in 1821 after removing a tumor from George IV's scalp, spent hundreds of pounds in this way. His personal accounts for 1818 show that he paid £14 7s as bail for one of his main suppliers, a man called Vaughan; 6s to Vaughan's wife; and £13 on "gaol comforts"—food, drink, and tobacco—for Vaughan when he was imprisoned.[4] It is likely that Sarah and Rhoda were in the process of applying to the various surgeons supplied by Bishop for assistance of this kind when they were arrested at the Fortune of War.

At Bow Street, Minshull advised Sarah that she was not legally obliged to say anything, but Sarah said that she was eager to defend herself. "I have nothing to fear, sir," she said to Minshull, "for I have done nothing wrong." She told Minshull that although she knew her husband had been a resurrectionist for several years and she had visited him in prison on a number of occasions, she had no knowledge of the crime of which he was now suspected. She pointed out that she had always worked in her own right, for her own money, supplementing whatever cash Bishop brought home with the income she received from doing needlework and taking in washing. She said that Thomas Williams "had only been out three times" with her husband and that he was a "very respectably connected" person. She claimed she knew her husband had been out at work the night before he was arrested because he had washed his hands in a basin, leaving a great deal of mud or clay in the bottom of it.

Rhoda also said that she knew nothing of any murder and that, while she was aware that her husband of seven weeks had been assisting Bishop with resurrection work, he was in fact a bricklayer by training, had also been a carpenter, and had worked in the glass trade, too. (Rhoda referred to Bishop as "my father"; he was, in fact, her half brother and stepfather.)

Minshull told the women that it was his duty to remand them into custody while the case against them was investigated. He also issued an order for the Bishop children to be placed in the Bethnal Green workhouse for the time being. It was quite likely, Superintendent Thomas had told him, that they would be able to give the magistrate damning evidence against their parents. A parish officer of St. Matthew's, Bethnal Green, needed John Bishop to swear to his place of settlement, in order that his children could be signed over to the care of the parish. Bishop signed the necessary papers, "with a very firm hand," and, in an apparently sarcasm-free act of courtesy, thanked Superintendent Thomas for having made the arrangements for his family.[5]

On the same day that the boy's corpse was disinterred—a full two weeks after the arrest of Bishop, Williams, May, and Shields—men from Division F undertook a thorough examination of 3 Nova Scotia Gardens, "it having been intimated to Mr Minshull that it would be advisable that the premises should be strictly searched," as the *Times* put it.[6] Today, such a delay would be unthinkable; in 1831, a detailed search of the home of a murder suspect, except to recover stolen goods, was not an obvious move. But somebody in the neighborhood had told Thomas that, before her arrest, one of the Bishop women had been seen scattering ashes in the garden—had they been burning incriminating items?

Thomas, along with Constable Higgins, laborer and gardener James Waddy, James Corder, William Cribb (the coroner's jury foreman, with no obvious official interest in the case), and a number of

Police officers begin their search of Nova Scotia Gardens, in this curiously compressed version of Bishop's and Williams's cottages.

Division F officers went to the deserted cottage at noon on Saturday, 19 November. Thomas was very interested in that long back garden. He noticed that a pathway running its entire length, from the house to the privy, looked uneven, and in places the soil appeared to be loose; there was indeed a thin layer of ashes on the surface at one spot. Bishop's eldest son stood by during the digging, and it is possible that Thomas had asked for him to be present in the hope that the lad might let slip something incriminating. Indeed, as Higgins started to prod the earth near the path with an iron bar, the boy told him to take care, since there was a cesspool lying immediately beneath. This warning made Thomas suspicious, and he told Higgins to explore exactly that spot. Here, five yards from the Bishops' back door and one yard from the palings, Higgins's bar came up against a spongy substance. Waddy dug and, about a foot down, unearthed a child's jacket, trousers, and shirt. The jacket was of good-quality blue cloth with two rows of covered buttons and expertly sewn buttonholes;

some gilt buttons also on the jacket had a star motif at their center. The black trousers looked as though they had been removed with force, since the buttonholes that connected them to their yellow calico braces were torn. A yard away, Waddy and Higgins dug up another set of clothes—a shabby blue coat of an unusual cut (later described in court as being like the sort worn by charity-school boys) with white buttons, a pair of coarse gray trousers with patched knees, an old shirt that was ripped down the middle, and a striped waistcoat that had bloodstains on the collar and shoulder and, in its pocket, a small piece of comb. The waistcoat had once been an adult's but had been cut down and restitched to fit a boy. Thomas noted that this had been done in a slipshod way, using cheap, coarse yarn. When the waistcoat was shown to Minshull, the magistrate pointed out that it could prove significant, since it might bring forward the man to whom it had originally belonged.

In the privy at the bottom of the garden of Number 3 Thomas found a human scalp with long matted brown hair attached; down among the feces, the officers worked to disentangle chunks of human flesh. Thomas and his men—and, later, the magistrates—assumed that this find was evidence of Bishop and Williams's resurrection work; there was a good trade in body parts if the entire corpse was not fresh, and the scalp had probably been removed for the sale of the hair to a wigmaker and discarded once it was known that the house might be searched.

At four o'clock in the afternoon, with the garden dug to a depth of one foot and the privy thoroughly probed, the men went home. Two days later, Thomas returned and searched the inside of the house once more. The downstairs room (the parlor) contained scarcely any furniture—there was a fireplace and the remains of a small, rickety cupboard. In one corner lay a heap of old, soiled clothes, many of them children's. Sarah Bishop worked as a washerwoman, taking in washing for locals; but the womenfolk of resurrectionists were known to make money from selling the clothing from pauper bodies stolen from mortuaries, hospitals, or workhouses. Superintendent Thomas was particularly interested in a woman's bonnet and a brown, furry cap—the color of dark fox fur—that was lying near the top of the heap; on his first visit to the cottage he had seen it hanging on a nail in the parlor and had taken little notice of it. But now it intrigued him. He took it to show Margaret King and her family in Crabtree Row, and then to Covent Garden to see what Joseph Paragalli made of it. The Italian told Thomas that Carlo Ferrari had worn a cap very like it when he first came to London; he added that Carlo's cap had been larger but that this one looked as though it had been taken in. The fur crown of the cap was English, Paragalli said, but its green visor had been made in France.

Thomas seems to have found it hard to keep away from Nova Scotia Gardens. No. 3 was now officially in police hands, and the superintendent continued to scour it for anything that would forge links in the story he was piecing together. He had told Minshull that he found the Gardens "remarkable," that there was not a street lamp within a quarter of a mile of the place, and that he considered No. 3 itself to be "in a ruinous condition," its garden little more than waste ground.[7] Thomas pointed out to Minshull that Bishop and Williams had access to around thirty other gardens, since they had only to step over the palings to reach the privies and grounds of their neighbors. Searching these would not be a problem, he said, since people were moving out swiftly, in horror and shame at the new notoriety of the Gardens. Minshull was pleased with the trophies the superintendent was bringing into his office and was agog at the news of his daily progress.

On Tuesday, 22 November, Thomas decided to take a look at 2 Nova Scotia Gardens. It had lain empty after Williams went to live with the Bishops in the last week of September until William Wood-cock, a brass worker, his wife, Hannah, and their twelve-year-old son, also called William, moved in on 17 October. Superintendent Thomas found nothing of significance in the house, but from the bottom of Woodcock's privy he retrieved a bundle: unwrapped, it contained a woman's black cloak that fastened to one side with black ribbon, a plaid dress that had been patched in places with printed cotton, a chemise, an old, ragged flannel petticoat, a pair of stays that had been patched with striped "jean" (a heavy, twilled cotton), and a pair of black worsted stockings, all of which appeared to have been violently torn or cut from their wearer. There was also a muslin hand-kerchief, a red pincushion, a blue "pocket" (a poor woman's equiva-lent of a purse or small everyday bag), and a pair of women's black, high-heeled, twilled-silk shoes. The dress and chemise had been ripped up the front, as had the petticoat, which also had two large patches of blood on it. The stays had been cut off in a zigzag manner.

Thomas decided to search the well in Bishop's garden; it was cov-ered over by planks of wood, onto which someone had scattered a pile of grass cuttings. From the bottom of the well he fished out a bundle that proved to be a shawl wrapped around a large stone.

During Thomas's inquiries at the anatomical schools of London he had been told by Guy's Hospital that two bodies—one of them a young female—had been bought from Bishop in the first week of November; St. Bartholomew's had told him that Bishop had offered them a boy and a woman within the month before his arrest; and George Pilcher and John Appleton—respectively, anatomy lecturer and porter at Grainger's school in Webb Street—had told him that a tall, thin, middle-aged woman had been sold to Pilcher by Bishop early in October. Several women had lately been reported missing in Bethnal Green and Shoreditch; two sets of worried relatives had already contacted Thomas. A number of local children had not been seen for months. It was dawning on the superintendent that what had been going on at Nova Scotia Gardens was not the processing of dis-interred corpses into saleable Subjects but systematic slaughter.

SIX

Houseless Wretches Again

Urban poverty, so often a disgusting and harrowing sight to the respectable, could also be a source of wonder and intrigue. A beggar with a certain look or air or "act" could feed on city dwellers' craving for novelty and display. Certain street people, moving around wealthy West End districts as well as the poorer locales, began to take on the status of peripatetic performers, with the slightly unreal aura of renowned theatrical or operatic artistes, standing out amid the rush and bustle, seeping into urban popular consciousness. Rarely mentioned in the newspaper columns or police reports of the day, they survived in the reminiscences of those who thought to note them down before their image faded forever. They were described as though they were apparitions, and they seem to haunt, rather than inhabit, the city, their connections to their environment mysterious and unfathomable.

One such phantasmagoric creature was Samuel Horsey, who trundled around in a wooden cart–cum–sledge. His story was that the celebrated surgeon John Abernethy had removed both his legs at St. Bartholomew's; some thought the amputations had been the result of

Samuel Horsey was one of London's most famous sledge beggars.

a war injury, others that they followed his participation in London's anti-Catholic Gordon Riots of 1780. He frequently frightened horses by rolling into their eyeline, then berating them loudly when they whinnied or reared in terror; and he would erupt into pubs and gin shops by bashing his cart at the doors until they burst open to let him in. Black Joe Johnson was a West Indian who wore a model of Nelson's ship *Victory* built onto his hat and would come up to ground-floor windows and move his head so that the ship appeared to be sailing along the sill as he sang a sea shanty. The Dancing Doll Man of Lucca played drum and flute as puppets danced on a board in front of him, worked by strings attached to his knee (in fact, there appear to have been at least ten Dancing Doll Men of Lucca in London at the same time). Possibly in imitation of such continental élan, blind Charles Wood exhibited a poodle, the Real, Learned, French Dog, Bob, who wore a frock coat and danced to the organ played by Wood ("Look about Bob, be sharp, see what you're about").[1] Tim Buc Too was an old African street-crossing sweeper, whose spot was at Ludgate Hill/Fleet Street; he arranged his profuse white hair so it looked as though he were wearing a pith helmet. In Camden Town, "TL," a fifty-four-year-old former servant unable to find work, exhibited in the street his own scale model of Brunel's Thames Tunnel—the "Great Bore" that was taking years longer than anticipated to complete.[2]

There was a sense that these people were unlikely to survive much longer in the type of city that London was becoming and in the kind of society that was coming into being. Journalist Charles Knight expressed concern that the street sights were being "shouldered out by commerce and luxury."[3] Writing in 1841, seventeen years after the passage of the Vagrancy Act and twelve years after the arrival of the Metropolitan Police, Knight regretted that girls carrying pails of milk, fresh herbs, and watercress from the country were less often to be seen selling their goods in the streets. It was, Knight wrote, a quieter, duller London, now that the muffin man could not scream out his wares, no bugle could be sounded to announce news and events, and "chaunters" were not permitted to sing the first few lines of a broadsheet to tempt a passerby. The itinerant traders were being driven off as much by competition from fixed-location shopkeepers as by legal prohibitions on noise and nuisance; the introduction of plateglass and gas lighting and the proliferation of cheaper, more diverse, and increasingly exotic goods in shops and bazaars were rendering the peddler obsolete.

Artistic attempts were made to capture some of the grotesque individuals who wandered the town, those who were felt to be under threat of extinction by "progress." J. T. Smith, keeper of the prints at the British Museum, compiled *Etchings of Remarkable Beggars* in 1815 and *Vagabondiana* in 1817—both compendia of destitute people. Smith's later work, *The Cries of London*, recorded the chants and ditties of dead, or soon-to-be-dead, trades. His sketches included Anatony Antonini, who carried a huge tray of silk and paper flowers ("All in full bloom!") with plaster birds attached to them; William Conway, an itinerant spoon seller of Crabtree Row, Bethnal Green ("Hard-metal spoons to sell or mend"), who once rescued Smith when he was surrounded and threatened by a crowd while sketching

Black Joe Johnson; Charles Wood and his Learned French Dog, Bob; an aged "sledge beggar"; and the Dancing Doll Man of Lucca; all sketched by J. T. Smith for his compendia of street people, Etchings of Remarkable Beggars, *1815, and* Vagabondiana, *1817.*

another beggar (the locals had thought Smith was an authority figure, sent to snoop on them); George Smith, a rheumatic brush maker, reduced to peddling groundsel and chickweed; and Jeremiah Davies, a Welsh weight-lifting dwarf, who performed his tricks around Chancery Lane. Eking a living from the bizarrest of trades—that was typical of the city, where people subsisted on a seemingly infinite sub-division of labor, associated trades spun out of associated trades.

But according to Charles Knight, "the high and rushing tide of greasy citizenry" needed the color and spectacle that poor folk such as these—even the idle or the impostor—brought to city streets. The architectural splendors of London were many; but most streets were notable for their monotony and dreariness (a look that the Victorians were to delight in defacing with large, florid buildings, from the 1860s on). Away from the main streets, deep gloom pervaded: Joseph Sadler Thomas complained that after sundown, Covent Garden mar-ket was hard to penetrate and patrol effectively since there was just one, centrally placed lamp. He could hardly see his hand in front of his face, he said: "I act in the dark."[4] Ornamentation had been severely limited by the 1774 Building Act—which imposed higher standards of house construction and fireproofing at the expense of architectural variety—and aside from the occasional flourish of stucco and portland stone, street after street was lined with brick buildings that were blackened by smoke and filth; some had even been painted black—a Georgian fancy. Houses were rarely higher than three stories, and in certain areas by the 1830s the products of the eighteenth-century building boom were proving unable to cope with the sheer numbers of people cramming into them. The squalid frowsiness of many parts of east and central London were well known ("foetid localities . . . infected districts," proclaimed the architect Sydney Smirke), but the Georgian terraces of the wealthy west were also seen as dismal regions—dark, featureless, cheerless canyons of blank brick wall.[5]

Nevertheless, by 1823, 215 miles of London street had been lit. The flickering glare of gaslight brought a theatrical quality to many central streets, an effect enhanced by the presence of music (players strolled the streets of the West End, and one Italian band seems to have taken up a regular perch in Portland Place, just north of Oxford

George Scharf captured many of London's street characters throughout the 1820s and 1830s, including itinerant vendors of many nationalities and an Italian "image boy," second from left.

Circus). The stagelike quality only enhanced the strange appearance of the crowds. Even the tide of greasy citizenry could provide a spectacle to the onlooker, a cavalcade of images not unlike the panoramas, dioramas, cosmoramas, and georamas that were enjoying such popularity in new, purpose-built venues. For writer Thomas De Quincey, Londoners passing along the street looked like "a masque of maniacs, a pageant of phantoms"; in a short story, Edgar Allan Poe described the giddy fascination of watching London's "tumultuous sea of human heads" rolling by as the hero attempts to sort them into "types"; while in 1837, a doctor writing about the effect of the city on human health described Londoners as appearing distracted, pallid, shattered, sallow-complexioned, and "paralytic of limb"—puppets or automata moving to some invisible mechanical force.[6]

A *huge unknowable*, a subject that greatly perplexed those who looked into the question of vagrancy, was the proportion of beggars who were frauds; even a central London magistrate of long standing admitted that he could rarely distinguish someone who was genuinely out of work and hungry from someone who was quite capable of making a living but instead preyed on public sympathy.[7] Appearance was an increasingly unreliable gauge: continental visitors noted that the English tended to wear clothes that did not necessarily reflect their class, and, from the start of the nineteenth century, the English working classes had reportedly shown a new interest in self-adornment.[8] There was a vast trade in secondhand clothing; many householders would dress their servants in their castoffs, further eroding class distinctions in dress. To add to the confusion, thieves were known to adopt the type of clothing that parish constables or local firemen wore, in order to loiter near or enter a house to commit a burglary unchallenged. Sometimes, only the shabbiness of a garment would mark the pauper, say, from a tradesman or clerk: a policeman reported that his decision not to arrest a group frequently seen loitering in the Bond Street area had been taken because "they are too well-dressed to be apprehended under the Vagrant Act."[9]

Journalist John Wade complained that the city dweller "is everywhere pestered with clamours, and his feelings lacerated by the spectacle of real or fictitious suffering, which ought ever to be excluded from his sight."[10] Wade believed that virtually all London beggars were fakes; many people agreed with him. Another type of compendium sprang up claiming to detail the various ruses that beggars used to fool the public and providing a glossary of street slang used by this emerging tribe of other Londoners. The anonymous pamphlet *An Exposure of the Various Impostures Daily Practised by Vagrants of Every Description*

"Walking advertisements" as rendered by George Scharf

appealed to the cynic who wanted to be bolstered in the view that all beggars were impostors; it also tapped into the apparently large market discovered by James Hardy Vaux, a twice-transported thief and fraud whose *New and Comprehensive Vocabulary of the Flash Language* was published in 1819, and by journalist and comic author Pierce Egan, whose *Life in London* tales had translated the slang of the criminal and sporting fraternities.[11] *An Exposure of the Various Impostures*, for example, reveals that "Lurkers" have fake documentation showing loss by wreck, fire, accident, and so on; typical scams include a Fire Lurk, a Sick Lurk, a Deaf & Dumb Lurk, a Weaver's Lurk. "High-flyers" are begging-letter writers. "Cadgers on the downright" beg from door to door, while "Cadgers on the fly" beg from passersby. A "Shallow Lay" stands about in rags on cold days, and "Screevers" chalk on the pavement such piteous appeals as "Hunger is a sharp thorn and biteth keen" or "He that pitieth the poor lendeth to the Lord, and He will repay," while assuming a mournful look to fool the "Flat"—the dupe, or mug. Loud groanings and lamentations were required in order to be heard over the roar of daytime traffic. (Traffic noise could be so loud that ordinary conversation was often impossible on main streets.) Ann Taylor, in her thirties, was found groaning on a doorstep in Red Cross Street, Barbican, having apparently just miscarried; when a police officer discovered that the bloody matter in her lap was a sheep's liver, he attempted to arrest her, recognizing her as the woman who had staged a fit outside the Dicity in Red Lion Square and received bread, cheese, and five shillings from passersby. Jane Weston was sentenced to three months' hard labor for playing the part of a starving woman with nine children; the infants were hired, and two accomplices impersonated benevolent society ladies, to provoke others into almsgiving. James Prior spent fourteen nights in jail for acting the part of a pilgrim unable to continue his journey to Canterbury without money.[12] John Wade claimed that he had seen a beggar chewing soap in order to produce a more convincing fit, while J. T. Smith wrote scathingly of Italian boys' "learned mice and chattering monkeys" and recalled seeing an Italian throw his mice at a terrified nursery maid who had refused to give him any money.[13]

Despite widespread concern with fraud, criminal convictions were a hit-and-miss affair, even after the passage of the Vagrancy Act.

The Parliamentary Select Committee convened in 1828 to consider the inadequacies of the old methods of policing the capital was told that it was well known that two of the four justices of the peace who sat at Great Marlborough Street magistrates office never convicted anyone of vagrancy if it was a first offense, even though they had the power to do so.[14] In 1827, the committee heard, 196 of the 429 vagrants arrested and brought to Great Marlborough Street were instantly discharged, much to the anger of the arresting constables. (Figures such as these cannot give a clear indication of the true level of vagrancy in the city, since many vagrants—most, perhaps—were never arrested in the first place.) By 1832, however, imprisonment figures for vagrancy had risen significantly, suggesting that the New Police were more active in apprehending and/or more persuasive before the magistrates: the number of London vagrants committed to prison rose from 2,270 in 1829 to 6,650 in 1832.

Still, many beggars or "disorderly" or "suspicious" characters escaped arrest because of both "old" police and New Police inactivity, or officers' genuine fellow feeling for the street poor, or their fear of attracting an angry crowd during an arrest; other beggars benefited from the territorial disputes between the New Police and the medieval watch system that persisted in the City of London until 1839. Thus magistrate Peter Laurie, who loathed the Metropolitan Police, advised the City aldermen to keep driving any unwanted characters found in their area through the Temple Bar in Fleet Street, across the City border for the Metropolitan force to deal with, since, Laurie claimed, he had heard that West End magistrates had advised the driving of the idle and itinerant over the boundary for the City to cope with. Policing the poor had become a game of "tennis ball," according to one City alderman. It was a spectacle that certain Londoners came to the Temple Bar to watch on a regular basis on a mild evening, enjoying the dance of pursuit and escape performed nightly between the police and the criminals.[15]

Who had the right to be in the streets? Who was entitled to space in the city? The much-discussed changes to the poor laws brought anticipation that all paupers—and thus, beggars—would soon be contained behind the high walls of grim new workhouses, with those unable to give a good account of themselves liable to imprisonment. A further crackdown was heralded in 1839 with an act of Parliament that gave the Metropolitan Police even greater powers to suppress noise and nuisance created by street sellers and the more enterprising beggars.[16]

The Poor Laws that existed in 1831 had been devised in 1601, and one of their most important innovations had been the giving by the parish of "relief" (cash, food, clothing, and so on) to needy parishioners who applied for it and who were considered poor enough to warrant such state charity. In 1662, another law, the Act of Settlement, had been framed to coerce the poor into staying put—into not traveling the land in search of work or better pay and thereby causing local labor shortages or forcing the hand of local employers. Settlement meant that individuals were tied to their parish—usually their place of birth, though women were entitled to settlement in their husband's parish upon marriage.[17] (The "beating of the bounds" is a medieval tradition that remains as spectacle in certain parts of England. On Ascension Day, a parish boy—usually an apprentice—was whipped with a willow wand at the parish boundaries, to remind him, illiterate as he probably was, of where he belonged and where he did not belong.) Parish authorities were responsible for providing help to the local poor; but this assistance was to be given only to those with a settlement in the parish. Admission to the workhouse was one way of feeding and housing those without work, the sick, and the old; another was the system of "outdoor relief," which meant that the poor could, in theory at least, receive cash payments, food, and fuel, along with advances to buy work tools, clothing, and shoes, while remaining in their own homes—or out on the street.[18] The economic depressions of 1815 and 1825 pushed up the poor-rate levy paid by householders; where the nation's poor rates had amounted to around £2 million at the turn of the century, in 1832 the figure stood at £8.6 million. One Briton in ten was wholly or partially dependent on poor relief. In 1821, Parliament had debated removing the right to any kind of relief to the able-bodied; but, with memories of Paris 1789 still fresh, it balked at such an inflammatory move.

The system of settlement was yet another antiquated, inadequate mechanism that was failing in the face of the needs of post–Industrial Revolution Britain. Casual, often factory-based, employment required a large influx of potential workers into town, though the jobs were often precarious or seasonal. Moreover, settlement disputes were a notoriously complex maze for even a lawyer to negotiate and took up an inordinate amount of time in the lower courts; the cost of such legal wrangles to the parishes of Great Britain was running at over £250,000 a year by the end of the Napoleonic Wars.[19] John Wade, writing in 1829, was amazed at the confusion and the potential for abuse of poor relief that the settlement system created. A surprising number of individuals, he claimed, were unable to name the parish to which they "belonged," particularly the London-born poor, who were "so little acquainted with themselves"—a striking phrase that prefigures much later writing about the effects of urban living on the soul. "The number of persons," wrote Wade, "who, with their families, find their way to the metropolis from the remote parts of Great Britain and Ireland, in hopes of finding employment, is inconceivable. . . . Having incurred the expense and fatigue of the journey, and entertaining hopes, probably, of a change in circumstances, they are loth to apply to the parishes where accident has fixed them and thereby subject themselves to forcible removal. In this dilemma, they often linger till all they possess in the world is sold or pledged, and then falling into utter destitution, the females do not infrequently resort to prostitution, the feeble-spirited among the males to begging, those of more profligate principles to petty thefts or more atrocious offences, contributing to swell the general mass of delinquency." Wade estimated that around thirteen thousand people were removed from London and "passed back" (that is, forcibly returned by wagon to their parish of settlement, and to rural destitution) each year. Yet he conceded that there was no practical way of keeping someone where he or she did not want to live. Those who did stay in London were not properly dealt with by the parochial authorities, he wrote, but were passed from parish to parish, "driven to and fro like a weaver's shuttle."[20]

A young woman named Elizabeth Warner jumped into the New River near City Road on the morning of Wednesday, 7 October 1829. Two men passing by dived in and rescued her, and when, later, she was able to speak, she explained that she had come to London from Chigwell in Essex to find a job and had not eaten for three days or slept in a bed for a fortnight. She said that she had been denied parish relief because she did not belong to any London parish, that the Dicity would not relieve her because she had not resorted to begging; that the Blackfriars Road Magdalen Hospital for repentant prostitutes would not take her in because she had never sold her body. Warner was brought to the hospital ward of the Islington workhouse to recover, with the aim of her being "removed" to Chigwell at Islington's expense.[21]

Diving into a river to save a stranger was a brave act and, like the harrying of constables arresting beggars, flew in the face of the increasingly gloomy pronouncements about city life and the urban dweller's excessive subjectivity and self-absorption. To John Wade, there was something sinister in the idea that "in the midst of a million people the Londoner can create for himself a social solitude." For Thomas De Quincey, "No loneliness can be like that which weighs upon the heart in the centre of faces never-ending, . . . eyes innumerable, . . . and hurrying figures of men and women weaving to and fro"; and as James Grant, the editor of the *Morning Advertiser,* saw it, "Everyone runs, as though their house were on fire, even when they have no purpose. Nobody wants to know each other's business."[22] But the poor did not appear either to dash about or to drift along withdrawn and uncommunicative—their intervention to help one another was noted with incredulity by some observers. One fact that disgusted many was that it was often those in poverty themselves who gave to beggars. J. T. Smith described a number of poor people pursuing a staggering drunk along High Holborn in order to hand coins to him because he had a piece of paper that read "Out of Employment" stuck to his hat; Smith found this deplorable and believed the message on the hat to be untrue.[23]

Such generosity may be evidence that the disparate groups that made up lower-class London felt something that could perhaps be described as emergent solidarity. "Hit him hard, he has no friends" was a saying among the London poor in the 1820s, a sardonic comment on the perceived lack of social justice for the powerless and impoverished.[24] While London was one of the most heavily unionized areas of the country, with most trades having at least some sort of representative body, most Londoners were never members of unions—whether trades bodies or organizations pressing for political reform. But class consciousness was on the rise even outside politicized groups. Friendly societies and cooperatives were developing in the capital as early as 1820, and, in more settled areas, fragments of community appeared to be forming. If society had been torn apart by economic change, it was also in the process of putting itself back together again. Even Viscount Melbourne declared himself "well aware of the obstinate fidelity with which the lower classes cling to one another."[25]

And the events of November 1831 were encouraging diverse types of Londoner to look at one another anew, to take note of the fates of those around them. Where once missing children had been consigned to privately printed handbills and the columns of the *Police Gazette,* not even making its front page but placed amid notices of absconding prisoners, deserting soldiers, absent fathers, and strayed livestock, the letters pages of national newspapers now throbbed with the concern of their gentleman readers. Thus in the *Times* of 29 November:

> Sir, I have forwarded to you two cases of the loss of children, which I trust you will give publicity to, as the parents are too poor to pay for printing; and as it may be the means of discovery, at least in the recent case. In the month of March last, Mrs Hughes, a widow, of No 5, Paradise Place, Frog Lane, Islington, went out one morning to wash, leaving, as was her custom, her little boy at home; and on her return in the evening he was missing, and she has never heard of him since. He was seven years old; had on a blue jacket, black trousers, blue waistcoat, old brown pinafore, cloth cap and hob-nailed boots.
>
> The other case was a boy about nine years of age, the son of a poor woman at Poplar. On the 15th of October last, he was at play with his little brother in the street, and told him that a man had promised him such lots of sugar—a great many basins

full—and that he would bring him some when he came back. He then left his brother and has never returned. He had on a corduroy dress that had been washed, a good linen shirt, and half-boots.

I should be glad to render any assistance in discovering what has become of these poor children, and will satisfy any inquiries as far as lies in my power.

I am, yours, obediently, W.H.

And from the *Weekly Dispatch:* "Among the supposed victims to the 'interests of science' who have disappeared lately is a youth named Smith, about seventeen years of age, the son of respectable but unfortunate people in Grove Place, Camden Town. He was about 5ft 3 in, of florid complexion, with full, dark eyes, and rather stout. He left his father's house on business last Tuesday evening, dressed in a blue coat and dark trousers, and has not been seen or heard of since."[26]

After the arrest of Bishop, Williams, May, and Shields, the *Morning Advertiser* gave regular bulletins of missing children: Caroline Brand, eight, of Wolverley Street, Hackney Road, sent out by her parents to sell bundles of firewood one evening and not seen again, just as her thirteen-year-old brother had disappeared, five months before; and Henry Borroff, a five-year-old, of Barton Court, Hoxton Old Town—gone.

SEVEN

Neighbors

William Woodcock was awoken in his bed at 2 Nova Scotia Gardens at around one or two in the morning of Friday, 4 November, by a loud noise from next door. As was his habit, he had gone to bed at half past nine in the evening. He slept downstairs at the front of the house in a room that was next to the Bishops' parlor. The sounds he heard were a "scuffling, or struggling," as he described it, like the sound of men's feet. The noises stopped suddenly, and he heard two sets of footsteps running from Bishop's house and the slamming of the gate. Then Woodcock heard the slow, heavy tread of one person in the parlor. "Everything was quite still at the time and I could have heard a mouse stir. Had I known that any thing wrong was going on, I would have put my ear closer to the wall and might have heard every thing that passed." After around a minute, the other two pairs of footsteps returned, and there was the sound of voices, though words were impossible to make out. Then all was quiet, and Woodcock fell back to sleep.

This was Woodcock's evidence to George Rowland Minshull on Friday, 25 November, the final day of the magistrates' hearings.

Outside, in Bow Street, several hundred people had gathered and remained put all day, in spite of the heavy rain that fell for hours. Fifty persons "of rank" had written to Minshull to request a seat alongside the magistrate.

Minshull was keen to establish how many men Woodcock had heard during the disturbance.

"I can speak to the voices of two of the men, but I cannot speak as to the third," said Woodcock. Minshull pressed him on whether he could recognize the voices. Would he be able to confirm that they belonged to Bishop, Williams, and May?

Woodcock replied that he had never heard the voice of Bishop—his neighbor of three weeks—or of May, though he believed that one of the voices had been Williams's.

Williams called out from the dock that what Woodcock had heard was a row between him and John Bishop. Bishop, said Williams, had smashed some of Williams's belongings and was about to start on Rhoda's. Williams claimed that he had grabbed his wife's looking glass, bonnet, and shawl and left the house at about two in the morning to fetch an officer of the New Police. The constable, however, had refused to come beyond the garden gate and had walked away.

"I distinctly contradict that," said Woodcock; that particular row, he said, had happened on the Sunday before.

No, Williams retorted; the argument had happened on the Thursday . . . or perhaps the Friday. . . . "The women can say which night it was."

At this point, Bishop, who was sitting alongside him, whispered something urgently in Williams's ear, and Williams fell silent.

The magistrates were attempting to place May in the Bishop family home. Woodcock's testimony that there had been three sets of feet and that there may have been three voices was an effort to make the cottage-sharing duo of Bishop and Williams a well-established trio, with May.

"To the best of your belief, were there three men?" Minshull asked Woodcock.

"There must have been three," said Woodcock.

Woodcock had moved into No. 2 with his wife and son on Monday, 17 October. Despite living next door to Bishop and Williams for three weeks, Woodcock claimed to have seen only Williams, Sarah, and Rhoda at No. 3; the first time he had laid eyes on Bishop had been at the Bow Street magistrates office. Woodcock's unfamiliarity with the man next door may well be explained by the very different rhythms they followed: Woodcock left at six in the morning to go to his job in a local brass foundry; Bishop, by necessity, worked at night. Alternatively, Woodcock may have heard local talk that made him wish to shun the Bishop ménage altogether. On Sunday, 6 November, Rhoda had asked Woodcock if she could borrow a shilling; his response is not in the records.

Other neighbors had equally fragmentary information to offer. Robert Mortimer, an elderly tailor who lived in Nova Scotia Gardens, testified that, to the best of his belief, Williams lived at No. 3 with the Bishops. Toward the end of September, Mortimer had made Williams's wedding coat for him. He had gone to No. 3 on a number of occasions to collect the money Williams owed him for his work, without success. That's all he knew.

Sarah Trueby told the magistrates that she had let No. 3 to Sarah Bishop in July 1830, and No. 2 to Thomas Williams in July 1831, and he had lived there for about two months. Trueby said she had often seen Williams in Bishop's house since he had left No. 2. Of Rhoda, all she could say was, "I have seen her without any bonnet on."

George Gissing, son of the Birdcage's publican, knew both Bishop and Williams and recognized them on the night of the fourth, but said he had never seen Rhoda.

Ann Cannell, the local girl who had also seen the men that night, said she had not recognized Bishop or Williams.

"There is no such thing as neighbors," wrote James Grant about London in the *Morning Advertiser*. "You may live for half a century in one house without knowing the name of the person who lives next door." And John Wade concurred: "There is no such thing as a vicinage, no curiosity about neighbours. It is from this circumstance London affords so many facilities for the concealment of criminality."[1]

Minshull had asked Superintendent Thomas whether it was true, as he had heard, that Bishop's house lay "in a very lonely situation," the sort of place where evil deeds could be committed unseen. Thomas had had to reply that in fact the Gardens was "a colony of cottages," divided from one another by low palings and that one had only to step over these to have access to at least thirty other dwellings. Also, Nos. 2 and 3 were at the very entrance to the Gardens, just off Crabtree Row and within sight of the Birdcage pub.

How unnoticed could someone live in London? How little did one know about one's neighbors? These questions intrigued those investigating Nova Scotia Gardens.

Superintendent Thomas had written up a statement for Margaret King of Crabtree Row to sign, confirming what she had already told the magistrates about seeing the Italian boy in Nova Scotia Gardens. The arrival of King's baby was imminent, and it was unlikely that she would be able to attend an Old Bailey trial should the case make it into the final session of 1831. But when she stood before Minshull again on 25 November, King said she was unable to swear to the detail of the clothing the Italian boy had been wearing when she saw him on Thursday, 3 November. She had been aware only of a "Quaker-fashion" dark blue coat or jacket, with a straight collar; it had seemed unremarkable. "The boy's dress appeared to be shabby, such as other boys wear who go about the streets," she said. It was odd in itself that she could tell the cut of the coat, when she had said that the boy had been standing with his back to her. She had made no mention of his wearing anything on his head. All the clothing that had been dug up at No. 3 was now placed in front of her, and Minshull asked King whether the poorer quality "charity-school" coat was the one she had seen on the boy. "The coat is, to all appearances, exactly like the one which the boy had on," she said, "but there is no mark about it to enable me to swear positively that it is the same coat."

"You are not being called upon to swear positively to it, but only to the best of your knowledge and belief," Minshull told her.

She replied, "All I can say is, the coat is exactly like, as far as regards colour, size, and shape, and it has every appearance of the coat which the boy had on when I saw him on Thursday. And so is the cap."

King's nine-year-old son, John, was more forthcoming. He told the court that he had seen the Italian boy too, from the Kings' first-floor window, and when he asked his mother if he could go and see what the boy had in his cage or box, his mother told him no. Minshull asked the boy to describe all he could about the Italian boy, and John recalled that the boy had been standing with his back to Nova Scotia Gardens and facing Birdcage Walk, the northern continuation of Crabtree Row; he had his right foot turned out, his arms rested on his cage, and he was wearing a brown furry cap with a visor lined in green fabric. Thomas then brought the cap he had found in Bishop's home over to John King, who said, "It looks exactly like the cap the Italian boy had on." (John Bishop had smiled oddly in court as Thomas revealed that the cap had been found in his parlor.) The King family had seen all the items of clothing before, since Thomas had taken them straight to their home after exhuming them. Despite this, much play was made in court of the fact that John had been kept out of the courtroom as his mother gave her evidence on the clothing.

Minshull asked John King if he had ever seen the boy before, and the child said: "I think I have seen him about before. He used to carry a doll with two heads in a glass case. I saw him about a month ago. He looked like the same boy. I have not seen him since the Thursday

Inside the Bow Street police office/magistrates court

I saw him in the Gardens. He was then standing still, to see if anybody would come out and see what he had to show. I did not see him go away." When asked how far the boy had been standing from Bishop's house, John replied, "It would not take me more than half a minute to get there."

His eleven-year-old sister, Martha, said she was not sure if it was a Wednesday or a Thursday on which she saw the Italian boy at Nova Scotia Gardens. She did not remember any of his clothing except for the brown cap and the string around his neck from which his box or cage was hung. She could not see the color of the cap's visor lining since the boy had his back to her. But when Thomas handed her the cap, she said it was like the one she had seen.

It must be supposed, since there is no evidence to the contrary, that Margaret, John, and Martha King were describing the same incident, that they were all looking at the boy from either the first floor (John) or the ground floor (Margaret and Martha) of their house, which stood on the south side of Crabtree Row facing Nova Scotia Gardens. Both Mrs. King and her daughter saw the boy with his back turned, but John claimed to have seen the boy full on, from above— even noting the color of the visor. And now all three were placing themselves within their home, though in her earlier evidence, Margaret King had stated that she and the children had been out walking when they had seen the Italian boy.

Superintendent Thomas would not relinquish his grip on the two elder Bishop children. He believed they would eventually reveal damning facts about the household since, Thomas stated, and reporters duly reported, Williams had been living with them in the cottage for eighteen months. But here, the superintendent had become confused: Williams had moved into No. 2 in July 1831, not July 1830, and had lived with the Bishops for just a few weeks. It was the Bishops who had moved into No. 3 in July 1830.

The Bishop children had been brought from the Bethnal Green workhouse to be lodged at the Covent Garden watch house in the hope that closer acquaintance with the police would encourage them to speak more openly. It had already been established that Bishop's youngest son had told another little boy who lived nearby that he had "some nice little white mice at home" but that his father had used the cage as firewood.

A change had come over the prisoners during the week of hearings, and, as they stood at the bar on this, their final day at Bow Street, gone were the sneering and jeering, the sarcastic comments about foolish questions and flimsy, ill-remembered evidence. On the preceding Monday, Williams had even loudly sung several songs in the prison van, handcuffed and leg-ironed as he was; he had complained to Bishop that he should not look so "down upon his luck." Now, though, Williams was extremely pale and fidgeted constantly, his mouth and nose twitching in an odd manner. Bishop looked crestfallen, his eyes were sunken, and he seemed as though he were in a trance; his weight had dropped dramatically. When Minshull told him that he could ask any questions he liked of the witnesses, Bishop bowed to the magistrate and said quietly, "Thank you, sir, we are aware of that." The *Sunday Times* even attempted a pun at Bishop's expense, saying that the body snatcher was now looking "cut up." The Reverend Dr. Theodore Williams, vicar of Hendon, magistrate, and prison visitor, had seen Bishop in jail and asked the resurrectionist if there was anything he wished to discuss with him; Bishop had burst into tears and said no, not yet. Michael Shields looked skeletal and appeared to be in a stupor, standing rigidly at the bar and barely moving for the entire three-and-a-half-hour hearing.

Only May's nerve appeared to hold, though he was noticeably quieter than before and listened intently to all that was said. May and Bishop had had a fight. May blamed Bishop bitterly for getting him "into this scrape" (according to Dodd, a jailer who listened in on conversations and reported them to Superintendent Thomas).[2] May had shouted to Bishop, "You're a bloody murdering bastard—you should have been topped years ago." The signs were that May would, at any moment, turn king's evidence. What was he waiting for?

After the neighbors had had their say, the summing up began, and all the evidence that had been gathered during the inquiry was read out in court: everything that had been told at the coroner's inquest, all the witness statements given at Bow Street, all Thomas's tip-offs and "information received." Then James Corder revealed that proceedings against Michael Shields were being dropped, no evidence having been found against him. Shields was now officially discharged but was called to stand in front of the bench. Minshull told Shields that he was now a witness—what did he have to say for himself? Shields repeated once again the story that had been prised from him at the coroner's inquest: that he had met Bishop on the morning of Saturday the fifth at the Fortune of War, had agreed to carry a large hamper—taken from just inside St. Bartholomew's railings by Bishop—from Guy's to King's, a job for which, Shields pointed out to Minshull, he had still not been paid his promised half crown.

Minshull said: "Do you still persist in saying that you were not aware of what the hamper contained?" and Shields replied, "Upon my word, your worship, I knew nothing about what the hamper contained. I carried it as I would any other job."

"Did you ever carry any load for Bishop or May before?"

"No, your honour, never."

A clerk warned him: "You know, Shields, you have carried bodies repeatedly to the hospitals. You should remember you are now on your oath."

"I mean to say that I did not know what the hamper contained that May and Bishop hired me to carry. I never saw Bishop and Williams at my house. I never gave them my address." At this point, James Corder produced a piece of paper that had been found at No. 3 Nova Scotia Gardens. "Is this paper, on which is written 'Number 6 Eagle Street, Red Lion Square,' in your handwriting?" Corder asked.

Shields studied the scrap for some time before saying, "Yes, sir, it is."

Corder turned to Minshull: "It is quite clear that this man cannot be believed upon his oath, and therefore it would be useless to make a witness of him. I think I should be acting wrong if I did not state that I would not believe anything he could say on oath."

Minshull agreed: "Every word he has spoken goes for nothing."

Though extremely annoyed with Shields for failing to be prosecution-witness material, Minshull couldn't quite let go of the idea of wringing from the man something that would incriminate May,

Bishop, and Williams, since the case against them still appeared worryingly slender. "Can you produce any security for your appearance at trial?" asked Minshull, wondering about the chances of binding Shields over to appear at the Old Bailey.

"I cannot," said Shields. "No one would be answerable for me."

Then Minshull changed his mind again and decided to let Shields go, warning him to keep Superintendent Thomas informed of his whereabouts—partly for Shields's own protection. He knew how the crowd could vent its ill-feeling toward resurrectionists.

Minshull now turned to the three men remaining in the dock and said: "If you wish to say anything, now is your time, as this is the last opportunity you will have of appearing before me."

Bishop: "No, sir. I have nothing to say at present. I will reserve what I have got to say for another place."

Williams: "Nothing, sir, but what I have already said."

But James May had plenty to say: "This man, Bishop, can clear me of every thing, if he likes to speak the truth. He knows I am innocent of the charge. The man says he got the body from the ground, but that he doesn't like to say where because he is loath to injure the two watchmen left to guard it. Things, however, have come to such a crisis now that he ought to speak the truth, for I defy him to say anything to implicate me." He turned to Bishop: "I knew nothing of the body until I went to take it from your house!"

"I have said nothing against you. It's true what you say—you knew nothing of it until then."

"That is the truth. I did not. I know that nothing you can say—if you will only tell the truth—can implicate me."

Minshull told them: "Prisoners, you will all be committed to Newgate to take your trial at the ensuing Sessions at the Old Bailey, commencing on 1st December, for the wilful murder of Carlo Ferrari, and there will be another count in the indictment, charging you with the wilful murder of a person unknown."

Downstairs in the lockup room, May burst into tears, swearing to Dodd the jailer that he had had nothing to do with the boy's death, that the first he had seen of the lad was when he lay curled up dead in the trunk in Bishop's washhouse. Even if he were to be acquitted, wailed May, how would he ever be able to find work again? He beat his breast and railed at Bishop and Williams, who both appeared to have rallied a little. But when the door was opened to take them to the prison van that would carry them to Newgate, they shrank down behind the double row of police officers who stood between them and the huge crowd that surged forward, screaming insults; someone broke through and Bishop's left shoulder was injured. May, though, insisted on walking tall, as he followed the other two into the van amid the jostling and shouting.

Around three hundred people chased the vehicle as it turned down into the Strand, along Fleet Street, and up Chancery Lane, the commotion startling horses on the roadway and causing numerous accidents; but in Chancery Lane, the van was held up by traffic and the crowd caught up and began to pelt it with mud and stones. At Coldbath Fields Prison, just to the north of Saffron Hill, the van dropped off two prisoners, and then it was on to Newgate with Bishop, May, and Williams, arriving at a quarter past five. It took a great deal of effort to move the three into the prison without letting the crowd seize them.

Back at Bow Street, Sarah and Rhoda were called from their cells to appear before Minshull immediately after the committal of their husbands to be told that they would not face any charges. They were too cold to speak—their teeth were chattering—but they curtsied to the bench to show their gratitude. Superintendent Thomas, it seems, had for the time being given up hope of building a case against them; similarly, it had now been decided, probably by Minshull and Corder, that the Bishop children were too young to be given the burden of incriminating their parents, and so they too were set free. Minshull was concerned for the women's well-being and insisted that they not leave until it was quiet in the streets outside. Bishop, told by Thomas of his wife's imminent release, replied, "I thank you, sir, and I hope you will look to her and see that she is not insulted by the mob."

Michael Shields was allowed out of the Bow Street office close to midnight. Though Minshull had decided not to pursue a case against him for his lies, he had advised Dodd to hold him as late as possible, for his own safety. The hearing had ended before four in the afternoon, but Shields found himself confronted by a large group still waiting in the street, who hissed, hooted, and groaned at him. He walked briskly northward and turned into Long Acre, heading east toward home in Eagle Street, but the crowd followed him. He dodged right into Drury Lane, hoping to throw them off, then ran into Vinegar Yard, a tiny thoroughfare alongside the Drury Lane Theatre. Still they gave chase, and, terrified, the old man ran round to Bow Street, where the officers took him back into custody, for his own protection. Here he stayed for hours, cowering in a corner of the office, gibbering and sobbing.

EIGHT

·······················

Meat—An Interlude

The Fortune of War stood in Smithfield, where Giltspur Street meets Cock Lane, a spot known as Pye Corner. Here, in 1666, the Fire of London was stopped in its westward tracks after having destroyed four-fifths of the City. Smithfield, the Smoothe Field of twelfth-century descriptions, was largely undamaged by the flames, with the consequence that by the early part of the nineteenth century, some of London's oldest buildings were to be found surrounding the large open space that was given over to the meat market. In the 1820s some one and a half million sheep, 150,000 cattle and 60,000 pigs were driven to Smithfield every year to be sold and slaughtered, even though meat consumption had been in slow decline since the final decade of the last century. Smithfield was the "live" market; Newgate Shambles, half a mile away and just north of St. Paul's Cathedral, was the main dead-meat market. "Prime," the best meat, cost between eight and nine pence a pound in the late 1820s, while "seconds" sold for five to seven pence. At Pye Corner, the poorest-quality dead meat was sold off; "cag-mag" could cost as little as two pence a pound and supplemented the diets of the desperately poor, along with condemned fish from Billingsgate, damaged and withered fruit and vegetables, and cheap starch in the form of potatoes. Cag-mag was often meat that had simply been around too long (in summer, freshness was limited to just twenty-four hours after a kill); but often it was the flesh of recently killed but worn-out, old, thin, or diseased beasts. Cag-mag's etymology is uncertain, though "cag" is likely to be derived from "cack," meaning excrement; and a "mag" was slang for a farthing—so, "cheap crap" is a reasonable guess. Just how bad the quality of food sold at Smithfield could be was shown by a witness to the 1828 Parliamentary Select Committee on the State of Smithfield who had entered the Bear and Ragged Staff inn on the northeast side of the marketplace, close to where, today, Charterhouse Street forks left into Charterhouse Square; the inn also did duty as a slaughterhouse. The witness, Adam Armstrong, told the committee he had seen hanging up in the pub a cow's carcass that was so rancid the fat was no more than dripping yellow slime. On questioning the slaughterman, Armstrong was told that this was cag-mag that was to be sent to a nearby sausage factory, for two pence a pound.[1] Other campaigners claimed that the most rotten cag-mag was fed to beasts awaiting slaughter: "Let the reader reflect on the bare possibility of having partaken of the flesh of an animal fed, perhaps, on the fetid refuse of a diseased or glandered horse," ran one warning about feeding meat to herbivores.[2]

Beasts came to Smithfield from all over Great Britain, with drovers walking the animals in their charge for fifteen to twenty miles a day. It was a skilled job to maneuver herds of up to a thousand animals across the country, and drovers would frequently sleep out in the open in order to keep watch for rustlers; animal theft was common, despite still being a capital offense (in London, four rustlers were executed in 1825, one in 1826, and three in 1827).[3] An ox lost around twenty pounds in weight for every one hundred miles it walked to market; and if the creature came from the Scottish Highlands, and many did, the three-week journey could affect the quality of its flesh unless it had had time to put weight back on. The cattle that were driven to the capital from the north were pastured in the "grazing counties" of Norfolk, Lincolnshire, and Leicestershire to fatten them; the last stopping place was the meadows of Islington before the final

A view of Smithfield Market, sketched from the Bear and Ragged Staff pub-cum-slaughterhouse, looking south to the top of Giltspur Street, home to the Fortune of War. St. Bartholomew's Hospital is the large building to the left of center.

thrust down St. John Street and into Smithfield. At Islington, the rural drover handed his charges over to London drovers, of whom there were around a hundred, appointed by the City of London and required by law to wear numbered badges on their arms. In reality, these badges were often not worn, or were pawned, or were lent out by master drovers to their apprentices for a daily fee; fake badges were regularly seized. After a sale was made, a butcher's drover would drive a beast to its place of slaughter, which was usually in Smithfield, in Whitechapel and Shoreditch in east London, or at Leadenhall Market in the heart of the City.

Country drovers avoided towns and turnpikes by using "drovers' roads," grassy tracks where hooves would be less likely to be damaged; but in London there came a point where no roads could be given over to animals alone, and beasts had to share city space, often with calamitous consequences. In the summer of 1828, a bullock went berserk in Hatton Garden and killed a woman who was looking in a jewelry shop window; three other people were knocked unconscious. The beast was being pursued by a gang of boys, though whether they were trying to stop it or had caused the stampede in the first place was never established. (One method of ensuring a richer haul when stealing from a person or a shop was for a gang of boys to select an ox from a passing herd, goad or terrify it into charging, then, when there was uproar, to pick pockets or snatch from window displays. Sometimes, a panic was caused simply for fun, not for gain.)[4] Around the same time, a woman who sold oranges in the streets was knocked down and badly wounded when an ox charged in Lad Lane, near Guildhall.[5] Many less serious injuries were the result of kicks by frightened or furious animals. Beasts that became separated from their herd would often panic and charge up the narrow courts and alleys of Smithfield, terrorizing pedestrians, disrupting sleep and work, even entering homes and harming the inhabitants.

Trades that had nothing to do with butchery intermingled with meat-market businesses in Smithfield and its immediate surrounds, and many shopkeepers complained that their revenues dropped on market days: it was said that women would not venture out to buy when beasts were being driven in town; that women would not shop where they had to pass by mounds of flesh lying on the pavement or in the gutters. (Women were frequently cited as potential or real victims of the herds, though it is quite possible that this appeal to chivalry was a calculated ploy by those who wanted to see the market reformed.) William Wilkinson, an upholsterer of Ludgate Hill, said that terrified women would often run into his shop to seek shelter from a passing herd and that his plateglass windows were frequently smashed when bullocks poked their heads through. Robert Padmore of Marriott's ironmongery in Old Bailey saw a woman run down by a drove of panicking sheep, one of which ran into his shop and fell down into his cellar, on top of his workmen.[6] Some animals simply wandered off: "Found, in Holborn, a black and white cow, which is dry, in very bad condition, and aged; she has long horns, and is supposed to be diseased. Apply at the Police Station, Covent Garden," said a notice in the *Daily Police Report* of 16 November 1831.[7]

Monday was the busiest day at Smithfield; it was the main beef-trading day, with two thousand cattle and fifteen thousand sheep changing hands. At eleven o'clock on Sunday night, the cattle that had been held at Islington were moved down into Smithfield, an operation that lasted until four or five in the morning. That Sundays should end with the most unholy noise of animals thundering along narrow residential streets, drovers cursing and their dogs barking, was felt by some to be an outrage: this was "a shocking conclusion of the Christian Sabbath," fulminated an anonymous pamphlet of 1823, *Cursory Remarks on the Evil Tendency of Unrestrained Cruelty, Particularly on That Practised at Smithfield Market.*[8] At Christmas 1827, the sheer volume of cattle coming to market meant that the streets to the east of Smithfield as far as Barbican were solid with a bovine traffic jam.[9]

On Fridays there was a second cattle market and, from mid-afternoon, a horse market. Many believed that Friday's horse trading attracted a large criminal population into the area because so many of the horses put up for sale were stolen—around eight thousand a year in London alone ("pladding a prig" and "prad-chewing" were slang phrases for stealing a horse)—earning the thief around twenty pounds a head. The *Hue and Cry/Police Gazette* was filled with advertisements for missing beasts: "A black gelding, from Mr Thomas, at Manor Place, Kennington, Middlesex, 21st ultimo, 5 years old, near 15 hands, star on his face, switch tail, hair rubbed off his back and legs"—this was a more detailed description than those of the missing citizens who appeared in the paper's columns.[10] Horse thieves and their hangers-on, it was claimed, flooded into Smithfield—more particularly, to its fifty or sixty pubs and inns. Defenders of the market's reputation and the integrity of its dealers and drovers pointed to "outsiders" as the source of much of the mischief. "There are a great many boys who are running about the market that come there for mere wantonness," said one beef salesman. "Those are the persons they ought to punish."[11] As with all London markets, many vagrants, and vagrant children, slept the night in the straw of the pens, beneath the wooden stalls, or in the doorways of surrounding houses and shops. Just what the overlap was between these waifs and the "wanton boys" identified by the salesman cannot be known; one man's juvenile delinquent is another man's object of compassion.

Another, more alarming market was held at Smithfield from time

Two contemporary views of the Friday horse market at Smithfield—one sedate, one wild

to time: making a "Smithfield bargain" referred to the sale by a husband of his wife and was believed in many working-class communities to be a perfectly valid form of divorce (it had its roots in Anglo-Saxon common law). The sale was usually prearranged, and the buyer was often a friend of the family or a neighbor who, motivated by pity, wanted to help bring an unhappy union to an end; the public nature of the sale was to validate for the community the ending of the marriage. At two o'clock on the afternoon of Monday, 20 February 1832, a man brought his twenty-five-year-old wife in a halter and tied her in the pens opposite the Half Moon pub, close to the gate of St. Bartholomew the Great. A crowd gathered and the auction began, with a "respectable-looking man" striking a deal for ten shillings; throughout, the woman made no complaint about her treatment.[12] Some twenty cases of wife selling at Smithfield are on record between the 1790s and the 1830s, though the true figure is likely to be higher.

Descriptions of Smithfield challenged even the most euphemistic of writers. It is clear that offal, excrement ("filth"), and urine ("steam") had to be negotiated by a pedestrian. Quite apart from the stink and refuse from the market and the slaughterhouses, associated trades helped to contaminate the nearby streets—the sausage makers, tanners, cat- and rabbit-fur dressers, bladder blowers, tripe dressers, bone dealers, cat-gut manufacturers, neat's-foot-oil makers. Here is Charles Dickens attempting to convey the aura of Smithfield to a family readership, in *Great Expectations:* "The shameful place, being all asmear with filth and fat and blood and foam, seemed to stick to me." And in *Oliver Twist:* "The ground was covered, nearly ankle deep, with filth and mire; and a thick steam, perpetually rising from the reeking bodies of the cattle, and mingling with the fog, which seemed to rest upon the chimney tops, hung heavily above. . . . Countrymen, butchers, drovers, hawkers, boys, thieves, idlers, and vagabonds of every low grade, were mingled together in a dense mass." [13] Dickens did not attempt to address the issue of animal slaughter itself, which frequently took place in the cellars or back yards of ill-adapted private houses; but others, intent on reform, did not spare the detail. For the Smoothe Field that had been just outside the medieval city walls was now right in the center of a busy metropolis, the capital of a great and growing imperial power—and its goings-on were, frankly, not respectable.[14] These matters were handled better in France, the Select Committee on Smithfield discovered, and the abattoirs of Paris were analyzed and eulogized by committee witnesses. While local bylaws forbade any emission of blood from a slaughterhouse, it was, nevertheless, a regular sight across the pathways of Smithfield, and pedestrians would get blasts of hot, stinking air through street-level gratings since animals were often kept and killed below ground.[15] Passersby glancing left or right into a court or yard where a butcher worked could find themselves witnessing a killing. It was alleged by various witnesses before the 1828 Select Committee on Smithfield that sheep were often skinned before being completely dead; it was observed that an unskilled slaughterman could require up to ten blows with an axe to kill a bullock; and while an inspector was supposed to be notified before the slaughter of any horse, the rule was said to be broken more often than kept, and horses were observed up to their knees in the weltering remains of their fellow creatures, maimed and starving and showing obvious signs of distress as their fate dawned on them.[16]

George Cruikshank's The Knackers Yard; or, The Horse's Last Home, 1830, *shows the appalling conditions in slaughterhouses.*

The cruelty that was meted out to creatures in Smithfield was quite apparent to the passerby. While a goad on the end of a drover or market man's rod or staff was supposed to be no longer than one-eighth of an inch, many were longer and were seen being used on the head, eyes, genitals, and shins of animals that were standing perfectly still; the "wake them" beatings just before daylight in winter were said to be particularly vicious. In the marketplace, cattle were arranged in "drove rings"—circles of around fifteen; nose in, tail out—and were kept in that formation by beatings. Hundreds of cows and bullocks stood crowded together in this way in the wide paved area just to the northwest of St. Bartholomew's Hospital; this section was criss-crossed by pathways for pedestrians, with only a wooden handrail between beast and bypasser.[17] Walking this route was a challenge, given the slippery Smithfield terrain and especially so in the "black frosts of November."[18] That Smithfield was often brighter by night than by day was confirmed by a witness before the Select Committee, who said that in winter the handheld lamps of the drovers and the street gas lamps meant that selling could continue after dusk fell in the afternoon. The newspaper columnist who wrote under the pseudonym Aleph, remembering the Smithfield of the 1820s, recalled that "if the day was foggy (and there were more foggy days then than now) then the glaring lights of the drover-boys' torches added to the wild confusion. . . . The long horns of the Spanish breeds . . . made it a far from pleasant experience for a nervous man to venture along one of these narrow lanes, albeit it was the nearest and most direct way across the open market."[19] Road traffic continued to travel across the quarter-mile stretch between the top of Giltspur Street and the southern end of St. John Street, and collisions with animals were common; beatings were used to move beasts out of the way of carts, coaches, and carriages, but hindquarters were frequently hit by passing vehicles.

The common, all too visible brutality at Smithfield was to prove a major impetus in securing the world's first legally enforceable animal-protection measures. In April 1800, a motion had been defeated in Parliament to ban bullbaiting and cockfighting; in 1809, a more broadly defined anti–animal cruelty bill was also defeated, though it had progressed farther than its predecessor before being lost. In May 1821, a similar bill was passed in the Commons but lost in the Lords; and then, in May 1822, a Bill to Prevent Cruelty to Horses, Cattle and Donkeys was passed by both Commons and Lords, gaining royal assent in July of that year. It was always to be known as Martin's Act, after its mover, Colonel Richard Martin, MP for Galway.[20] Martin was popularly known as Humanity Dick, a nickname thought to have been given to him by George IV, with whom he was friendly, despite the king's love of hunting and cockfighting.[21] He was also called Hair-Trigger Dick because of his overexcitability and his readiness to fight duels (he killed no one but inflicted and received a number of gun-shot wounds). Martin was nearly seventy when his act was passed, but he was tireless in his drive to seek out brutality to animals and drag offenders before the magistrates; within a year of the act's becoming law, 150 people were prosecuted in police courts for cruelty. Martin lived, like many other MPs of the day, in Manchester Buildings, a court of rented rooms on the river next to Westminster Bridge, and was often to be seen parading Whitehall and Charing Cross Road inspecting cabmen's behavior and the condition of their horses.[22] A contemporary described him as "a meteor of ubiquity" who appeared to be all over London at the same time, ferreting out and exposing the ill treatment of animals.

The first prosecution to be brought under his novel piece of legislation came about after Martin paid a visit to the Friday horse market at Smithfield and secured the arrest of Samuel Clarke and David Hyde. Clarke was a horse dealer who had repeatedly struck a horse on the head with the handle of his whip to make it look more lively as it stood tethered to a rail; Hyde had severely beaten a horse as he was riding it, for the same reason. Both men were fined twenty shillings each. (The minimum fine was ten shillings, the maximum five pounds or up to two months in jail.) Martin also undertook a citizen's arrest of a Smithfield butcher whom he saw breaking the leg of a sheep; Martin forcibly pulled the man away, even though a gang of drovers appeared on the scene and threatened him. He gave eyewitness evidence at the successful prosecution of a Smithfield dealer who regularly flung calves into a van with their legs tied together and cords around their necks; the creatures piled on top of one another and many suffocated. (In his defense, the dealer said that, if he was not allowed to do his job the way he saw fit, "gentlefolk would get no veal.")[23]

Martin was particularly alarmed at the use of vivisection in medical research. During the 1825 House of Commons debate on a bill that would broaden the scope of Martin's Act, the member for Galway told the House how the French anatomist François Magendie ("this surgical butcher, or butchering surgeon," Martin called him) had, on a visit to London, bought a greyhound for ten guineas (the going rate for a dead human) and nailed the dog's paws and ears to an operating table and dissected its facial and cranial nerves one by one, severing its senses of taste, then of hearing, and announcing that he would perform a live vivisection the next day—if the dog was still alive.[24]

Within the medical community, many London surgeons voiced their opposition to vivisection—in public, at least. The great John ("Fear God, and keep your bowels open") Abernethy saw little value in such research, believing that observation, not experiment, was the key to physiological knowledge; whenever Abernethy did investigate animal anatomy, he insisted the beast be killed quickly and humanely before dissection. Sir Charles Bell, the eminent physiologist, believed there was little of use to humans to be learned from exploring animal physiology, and he had moral scruples, too: "I cannot perfectly convince myself that I am authorised in nature or religion to do these crudities," he wrote in a letter to his brother George in 1822. Elsewhere Bell wrote: "Experiments have never been the means of discovery; and a survey of what has been attempted in late years in physiology will prove that the opening of living animals has done more to perpetuate error than to confirm the just views taken from the study of anatomy and natural motions." To which Magendie, who was determined to fathom the mysteries of muscle movement, particularly that of the facial muscles, replied: "One should not say that to perform physiological experiments one must necessarily have a heart of stone and a leaning towards cruelty."[25] In 1824, before a crowd of physicians, Magendie severed part of the brain of a dog, which fell down, stood up, ran around, then died.

Edinburgh's Dr. Knox, purchaser of Burke and Hare's produce, was another who preferred to work on humans: "I have, all my life, had a natural horror for experiments made on living animals, nor has more matured reason altered my feelings with regard to these vivisections. . . . A minute and careful anatomy, aided by observation of the numerous experiments made by nature and accident on man himself, seems to me to present infinitely the best and surest basis for physiological and pathological science."[26]

Humanity Dick was never able to bring an action against a vivisectionist; his attempts to pass such a measure failed in Parliament. But in pursuing cases of ordinary, everyday cruelty, he became legendary, and his London court appearances—as prosecutor—often found him in front of George Rowland Minshull, who obtained many contributions to the courtroom swear box (proceeds to the poor) as a result of Martin's endless stream of exasperated "By God"s and "Oh God"s. The two men seem to have enjoyed a part-jocular, part-peevish series of exchanges in the mid-1820s, such as this, at Bow Street. Minshull had suggested that a man could judge for himself how much chastisement his own horse might require, to which Martin called out, "By God, if a man is to be the judge in his own case, there is an end of everything!"

"I fine you five shillings for swearing," said Minshull.

"I'll pay up," said Martin.

"No, I was joking," said Minshull, who went on to acquit the defendant, who had been charged with cruelty to a horse. Martin was furious, quoting Macbeth (and shouting): "Time has been, that when the brains were out, the man would die," as he leapt across the courtroom to make his point.

"My brains may be out," said Minshull, "but I cannot make up my mind to convict in this case."

"Then it is time that you were relieved from the labours of your office!"

"Well that was a very kind and gentlemanly remark, I must say," said Minshull, "but I am going to keep my temper, whatever you do, and I dismiss the case." And Martin flounced out.[27]

Martin was determined to extend his 1822 anticruelty act to protect all animals, including domestic pets, to ban bull- and badgerbaiting, cock- and dogfighting, and to improve conditions in abattoirs. He failed to get further bills passed in 1823, twice in 1824, three times in

1825, and three times in 1826. On 16 June 1824, the day after the loss of Martin's Slaughtering of Horses Bill (an attempt to force slaughterhouse owners to keep horses well fed while they awaited death), a meeting took place at the inappropriately named Old Slaughter's Coffee House.[28] The Friends of the Bill for the Prevention of Cruelty to Animals resolved to become a more permanent body, the Society for the Prevention of Cruelty to Animals (to be given its "Royal" prefix by Victoria in 1840). Those assembled pledged to redouble their efforts to police the behavior of cabmen and drovers and to publish tracts and write letters to the great and good on why mistreating brute beasts was immoral. Such activities could take time: one Charles Merritt told the 1828 Select Committee on Smithfield that it had taken him the best part of a day to get a drover's boy arrested for injuring a bullock in Oxford Street. A growing number of anticruelty campaigners took to patrolling Smithfield, reflecting a growing passion for personal intervention in the face of the apparent unwillingness or inability of the constables appointed by the Corporation of London to police Smithfield Market effectively. (The Metropolitan Police had no jurisdiction in Smithfield; not until 1839 did the City exchange its parochial constables for a body modeled on the Met.) Eight to ten constables were supposed to be on hand at any time during the day, but there were frequent complaints that officers were never to be found or, if found, would do little to act against a cruel drover.[29]

Shifts in attitudes toward animal cruelty had wide-ranging implications. Opposition to the 1800 and 1809 anticruelty bills had largely focused on two issues. First, it was felt to be a gross infringement of liberty for a man to be prohibited from doing as he saw fit with his property—living property included (the same reason that, short of murder, a man could do as he pleased with his wife). Undue interference in private lives was to be avoided as far as possible (though some private lives were considered more worthy of protection than others). Martin's Act cleverly got around the freedom-of-the-individual objection by framing the legislation to apply to those who had *charge* of a beast; its result, though, was a crackdown on workingmen, who merely had charge—not ownership—of horses, cattle, and donkeys. Second, there was doctrinal objection to animal protection, at least when the Lords came to debate the measure. Why should animals be considered the equal of man when he was given dominion over every living thing that moves upon the earth? The concept of an animal's having feelings and legal rights was seen as yet one more eccentric notion held by Methodists, Quakers, Baptists, Evangelicals, and other nonconformists who made up a large and vocal part of the anti-cruelty lobby.[30] Many of Martin's supporters conflated their attacks on animal cruelty with opposition to ancient aristocratic privilege and to arcane, outmoded civil processes and institutions, and many different threads of protest were to be interlinked in the literature of animal-cruelty campaigners. The 1823 *Cursory Remarks on the Evil Tendency of Unrestrained Cruelty* pamphlet, for example, worked itself up into a purple passage eliding all manner of social ills perpetrated in unreformed, aristocratically misruled Britain: "Man has the vanity, the preposterous arrogance, to fancy himself the only worthy object of divine regard; and in proportion as he fancies himself such, considers himself authorised to despise, oppress, and torment all the creatures which he regards as his inferiors . . . and thus the proud and voluptuous in the higher ranks of society too often regard the humble and laborious classes as beings of a different cast, with whom it would be degrading familiarity to associate, and whom, whenever they interfere with their pleasures, their interest, or caprice, they may persecute, oppress and imprison. [This last was a reference to the Vagrancy Act, then being debated in Parliament.] . . . Thus men in the lowest stations become, in their turn, the persecutors and tormentors of the brute creation, of creatures which they regard as inferiors." The chain of evil passed downward from the aristocracy to Smithfield, where the cattle appeared to take on Christlike attributes, exhibiting, according to *Cursory Remarks,* "the most patient endurance of every kind of persecution" and having "a harmless, unresisting, uncomplaining nature."[31]

Impassioned rhetoric such as this, combined with zealous personal intervention, appeared to be winning the day. Humanitarianism was becoming attractive to those seeking a new respectability—those who felt themselves on the verge of getting the vote—and increasing support was being shown for moves that would distance the new industrial/mercantile age from a past perceived as barbarous. Some of the more obvious excesses were being eradicated by legislation: the slave trade was abolished in the British Empire in 1807, and the ownership of slaves in 1833; the use of child labor began to diminish with the passing of the first Factory Act in 1833. The Bloody Code was crumbling: the burning of female felons ended in 1790; hanging, drawing, and quartering was abolished in 1814; the last beheadings were in 1820; the stocks, the whip, the pillory, and the gibbet would all fall idle by 1837. (London's last set of stocks would stand disused for many years in Portugal Street, James May's former haunt.) One of the last public whippings in London took place in 1829, when a thirteen-year-old boy was flogged for 150 yards while tied to the end of a moving cart for stealing a pair of shoes; though no one attempted his rescue, the crowd that gathered was vocal in its opposition.[32] The old was becoming repugnant, and Smithfield offended on many levels; everything about the place stood in direct opposition to the impulses of those bent on reforming, modernizing, cleansing, ordering, making open and visible. The very topography of "this old field of cruelty" appeared to modern eyes to embody and perpetuate the sins of ages past.[33] Until the middle of the thirteenth century, a small wooded section of the Smoothe Field called the Elms, which lay between today's Cowcross and Charterhouse streets, had been the place of public execution. In 1542, Henry VIII devised the spectacle of the boiling to death of offenders, to take place in Smithfield (one of his kitchen staff, who had been accused of poisoning, died in a vat, slowly, in this way; a serving woman met the same fate the following year). In the next decade, Mary Tudor had forty-five Protestants burned close to the gates of St. Bartholomew the Great, and her sister, Elizabeth I, sent Catholics to the flames. Two centuries later, the convoluted lanes running around Turnmill Street, West Street, Field Lane, Saffron Hill, Cowcross, and other thoroughfares near the Fleet were colloquially known as Jack Ketch's Warren, after the seventeenth-century executioner; the Warren was where gallows fodder hid from the law and bred new sinners. These festering piles of wooden buildings cut off the south from the north, while the higgledy-piggledy, queer, and quaint alleys and courts, with their antique names (Black Boy Alley, Swan Inn Yard, Bread Court), were increasingly seen as harboring immorality, criminality, disease, and civil unrest—right in the heart of

Tudor/Stuart housing in Cloth Fair, Smithfield. Although it was con-
sidered squalid in the 1830s, its destruction at the end of the nine-
teenth century provoked an outcry.

the wealthiest city in the world.[34] The sinuosity and complexity of the
Warren confounded those who attempted to enter and investigate
these ancient spaces: to the horror of one surveyor and public health
campaigner, Frying Pan Alley, off Turnmill Street, was found to be
twenty feet long but just two feet wide.[35]

But it was only the outsider who was bewildered by the twists and turns of Smithfield. Those who lived there or worked there were able to negotiate it with ease. When Thomas Williams was sought for the theft of the copper from his parents' lodgings at 46 Turnmill Street, James Spoor, his parents' landlord, was told that he could probably find the culprit at the Bull's Head.[36] This pub was a right, a right, and a right again walk from Turnmill Street—and sure enough, there was Williams. The pub stood in a secluded court within a morass of tiny streets; but to those in the know it was simple to locate.[37]

Cleanliness, godliness, and commercial progress—the Victorian trinity—would sweep much of the district away; the alleys and courts that remained were often no more than amputated stumps abutting the fine new thoroughfares that thrust through the region: Farringdon Road, Clerkenwell Road, Holborn Viaduct, Charterhouse Street, the Metropolitan railway line. The filthy Fleet would be locked into a conduit beneath Farringdon Road. Disease, the Victorians believed, was airborne; petty, and not so petty, criminality festered in dark, unseen quarters; trade was shackled by poor lines of communication and slowed traffic. Before the century's end, Smithfield's secrets would be laid open to the skies.

NINE

Whatever Has Happened to Fanny?

On Thursday, 24 November, two admission booths were set up outside Bishop's House of Murder, as No. 3 Nova Scotia Gardens was
now known. The police had asked John and Sarah Trueby, owners of
Nos. 1, 2, and 3, if some arrangement could be made for visitors to
enter the House of Murder five or six at a time, paying a minimum
entrance fee of five shillings—a move officers hoped would prevent
the houses being rushed by the hundreds who were thronging the
narrow pathways of the Gardens and straining to get as close to the
seat of horror as possible. Sarah Trueby's grown-up son told Constable Higgins that he was concerned about his family's property sus-
taining damage and asked Higgins and his men if they could weed out
the rougher element in the crowd. Somehow, Higgins managed to
maintain at least the pretense of decorum, and the *Morning Advertiser*
later claimed that "only the genteel were admitted to the tour." Nevertheless, the two small trees that stood in the Bishops' garden were
reduced to stumps as sightseers made off with bark and branches as
mementoes—ditto the gooseberry bushes, the palings, and the few
items of worn-out furniture found in the upstairs rooms, while the

floorboards were chopped to pieces for souvenir splinters. Local boys were reported to have already stolen many of the Bishops' household items, and around Hackney Road and Crabtree Row a shilling could buy the scrubbing brush or bottle of blacking or coffeepot from the House of Murder. All of which prompted journalist and historian Albany Fontblanque to ruminate on English morbidity and enterprise in the *Examiner* magazine: "The landlord upon whose premises a murder is committed is now-a-days a made man. . . . Bishop's house bids fair to go off in tobacco-stoppers and snuff-boxes; and the well will be drained—if one lady has not already finished it at a draught— at the rate of a guinea a quart. . . . If a Bishop will commit a murder for £12, which seems the average market price, the owner of a paltry tenement might find it worth while to entice a ruffian to make it the scene of a tragedy, for the sale of the planks and timbers in tooth-picks, at a crown each."[1]

One of the assistants to architect John Soane came to take a detailed sketch of No. 3 in order to create a scale model for use at the Old Bailey trial, while celebrated solicitor James Harmer (who had

Sightseers at Nova Scotia Gardens. This drawing shows a third variant impression of Bishop's House of Murder. The Gardens differed as much as the faces of the accused in the various visual representations of the day.

offered his services as prosecution lawyer to the impoverished parish of
St. Paul's, Covent Garden, for free) undertook a full survey of the cottage.[2] The sketch and the written survey were intended to show that all
the inhabitants of No. 3 must have been aware of any killings that
were taking place within; Sarah and Rhoda were not yet in the clear.
Indeed, they never would be, in the minds of locals. In the streets
of Bethnal Green, Shoreditch, and Hoxton, a number of women had
been jeered at and jostled by people who mistook them for Sarah or
Rhoda. On Monday, 28 November, the real Sarah and Rhoda made an
ill-advised visit to the neighborhood and were spotted and chased by a
crowd. A Shoreditch publican hustled them into the garden at the
back of his premises and helped them escape over the back wall.

Reports of attempted burkings on the streets of the metropolis after
dark began to fill the news pages of the national papers; but it is likely
that panic and paranoia were contributing to making perfectly ordinary robberies and attempted sexual assaults appear bungled efforts
to supply the surgeons. William Burke had been hanged in January
1829, and in that year the *Times* carried thirteen stories of attempted
or alleged burkings, ten of them in January and February; throughout
1830, however, just one such story appeared in the paper, though
there had been no diminution in anatomists' need for Subjects. After
the Italian Boy arrests, five supposed attempted burkings were
recorded by the *Times* within four weeks. Typical is this account,
from the edition of 24 November 1831: "On Tuesday evening
between eight and nine o'clock, Charles White, a young lad about
thirteen years of age, was returning from Messrs Fowlers manufactory in the Belvedere Road, near Waterloo Bridge, to his own home at
8 James Street, Lambeth, when he was seized by two men in a place
called Sutton Street, leading into the York Road. One of the ruffians
held him while the other clapped a large plaster over his face and
endeavoured to stifle him. The poor lad struggled violently, got one of
his hands loose and took the plaster from his mouth. The boy
screamed for help and the villains, finding that they could not accom-
plish their diabolical purpose, and again clap the plaster on his face,
became alarmed. The cries of the lad were fortunately heard when

one of the villains, with a ruffian's grasp, seized him by the neck and threw him over a paling into an unused plot of ground and then ran away. A number of persons came to his assistance, and he was conveyed to the station house in Waterloo Road. . . . A description of one of the men, who was dressed in a smock frock, was taken down and the constables placed on alert."[3] The smock-frock reference is interesting; it had been widely reported that May and Bishop had been arrested wearing this common item of rural laborer's clothing, which was coming to be associated, in the London mind, with resurrection and burking. Also, at the time of the attack on White, no modus operandi had been suggested for the murder of the Italian boy; but no one had forgotten the iconic woodcut images in various broadsheets of Burke and Hare suffocating their victims by placing adhesive bandages over the mouth and nose—a mythical method of killing, since by their own admission, Burke and Hare had simply pinched shut the noses and clamped closed the jaws of their victims.

There were a number of other reported attacks on south London youngsters while the Italian Boy hearings were in progress. Henry Edward, fourteen, of Felix Street, Westminster Bridge Road, was assaulted in Waterloo Road; Henry Morgan, eighteen, was being attacked in Fore Street, a street running alongside the Thames, in Lambeth, when the police arrived and scared away his assailant; Martha Allenby, sixteen, of Bronti Place, off Walworth Road, thwarted an attempt to place a pitch plaster across her mouth; Elizabeth Turner, eight, of Waterloo Road, was lured from her doorstep by a man offering her sweets, then tied with a rope and beaten before being rescued by passersby.[4] All these assaults were reported as attempted burkings.

The man who swept the crossing at the Stamford Street junction with Waterloo Road suddenly stopped turning up for work, though those who knew him said he was someone of regular habits. The *Sunday Times* of 27 November stated that "little doubt is entertained that he has been murdered." Meanwhile in the East End, a boy who had claimed that he was the victim of an attempted burking on open ground opposite the Salmon and Ball pub in Bethnal Green Road later admitted that he had lied, concocting the story as an excuse to his family for having stayed out late.[5]

On the evening of the Monday after the Italian Boy arrests, residents of Chalton Street, Somers Town, heard the screams of a local girl named Eliza Campbell as she ran from the pathway that led north through the fields to Camden Town, north London. She told those who came to help her that on the unlit path two men had thrown her to the ground, stuffed something into her mouth, and placed a noose around her neck. She fought hard and screamed so loudly that the two ran off across the fields. "We again caution the public to be on their guard," warned the *Morning Advertiser,* in its report of the incident, stressing that there were thousands of hardened villains in London who were likely to be tempted to commit murder by the high price of bodies (in fact, prices were down to eight to twelve guineas a corpse, from an earlier high of fifteen to twenty guineas). "It is impossible to find any excuse for persons thus imprudently placing themselves in the way of danger," admonished the *Advertiser.* "It is to be hoped that the publicity of this transaction, the narrow, nay miraculous, escape of this young woman, will be a warning to both sexes to avoid at night the lonely paths of the suburbs of this town."

At twenty to ten on the night of Saturday, 3 December, Mary Cane went to the public three-seater privy that served the tenements of Hartshorn Court, in the poor, rundown parish of St. Luke's, Old Street. Opening the latch with a method known only to those familiar with its faulty mechanism, Cane stumbled in the dark upon a small body lying just inside the door. Her screams alerted a twelve-year-old neighbor, William Newton, who took a candle and opened the privy door. A man and a woman rushed out, knocking hard against Newton and blowing out his candle; the man was wearing a long black coat, Newton later said, and the woman a light shawl and pale-colored bonnet. Other neighbors gathered and, when they entered the privy, found the body of a five-year-old girl, lying on her back, with her frock pulled above her knees and her stockings removed; one of her legs was drawn up. She had been strangled.

Half a mile away in Broad Arrow Court, near the Barbican, Mary Duffey was distraught; her five-year-old daughter, Margaret, had last been seen being led away by Duffey's next-door neighbor, Bridget Culkin, a twenty-eight-year-old who had recently moved to Broad Arrow Court from Hartshorn Court—where she had lived opposite the privy. "If you come along with me, I'll give you a penny," Culkin was overheard saying to the child at around six o'clock in the evening. Culkin had often played with the child and was said to have always shown her kindness. When Mary Duffey's older daughter asked Culkin, just before nine o'clock, what she had done with little Margaret, Culkin openly stated that she had left her in Hartshorn Court; Culkin then became aggressive and refused to give a good reason for abandoning the child. She was arrested half an hour before the body was discovered.

At her Old Bailey trial, Culkin was proved to have supplied two false alibis for the hours between six and nine o'clock on the third, and several witnesses—people who knew Culkin by sight—told the court that they had seen her that night, leading a crying, shoeless child up Whitecross Street and into Hartshorn Court. What looked even worse for Culkin was that she was the lover of one Robert Tighe (or Tye), who also went by the name of James Kettle (or Cattle), a known resurrectionist who worked with a gang that usually included William and John Shearing, William "Boney" Dunkley, and George Long. The landlord and landlady of the Fortune of War went to the authorities to denounce Bridget Culkin as an associate of snatchers; even more damningly, they claimed that she had often been seen in the pub with Bishop, Williams, and May and had been observed receiving money from them.[6] It is quite possible that Culkin knew May and Bishop and other resurrectionists, and perhaps the payments were for information about where a body was likely to be found.

The publican of the Fortune of War appears to have been a poacher turned gamekeeper, and he may well have been retained as a police informer for the purpose of keeping an eye on the resurrection trade. The New Police were not supposed to behave in this way; but in trying to keep such a covert community as the snatchers under surveillance, doubtless they felt they had little choice but to cultivate certain publicans.

Culkin was found not guilty at her Old Bailey trial—though people were often hanged on the basis of far less compelling circumstantial evidence of involvement in murder—and no one else was ever tried for Margaret Duffey's killing.

There is a curious feeling for the modern reader that the Culkin case may have been a sex crime. Though couched in euphemism, sexual assaults on children were reported in the newspapers of the day, even when they occurred within the family.[7] The point of a burking was to obtain a body, not to abandon it when interrupted, and the public nature of the scene of the killing—a privy in an overpopulated court—seems strange. If Margaret Duffey had been murdered to supply the surgeons, this was a peculiar choice of venue.

Meanwhile, imaginations were running wild in Bethnal Green. Superintendent Thomas repeated to the Bow Street magistrates tales of local women who had gone missing, of one John Bishop trying to tempt girls back to his house for a nip to drink. A police handbill had been circulated detailing the female clothing found in the privy of 2 Nova Scotia Gardens, and a number of people had come forward but failed to recognize the items, when, on Saturday, 26 November, the identity of the owner was established: Fanny Pighorn, or Pickbourne, or Pigburn—the latter being the choice eventually settled on by most reporters. The *Times* recorded the proceedings at Bow Street as follows:

> Mr Thomas stated that the female dress found in the privy of No 2 Nova Scotia Gardens, next door to the residence of Bishop, had been identified by two females, Mrs Hitchcock and Mrs Low, who had called upon him in consequence of having seen an advertisement stating that such clothes had been found. It appeared that a poor woman called Fanny Pighorn, who used to obtain her living by washing, left the house of her sister, Mrs Low, one of the applicants, who resided in Chart Street East, City Road, about six weeks ago, at eight o'clock in the evening, and had never since been either seen or heard of. When she left her sister's, she said she should not be long, as she was going as far only as Mr Campion's in Church Street, Bethnal Green. It appeared that she had called there on the evening in question, and left the house at about

nine o'clock for the purpose, it is supposed, of returning to her sister's. Mrs Hitchcock, who had known the missing woman for 35 years, described the dress which she used to wear, which exactly corresponded with the clothes found in the privy. She spoke particularly to the shawl, which she said she herself had worn and afterwards gave it to Fanny Pighorn; and she also identified the blue cloth pocket found with the other articles, and the fellow of which she produced, saying that they had both belonged to a Mrs Bell, who on her death had bequeathed one of them to her, Mrs Hitchcock, and the other to Fanny Pighorn. The moment that the clothes were produced, they were identified by both women, and Mrs Low positively declared that they were the same which her unfortunate sister had on when she left her house to go to Church Street.

Thomas then asked the women to swear the truth of their statements before the magistrates, which they did, Mrs Low weeping.

Mrs Low said that her sister was about 45 years of age, that she was of a cheerful disposition, in the enjoyment of good health and of particularly sober habits. Mr Thomas said that the shawl which Mrs Hitchcock had so fully identified was not found with the rest of the clothes, but in a deep well in Bishop's garden, where it had been sunk by means of a large stone, and he had ascertained that about the time spoken to by the applicants, Bishop had disposed of the body of a woman at one of the hospitals. He had also been informed that cries of "murder" were heard to proceed from the direction of Bishop's cottage, late one night about six weeks ago.

At a subsequent period of the day, the two women were brought by Mr Thomas before Mr Minshull in the private room, when the clothes were produced and again fully identified by them, except the petticoat and shift, which could not be distinctly sworn to, as the clothes of Fanny Pighorn. [Solicitor] Mr Harmer was present and submitted that a warrant should be lodged at Newgate against Bishop and Williams, charging them on suspicion with the wilful murder of Fanny Pighorn. Mr Thomas said he should use every exertion for the purpose of ascertaining the hospital at which Bishop disposed of the body of a female about the period stated, with a view to obtain further evidence tending to identify it with that of Fanny Pighorn.

The *Morning Advertiser*'s version of these events contained further interesting snippets. Fanny had a ten-year-old child who was in the Shoreditch workhouse, and Mrs. Low confirmed that a straw bonnet found by Superintendent Thomas in the parlor of 3 Nova Scotia Gardens had belonged to Fanny. It had once been white but was dyed black; Mrs. Low had dyed it herself, because Fanny had said that a white bonnet was too smart for her to wear.[8]

The district in which Fanny and her relatives lived was notoriously poor, and getting poorer. Paintings and sketches from the start of the nineteenth century show that the area to the west of Shoreditch High Street largely comprised meadows, ponds, copses, and tenter grounds, but by the 1820s, noxious industries, warehouses, tenement housing, the inevitable pubs (and, by extension, the inevitable chapels and tabernacles) had obliterated these and dispelled the rich romance of its past. Holywell, Shoreditch, had been the site of an Augustinian priory, founded in 1128; with the dissolution of the monasteries, the quarter was commandeered by actors, who, in the 1570s, founded London's first two theaters—the Theatre and the Curtain—in the little enclave that centers on New Inn Yard.[9] In the 1780s, the grassy hillock immediately to the west of this spot, Holywell Mount, was leveled and became a private burial ground run by two elderly women who lived on the site. Here, a notorious feud between local resurrectionists had contributed to the bad repute of a desperately poor neighborhood. In the years between 1810 and 1820, a two-man team of body snatchers was said to be emptying the Holywell Mount burial ground. One of the men was known only as Murphy; the other was tentatively identified as Patrick Connolly; both were among surgeon Sir Astley Cooper's elite of lifters and were helped in their work by the ground's corrupt sexton and gravedigger, a man called Whackett.[10] Two envious rivals, Hollis and Vaughan, wanted to put a stop to this lucrative source of corpses, and so they went along to the local magistrates office, at a time when they knew the courtroom would be full of members of the public, as well as police officers, and shouted this information out loud. The people in the courtroom, hearing the accusation about Holywell Mount, rushed en masse to the graveyard, dug up some of the most recent graves, and found the coffins to be empty. Whackett, his wife and children, and the old women (who had, apparently, been unaware of any body trafficking from their ground) were assaulted and their homes attacked. Now here were Shoreditch and Holywell once again linked to one of the most reviled crimes.

The evidence in the Fanny Pigburn affair was coming in thick and fast. Corrupt gravedigger and snatcher's assistant Michael Shields read one of the accounts of her identification and on the night of Monday, 28 November, paid a visit to Superintendent Thomas. Having earlier decided that Shields's word on any matter was worthless, Thomas and the magistrates now appeared to give weight to the tale he told them.

Shields recalled that he had been woken at five o'clock in the morning on Sunday, 9 October, by John Bishop and Thomas Williams banging on his door in Eagle Street. They wanted him to carry a trunk to St. Thomas's Hospital. Shields walked at dawn the two miles to Nova Scotia Gardens with Bishop and Williams. There, Bishop placed a large but fairly light trunk on Shields's head and told the porter that he was to proceed to St. Thomas's on one side of the road, accompanied by Williams's wife; Rhoda would be carrying a small box tied up in a handkerchief, and the two of them were to give the impression that Rhoda was a servant going to a new position and Shields a porter employed to carry her possessions for her. Bishop and Williams would walk on the other side of the street and would pretend, if anyone stopped them, to have no connection with Shields and Rhoda.

In this formation they walked from Nova Scotia Gardens to St. Thomas's—a distance of nearly two miles—crossing new London Bridge on opposite sides of the roadway. Rhoda waited outside as the three men entered the hospital dissecting rooms and failed to make a sale; Bishop had asked the footman of Dr. John Flint South, demonstrator of anatomy, if he was in need of a body, and his footman said that South was in need but did not have time to come down and look at the corpse—could Bishop come back tomorrow?[11] The men decided to leave the trunk at St. Thomas's and go to a nearby pub to ponder the offer. Rhoda was then left at the pub as a pledge, since there was no money to pay for the beers they had just drunk.

They walked to Grainger's school in Webb Street, and Bishop spoke alone with John Appleton, porter to the dissecting room. The conversation lasted only a few minutes; then the three went back to St. Thomas's for the trunk. At Grainger's, Bishop pulled from it a corpse for Appleton to inspect. It was the body of a thin, middle-aged female, extremely fresh and with no grave dirt on it, thought Shields. The Subject's hair was dark and short. Appleton and Bishop spent some time striking a bargain, and when the sum had been agreed on—ten pounds—Appleton paid Bishop half and promised to pay him the remainder the following day. Gin was then sent for, and all four men had a genial drink together.

Bishop, Williams, and Shields went back to the pub to collect Rhoda and found her weeping. The innkeeper wanted his payment and had been unpleasant to her. Bishop flew into a rage and, as he paid up, shouted that he would never drink there again and would tell his friends not to drink there either. They all left together and walked over London Bridge and up Bishopsgate Street, where Bishop bought them all some gin at the Flowerpot.[12] Bishop paid Shields his ten shillings for the job and even offered to pay him a little more when he got hold of the rest of his earnings the next day. At this point, Shields went home.

Shields told Thomas that the reason he had not mentioned any of this at the various hearings was that he had been too frightened of implicating himself. He now wished to atone, he said. Superintendent Thomas was quite satisfied, since Shields's chronology seemed roughly to tally with the time that Fanny Pigburn was last seen, and the corpse that Shields described appeared to match Fanny Pigburn in age and stature. The information also confirmed the superintendent in his suspicion that the women of 3 Nova Scotia Gardens were implicated in murder. He gave orders for Rhoda to be rearrested, which she was, the following afternoon, as she sat at the porter's lodge at Newgate, waiting to visit her husband.

She was brought before Minshull at Bow Street, and charged

with being an accessory after the fact in the willful murder of Frances Pigburn. Thomas declared that he expected to be able to produce further evidence against her. Rhoda wept. Minshull asked her if she had anything to say, warning her that whatever she did say would be taken down in writing and might be used as evidence against her, and she said: "I thank you, sir, but I want to say what I know. I wish to speak the truth."

She told of how her "father" had awoken her at six o'clock on a Sunday morning "about six or seven weeks ago." He asked her if she would carry a small box for him to the Borough. She agreed and walked with Bishop, her husband, and Shields over London Bridge. Just across the bridge, they came to a pub and Bishop told her to go in and wait until they returned. They came back again in about half an hour, and then they all went together to another pub, and had a pot of "half-and-half" (half ale, half porter) and smoked pipes. There was no money to pay for the drinks, and Bishop told her to wait there. When he came back, he paid the barman, and then all four of them went to Bishopsgate Street and drank gin in a pub. Shields then left, and later Rhoda, her father, and her husband went home. "That is all I wish to say, I have nothing more to add."

Minshull remanded her for a fortnight, though Thomas said he would be able to find further evidence against her within a week. As Rhoda rose to be taken away, Thomas said he believed she had not eaten all day and he hoped she would be given some food, since she was now passing out of his jurisdiction. Minshull replied: "Most certainly—the jailer shall provide her with what is necessary. No prisoner shall want food while I sit here as a magistrate."

It was all shaping up very nicely now, which was just as well, because the Old Bailey trial, at which Bishop and Williams would now be charged with three counts of murder and May with one, was set to begin in three days' time, on Friday, 2 December. Even though no name had yet been suggested for the missing and presumed-burked owner of one of the sets of clothes unearthed in the garden of the House of Murder, the identities of Carlo Ferrari and Fanny Pigburn now seemed reasonably well fixed.

On Wednesday the thirtieth, Minshull received his first visit from an anatomist. George Pilcher was a lecturer in anatomy—and keeper of the Anatomical Theatre of Medical Specimens—at Grainger's school.[13] He had read Shields's statement in the newspapers and came to Bow Street to give Grainger's side of the story with regard to Fanny Pigburn. He also wanted to point out that he had in fact come forward to Superintendent Thomas as soon as the discovery of the Italian boy's body had been made and had explained that Grainger's had refused to buy it but had bought the body of a woman early in October. Did the policeman not remember his visit?

Minshull asked when he had first seen Fanny's body.

Pilcher: "The body, I understand, was brought to the theatre on the morning of Sunday 9th October, but I did not see it until the following day."

Minshull: "In what state did the body appear to you then?"

Pilcher answered that the body had seemed far fresher than most Subjects brought in for dissection. He thought that it looked as though it had never been buried or prepared for burial, and he had assumed that Bishop, as a resurrectionist, had probably stolen it from a bone house or an undertaker's premises. Pilcher said that Appleton, the dissecting-room porter, had thought the same thing; and both men took Bishop's willingness to accept only part of his payment on the Sunday as further proof that there was nothing unusual about the way in which the corpse had been procured (the inference being that a man guilty of murder would want all his money at once). "Of course, had there been any suspicion that the woman had been unfairly dealt by, the body would not have been purchased at all," said Pilcher.

Minshull: "Did you perceive any marks of violence on the body when you saw it on the Monday?"

Pilcher: "I was not aware of any, but Mr Dunn, the pupil by whom the body was dissected, is now present and ready to be examined."

Minshull said that he "did not think it proper to put any questions to Dunn then." That decision did nothing to assist the case but was likely to have been an example of Minshull's characteristic, if sometimes misdirected, courtesy. The young man risked implicating himself, his tutors, and his school in body trafficking, since his statements would be printed in the press.

Pilcher then took it upon himself to speak on behalf of the London medical profession. He told the magistrate, with the court reporters sitting nearby, that he regretted "as much as any man, the horrible disclosures that had taken place; and he was truly sorry that the profession was driven to the necessity of dealing with men such as Bishop, Williams and May. He, however, begged to repeat that no suspicion existed in his mind of anything wrong, until he heard that Bishop and Williams were charged with the murder of the Italian Boy; and then he immediately came forward to state that the body of a woman had been sold at Webb Street by Bishop early in October." Thomas said yes, that was right, Mr. Pilcher had indeed come forward straightaway to tell of that particular purchase, he remembered now.

Minshull had had his curiosity about dissecting-room etiquette stimulated, and in a reply to a question by the magistrate, Pilcher said that the normal practice was for the porters to wash and prepare for dissection any Subjects that were brought in. Appleton had washed the middle-aged thin woman before the student Dunn had wielded the scalpel.

Minshull: "Do you remember whether or not the face of the woman was marked with the small-pox?"

Pilcher: "Mr Dunn told me that the face was slightly marked with the small-pox. But I did not perceive any such marks myself. Generally speaking, they are not easily discoverable after death."

Thomas, still dwelling on an earlier point, said that it was utterly out of the question that the woman's body could have been stolen from a mortuary because he had obtained additional evidence that left him in no doubt that the woman had been murdered. He said he now knew that Fanny had left the house of Mr. Campion in Church Street, Bethnal Green, at half past nine on the night of Saturday, 8 October, and that at half past eleven Bishop and Williams had been seen dragging a woman, who appeared to be intoxicated, in the direction of their home. About an hour later, said the superintendent, cries of murder were heard proceeding from Nova Scotia Gardens. Meanwhile, he said, at seven o'clock the next morning, Shields was hired by Bishop and Williams to carry the body of a woman to St. Thomas's Hospital. They arrived at the hospital at eleven in the morning but failed to make a sale, but between noon and one o'clock the body was sold at Grainger's school in Webb Street.

Thomas had got much of his information from Bethnal Green pub goers. They told him that on the night of the eighth, Fanny had been seen drinking porter with two men in a public house called the London Apprentice, in Old Street, near Nova Scotia Gardens. Concerned, they decided to keep an eye on Fanny—the conversation they had overheard between the trio had seemed rather odd to them. When Bishop, Williams, and Fanny left the London Apprentice, the concerned drinkers followed them and watched as Bishop and Williams persuaded Fanny to come to another public house, the Feathers, just behind Shoreditch Church. There, they bought her some mixed spirits and beer called "hot," after which Fanny seemed to be incapacitated and was last seen with her arms linked in those of Bishop and Williams, staggering in the direction of Nova Scotia Gardens.

Furthermore—quite a coup this—Thomas announced that he now had reason to believe that Fanny had died by drowning: he had found her shawl at the bottom of the well in Bishop's garden; this well consisted of a wooden barrel sunk into a hole in the ground, and he wondered whether the victims were told to bend down and drink from the well and were then pushed in headfirst. He had learned that the vessels of Fanny Pigburn's heart had been engorged, which, as he understood it, was generally the result of drowning—the medical gentlemen present would correct him if he was wrong.

A Horrid System

The medical men had been keeping a low profile since their original announcement that the King's College corpse had been a victim of murder; but no group was watching the unfolding events with more interest. Herbert Mayo, professor of anatomy at King's College, and his junior colleague Richard Partridge, "demonstrator," or lecturer, in anatomy, both had reason to take particular notice of the Italian Boy case. At thirty-six, Mayo had established a formidable reputation as an anatomist, having been made house surgeon at Middlesex Hospital at the age of twenty-two, in the same year that he published his *Anatomical and Physiological Commentaries,* in which he revealed his discovery of the functions of individual facial nerves. A bitter quarrel followed publication, with Mayo's former teacher, Sir Charles Bell, claiming it was his own unattributed groundwork that had made Mayo's discoveries possible. Mayo replied that the opposite was true, that Bell's work had been based on research by Mayo. The dispute became one of the most famous medical wrangles of the day, and those who mulled it over later in the century tended to concur that most of the glory should have been Mayo's. (Had the junior man won his argument, a temporary paralysis of the face might today be referred to as Mayo's palsy.)

Mayo had been chosen as King's College's first professor of anatomy—properly, professor of morbid anatomy and physiology—just as his own private school and anatomical theater in Great Windmill Street, Soho, was going into decline.[1] But, like most of his peers, Mayo was not quite so acute in the new field of forensic medicine. King's College (which had officially opened in October 1831, just one month before Bishop, Williams, May, and Shields made their troubling delivery to its dissecting rooms) had been founded as a response to the new University College—"the godless institution of Gower Street," as its critics called it. University College had been refused a royal charter since no religious instruction was given there and Catholics, Jews, and Dissenters were allowed to take courses. King's, by contrast, was built on Crown land and reeked of Anglican religiosity; its founder (Rev. George D'Oyly) was a future chaplain to the archbishop of Canterbury; its first principal (Rev. William Otter) would soon be made bishop of Chichester. Present at the inaugural meeting of the council of King's College in June 1828 were George IV (patron), the duke of Wellington (governor), and three archbishops and seven bishops, while the governors of the medical school included two baronets. The bishop of London's address at King's opening ceremony was entitled "The Duty of Combining Religious Instruction with Intellectual Culture." The lower orders were not overlooked: a (never observed) rule in King's constitution stated that "post-mortems must not be performed at such times as would interfere with the presence of the hospital porters at divine service in the chapel."[2]

The college, according to its charter, would attract those whose ambition for their sons was "to fix in their minds the true principles of morality." Perhaps it was this kind of earnestness that urged Partridge and his students to look further into the matter of the too fresh corpse that Bishop, Williams, May, and Shields had delivered and so make King's stand apart from other, conniving medical schools. Or perhaps the new school was receiving so steady a supply of bodies from St. Clement Danes workhouse just across the Strand in Portugal Street that it felt secure enough to raise the alarm when a suspect Subject turned up; though King's was attached to no hospital, the workhouse provided plenty of useful case studies.

The medical journal the *Lancet* missed no chance to pillory King's for its ultraconservatism. Refusing to defer to King's royal links, the journal nicknamed it Strand Lane College, and the Church and Tory College in the Strand, while the cap and gown that King's students were required to wear were, it said, "disgusting mummeries." Herbert Mayo was regularly mocked in the *Lancet*. Dubbed the Owl because he lectured with his eyes half closed, he was castigated for his "Cockney" accent, in a strangely snobbish attack (for a Radical publication) on his nongentry background, and a contributor pondered how very un–King's College it was that Mayo had taken out advertisements in the newspapers to publicize his book *Observations on Injuries and Diseases of the Rectum*.[3] Mayo was further criticized for the fact that upon joining King's he had asked for (and received) the enormous sum of nine hundred pounds for his jars and bottles of interesting specimens (human parts showing rare pathological conditions, unusual animals, "monster" stillborn babies) that had been stored in the anatomical museum of the Great Windmill Street School.[4] The nine hundred pounds included a payment of three hundred pounds for "assistance," which may or may not have been money to pay resurrectionists. Mayo was also taken to task for being a poor lecturer, with bad diction; a student complained to the *Lancet* about the Owl who "does not whoop with a clear voice."[5]

That Mayo's lectures were hard to follow would have been of significance to Thomas Wakely, surgeon, founder of the *Lancet,* and, later, member of Parliament. The *Lancet* had been set up, in October 1823, to prod the medical establishment (mainly, but not solely, those men who ran the hospital-linked anatomy schools) into reforming itself. Wakely perceived the men in charge of the profession as mediocre, highly resistant to change, and, in certain cases, driven less by interest in science than by petty rivalries, indulging in rancorous feuds that could last for years. His name for them was "bats"—creatures that thrived in the dark, in the gloom of an aristocratic system of patronage that exhibited all the perceived corruption and skulduggery of the Hanoverian age. And now, many influential people believed, it was time for this age to end.

Herbert Mayo

To Wakely, nothing embodied the establishment more than the Royal College of Surgeons of England, and he labeled it a "selfish oligarchy," even a "junta."[6] The Royal College had been granted its charter in 1800, changing its name from the Company of Surgeons, the organization formed in 1745 when the surgeons broke from the medieval Barbers and Surgeons Company, thereby throwing off any connection with tonsure, shaving, and teeth pulling. Run by a small, self-selecting council of senior surgeons/anatomists, the Royal College was the only body entitled to grant qualifications in surgery in England; whoever wanted to qualify as a surgeon—and thereby become a member of the college—had to fulfill its requirements. And as of 1823, these requirements underwent a controversial change. Summer courses in anatomy, which were taught only at private schools, were delegitimized, and the sole acceptable lectures in surgery and anatomy were those given at London's teaching hospitals (St. Thomas's and Guy's, known until 1826 as the United Hospitals;

St. Bartholomew's; and the London Hospital, in Whitechapel) or, later, at a university-linked institution such as King's College's medical school and, even later, the one at University College London. Before undergoing examination at the Royal College, a candidate had to produce certificates of attendance from one of these schools (and then cough up fees for the examiner). So, no matter how good the anatomy teaching at London's various private schools—and much of it was said to be excellent, with Joshua Brookes, Edward Grainger, Joseph Carpue, and Edward Tuson reputed to have superior learning and technical skill—these courses would no longer count toward qualification.

Teaching standards were of particular concern to Thomas Wakely, since he believed that medical education was the field in which change was most urgently needed. Students paid fees directly to the teaching surgeon/anatomist; the more pupil revenues, the wealthier the institution. But, as Wakely revealed, pupils rarely got their money's worth at the hospital schools. Teachers who did not turn up for lectures, who were too busy or too lazy to field questions, who refused even to acknowledge complaints, whose information was out of date or simply wrong, who would peremptorily shun or exclude any student—these were the men Wakely was out to shame.

Wakely's views were not unusual within medical circles. Comparatively few autobiographies and reminiscences from these years are free from at least implicit criticism of senior surgeons and how they ran the medical profession. Joseph Carpue—founder of the Dean Street School of Anatomy, where John Bishop had tried to sell the fresh boy on 4 November—told the Parliamentary Select Committee on Medical Education that he was "disgusted" by the council of the Royal College of Surgeons: "I considered the council a select vestry, which did not like to let in any but the friends, allies and connections of their own body."[7] Its exclusivity expressed itself in the college building: the council entered through the main entrance fronting Lincoln's Inn Fields; mere members came and went by the back door, which opened onto filthy, tumbledown Portugal Street— the haunt of James May and site of the noxious, much-pillaged St. Clement Danes graveyard.

Quite apart from alleged poor teaching and social and familial exclusivity, hospital schools had two major drawbacks for the medical student: their courses were expensive and instruction stopped in April for five months. A pupil who wanted to study under England's most famous surgeon, Sir Astley Cooper at Guy's, would pay the baronet ten pounds and ten shillings for his course of lectures and a further ten pounds and ten shillings for his dissection course.[8] But for ten guineas total a pupil could, for instance, attend lectures and perform dissections at Joshua Brookes's school in Blenheim Steps, in the West End.[9] Brookes was an outstanding anatomist and had founded his school in 1787, closing it down in 1826 because of ill health—he was by then sixty-seven and had worked for nearly forty years in typically appalling conditions: his school stank of rank meat because of his unique method of preserving Subjects by injecting them with potassium nitrate (which was more usually the method of extending the shelf life of ham and sausages) and filth was present on every floor of the school. (Such an environment was the norm in these pre–Florence Nightingale, pre–Joseph Lister days. Joseph Carpue was remembered as having dirt-encrusted hands and nostrils exuding snuff, no doubt placed there to keep out the stench; Edward Tuson's Little Windmill Street School was said to be rat-ridden.)[10] The Brookesian Comparative Osteological Museum filled the two upper stories of the tall, narrow house in Blenheim Steps, and, with around six thousand specimens— including three elephants and a number of whales—it was said to rank second only to the famous collection amassed by celebrated eighteenth-century anatomist John Hunter; many of Brookes's exhibits had been donated by his brother, who kept a small indoor zoo in a crumbling house in Exeter 'Change in the Strand.[11] While it was debatable whether much of use could be learned from pickled oddities in jars, the Royal College used as one of its weapons against private schools the argument that since private schools did not have access to museums, their teaching was likely to be defective. In fact, the existence of the Brookesian collection and those of Sir Charles Bell and Herbert Mayo proved that private anatomists often had very good museums in the 1820s; but the Royal College and the hospital schools bought up the private museums (starting with the Hunterian collection as soon as the Royal College was formed), thereby making its original accusation become true in time.[12]

The top floors of Joshua Brookes's private school, the Brookesian, in Great Marlborough Street, housed a museum of six thousand specimens. His garden contained his Vivarium—a chunk of Gibraltar Rock to which were chained unusual animals and birds, many of which were on loan from his brother's private zoo in the Strand.

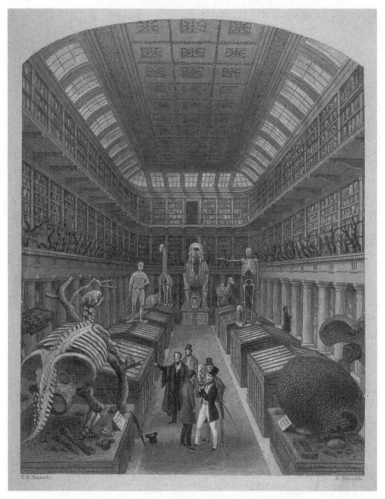

The Hunterian Museum at the Royal College of Surgeons

Upon qualification, the next step for the surgeon-to-be was to become a "dresser," or paying apprentice, to a surgeon, the more illustrious the better. These positions earned the surgeon around fifty guineas a year per dresser; and as each surgeon had between four and six dressers, he was ensured an annual income of at least two hundred pounds. Only students who could afford such fees were likely to make it into the top echelons of medicine, and those who had blood ties or who enjoyed other forms of favoritism were first in line for dresserships. As "A Student of 1815" commented in the *Lancet*: "Tell me the name of the successful individual and I will tell you who his uncle was."[13] The consequent waste of talent was lamented by those campaigning for reform. Sir Astley Cooper played straight into their hands when he expressed his pride that, of the surgeons at St. Thomas's and Guy's, Joseph Green was his godson, while Charles Aston Key, Bransby Cooper, and Frederick Tyrrell were his nephews.[14] Bransby Cooper was a mediocre surgeon, as Thomas Wakely pointed out in the *Lancet* and was sued for his pains. To accusations that the wrong man had reached the wrong position for the wrong reasons, Sir Astley said: "I do not say that he is a perfectly good surgeon, but give him time, gentlemen, give him time. Do not crush him in the outset of his career."[15] At this point, Bransby Cooper had been operating for three years. It was a reply that would be extremely funny if it could be forgotten how many lives Bransby brought to a painful, premature end.

Wakely persistently depicted the iniquities and inequities of the London medical establishment as stemming from an as yet unrevoked age of aristocratic misrule; unfair systems, networks, and behaviors were, he and others believed, poisoning all of Great Britain's institutions. Wakely had written: "We hope the age of Mental Delusion has passed and that mystery and concealment will no longer be encouraged." And of Bats, he wrote: "In youth they are always, by the instinctive precautions of their parents, kept from contact with the ground; and before these disgusting creatures are allowed to take their flight in the air, they are invariably either forced upon some eminence by parental exertion, or they succeed in crawling to some elevated point, through, possibly, the most filthy channels of rottenness and corruption."[16] Many (perhaps most) Bats were in fact "self-made" men of comparatively humble beginnings, but it is true that their careers flourished only when they managed to get patronage to work on their behalf; it was vital that they accepted and manipulated the networks and never challenged them.[17] And once they rose up the hierarchy, the Bats ensured that their own offspring or relatives were favored over "outsiders." George Guthrie would not resign his post at the Westminster Hospital until his son was ready to take it over in 1843.

Wakely was to feel badly let down when two of his medical-reform allies went over to "the other side" as soon as they achieved good positions within hospitals. The more usual fate of the bright and able but not well connected was either to become a surgeon in the army or navy or to set up practice in the provinces. Sir Astley Cooper told the talented and assiduous Edward Grainger to try his luck in Birmingham; Cooper had refused Grainger the post of demonstrator of anatomy at Guy's, appointing instead his own unremarkable nephew, Charles Aston Key. But Grainger decided to join the ranks of London's independent anatomy teachers and in June 1819, at the age of twenty-two, he rented an attic in a tailor's shop on the edge of the graveyard of St. Saviour's church, Southwark, just across the street from Guy's, and began to teach a summer course in anatomy. A few months later he moved the school to a former Catholic chapel in nearby Webb Street, where he was able to offer year-round classes at around half the price of those at the United Hospitals of St. Thomas's and Guy's. It is not known whether Grainger availed himself of the slumberers in St. Saviour's graveyard, but what is certain is that, like all other private teachers, he relied on the resurrectionists for Subjects, since he had no hospital morgue to supply any of his teaching material. Between 1819 and 1824, the year of his death from consumption, a turf war seems to have broken out, not among the resurrectionists but between London's anatomy teachers—a battle between the buyers, not the sellers. The story goes that Sir Astley, furious at the success of what he called "the cheap school of anatomy," sought to pay resurrectionists *not* to supply Grainger, with the aim of driving him out of business. The resurrectionists, seeking to capitalize on this schism, chose instead to supply Grainger almost exclusively, in order to bolster his school and maintain another outlet for their goods. The hospital schools had therefore to offer higher prices to the resurrectionists, forcing the hospital surgeons to break their own club-cum-cartel, the Anatomical Society (set up some time in the first decade of the century to keep fees to resurrectionists as low as possible); prices, as a result, were said to have hit a high of twenty guineas per corpse. Grainger, in reply, offered even higher prices, thereby securing for himself a good supply of corpses and, as a result, more pupils.[18] According to Grainger's friend and competitor Joseph Carpue, an estimated 250 to 300 pupils a year were enrolling at the Webb Street School in the early 1820s, a very impressive figure, particularly since the number of medical students in London was declining. Pupils

The lecture theater at King's College; the brand-new institution boasted bright, airy teaching facilities, but nevertheless included a room set aside to receive body snatchers' produce.

were increasingly heading for Paris to study surgery, since the French state supplied a steady—and free—flow of corpses for dissection from centralized public morgues.[19] And fewer students meant lower revenues for the hospital surgeons of London.

Edward Grainger had managed to upset the medical hierarchy in a way that Joshua Brookes, Joseph Carpue, Edward Tuson, and other noteworthy private teachers in London had not. Perhaps it had seemed like a personal affront to Sir Astley that a man who was not related to him had defied his patronizing advice and set up in direct opposition, geographically and commercially, to Guy's and prospered, all the while disturbing the uneasy but workable relationship between the Bats and the body snatchers. Sir Astley had in the past praised Joshua Brookes's academy, saying that his summer courses could be a useful adjunct to hospital teaching; and he would, in the future, support Richard Dugard Grainger, who would take over the running of the Webb Street School on his brother's death. But Edward Grainger's refusal to accept the status quo would not be forgiven.

In her book *Death, Dissection and the Destitute,* historian Ruth

Richardson notes that Edward Grainger's action, and the Anatomical Society's reaction, in part triggered the events that would lead to the passage of the 1832 Anatomy Act, which made legally available to surgeons the bodies of paupers unclaimed by family or friends. Richardson writes: "In 1823, probably as a result of the failure of the Anatomical Society to control corpse prices, Astley Cooper solicited from several fellow anatomists ideas about what could be done to break the power of the bodysnatchers. . . . It is remarkable that most of the replies seem to favour covert official connivance at existing supply routes."[20] As Richardson points out, "official connivance" was vital to the nation's surgeons if they were to avoid the implications of the *Rex v. Lynn* case of 1788, which made taking a body from a churchyard a misdemeanor. For thirty years, only resurrectionists had gone to prison or been fined for obtaining or possessing corpses for dissection; the price paid by the surgeons was comparatively low, consisting of coming up with bail fees and legal defense costs, providing jail "comforts," and helping to support the family of the imprisoned man. (The "humble petition" found on Sarah Bishop when she was arrested at the Fortune of War was just such a calling in of a debt.) But in February 1828, a Liverpool anatomy teacher was convicted of causing a body to be disinterred, and one month later, a Lancaster court convicted three of a gang of five—which included a surgeon and a medical student—of possession of a body that had been obtained illegally. The Edinburgh Horrors provided another spur to legislation, and the first Anatomy Bill was introduced to Parliament by Henry Warburton in March 1829, just six weeks after William Burke had been hanged for the murders he had committed with William Hare. The bill's supporters declared that burking would end as soon as a legal supply—the unclaimed poor from workhouses and hospitals—was made available to the surgeons. But while Warburton's bill passed in the Commons, it failed in the Lords; and not until 1832 would its heir successfully proceed through Parliament.

So, in 1831, London's anatomy teachers—at both hospitals and private schools—were still relying on the authorities to turn a blind eye to the trafficking of corpses, on policemen not to make arrests or at least to leave the buyer out of the charge, and on magistrates and the higher courts to ensure that a surgeon or school was not implicated when a resurrectionist was in the dock. Discretion was also paramount if doctors, schools, and hospitals were to avoid being the target of the angry crowds that seemed to materialize as though from nowhere whenever resurrection was suspected—just as they did when a beggar was being arrested. Reliable reports of attacks and threats by the London public on individual doctors or medical institutions are not easy to come by; whether this indicates that there was less interest in the issue in London than elsewhere in the country or whether it reflects the under-reporting of popular dissent in the metropolis cannot now be known. There were violent attacks on provincial medical schools both before and after the passage of the Anatomy Act, and the Burke and Hare case caused citywide civil disturbances in Edinburgh in 1828–29; but in London, no medical school was burned down, no doctor hanged in effigy.[21] The extent of opposition to London anatomists, and the risks that doctors ran of exposure and attack, can only be guessed at by the ripples—memories, anecdotes, hearsay—caused by individual events. One old, oft-repeated story underlined the perils of treating dead flesh irreverently: in 1810, a medical student at the Great Windmill Street School climbed onto the roof of the building carrying a human leg and dropped it down the chimney of the house next door, where it fell into a pot of stew cooking over the fire. A hue and cry was raised, angry citizens gathered, and they were dispersed only when the surgeons of the school paid them to go away.[22] Nineteen years later, after Burke and Hare, the misdeeds of medical students were more likely to lead to a hearing before the magistrates, even if it was quite cursory. In October 1829, London's chief magistrate, Sir Richard Birnie, found before him at Bow Street a "very elegantly dressed young man" who was charged with attempting to burke a seventy-year-old woman in St. Martin's Court, off St. Martin's Lane. The young man was a medical student and along with three other students had been drinking in the Shades tavern on Leicester Square; by seven o'clock in the evening the four were very drunk. The student in the dock had seized the old woman by the throat and she had lost consciousness; when passersby

*Anatomist Joshua Brookes was frequently attacked by resurrection-
ists for failing to pay them properly.*

rushed to help her, the students assaulted them. Birnie made light
of the matter, chortling that it looked to him as though they were
carrying out some sort of experiment on the woman but that "the
burking system, thank God, was not prevalent in the metropolis."
He remanded the student for a further hearing, however, perhaps
fearing public reaction if he did anything less.[23]

Joshua Brookes, an unlucky man in so many ways, comes down to us as the London anatomist most closely connected with public fury. Perhaps he did not have the guile to be as circumspect as other medical men; perhaps he was too proud to care about discretion. One night, date unknown, disgruntled resurrectionists, angry that Brookes would not pay them a retainer, dumped two badly decomposed bodies near his school. Two "well-dressed ladies" stumbled over them in the dark, and their screams caused a mob to assemble outside the Brookesian; the anatomist, afraid of a lynching, sought refuge in the Great Marlborough Street police court and magistrates office.[24] Brookes's refusal to agree to resurrectionists' financial terms got him into trouble on at least one other occasion, when a resurrection gang broke into his school at night and slashed to pieces a body lying on his dissection table; again, Brookes needed help from Great Marlborough Street. In addition to his having to flee to the magistrates office for protection, it was reported that Brookes's school was frequently raided by constables from that very police office. He is likely to have been the victim of informants, both snatchers and Bats, having managed to arouse the dislike of both.

Brookes is the nearest London has to a Dr. Knox figure. When Knox was discovered to have been the buyer of Burke and Hare's victims and suspected of having known how the corpses had been obtained, he was besieged in his Edinburgh home by crowds and his windows were smashed, while his effigy was hanged, then torn apart; in another part of the city his image was burned. But the greater damage was done to Knox by his peers; gradually, colleagues and acquaintances began to withdraw support, and Edinburgh's most brilliant surgeon found himself unable to obtain the humblest post. The social shunning forced him to leave Edinburgh for London, where he was also ostracized, and dwindled into poverty and a lonely death in 1862. Brookes, too, died poor and alone, in 1833, but without the ignominy endured by Knox.[25]

There are other, smaller, ripples. Here is poet Thomas Hood's 1826 portrayal of Londoners' anxieties about the fate of their bodies after death:

'Twas in the middle of the night
To sleep young William tried;
When Mary's ghost came stealing in
And stood at his bedside.

Oh, William, dear! Oh, William, dear!
My rest eternal ceases;
Alas! my everlasting peace
Is broken into pieces.

I thought the last of all my cares
Would end with my last minute,
But when I went to my last home
I didn't stay long in it.

The body-snatchers, they have come
And made a snatch at me.
It's very hard them kind of men
Won't let a body be.

You thought that I was buried deep
Quite decent like and chary;
But from her grave in Mary-bone
They've come and bon'd your Mary!

The arm that us'd to take your arm
Is took to Dr. Vyse,
And both my legs are gone to walk
The Hospital at Guy's.

I vowed that you should have my hand,
But Fate gave no denial;
You'll find it there at Dr. Bell's
In spirits and a phial.

As for my feet—my little feet
You used to call so pretty—
There's one, I know, in Bedford Row,
The other's in the City.

I can't tell where my head is gone,
But Dr. Carpue can;
As for my trunk, it's all packed up
To go by Pickford's van.

I wish you'd go to Mr. P.
And save me such a ride;
I don't half like the outside place
They've took for my inside.

The cock it crows—I must be gone;
My William, we must part;
But I'll be yours in death, altho'
Sir Astley has my heart.

Don't go to weep upon my grave
And think that there I'll be;
They haven't left an atom there
Of my anatomie.[26]

The link between anatomists and resurrection men had become part of urban folklore. "If you go to stay at the Cooks, they'll cook you!" Anne Buton told her grandmother on 19 August 1831. The impoverished eighty-four-year-old Caroline Walsh had decided to take up the offer made to her by one Edward Cook and his common-law wife, Eliza Ross, of a bed in their rooms at Goodman's Yard, Minories, east London. Buton told Walsh that the pair were body snatchers, warning, "They're sure to sell you to the doctors."

Buton never saw her grandmother alive again, and when Eliza Ross eventually told Buton that Walsh had left Goodman's Yard after just one day, Buton mounted her own search of east London's streets, workhouses, and hospitals. By late October, the newspapers had begun to take Buton's worries seriously, and under the heading "Mysterious Disappearance" the *Globe and Traveller* of 28 October reported that the old woman may have been "burked for the base object of selling the body for anatomical purposes." Nine days before the Italian Boy arrests, Ross was taken into custody on suspicion of murder; her twelve-year-old son had told the police that Ross, acting alone, had suffocated Walsh on the evening of 19 August, had put her body in a sack, and had lugged her off to be sold at the London Hospital, three-quarters of a mile away in Whitechapel Road. On 6 January 1832 at the Old Bailey, Eliza Ross was found guilty of murder and was executed three days later.[27] Surgeons at the London Hospital vigorously denied that they had bought any cadavers in August, and there is evidence to suggest that Cook and Ross's neighbors were intent on blackening the couple's name. One of the lodgers who gave evidence claimed that he had often seen coffins in their parlor—an obvious concoction, since no resurrectionist ever went to the trouble of lugging a coffin up out of the grave.

As with the dead boy in the watch house of St. Paul's, Covent Garden, identity proved problematic in the Walsh case. An old woman who had died on 3 September after being taken to the London Hospital with a broken hip was twice exhumed for Anne Buton to identify. But this old lady proved to be Catherine Welch, sixty-one, originally from Waterford in Ireland; she was tall but stooped and feeble, with no front teeth, feet in very poor condition, and filthy skin and matted hair. She had been wearing a blue gown and a black silk bonnet, all her clothing being verminous. Welch had made her living selling matches in the streets but had broken her hip in a fall in Whitechapel on 20 August. Caroline Walsh, Anne Buton's grandmother, hailed from Kilkenny, was energetic, did not stoop, had a full set of teeth, and looked clean. She was a peddler of laces, tapes, and ribbons. Her clothing consisted of a black gown, a black bonnet, and a blue shawl (stained), and she wore men's shoes. In a telling detail of the case, Buton had also searched for her grandmother at the houses of those "who were very kind to her [Walsh] for many years by giving her victuals &c."

But where had Anne Buton got her notion that burkers cooked or boiled their victims? Poet John Clare, on his first visit to London from his native Northamptonshire in March 1820, learned some "fearful disclosures" from his city-dwelling friend the artist Edward Rippingille, who described to Clare "the pathways on the street as full of trap doors which dropped down as soon as pressed with the feet, and sprung in their places after the unfortunate countryman had fallen into

the deep hole . . . where he would be robbed and murdered and
thrown into boiling cauldrons kept continually boiling for that purpose and his bones sold to the doctors."[28] Perhaps Clare's friend was
simply having fun frightening a naive countryman; but as with Anne
Buton's warning to her grandmother, the notion of boiling, cooking,
and consuming had become intermingled with the notion of dissection and anatomy. It crops up again in the Nattomy Soup incident of
May 1829, in which an inmate at Shadwell workhouse in east London claimed that the institution's broth included human remains; a
local magistrate sentenced the man to twenty-one days in jail for
making such an allegation.[29]

Dr. James Craig Somerville, who was teaching at the Great Windmill Street School in the late 1820s, had a curious experience of the
public's anxiety. He told the Select Committee on Anatomy that he
had only started to be "annoyed" by locals since the occasion on
which he took in a murderer's corpse to dissect.[30] The dissection of a
felon was an event that the public could—and did, in great
numbers—pay to witness. Many surgeons believed that allowing the
public in helped dispel ignorance about dissection; others worried
that it would have exactly the opposite result. (Dr. Knox himself
believed that "the disclosures of the most innocent proceedings even
of the best-conducted dissecting rooms must always shock the public
and be hurtful to science.")[31] Somerville said that he was now
plagued by members of the public wanting to see each body "whom
they believed may be a victim." A victim of what? Of being resur-
rected? Of dying accidentally and ending up as a Subject? Or a victim
of something more sinister? This tantalizing throwaway remark is the
best evidence we have that, even before Burke and Hare, there may
have been widespread suspicion that individuals were being killed in
order to supply the surgeons.

Sir Astley Cooper's efforts to shield his activities from public view
also testify to the general mood. The ground floor of Cooper's private
house in St. Mary Axe, just east of Bishopsgate, contained a dissecting

room, with windows painted so that his neighbors would not be offended or passersby alarmed. Upstairs, in his attic, up to thirty dogs at a time were kept, stolen from the street by Sir Astley's butler, Charles, who would also inveigle youngsters, Fagin-style, into stealing stray dogs or luring them from their owners, paying the boys half a crown per beast. (And Sir Astley had once called body snatchers "the lowest dregs of degradation.")[32] According to his biographer—and nephew—Bransby Cooper, Sir Astley killed the dogs in order to discover whether a catgut ligature tied around the carotid artery would dissolve (it wouldn't).[33] In a gorgeous example of the hypocrisy and arrogance to which the clan Cooper seems to have been so prone, Bransby makes the perpetrator the injured party: "These circumstances, to which surgeons were unavoidably rendered victims, perhaps may be considered as some of the principal causes which have prevented the members of the medical profession maintaining that rank in society of which the usefulness of their purpose rendered them justly worthy."

Secrecy such as Sir Astley's tended to provoke suspicion rather than deflect it. Mysterious attics, rooms with opaque windows, creatures pickled in bottles, body parts in cooking pots, disappearances, strange goings-on after dark: it was the stuff of gothic fiction and fairy tales. A physician, Dr. James Johnson, used another gothic trope when he wrote that in comparison with London hospitals "the cells of the Spanish Inquisition were not sealed up from public observation with a much stricter secrecy."[34] But surgeon George Guthrie was having none of this, and in an open letter to the home secretary he claimed that dissection and the teaching of anatomy involved no secrecy or need for circumspection whatsoever: "The doors of every dissecting-room in London are always open, there is nobody to watch them, they swing backwards and forwards on a pulley weight, they may shut of themselves, in case anybody leaves them open; every man may walk in and walk out wherever he pleases; many persons do, but no one gives himself any concern about what is going on. The neighbors care nothing about it, and unless, from some accident, the place becomes offensive, no one interferes; although the resurrection men, for their own purposes, sometimes endeavor to excite a little commotion. . . . In London . . . no one knows or cares what is going on, unless he is interested in it."[35]

Guthrie's diagnosis of metropolitan apathy was in keeping with the growing view that Londoners were self-absorbed and unobservant, though it clashed with the simultaneously increasing wariness of the Mob, which dictated a great deal of establishment behavior. But London street protest in these years is notable for the fact that it never truly evolved into systematic revolt. Insulting or striking a constable who was arresting a beggar was a familiar enough rumpus; setting up a hue and cry when a graveyard was discovered to have been plundered by resurrectionists was not unusual. But public outcry at the defeat of the Reform Bill—what had that amounted to in London? One abandoned mass meeting at the bill's second failure to pass; early closing for the shops of the West End; a few Tory windows put out; smaller meetings and marches here and there. Five hundred Metropolitan Police officers lined Whitehall and Old Palace Yard when Parliament reconvened after the bill had been rejected by the Lords in October 1831: a huge crowd jeered the carriages of the anti-Reform members and cheered the supporters of the bill. The Mob laughed when they realized they should have been jeering, not cheering, Lord Ellenborough. A piece of orange was thrown at the anti-Reform duke of Wellington.[36] No soldiers were needed, no firearms. Six months earlier, demonstrators had marched through town and smashed windows where no light was showing on the night of the General Illumination; when they reached Apsley House—Wellington's London home, at the southern end of Park Lane—and had commenced stoning, they were informed that the duchess of Wellington had died and was lying in state within. The Mob withdrew immediately as a mark of respect.[37] There was nothing here to compare to London's last mass civil action, the Gordon Riots of 1780; only No-Popery seemed to galvanize Londoners, who had shown atypical vigor in the Puritan/Parliamentarian cause during the English Civil War. In the Reform era, the capital's citizens failed to match the organized, planned mass protests in other British cities and the countryside.

"No one knows or cares what is going on," said Guthrie, who in his letter went on to state his belief that there was far less popular opposition to becoming a Subject than was generally supposed. "Few individuals really care much what becomes of their bodies after they are dead," he claimed, adding that he had heard the poor in hospital wards laughing and joking about the idea of their bodies being lectured over or being preserved in bottles. But his assertion that there was nothing secretive about hospital dissecting rooms is hard to fathom. That the doors were not closed is not proof that anyone other than medical men ever passed through them. And against Guthrie must be set the rest of London's teachers, who certainly acted as though there was very good reason to be cautious. The more secret, the better; the less the public knew, the quicker science could advance.

The Italian Boy hearings were shining an uncomfortably bright light on the mysteries of the dissecting room. If, as Guthrie claimed, anyone could easily penetrate London's anatomical theaters, it was quite clear that George Rowland Minshull and other justices had never taken advantage of that freedom. A number of procedural niceties from London's dissecting rooms were revealed as the evidence against Bishop, Williams, and May piled up: the hampers left by hospital railings for resurrectionists to use; the convivial relationships between the porters and Bishop, May, and Shields; the small-change tips given to porters by resurrectionists; the fact that there was, in October and November 1831, a body glut in London; the preference of anatomists for adult male corpses rather than female; and the acceptability of children in the absence of either.

Such revelations were not likely to inspire confidence in the medical profession. A tailor named West said he had seen strange goings-on in his neighborhood. West lived close by an anatomical theater "near to Golden Square." (It was not named and could have been one of several in the Soho area.)[38] He claimed that three or four days before the arrests at King's College, he had seen Bishop and Williams bring to the theater the body of a boy "supposed to be about ten." It seems curious that Bishop and Williams would allow themselves to be spotted carrying about a corpse so badly wrapped that an onlooker could describe its gender and age. The next day, Superintendent Thomas called on the theater in question and was told that Bishop had indeed sold to the surgeon there a child—though a three-year-old, not a ten-year-old—along with the corpse of a fifty-year-old woman.

The official connivance in the trafficking of corpses could not withstand such direct evidence of doctors' participation. The testimony of King's College porter William Hill with regard to the events of Saturday, 5 November, was similarly disturbing.

Hill: "The prisoners then asked me for the money."

Minshull: "Do you mean the price of the body?"

Hill: "Yes."

Minshull: "Did you not inquire of the men how they got possession of a body so fresh as they described?"

Hill: "No. We never ask that question. We are not in the habit of doing so."

Hill had given a similar answer to the Covent Garden coroner: "I did not ask them how they got the body because I never ask such a question. It is not likely they would have answered me truly if I did."

So far, so good: only the porters had besmirched themselves, and the only anatomist placed in an awkward position had been the unnamed Golden Square private tutor. But an error in the proceedings now forced a hospital surgeon to come forward. John Hilton (nicknamed "Anatomical John" since he was rarely out of the dissecting room and would always do "an inch or so" of dissecting before starting work in the morning) was demonstrator of anatomy at Guy's.[39] He wrote to the *Times* on 30 November: "Through the medium of your journal and some others, a most unfounded report prevails respecting the teachers of anatomy of Guy's Hospital having sanctioned an easy disposal of any subject which might have been offered to them for dissection by the prisoner Bishop. It was stated at Bow Street that a female had been recently purchased by us from him. As you have participated in this mistake by giving circulation to it, I trust, in justice to the school, you will insert the following remarks in reply not only to this point, but as a general refutation to several most unmerited errors, at any rate as regards the dissecting-room to which I am attached. Allow me to assure you not one subject of any kind has been purchased of Bishop since October 19th 1829.

The last boy dissected was in March 1831, and no bodies were obtained during the past summer of any person, from April 15 to October. Lastly, . . . detached portions of the body have never been purchased for our dissecting-rooms, although it may be the practice at other schools."

Hilton's protestations were disingenuous. Guy's dissecting-room porter, James Davis, had already admitted at Bow Street that he had bought two corpses from James May on the second or third of November, and at the Old Bailey he would repeat this evidence. So while no Subject had been bought between April and October—which was, in any case, the summer recess—purchasing had resumed by early November. Even more compromising was the reported exchange between Davis and May when the body snatcher turned up on the evening of Friday, 4 November, with Bishop and Williams—a friendly, chatty conversation that made it clear how cordial such relationships could be.

But Anatomical John was correct about the error. The source of the mistake was Superintendent Thomas, who had told Minshull in open court that he had ascertained that the bodies of two women had been sold to Guy's Hospital. What Thomas had meant to say was "Grainger's," not "Guy's." Nevertheless, Guy's and missing women were now linked in the minds of newspaper readers, and Hilton's efforts to disengage them looked like trying just a little too hard.

Richard Grainger of the Webb Street School was also tying himself in knots. With a citywide panic aroused, the condition of Subjects being brought into dissecting rooms by resurrectionists was under scrutiny, and one of Grainger's own pupils had gone to the magistrates when the corpse of a forty-year-old man with a head injury turned up at Webb Street. Grainger came forward to explain that this was a disinterred convict who had died on the Woolwich Marshes. The body had been caked in mud and the injury had, Grainger believed, occurred when the body was pulled from the grave. The *Morning Advertiser* reported

> that in consequence of the misstatements which had appeared
> in some of the public journals, respecting the connection of

the Webb Street School with Bishop and his gang, he was extremely anxious to remove an unfavourable impression which had been in the minds of many on the subject. In the first place, the body of the unfortunate Italian boy was not brought to Webb Street, nor was it ever seen by Appleton, the porter. Bishop merely called to inquire if a Subject would be purchased, and was answered that none was wanted. Secondly, that with the exception of one body, bought in October, no Subjects had been received from Bishop and Williams in two years. Thirdly, that on its being known that Bishop and his vile associates were apprehended on the charge of having murdered the Italian boy, information was given by Mr Pilcher, one of the lecturers, to Mr Thomas, the superintendent of police, of the fact that those men had brought the body of a female to Webb Street early in October. The circumstance of Mr Thomas having omitted to mention this fact, when he communicated Shields's confession, although he acknowledged it at Bow Street on Thursday last, has led the public to suppose that the lecturers in Webb Street had concealed this important circumstance, when, in point of fact, they had done everything in their power to assist the cause of justice. . . . The circumstance of bodies being occasionally stolen from dead houses before interment, and disposed of for dissection, no suspicion was excited in Appleton's mind by the state of the body brought early in October.[40]

This denial only served to underline Webb Street's involvement in flesh trading and suggests that the public had in some way been making known its disapproval of the school's anatomists.

One surgeon was covering himself with glory in this affair. Richard Partridge would distinguish himself in little else during the rest of his career (one epitaph would claim "he was best operating on a body that was already a corpse"), but he would be credited with uncovering the Case of the London Burkers.[41] He had arrived in London from

Richard Partridge as a young man

Birmingham four years earlier and had studied under John Abernethy at St. Bartholomew's. He was just twenty-seven when he was appointed King's first demonstrator of anatomy. He dressed in dandyish fashion—highly polished boots, beautifully tailored trousers—and drove a very smart coach and horses. He was no Bat, but—like so many other self-made men of the nineteenth century—he quickly adopted the condescension and waggishness of the gentleman born. He told his class one morning that his carriage had just run over "a little street urchin" but that the child had jumped straight up and made a rude gesture to him. "Really, you cannot break the bones of these street arabs—they're so elastic!" he joked.[42] Confidential details about colleagues and off-color jokes about the corpses in front of him punctuated his lectures. (Partridge was not alone in this facetiousness: Joseph Carpue claimed in classes to have known some of the Subjects that ended up on his dissecting table. "That skeleton is one of the prettiest girls I ever saw," he once told his students.)

It was dissecting-room porter William Hill who had raised the alarm about Bishop's fresh Subject, with a still-weeping wound, but it was Partridge who received the credit.

Minshull asked Hill: "Was it by direction of the persons in the

College, under whom you act, that the prisoners were taken into custody?"

Hill: "Certainly. Mr Partridge and the gentlemen who belong to his class agreed that the appearance of the body was so suspicious that information should be given to the police."

Minshull: "In doing so, they acted very properly."

With King's College in receipt of so much praise, certain sections of the press now felt able to criticize the rest of the medical profession for its inability, or unwillingness, to differentiate between a burking victim and an honestly-dishonestly obtained Subject. The *Times* of 2 December editorialized thus: "In the case of Frances Pighorn, who was seen alive on the evening of 8th October, and whose body was disposed of early on the morning of the 9th at Mr Grainger's, there must have been appearances to excite suspicion, had attention been properly directed to them. Though no marks of violence on the surface betrayed the hand of the murderer, yet the freshness of the body, which could scarcely be cold, the absence of all signs of interment, and the certain evidence supplied by the corpse of the unfortunate woman, that she must have died suddenly, and in the enjoyment of perfect health, ought to have suggested to the purveyors for the dissecting knife in Grainger's establishment, or to the lecturer himself, the necessity of putting some questions to such customers as Bishop and Williams about the history of their prize. We should be sorry to accuse the purchasers of the body in this case of being accessories to murder after the fact, or to excite any vulgar clamor against a most useful and honorable profession, whose necessary means of instruction the law has rendered unattainable, except by the commission of an offence; but we cannot help stating that in our opinion a culpable negligence appears on the face of this transaction. . . . If the deposition of Shields be true, it will require a good deal of explanation to remove the charge of blameable carelessness from the parties which it implicates."

It is curious to note that in showing concern at the moral inertia of surgeons in general, the *Times* singled out for criticism the most successful of the private schools, Grainger's. Guy's willingness to buy May's corpses and to store Bishop and Williams's dead boy overnight did not bring Sir Astley Cooper's former hospital into disrepute.

Many alarmed individuals wrote to urge all surgeons and their porters never to accept corpses that looked suspiciously fresh—to be always alert to the signs of murder. But this assumed a level of skill in forensic medicine that had not yet been achieved. Hope and expectation were running ahead of scientific advance. Of the medical men who had examined the dead boy brought to King's College, and those who had seen Fanny Pigburn's body, not one had come close to identifying the cause of death. Three people knew it, and none was a doctor.

ELEVEN

At the Bailey

At eight o'clock on the morning of Friday, 2 December, the public gallery of the Sessions House in the Old Bailey was already crowded, and surgeons made up a sizeable proportion of the onlookers. Offers of over a guinea were being made for a seat (the sheriffs normally pocketed a shilling a head but raised prices for the more interesting cases), and some people had tried to pass themselves off as court officials, newspaper reporters, and even jurors in an attempt to get into the room. One man rented a barrister's wig and gown at a theatrical costumers for three shillings and six pence and sat unchallenged in the well of the court. Even though the hearing was not due to "come on" until ten, the customary aromatic herbs had been strewn about the courtroom—an attempt to block out the infamous Newgate Stink from the prison adjoining the court. (Not just Newgate: to legal noses, those appearing before the court typically had the aroma of last night's gin, cheese, and onions on their breath, clothes, and skin.)[1]

The dock in the courtroom had a notable feature, a mirror that was fixed above the heads of the accused, tilted in such a way that the bench and most of the room had a view of the back of the prisoners, from the crown of the head down to their boots. Three heads now appeared in the mirror. The thick, dark, wavy hair of John Bishop; the dark-blond mop of James May, and the nondescript mousiness of Thomas Williams. Still in his smock frock, which was by now filthy, Bishop looked like a rustic, according to the *Morning Advertiser*, but "tinged with metropolitan cunning"; he stood at one side of the dock and gazed at the floor. Alongside him, and seeming to hang back slightly, was Williams in a fustian jacket with a brown neckerchief at his throat; he looked, wrote one reporter, "extremely inoffensive" and "shorter than average"—though at five foot four he was by no means short for a workingman of the time. May, also in fustian, and with a yellow silk cravat carefully tied at his neck, appeared to be brimming with life—athletic and alert, with lips pressed tight together and a stern, determined expression on his face. "Their appearance rather indicated low cunning than hardened ferocity," declared the *Times*'s man of the trio.[2]

At nine o'clock, the assistant judge, Serjeant Arabin, deputy recorder of London, entered the court to open the proceedings. William St. Julien Arabin was a notorious figure of fun on the circuit, so much so that one young lawyer, Henry Blencowe Churchill, had

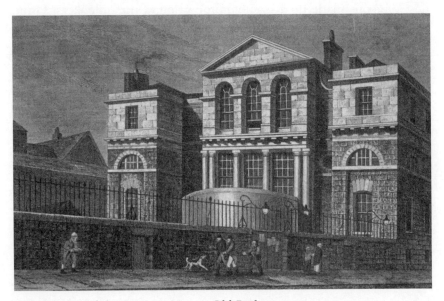

Exterior view of the Sessions House, Old Bailey

started to scribble down verbatim his bizarre sayings, non sequiturs, and eccentric decisions; these were privately published and circulated among cognoscenti in 1843 as *Arabiniana; or, The Remains of Mr Serjeant Arabin*. They included such oddities as: "A man with a cold is not fit to try on a ladies shoe"; "Woman, how can you be so stupid. You are tall enough to be wise enough"; "She goes into a shop and looks at several things, and purchases nothing. That always indicates some guilt"; and "No man is fit to be a cheesemonger who cannot guess the length of a street." On the notorious draftiness of the Old Bailey Sessions House: "When I sit here, I fancy myself on the top of Mount Breeze, and the first thing I do every morning of the Session is to go to the glass and see if my eyes have not been blown out of my head." One of those who would come to own a copy of *Arabiniana* was William Henry Bodkin, cofounder of the London Society for the Suppression of Mendicity, chairman of the Houseless Poor Association, member of the 1828 Select Committee on policing London, Tory member of Parliament to be (from 1841), and one of the three prosecution barristers at the trial of Bishop, Williams, and May.[3] Bodkin's colleagues that day were John Adolphus, who had also interested himself in the administration of the poor laws, publishing in 1824 a pamphlet called *Observations on the Vagrant Act,* and William Clarkson, of whom a contemporary recalled a loud, swaggering demeanor in court and a habit of bullying junior members in chambers.[4] In their wigs, the assembled lawyers looked, according to one of the more astute reporters in court that day, like nothing so much as "a row of cauliflowers."[5]

Serjeant Arabin began by reading the charges. The indictment was all one sentence, weaving its way past many points of interest before coming to rest; the "Jurors" were the grand jury, who decided ahead of a trial whether there really was a case—A True Bill—for the accused to answer:

> The Jurors for our Lord the King upon their oath present that John Bishop, late of the parish of St Matthew, Bethnal Green in the county of Middlesex, Labourer, Thomas Williams, late of the same, Labourer, and James May, late of the same, Labourer, being evil disposed persons and not having the fear of God

before their eyes and being moved and seduced by the instigation of the Devil on the fourth day of November in the second year of the Reign of our Sovereign Lord William the Fourth by the Grace of God of the United Kingdom of Great Britain and Ireland King Defender of the Faith with force and arms at the parish aforesaid in the County aforesaid in and upon Carlo Feriere otherwise called Charles Ferrier in the peace of God and our said Lord the King then and there being feloniously, wilfully and of their Malice aforethought did make an assault—And that the said John Bishop, Thomas Williams and James May with a certain Wooden Staff of no value the said Carlo Feriere otherwise called Charles Ferrier then and there feloniously, wilfully and of their Malice aforethought did strike and beat—And that the said John Bishop, Thomas Williams and James May by such striking and beating the said Carlo Feriere otherwise called Charles Ferrier in and upon the back part of the neck of him the said Carlo Feriere otherwise called Charles Ferrier as aforesaid then and there feloniously, wilfully and of their Malice aforethought did give unto the said Carlo Feriere otherwise called Charles Ferrier divers mortal bruises and contusions in and upon the back part of the neck of him the said Carlo Feriere otherwise called Charles Ferrier of which said mortal bruises and contusions the said Carlo Feriere otherwise called Charles Ferrier did then and there instantly Die—And so the Jurors aforesaid upon their Oath aforesaid do say that the said John Bishop, Thomas Williams and James May the said Carlo Feriere otherwise called Charles Ferrier in manner and form aforesaid feloniously, wilfully and of their Malice aforethought did Kill and Murder against the peace of our said Lord the King his Crown and Dignity—And the Jurors aforesaid upon their Oath aforesaid do further present that the said John Bishop, Thomas Williams and James May not having the fear of God before their eyes but being moved and seduced by the instigation of the Devil afterwards to wit on the same day and in the year aforesaid with force and Arms at the parish aforesaid in the County aforesaid in the peace of God and our own said Lord the King then and there being feloniously, wilfully and of their Malice aforethought did make an assault and that the said John Bishop, Thomas

Williams and James May with a certain Wooden Staff of no value the said Male person whose name is unknown as aforesaid in and upon the back part of the neck of the said Male person whose name is unknown to the Jurors aforesaid in the peace of God and our sovereign Lord the King then and there did strike and beat—And that the said John Bishop, Thomas Williams and James May by such striking and beating the said Male person whose name is unknown as aforesaid then and there feloniously, wilfully and of their Malice aforethought did give unto the Male person whose name is unknown as aforesaid divers mortal bruises and contusions in and upon the back part of the neck of him the said Male person whose name is unknown as aforesaid of which said mortal bruises and contusions the said Male person whose name is unknown as aforesaid did then and there instantly Die—And so the Jurors aforesaid upon their Oath aforesaid do say that the said John Bishop, Thomas Williams and James May the said Male person whose name is unknown as aforesaid in manner and form aforesaid feloniously, wilfully and of their Malice aforethought did Kill and Murder against the peace of our said Lord and King his Crown and Dignity.

Well, at least it wasn't Latin or Norman French: from 1730 on, indictments had to be written in English, albeit of an archaic kind. The strange, meandering prose reflected the need for something that would stick: the accused could be acquitted if a charge was not accurate; and in a case as serious as murder, as many variations on a theme as possible were included in the indictment.[6] The victim would have to be proved to have been Carlo Feriere/Charles Ferrier in order for a conviction to be secured. So a second boy, "Male person whose name is unknown," appeared in the text, to cover the possibility that witnesses might be unable to convince the jury of the identity of the King's College body. However, it didn't matter that "Thomas Williams" was an alias; this was the name that Thomas Head had let himself be known by and would therefore be the name by which he faced conviction.

The killing of Fanny Pigburn was not in the indictment. Despite Shields's testimony, Rhoda's statement, the clothes found at 2 Nova

Scotia Gardens, and the admission by the Webb Street porter John Appleton and the medical student Dunn that a woman resembling Fanny had been delivered to Grainger's at about the right time, there was no body and thus no forensic evidence to substantiate a charge. What's more, Fanny's case would have brought a surgeon in the role of receiver into the witness box. No hint of any connivance in murder by doctors would be heard in so public an arena as the Old Bailey.

Next, Serjeant Arabin addressed the prisoners and asked how they pleaded; each said "not guilty." Then the jury was sworn in—twelve good men and true, between twenty-one and sixty years of age and, since they each inhabited a property of ten pounds per annum freehold or twenty pounds per annum leasehold, deemed "respectable." No one else might sit in judgment on his fellow Londoner. At ten o'clock, the three judges took their place on the bench: Sir Nicholas Conyngham Tindal, lord chief justice of the Common Pleas and Tory member for Cambridge University; Sir John (Baron) Vaughan; and Sir Joseph Littledale. Each man had around thirty-five years' legal experience. Sitting alongside them were the lord mayor of London, John Key; two sons of the prime minister, Earl Grey; and the duke of Sussex, younger brother of the king and England's highest-ranking Freemason. Augustus Frederick Hanover was an enthusiastic amateur follower of many matters scientific, literary, and political. (He had been keen to leave his body to medical science but in the event ended up in a sealed vault at the brand-new Kensal Green cemetery, in 1843.) The duke had requested and been granted a place on the bench for the Bishop, Williams, and May trial in order to see for himself the workings of England's judicial system. But it is possible that as grand master, he was concerned as to how the trial would affect London's surgeons, many of whom were Masons. (The Anatomical Society met at the Freemasons Arms, in Great Queen Street, Covent Garden.) The duke of Sussex clamped a pocket telescope to his eye and took particular interest in the appearance of Williams, who was seen to return the royal gaze with a glare.

The average Old Bailey trial lasted eight and a half minutes, from opening address to sentencing, though some "capitals"—cases that could end in the donning of the black cap—might take hours.[7] Today was going to be different: everyone knew there was little chance of a

Interior view of the Sessions House, Old Bailey

verdict coming in before nightfall. Charles Phillips, barrister at law, knew it, and only the night before had withdrawn from acting as the prisoners' defense attorney since he felt unable to commit himself to a trial that was likely to last the whole day. It is probable he had a number of more lucrative cases lined up in the second courthouse, adjacent to the Sessions House; he would earn a great deal more money from several eight-and-a-half-minute jobs than from an all-day capital case, and there was nothing to stop him from simply abandoning his clients without notice—plenty of attorneys did likewise every day.

Prisoners were obliged to seek out legal representation (and to corral witnesses) from their prison cell—no easy task—and Bishop and Williams had asked for the trial to be delayed because of their problem in finding a barrister: Phillips had been acquired only with difficulty. Their request had been rejected, however, even though Minshull and Superintendent Thomas had publicly stated that the case should go to court only when it seemed "perfect." Both had been hoping for a postponement, and even the recorder of London, the city's most senior judge, had given his opinion that it would be wisest to wait until January. Whichever mysterious power ordered these matters, though, had decided that the swifter the better with this trial. At the last minute, John Curwood and J. T. Barry, a barrister who campaigned against the death penalty, volunteered to act as defense counsel. To modern eyes reading the trial, it looks as though Curwood and Barry barely acted at all; but there were reasons for their apparent passivity. An attorney hired by a defendant did not mount a defense case as we understand it; he was restricted to calling defense witnesses, cross-examining prosecution witnesses, and reading to the court any statements the prisoner wanted to submit, but he could not address the jury. Since he had no right to know what evidence was going to be given against the prisoner, the prisoner's statement, prepared before the trial began, had limited effectiveness. Not until 1836 would a barrister in a criminal case be able to make a narrative defense on a client's behalf; and not until 1898 would the accused be able to take the stand in an English court of law, the idea having earlier been held that defendants should not be allowed to incriminate themselves. But with the defense attorney's actions so restricted, this right to silence acted against the prisoner, since he or she had no chance to put forward an alternative version of events or to impress a jury with an appearance of honesty through speech or gesture. Silence had a tendency to look like guilt.

The prosecution, too, faced a number of difficulties. It was a growing criticism in legal circles that cases often had to be abandoned and prisoners discharged because witnesses for the prosecution failed to show. For, unless subpoenaed, a witness (both for the defense and for the prosecution) was not obliged to come to court; and, given the possibility of reprisals on the part of the accused, plus the loss of earnings as a result of attending court, many people chose to absent themselves from the witness box. Subpoenas proved hard to enforce, and there was even a name for evading a summons: "running up and down" was street slang for making sure you were not at home, and not to be found anywhere around town, when an official came to deliver a subpoena. Many witnesses who did come forward were found to be drunk by the time they testified; the order of trials at the Old Bailey was only very loosely fixed, and those waiting to be called would often repair to the King of Denmark, the George, the Bell, the Plough, or any of the many other pubs and inns around the Sessions House. It wasn't just the sobriety of witnesses that gave cause for concern; evening sittings, which would be abolished in 1845, were notable for the inebriation of lawyers after lunch and dinner—at which wine was plentiful—and one judge was regularly seen clutching the banisters as he lurched back to the Old Bailey bench after meals.[8]

Forty individuals had turned up to assist the prosecution of Bishop, Williams, and May; six had come forward for the defense—Sarah, Rhoda, and the three little Bishops were not among them, since spouses and offspring were deemed "incompetent witnesses." Surgeon Edward Tuson of the Little Windmill Street School had been subpoenaed by the defense but protested that he had no idea what the prisoners expected him to be able to say in their favor. Perhaps they were prepared to make embarrassing disclosures about his practice if he would not speak for them; perhaps he had accepted too many "smalls" and "large smalls" than was compatible with respectability; perhaps he had made off-color jokes about the produce or even made comments that could be construed as instructions to murder.

Henry Bodkin opened for the prosecution, saying that he wished to place particular emphasis on the exchanges between Bishop and May overheard by porter Thomas Wigley at the Fortune of War on Friday, 4 November; the conversation that evening had excited suspicion in all who had heard it. (All of Thomas Wigley, Bodkin must have meant; no one else had claimed to have heard it.) Next, John Adolphus rose to instruct the jury not to allow the "interest" that the case had "excited out of doors" to affect their judgment in this "painful and extraordinary enquiry." It was a revolting crime, he said, precisely because it had not stemmed from any strong feeling or passion: "Nothing but the sordid and base desire to possess themselves of a dead body in order to sell it for dissection had induced the prisoners at the bar to commit the crime for which they were now about to answer." Bodkin acknowledged that the case relied on circumstantial evidence, "but he contended that a large and well-connected body of circumstantial evidence was in many cases superior to the positive testimony of an eye witness." He concluded that he relied utterly on the good sense and integrity of a British jury, "which a long life of practice had left him no room to doubt."

William Hill, dissecting-room porter at King's, was the first witness called by the prosecution. He repeated his earlier evidence of the events of the afternoon of Saturday, 5 November, though this time there was a little more local color, and the role that May, though "tipsy," had taken in the negotiations was foregrounded. (Williams, Hill admitted, had been party to none of the bargaining; like Shields, he had been a silent partner on that day.) It came out that with regard to resurrectionists, even so modern a building as King's anatomical department had "a place appropriated for them." Hill recalled asking Bishop and May, "What have you got?" and "What size?"; on hearing that it was a boy of around fourteen, Hill had merely asked the price. Hill said that the freshness, the strangeness of the boy's bent left arm with clenched fingers, together with the absence of any sawdust in the hair (which would indicate that the corpse had been in a coffin), had triggered his suspicion. Hill's testimony also revealed Richard Partridge haggling in person with May over the price of the child, no doubt to the discomfort of the anatomist, who was next into the witness box. Partridge, when his turn came, told the Old Bailey, "I do not recollect whether I saw the prisoners before I went to the police," in response to Hill's clearly remembered "He was talking with May in the room." Partridge then explained his findings during the postmortem on Sunday night in the Covent Garden watch house. "There was a wound on the temple, which did not injure the bone. That was the only appearance of external injury. Beneath the scalp on the top of the skull, there was some blood effused . . . the skull was taken off and the brain examined. That was perfectly healthy, as well as the spinal part. In cutting down to remove the bone which conceals the spinal part at the back of the neck, we found a quantity of coagulated blood within the muscles, and on removing the back part of the bony canal, some coagulated blood was found laying in the cavity opposite the blood found in the muscles of the neck. There was blood uncoagulated within the rest of the spinal canal. The spinal marrow appeared perfectly healthy. I think these internal marks of violence were sufficient to produce death. I think a blow from a stick on the back of the neck would have caused those appearances and I think it would produce a rapid death, but perhaps not an instantaneous one."

He had noticed that the face was flushed and swollen and the heart empty of blood.

"What do you infer from the heart being empty?" asked Bodkin.

"I do not infer anything from it, except that, accompanied with bloodshot eyes, it has been found in persons who have died suddenly and evidently from no violence."

Curwood, cross-examining on the blood in the spinal canal, asked, "Mightn't this have been caused by other means as well as by a blow—by pressure otherwise applied?" Perhaps Curwood was recalling a forensic detail from Burke and Hare: in Edinburgh, surgeon Robert Christison had stated that, in his view, extravasated blood—that is, blood that has escaped from blood vessels into surrounding tissue—would have the same appearance regardless of whether the injury happened before or after death. Christison had pointed this out when Burke and Hare had claimed that the injuries found on Mary Docherty had been caused when her body had been doubled up to be packed into a tea chest for delivery to Knox; she had died of drink and old age, not from violence, they had said. In Burke's confessions, the Edinburgh killers' modus operandi was revealed—suffocation with bare hands and no blows struck, to keep the corpses looking as though they had died from natural causes. Partridge had evidently never read this aspect of the famous case or, if he had, he had rejected Christison's (and Burke's) findings, for he answered Curwood: "I think not. I cannot conceive any thing but a blow would produce those appearances."

George Beaman knew a thing or two about spinal injuries, having killed many animals with a blow to the back of the neck to observe the results upon dissection. But he, too, thought spinal injury had been the cause of death: "On the top of the skull we detected a patch of blood. . . . This appearance must have been produced by a blow given during life. . . . On removing the skin at the back part of the neck, I should think from three to four ounces of coagulated blood were found among the muscles. That blood must have been effused while the subject was alive. On removing a portion of the spine to examine the spinal marrow, a quantity of coagulated blood was laying in the canal, which, by pressure on the spinal marrow, must cause death. There was no injury to the bone of the spine, nor any displacement. All these appearances would follow from a blow with a staff, stick or heavy instrument." Cross-examined by Barry, Beaman admitted that there was no injury to the skin at the back of the neck; he saw nothing odd in that, claiming that the boy had died too quickly to have developed a bruise or weal.

The body had been in "very good health," Beaman added, and had been generally clean, apart from some obviously smeared-on mud or clay. All the other organs had been in good condition, though Beaman had never before seen a heart empty of blood; along with Partridge, he took this to indicate a very quick death—probably within two or three minutes of the fatal blow.

Beaman estimated that the body had been dead for thirty-six hours by the evening of Saturday the fifth, when he had opened it prior to the full postmortem the following day; though, as he pointed out to the court, the coldness of the weather "was very favourable to the preservation of dead flesh." He believed that the teeth had been removed two to three hours after death and that the boy had eaten a meal around three hours before being killed. (Thirty-six hours before the "evening" of Saturday the fifth was between 5 A.M. and 10 A.M. on Friday, 4 November, if "evening" could be interpreted as anytime between 5 P.M. and 10 P.M.) Cross-examined, Beaman would not swear to the time of the teeth's being removed but said that he was certain twelve hours had not passed between death and extraction. James May claimed to have removed them at around half past six on the Friday evening.

To give some weight to the findings of the unillustrious Beaman (he was just a parish surgeon) and the young Partridge, Frederick Tyrrell, a nephew of Sir Astley Cooper, was called. He backed up Partridge and Beaman, stressing that the child had certainly not died from a stroke; the injuries could have been caused "only by violence."

That ended the medical evidence. Next, PC John Wilson of F Division told of the violent struggle that James May had put up as he was being taken into custody: "He struck me because I would not let Bishop and him talk together." Superintendent Thomas took up the story, saying, "I should observe that the prisoners were under the effects of liquor, in my judgement—May and Bishop more particularly so. May was carried in on all fours and his frock over his face. He was scuffling." The noose was tightening.

May, for reasons the prosecution could not fathom, had refused to secure immunity for himself by revealing when, where, and how the child in the trunk had met his death. This was unforgivable: he was going to be made to pay.

Two of the more foggy, fluid parts of the story were next recounted by Henry Lock, barman at the Fortune of War, and Thomas Wigley, beer drinker at the same—with new emphases on May and the other prisoners acting in concert. It had been May and Bishop's claim that their meeting at the Fortune of War that Friday morning had been a chance encounter, that they had arrived separately, though neither had been able to give specific times. May had remembered being there already, sometime after eleven or twelve, when Bishop and Williams walked in. Lock now pinned the time to "about eleven o'clock. . . . I remember seeing them all three at the Fortune of War, they had some drink there and stayed till about twelve." Lock claimed that Bishop, May, and Williams were accompanied by another man, "a stranger to me." (Shields would not meet them at the Fortune of War for another whole day; even Superintendent Thomas had given up the goose chase of trying to place the four original prisoners together in the pub on the Friday morning.) Lock told the Old Bailey that Bishop, Williams, May, and the stranger all left the Fortune of War "together"—"together" now being the motif of his evidence. He said that Bishop, Williams, and May came back at around three o'clock, left at dusk, returning at about eight o'clock with a different fourth man, "who appeared to be a coachman." The three prisoners were in the taproom for quite a while, said Lock, and then a little before nine, May came to the bar, rubbing a set of teeth with his handkerchief. "They all left together, some short time after this," said Lock. At around eight o'clock the next morning, Lock saw Bishop and Williams with Michael Shields at the Fortune of War; the latter was heard to refuse to go across the road and take a hamper from just inside the railings of St. Bartholomew's Hospital, so Bishop went and collected it himself.

Thomas Wigley gave the gist of his former evidence, and the prosecution attempted to show that May—aware that his conversation with Bishop was being overheard by Wigley, sitting at the same table at the Fortune of War—had tried to make out that he did not understand Bishop's resurrection slang. Wigley said that Bishop had asked May, "Did not he go up to him well and collar him—was he not a game one?" to which May had said, "I don't know what you mean."

Next, May's role in procuring a cab was highlighted by the drivers he and Bishop had approached. Then the eyewitness accounts were heard from the neighbors who had seen Bishop, Williams, and May arrive at Nova Scotia Gardens in a yellow chariot, then carry something away in a sack; though twelve-year-old George Gissing inconveniently said that "the strange man" in the smock frock he had seen that evening with Bishop and Williams was not the third man in the dock, and neighbor Ann Cannell—who had failed to pick out Bishop at Bow Street when taken there to do so—now maintained that she hadn't seen enough of any of the three to recognize them at the time or on any subsequent occasion.

When Robert Mortimer, the elderly tailor who lived near the Bishops and who had cut Williams a coat for his wedding day just ten weeks earlier, was not found to be among the prosecution witnesses at the Old Bailey, two sheriff's officers were dispatched to Nova Scotia Gardens to collect him. Mortimer welcomed the men into his cottage, apologized for having forgotten the day of the trial, and asked them to excuse him while he shaved. He picked up his razor and, in front of the officers, drew the blade across his throat.

Guy's Hospital porter James Davis and his assistant, James Weeks, repeated that they had bought two bodies from May earlier in the week of the arrests, that they knew both Bishop and May well; that the two had delivered to them a sack from which protruded the foot of what they took to be a woman or a child; that Guy's had stored it overnight and delivered it up safely to the resurrectionists on Saturday morning. Like William Hill, Davis said that Williams had taken no part in the brokering of the body on the Friday night—it had all been done by Bishop and May; Davis hadn't even seen Williams until the latter's appearance at Bow Street. John Appleton of Grainger's school hadn't seen Williams either—he had dealt with only Bishop and May. And May's apparently detailed knowledge of the boy's corpse was reiterated by dentist Thomas Mills. May, said Mills, had called between nine and ten o'clock on the Saturday morning and, when challenged about whether the teeth were in fact a set, said "upon his soul to God, they all belonged to one head, and not long since, and that the body had never been buried. He said, 'The fact is, they belong to a boy between fourteen and fifteen years old.'" In Mills's opinion, great violence must have been used to get the teeth out of the head, since part of the jaw socket was still attached; he said that the brad awl found in May's room in Dorset Street, and produced in court, was exactly the sort of implement that would have been used to extract the teeth.

Augustine Brun, the Birmingham padrone, was interpreted to the court by Joseph Paragalli. According to the *Times,* this was not a satisfactory arrangement, and the judge reprimanded Paragalli for appearing to alter the questions and Brun's answers and for "impertinence and frivolity not at all in character with the solemn investigation which was then pending." There was laughter when Brun said that he had not seen the boy alive since July 1830 and, presumably in reply to a clumsily worded question, said that he couldn't have seen the boy alive after he was dead. That aside, it is difficult to make out, in the official transcript of the trial and the various newspaper reports, where Paragalli would have been criticized for levity, and how much of the following testimony represents what Brun really meant to say cannot be known: "I knew an Italian boy named Carlo Ferrier. I brought him over from Italy about two years ago, he was then about fourteen years old. He lived with me for about six weeks. I saw him alive on 28th July 1830. The last place I knew him to lodge at was Mr Elliott's, No 2 Charles Street, Drury Lane. On 19th November I saw the body of a boy at the burial ground near Covent Garden. I can only say that I suppose it to be the boy of whom I have spoken, by his size and hair, but the face I cannot give an opinion upon, from the state it was in, and the teeth were taken out. The size and the hair were exactly the same as Ferrier's. I have not seen that boy alive since."

Brun said that he could perceive no trace of resemblance to Carlo in the corpse's face, which, in any case, he had not had the heart to look at for very long.

Curwood asked him: "Supposing you had heard nothing about

Carlo Ferrier, and had looked at that body. Should you at all have known it?"

"Yes, I should, from the hair and size. If I had known nothing about this occurrence and had seen the body, I should be of the opinion that he was 'my own.'"

Curwood wanted Brun to confirm that he was completely sure, and Brun said: "At first sight, if anybody had asked me who the body was, the face was so disfigured, I could not tell."

"Have you seen him since July twelve months?"

"No. He might grow a little in fifteen months, but not much."

It is difficult to guess how much a poor boy, aged around fourteen, would have grown in fifteen months; malnourishment meant that in the early part of the nineteenth century, the poorest London fourteen-year-olds were, on average, between four and six inches shorter than the fourteen-year-old sons of the gentry.[9] But George Beaman had found this child to be healthy, even slightly "stout."

Giving his own testimony, Joseph Paragalli said: "I play an organ and pandean pipes about the streets, with my wife and three children. I knew Carlo Ferrier. I saw him every morning at Mr Elliott's. I knew he was once in Brun's service. I have known the boy from 22nd May 1830. I saw him alive in the Quadrant, Regent Street, at half-past two o'clock on a Saturday afternoon, four weeks before I saw him at the station house. He was then dead. When I saw him in the Quadrant he had a little cage round his neck, and two white mice in it. He was the same boy as I saw dead at the station house, undoubtedly."

Paragalli also revealed that Carlo had been brought to England with his sister, who had died in Scotland. Extraordinarily, he offered the information that Carlo was the only Italian boy who made money exhibiting animals in the streets of London. The boy he had seen in the Quadrant could only have been Carlo.

He was now handed the brown furry cap, which had been sitting in court all morning alongside the sack, hamper, trunk, set of teeth, and all the articles of clothing exhumed at 3 Nova Scotia Gardens; the garments had been described in great detail in every national newspaper the day after Superintendent Thomas had brought them back in triumph to Bow Street. "I cannot swear to this cap," said Paragalli. "He always wore a cap. I cannot say whether I ever saw him in one like this. He had one on in the Quadrant, but I cannot say whether it was cloth, leather or skin. I am sure the shade [visor] of this cap is of foreign manufacture."

Barry asked: "Is it not eleven weeks since you saw him?"

"It was four weeks before I saw him a corpse. He lodged close to me. The rest of the Italian boys live by Saffron Hill. I have seen many about town. I do not keep company with my countrymen here."

Paragalli's wife, Mary, said, "I knew a boy who carried two white mice about. I do not know his name. I saw that boy on Tuesday 1st November in Oxford Street, near Hanover Square, exactly at a quarter past twelve o'clock. He had a little cage, like a squirrel's cage, which turns round, with two little white mice in it. I did not speak to him. I do not recollect how he was dressed. He had a little cap on but it is impossible for me to say what color, or what it was made of. On Sunday morning, 6th November, about nine o'clock, I saw the dead body of the very same boy at the station house, Covent Garden. I had known him all the summer. I know Brun, but did not know him till the boy had left him. I do not know what name the boy went by. I never spoke to him much. I was with my husband when we saw him in the Quadrant. That was the same boy that I saw dead. I have a son eight years old, who knew the boy well. He went with me to the station house and knew him. He is not here." Hearsay had not been allowed in an English court of law since the seventeenth century; Mary Paragalli should have been allowed to mention her son's views only if he was there himself to be questioned on them.

A new Italian witness had come forward. Andrew Colla lived at 4 Saffron Hill and was a peripatetic seller of birdcages, which he constructed in his home. "I knew Carlo Ferrier by seeing him about the street," he said, without an interpreter. "On Tuesday 1st November, I saw him in Oxford Street and spoke to him. I saw a dead body at the station house in Covent Garden on the following Monday—it was the body of the same person as I had seen in Oxford Street. He had a cage with white mice in it, and a tortoise." The tortoise had absented itself from the story quite some time ago; now here was Colla resurrecting it. Asked to identify the cap and disinterred outfit as belonging to the victim, Colla continued: "He had a cap on his head, something like the one produced. It was torn on one side. I believe this to be the same cap. He had on a blue coat and grey trousers. I observed a large patch on the left knee and from the patch on the left knee of these trousers I believe them to be the same he had on. They are the same kind. I did not so particularly notice the color or patch as I did the stitches, being so great a distance from each other as these are. I do believe these to be the trousers. I have not seen them since I saw them on the boy in Oxford Street."

Colla had taken in a great deal of detail that day in Oxford Street; Superintendent Thomas must have been extremely pleased. As he must have been with little John King. Children of any age could give evidence at the Old Bailey, provided the judge was satisfied that the child knew good from evil and understood the nature of an oath. John King was nine, old enough in their honors' view to give testimony at a capital trial. "I live with my mother, who is now confined. I remember one day when my mother was washing seeing a foreign boy near Nova Scotia Gardens. I believe it was on the Thursday before Guy Fawkes day, and between one and two o'clock. I was looking down upon him from the loft window and could not see whether he had a cage or a box as my mother would not let me go down to him. I believe it was a cage for I saw some wire on the top of it. He was standing still, with the cage hanging around his neck by a string. He had a brown hairy cap on his head, the peak of it was lined with green. The cap produced looks exactly like it. I do not know how long he remained there. I was looking at him for a few minutes."

Barry asked: "Were you in the first or second floor?"

"In the first, not very high from the ground. I was looking out at the loft door and could see the green of the peak." The child must have realized the import of the question: how could he have seen the color of the cap's visor but not the cage?

Martha King, aged eleven, said: "I remember seeing an Italian boy near the Birdcage public house. I was at the front part of the house. It was on the Wednesday or Thursday before Guy Fawkes day, and about twelve o'clock. I am sure it was either Wednesday or Thursday. He was standing still opposite the Birdcage with his box slung round his neck and a cap on his head. The cap was just like this. Bishop's house is about a minute's walk from our house. I have never seen the boy since."

Rebecca Baylis was a new witness; she also lived opposite the Birdcage, at 1 Virginia Row, which approached the pub from the southwest. "On Thursday 3rd November, about a quarter before twelve o'clock, I saw an Italian boy. He was very near my own window, standing sideways. I could see the side of his face and one end of the box, which he had in front of him. I think it was slung round his neck. He had a brown fur or seal-skin cap on, a small one, rather shabby. I could see the peak was lined with green and cut off very sharp. [Here, she looked down at the cap in her hands.] It was this color . . . but the front appeared to me to come more pointed. It was a cap much like this. I cannot swear whether this is it. He had on a dark blue or a dirty green jacket and grey trousers, apparently a dark mixture, but very shabby. About a quarter of an hour after, I had occasion to go to The Virginia Planter [a pub in Virginia Row] to see if it was time to put on my husband's potatoes. I went a little way down Nova Scotia Gardens to look for my little boy. I saw the Italian boy standing within two doors of Number 3. There are three houses together and he stood by Number 1. I do not think the jacket produced is the one he had on. . . . I thought it was darker. These have the appearance of the trousers he had on." Curwood pressed her about the jacket. "No," said Baylis, "it appeared darker at the distance I was, which was about six yards. I will not say it is the same."

Another new witness, John Randall, laborer, told the court: "On Thursday morning 3rd November, between nine and ten o'clock, I saw an Italian boy standing under the window of the Birdcage public house, near Nova Scotia Gardens. He had a box or cage with two white mice—the cage part of the box went round. I turned round to the boy. I saw he looked very cold and I gave him a halfpenny and told him he had better go on. He had on a blue coarse jacket or coat, apparently very coarse, and a brown cap with a bit of leather in front. I did not notice whether it was fur or not. It was similar to this in color, and the jacket was this color. I did not notice his trousers."

Sarah Trueby once again described the topography of Nova Scotia Gardens. Her husband, she said, owned Nos. 1, 2, and 3 and rented

John Bishop
Thomas Head *alias Willi...* James May

Two unconvincing Old Bailey courtroom sketches of Bishop, Williams, and May

them out. The well in the Bishops' garden was easily accessible: gates in the palings between Nos. 1 and 2 and Nos. 2 and 3 showed that this well was meant to be used by all three sets of residents. Many others could easily reach it too, though.

All the Woodcocks, of 2 Nova Scotia Gardens, took the stand—twelve-year-old William to repeat his belief that Williams was living with the Bishops and that he had from time to time seen Rhoda doing her washing at No. 3; his mother, Hannah, to say the same; and William Woodcock senior to repeat his evidence about the noises that had awoken him in the early hours of Friday, 4 November, after what he guessed had been four or four and a half hours of sleep. He claimed that, without any doubt, one of the three voices he had heard during the scuffle belonged to Williams. Woodcock had chatted with him for around two hours on the afternoon of Sunday, 23 October, when Williams came up to the palings while Woodcock was gardening and dissuaded him from digging the soil at the bottom of the garden of No. 2, suggesting instead the area close to the cottage where, Williams said, some lily bulbs could be found.

Abraham Keymer kept the Feathers public house in Castle Street (the southwestern continuation of Virginia Row). He said that "about a quarter before twelve o'clock on Thursday night, 3rd November, Bishop came to my house with another person, who I think was

Williams, but I am not quite certain of him. My house is one or two hundred yards from Bishop's. I think they had a quartern of rum and half a gallon of beer—they took the beer away with them in a half-gallon can. This is the can." Superintendent Thomas had seized it at No. 3 and proffered it as evidence. Keymer added that he could not be positive that Williams had come that night "as I had never seen him before." This statement contradicted eyewitness evidence that Bishop and Williams had made the Feathers their last port of call when they made Fanny Pigburn drunk on the night of 8 October.

PC Joseph Higgins told of the digging up of Bishop's garden and detailed the state of the clothing he had found one foot down, below a spot that had been scattered with cinders and ashes "which would prevent my noticing its having been turned up." He told of the implements found in Bishop's house and at May's lodgings. The blood had been fresh on the brad awl and on the breeches found at May's. The dug-up clothing was passed around the jury. The prosecution asked Higgins whether such clothes would have been "useful" to Bishop's own children. "The coat would be very useful and has not got a rent in it. It would be very useful for a working boy." So why would a family bury clothing that still had plenty of life in it? was the unvoiced question. Superintendent Thomas told the court that he had been requested by May to point out that the blood on the breeches had been so fresh that it must have been shed after his arrest; Thomas felt it only right to make that point clear on behalf of the prisoner.

Edward Ward of Nova Scotia Gardens came into the witness box. He told the court that he knew that it was a very bad thing to tell a lie, that it was a great sin. He said he knew that people who lied went to hell and were burned in brimstone and sulfur. Then he took the oath. He was six and a half years old. "I remember Guy Fawkes day—my mother gave me a half-holiday before Guy Fawkes day. I do not recollect what day of the week it was. I went to Bishop's house on the day I had the half-holiday. He lives in Nova Scotia Gardens at a corner house. I have seen three of his children—he has one big boy, another about my age, and a little girl. I saw them that day in a room, next to the little room, and the little room is next to the garden. I played with the children there. I had often seen them before."

"Did the children show you anything that day?" the prosecution asked their witness.

"Yes. Two white mice—one little one and one big one. They were in a cage, which moved round and round. I never saw them with white mice before, nor with a cage. I often played with them before. I saw my brother John when I got home and told him what I had seen." Brother John confirmed that Edward had told him about the mice and the cage, and said that the half holiday from school had been on Friday, 4 November.[10]

PC John Kirkman of F Division stepped up and reported that he had been watching over the prisoners in the Covent Garden station house late in the afternoon of Saturday the fifth. Repeating what he had told the coroner's court, he testified that Bishop stood and read a printed bill on the wall about the King's College corpse. "It was the blood that sold us," Bishop had muttered to May, over the head of Williams.

This was the case for the prosecution. Curwood announced that he felt it was his duty to ask that the murder charge against Thomas Williams be dropped; his client was clearly not a principal in the crime, though Curwood conceded that he may have acted as an accessory after the fact. It was true that very little of what had been presented in court connected Williams even to the bartering of the body; by Bishop's own admission, his stepson-in-law/half-brother-in-law was very new to the trade; and none of the resurrection community had appeared even to recognize Williams. But Lord Chief Justice Tindal was having none of it. He told Curwood that it would be up to the jury to decide the guilt or innocence of Williams, as charged.

Now the defense did what the defense was restricted to doing: putting forward the written statements of the accused and bringing forth the defense witnesses. An officer of the court read the statements out. Bishop admitted that he had been a body snatcher for twelve years, though, probably on the advice of his attorney, he described his work as "procuring bodies for surgical and anatomical purposes." Then he stated:

> I declare that I never sold any body but what had died a natural death. I have had bodies from the various workhouses, together with the clothes which were on the bodies. I occupied the house in Nova Scotia Gardens fifteen months. It consisted of three rooms and a wash-house, a garden, about twenty yards long, by about eight yards broad, three gardens adjoin, and are separated by a dwarf railing. I could have communication to either cottage, or the occupiers of them to mine. The well in my garden was for the joint use of all the tenants. There was also a privy to each house. The fact is, there are twenty cottages and gardens which are only separated by the paling already described, and I could get easy access to any of them. I declare I know nothing at all about the various articles of wearing apparel that have been found in the garden, but as regards the cap that was found in the house and supposed to have belonged to the deceased Italian boy, I can prove that it was bought by my wife of a Mrs Dodswell, of Hoxton Old Town, clothes dealer, for my own son, Frederick. The front I sewed on myself after it was purchased. The front was bought with the cap but not sewed to it. They were sold to my wife along with other articles. Mr Dodswell is a pastry cook, and has nothing to do with the business of the clothes shop—the calling of Mrs Dodswell, therefore, as evidence to prove the truth of my statement, will put it beyond a doubt that the cap never did belong

to the deceased boy, and Mrs Dodswell should also prove how long she had the cap in her possession, and how she came by it. As much stress has been laid upon the finding of several articles of wearing apparel, and also the peculiar manner in which they appear to have been taken off the persons of those supposed to have come in an improper way into my hands, I most solemnly declare I know nothing whatever of them. The length of the examinations and the repetition of them have been so diligently promulgated and impressed on the public mind, that it cannot but be supposed that a portion of the circumstances connected with this unfortunate case (if not all) have reached and attracted the attention of the jury. But I entreat them, as they value the solemn obligation of the oath they have this day taken, that they will at once divest themselves of all prejudice and give me the whole benefit of a cool, dispassionate and impartial hearing of the case, and record such a verdict as they, on their conscience, their honour, and their oath, can return. May and Williams know nothing as to how I became possessed of the body.

Toward the end of Bishop's statement, lawyer language is clearly detectable; Williams's brief statement bore the mark of a legal hand to a far greater extent: "I am a bricklayer by trade, and latterly worked at the glass-blowing business. I never was engaged in any instance as a procurer of dead bodies or Subjects. Into the present melancholy business I was invited by Bishop. I know nothing whatever about the manner in which he became possessed of the dead body. Bishop asked me to join him on the Friday. I made no inquiry about the nature of the business. I shall, therefore, leave my case entirely to the intelligence and discrimination of the jury and the learned and merciful judge, but I trust I may be allowed once more to state that I am entirely innocent of any offence against the laws of my country."

May's statement said that he had had a "moderate" education and

first became engaged in the traffic of anatomical Subjects six years since, and from that period up to the time of my apprehension have continued so, with occasionally looking after horses. I accidentally met Bishop at the Fortune of War, a house that persons of our calling generally frequent and are known there as such. Bishop wanted to speak to me, called me outside the door, and asked me where the best price could be procured for Things. I told him where I had sold two for ten guineas each, at Mr Davis's, and I had no doubt I could get rid of that Thing for him at the same price. He said if I did, I should keep all I got above nine guineas to myself. There was no questions asked as to the manner in which the body had been procured, and I knew nothing about it. As to what has been said in the public papers, or the prejudice that exists against me, and the other prisoners, it is of no moment. I here declare that during all the years that I have been in this business, I never came into possession of a living person, nor used any means for converting them into Subjects for the purposes of dissection. I admit that I have traded largely in dead bodies but I solemnly declare that I never took undue advantage of any person alive, whether man, woman, or child, however poor or unprotected. I have not been accustomed to make application for bodies at the different workhouses and I now solemnly declare that I know nothing at all of the circumstances connected with the procuring of the body, which is suspected to be that of the one named in the indictment, nor did I ever hear, nor understand, how Bishop became possessed thereof. I shall, therefore, leave my fate entirely to the intelligence and discernment of the jury and the learned judge.

May's cavalry had arrived: Rosina Carpenter was the woman with whom May said he had spent the night of Thursday, 3 November—the suspected, though not named, murder night, if George Beaman's time-of-death estimate and William Woodcock's disturbed sleep were accepted. Rosina said: "I have known May fourteen or fifteen years but have not seen him for four or five years till within the last four months. On Thursday 3rd November he came to my house in Nag's Head Court, Golden Lane, between four and five o'clock in the evening. I am sure it was Thursday. He stopped with me till between eleven and twelve o'clock the next morning, which was Friday. I am sure he never left me." But as a single woman seeing a married man on a casual, adulterous basis, Rosina's word was not considered enough. "Nobody is present in court who saw him at my residence, although there were several persons at my house drinking with us at the time May was there. I cannot particularly name the persons who drank with us. He had passed several nights with me before this. I didn't know he was married."

Next, Mary Ann Hall said: "I am single and live at Number 4 Dorset Street, New Kent Road. On Sunday morning, 30th October, May left me and said he was going into the country. I saw no more of him till the Wednesday night following, when I met him at the corner of William Street and we went home and May went to bed. I sat up till three o'clock in the morning to air his jacket, which was very wet indeed, and also his under jacket. He got up on Thursday morning, put on a clean shirt, clean waistcoat and breeches and went away. I saw no more of him till Friday night when I met him by the Alfred's Head, facing Elephant and Castle, at half-past eleven o'clock. He went home with me, got up about eight o'clock and went out. I asked if he could give me a little money. He said he should be back by the time I wanted any. My landlady kept a jackdaw. She is Mrs Carroll—she is not here. I and May live upstairs. We do not live together exactly, but I think he is more with me than with anybody else. He did not come home at all on Thursday night—he left me at half-past seven o'clock on Thursday morning, and I saw no more of him till half-past eleven on Friday."[11]

Charlotte Berry, who had the room along the landing at 4 Dorset Street, and Jane Lewis, another lodger, told the jackdaw story, helping to explain the bloodied breeches, though the prosecution had given up on that item long before. Charlotte and Jane both admitted that they were "in the habit of seeing gentlemen," while Mary Ann Hall, when asked by Adolphus how she made a living, had offered the fact that she had been in custody twice at Bow Street on charges of prostitution and for the past two years had made her living walking the streets. Prostitutes defending a body snatcher: it was not likely to look good to the jury.

It was Bishop's turn: he had lined up Sarah Trueby, Mary Dodswell, and anatomist Edward Tuson. They were to prove catastrophic choices. Tuson got out of the witness box very quickly, saying of the prisoners, "I know them by seeing them. I believe I have seen

Bishop once or twice, but I do not know what I am to prove." He was asked no questions, and the *Times* report chivalrously omitted even to mention that he had appeared.

Sarah Trueby was recalled, and Bishop, abandoning Curwood and Barry and interviewing his witnesses himself, asked his landlady to recall the time she had seen white mice at No. 3, in an effort to undermine six-year-old Edward Ward's testimony. Trueby said: "I never saw any white mice in the possession of you or your family."

"Do you not recollect any mice running out of my garden and into yours?"

"No, Mr Bishop. Never."

"Not about six months ago? Don't you recollect your cat having killed some in my garden?"

"Never."

Mary Dodswell was supposed to explain away the furry cap. It's possible that as a secondhand clothes dealer, Dodswell received and sold the garments that clothed the bodies stolen or obtained fraudulently from workhouses by snatchers; perhaps Bishop had threatened to expose her trade, and perhaps Superintendent Thomas had then told her not to worry about any threats from Bishop. "I am the wife of George Henry Dodswell, we live at 56 Hoxton Old Town and sell second-hand clothes—my husband is employed as a pastry cook. I know Bishop's wife perfectly well. I sold her a cap about two years ago—it was a cloth cap with a leather peak at the front. I am perfectly sure it was cloth—the front was attached to the cap when I sold it. It had a black front but I am not sure how it was lined."

"My wife bought two caps of you."

"She only bought one. I am quite confident."

"Mrs Dodswell, recollect, you sold two caps to my wife—one for each of my boys. My wife gave you three pence for the peak, which you sold separately."

"I never sold but one cap to her. I never sold a peak."

She told the court, "I never saw Bishop or any of the family but his wife," though she added, "His daughter [Rhoda] lived servant with me twelve months ago."

It was half past five in the afternoon, and Lord Chief Justice Tindal began his summing up. He reminded the jury to base their decision only on what they had heard that day, to disregard anything they might have read or heard about the prisoners. They had first to consider whether the child had died of natural causes or not and, if not, whether each of the three prisoners was involved in the murder and to what degree they were implicated. With regard to the first point, his lordship said that he felt the jury would have little trouble "after the explicit evidence of the medical gentlemen who had been that day examined and whose conduct it was but justice to say was an honourable rebuke to any calumnious imputations on the medical profession to which the present case may have given birth." (The duke of Sussex here whispered into his lordship's ear.) He said that in order to convict the men of murder, the jury must be satisfied that all three were present aiding, assisting, and abetting the actual commission of the crime. If a man was not actually on the spot of the killing but nearby, ready to lend his assistance, or was watching a door to prevent the detection of the parties within the house, the law considered him as much a principal offender as if his hand actually committed the deed.

Justice Tindal reminded the jury that witnesses had placed the Italian boy close to Bishop's home at noon on Thursday, 3 November, the day on which the murder was most likely to have taken place. It was late that night that a scuffle was heard, and Williams's voice was discerned. But it was by no means certain that May was present at that time, and it was for the jury to decide whether he was a principal or an accessory. If they had any reasonable doubts, they must acquit May. There was no convincing evidence that May had access to, or was connected with, the other two prisoners previous to the death of the deceased. But he asked the jury to bear in mind the "loose and obscure" conversation overheard in the Fortune of War by Thomas Wigley, which could be taken to indicate that Bishop and May were a well-established team, with Williams the novice to be welcomed into the trade; and then there was Bishop's comment to May—"It was the blood that sold us"—overheard by PC Kirkman. And May had claimed the body as his property, both at Guy's Hospital and to Mills the dentist. Would they then feel justified in considering May a principal? The jury might perhaps decide that only Bishop and Williams had committed the deed—or perhaps Bishop alone. Or they might decide that all three were equally guilty or that all three were guilty but not to an equal degree. Simply standing by and offering no help to the boy made a prisoner guilty of murder. The jury must accept the fact that there were no eyewitness accounts of the killing, that they would be relying on circumstantial evidence. He then went over the day's evidence with what the *Times* called "the most painstaking minuteness." Alas, no full transcript of the summing up has come down, so we cannot know how Tindal chose to interpret the witnesses' statements. But his speech must have been painstaking indeed, because it did not end until eight o'clock, at which time the jury went out and the prisoners were removed from the dock.

Half an hour later, the jury came back. The talk around the courtroom had been that Bishop and Williams were likely to be convicted but that May was probably in the clear. The reporter whose account appears in the *Times* (and was syndicated in various other newspapers and broadsheets) takes up the tale:

> The most deathlike silence now prevailed throughout the court, interrupted only by a slight buzz on the reintroduction of the prisoners. Every eye was now fixed upon them; but though their appearance and manner had undergone a considerable change from what they exhibited on being first placed at the bar and during the greater part of the trial, they did not seem conscious of the additional interest which their presence at this moment excited. They scarcely raised their eyes as they entered, beyond a glance or two at the jury box.
>
> Bishop advanced to the bar with a heavy step, and with rather a slight bend of the body, his arms hung closely down, and it seemed a kind of relief to him, when he took his place, to rest his hand on the board before him. His appearance was that of a man labouring for some time under the most intense mental agony, which had brought on a kind of lethargic stupor. His eye was sunk and glassy; his nose drawn and pinched; the jaw fallen, and, of course, the mouth open; but occasionally the mouth closed, the lips became compressed, and the shoulders and chest raised, as if he was struggling to repress some violent emotion. After a few efforts of this kind, he became apparently calm, and frequently glanced his eye towards the bench and

jury box; but this was done without once raising his head. His face had that pallid, blueish appearance which so often accompanies and betokens great mental suffering.

Williams came forward with a short, quick step, and his whole manner was, we should say, the reverse of that of his companion in guilt. His face had undergone very little change, but in his eye and manner there was a feverish anxiety we did not observe during the trial. When he came and laid his hand on the bar, the rapid movement of his fingers on the board shewed the perturbed state of his feelings. Once or twice he gave a glance round the bench and bar, but after that, he seldom took his eye from the jury box.

May came forward with a more firm step than either of his fellow prisoners, but his look was that of a man who thought that all chance of life was lost. He seemed desponding, but there appeared that in his despondency which gave an air of— we could not call it daring, or even confidence—we should rather say, a physical power of endurance, which imparted to his whole manner a more firm bearing than that of the other prisoners. He was very pale, but his eye had not relaxed from that firmness which was observable in his glance throughout the whole of the trial.

Ordinary physiognomists, who, without having seen the prisoners, had read the accounts of their examinations at the police office, of their habits and mode of living, and of the horrible atrocities with which there is now no doubt they are familiar, would have been greatly disappointed in the appearance of all of them as they stood at the bar yesterday. . . . There was something of heaviness in the aspect of Bishop, but altogether his countenance was mild. Williams had that kind of aspect with which men associate the idea of sharpness and cunning, and something of mischief, but nothing of the villain. May, who was the best looking of the three, had a countenance which most persons would consider open and manly. There was an air of firmness and determination about him, but neither in him nor his companions was there the slightest physiognomical trait of a murderer, according to the common notions on the subject. They were all those kinds of common vulgar men in appearance of which one sees hundreds every day, without being struck with any indication in them of good or evil disposition.*

There was silence. The duke of Sussex raised his telescope to observe the accused. The jury was asked if they had reached their verdict on each man, and the foreman said yes. John Bishop, guilty of murder. Thomas Williams, alias Head, guilty of murder. James May, guilty of murder. In court, more silence; but as soon as the vast crowd outside heard the verdicts, a tremendous roar of cheering and applause began, so loud that court officials had to shut every window so that the sentence could be heard. The judge first praised the jury and recalled that he had often had occasion to note of Old Bailey juries that nothing but the most satisfactory evidence and a conviction of the solemn obligation they owed to their Maker and to their country could induce them to pronounce a verdict that was to condemn their fellow man to a disgraceful death. He heartily agreed with their verdict, which was supported by the most conclusive evidence. "By false evidence, my Lord," said John Bishop. The judge now turned to the dock and said he would not take up any more moments than were necessary of the short time they had left before appearing before their Creator. He hoped that in the month since their arrest they had taken time to reflect on "the horrible agony which they had inflicted on the feelings of so many of their fellow men." He expected they would spend every instant remaining to them in fervent prayers to the Almighty for pardon through the merits of their Redeemer. They would find plenty of help in this regard at Newgate, he said. He concluded by saying that each of them would be hanged on Monday morning and their bodies handed over to the anatomists for dissection.

---

*There is a striking similarity between this passage and the paragraphs in chapter 52 of *Oliver Twist* that describe Fagin's trial at the Old Bailey, and it may well be that Charles Dickens reported the Italian Boy case from the press benches.[12]

TWELVE

A Newgate Stink

They said nothing, initially; they just stood there, as though they expected something more to happen. After a few moments a court official indicated that it was time for them to leave the dock, and James May, in a firm voice, told the bench, "I am a murdered man, gentlemen—and *that* man knows it," and he pointed to Bishop. Bishop made no reply, still appearing to be deeply self-absorbed, but Williams responded, "We are all murdered men." He had turned a ghastly pale color on hearing the verdict, but soon a scornful smile appeared on his face. He leaned over the edge of the dock and shook his fist at Andrew Colla, saying, "I hope you and that other Italian will be somewhere else as well as us on Monday morning," and shouted to the Italian witnesses that within three months they would pay for the lies they had told about him. Then he looked up to the public gallery and, spotting somebody among the huddle, raised his hand and called out, "Goodbye, goodbye."

They left the dock and were escorted back down the winding stone tunnels that led between the Sessions House and the prison, and up and across the Press Yard to Newgate's condemned cells.

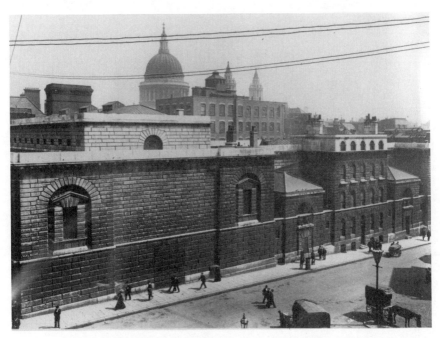

Newgate Prison and Debtors Door, photographed shortly before the building's demolition in 1902

Walking with them was the Reverend Dr. Theodore Williams, vicar of Hendon, magistrate, and prison visitor, who had called on Bishop every day while he was on remand; Bishop had been the recipient—willing or unwilling, it is not known—of the vicar's visits during previous incarcerations. Now as they walked, Bishop told Dr. Williams that he wanted to confess to him at once; but the vicar said no, wait awhile, and urged him to speak when he was feeling calmer; the reverend would be happy to hear Bishop's tale first thing the next morning.

Sir Nicholas Conyngham Tindal, his fellow judges, the lord mayor, and the duke of Sussex had repaired to the private apartments above the Sessions House. Here, over dinner, the duke told the lord mayor that trials such as these made him proud of England, which had "the most perfect, intelligent and humane system."[1] Evidently overheard by someone who was transcribing his words, the duke continued: "The judges of our land, the learned in our law, nobility, magistrates, merchants, medical professors and individuals of every rank in society, anxiously devoting themselves and co-operating in the one common object of redressing an injury inflicted upon a pauper child, wandering friendless and unknown in a foreign land. Seeing this, I am indeed proud of being an Englishman, and prouder still to be a prince in such a country and of such a people."

In the condemned block, the three were searched to ensure they had no means of cheating the hangman and were then locked into their separate cells, each with two guards. The fifteen condemned cells (built in 1728 and retained when the prison was reconstructed, along with the Sessions House, in the 1770s) stood at the northern end of the Newgate/Old Bailey complex, three stories of five rooms, each nine feet by six, and nine feet high. A dark staircase leading between the floors, Charles Dickens would later note, was luridly lit by a charcoal stove.[2] The condemned block was built of stone that was three feet thick, and each cell was paneled with planks of wood. In summer, these were chilly rooms; in winter, bitterly cold. The cell door was four inches thick with a small, grated hole; the cell window was five feet from the ground and a foot high, double-grated and barred. At best, the cells were in semidarkness, and after sundown each was lit by a single candle. On the floor was a hemp mat, which acted as a mattress and was tarred to keep out damp and vermin, and a couple of horse rugs, which served as blankets.[3]

Separating the condemned cells from the rest of Newgate was the Press Yard, at the southern end of which were two "press rooms"—wards containing tables, benches, and a fire where the condemned were allowed to spend their daytime. In the Press Yard, remand prisoners used to be pressed to death by iron weights placed on a board if they refused to enter a plea of guilty or not guilty, an act that was viewed as treasonable; this *peine forte et dure* had squashed its last victim in 1726, but the memory of the ancient cruelty was retained in the name of the yard. It was just ten feet wide but seventy feet long, running down from the Newgate Street wall to the garden of the Royal College of Physicians (the college once backed onto the prison/Sessions House complex) and to another icon of the medical profession, Surgeons Hall, where, between 1752 and 1796, members of the Company of Surgeons had taken apart the bodies of the executed. (This had been the site of Sir Astley Cooper's earliest triumphs, by his own admission: "The lectures were received with great *éclat,* and I became very popular as a lecturer. The theatre was constantly crowded, and the applause excessive.")[4]

Dare it be said, Newgate was not so bad. Not so bad as it had been. John Wontner had been in charge since 1822 and his governorship was regarded by many at the time as something of a golden age, though overcrowding continued to be a problem.[5] George Dance the Younger's building was supposed to hold 350 prisoners, but in 1826 the population had reached 643, down from over 900 in 1815. (If two men were kept in the same cell, the warders had noted that "crimes have been committed of a nature not to be more particularly described.")[6] Newgate housed both men and women (the ratio was four to one), though they were segregated, while children between the ages of eight and fourteen were kept in the "school" area. One of the most serious criticisms was that those awaiting trial mixed with the already convicted, the innocent and the novice being "contaminated" by the older felon, with the result that the same old faces would come back into the jail time and time again. No strenuous efforts were made here to "redeem" the criminal, unlike at Millbank Penitentiary. Compared

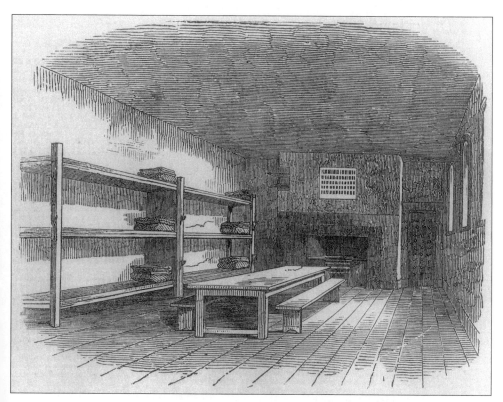

A sketch of the Newgate press room, where the condemned passed their remaining daytimes

with that at many other London jails, however, Newgate's death rate was low, at three a year; and suicide was uncommon.

There were no limitations on the number of visitors, and family and friends could bring in food and drink to augment the prison ration, which was in itself not ungenerous. Every day, breakfast consisted of half a pint of gruel; each prisoner had a pound of bread a day; and dinner alternated between half a pound of beef on one night and soup on the next, with vegetables and barley. The Newgate diet was a source of criticism, since it was said by many to be more plentiful and of better quality than the food eaten by the nonoffending poor outside the prison walls. There was no restriction on the amount of porter that could be drunk (it was safer than the water), and visitors noticed high levels of drunkenness among the inmates. The tradition of "garnish," or "chummage," had each new arrival buy a round of drinks for those who shared his cell or ward—under threat of humiliation, such as removal of his trousers. It is impossible to gauge the extent to which psychological bullying went on, though an idea of the mores of Newgate thieves in the late 1820s is suggested by the tale of one prisoner who found himself being shunned when it became known that during the robbery at the London Docks for which he was imprisoned, he had knocked unconscious his victim, an aged sea captain.[7]

Physical violence among inmates was said to be rare, and rioting even rarer, with the only dissent tending to occur after lockup on the nights when the "transports" were announced—those who the next day would be taken, in "drafts" of twenty-five, to the hulks, either to finish their jail term there or to set sail for the other end of the earth. These announcements seemed to trigger anger and despair across the jail.

John Bishop slept soundly in his cell and woke at around six on Saturday morning. The Reverend Dr. Theodore Williams, true to his word, turned up at ten. The vicar took Bishop into the room of Brown, the turnkey of the condemned block, and here, as the two men sat on either side of Brown's table, Bishop began to reveal a number of most interesting matters—one of which was that James May had had no knowledge of how the boy's body had been obtained, that he was entirely innocent and must have his death sentence overturned. Bishop continued, and the vicar's pen flew over his notebook as he tried to capture the killer's account. Suddenly there erupted into the room a party of furious men: Dr. Horace Cotton, the chaplain (or "ordinary") of Newgate; prison governor John Wontner; and Alderman Wood, City sheriff. "Come, come, Mr. Williams," said Dr. Cotton, "what is all this about? I suppose you want to extract confessions with a view to publishing them." Dr. Cotton demanded that the confession stop immediately, and Bishop was ordered from the room and told to walk awhile with Brown in the Press Yard. Dr. Cotton told Dr. Williams that he had no right even to be in the prison, since these were condemned men and therefore came under the jurisdiction of the ordinary of Newgate. The extraction and publication—for money, via the newspapers—of condemned men's confessions within twenty-four hours of an execution was among the perks of the ordinary's job; it was one of Newgate's many interesting old traditions, a practice sanctioned by the lord mayor of London and his court of aldermen. Alderman Wood told Dr. Williams that any written account of Bishop's story would not be allowed out of the prison—it would have to be surrendered at the sheriff's office. If Bishop were to go giving his account of events, it was highly likely that he would implicate others—hadn't Dr. Williams remembered that Rhoda Head was still in custody on suspicion of being an accessory after the fact of murder?

The vicar of Hendon was astonished but not daunted, and when the party had swept out of Brown's room and Bishop was brought back in, he asked the killer to pick up the tale—Bishop had just reached the most extraordinary part of it when the interruption had occurred. But Bishop would not go on. He had become dejected again, and said, "It is now of no use to implicate others."[8] He was

Theodore Williams, the controversial vicar of Hendon, photographed in old age

returned to his cell by Brown, and the vicar of Hendon went off to see if Thomas Williams had anything to say for himself. He did.

At around noon, solicitor James Harmer was informed by Dr. Cotton that Bishop and Williams were in the process of making confessions and that anything they might say could compromise Rhoda. So on Saturday afternoon, Harmer went along to Bow Street and asked Minshull to set Rhoda free, on the legal grounds that she could not be held accountable for any crimes that her husband may have compelled her to commit. Besides, with Rhoda out of danger, the men would feel able to tell everything. Minshull saw the wisdom of this stratagem, and so it was that late on Saturday afternoon, Rhoda found herself in a coach with James Harmer traveling to Newgate. There, in one of the press rooms, "a most affecting scene" (according to the *Morning Advertiser*) took place, as Rhoda was reunited with Bishop and Williams. All three wept, and she told them that they must feel free to make the fullest confession possible and not worry about her and Sarah.

James May, the former legal clerk with beautiful handwriting, had expressed himself in verse:

> *James May is doomed to die,*
> *And is condemned most innocently.*
> *The Lord above, he knows the same,*
> *And will send a mitigation for his pain.*

He had written these lines on some sheets of paper on which he was revealing the secrets of the London resurrection world.[9] When the vicar of Hendon came calling at May's cell and urged him to unburden his soul, May told him, "I've been guilty of many offences, but I never committed murder." Even as he faced execution, May was proving unable to supply information on any part of the story before the encounter at the Fortune of War on the morning of Friday, 4 November. He told Dr. Williams everything he had ever known about both

Bishop and Williams, but none of it was new or remarkable. And it wasn't as if May was above snitching: Superintendent Thomas had been among the Newgate visitors on that busy Saturday morning. The superintendent and others had compiled a list of all the London resurrectionists they had ever come across or heard talk of; it numbered fifty men. Thomas placed the list in front of May and asked him to make a pen mark against the name of any whom he considered to be capable of burking. When he handed the list back, May had marked six names.

Bishop had some surprise visitors too. Magistrates from the Lambeth Street police court applied to him to see if he could help in the case of Caroline Walsh, the supposed victim of Eliza Ross, who was being held on suspicion of murder. No hospital dissecting-room porter had been able to assist with this case, though John Appleton of Grainger's school had been keen to impress the magistrates by coming forward with a dissecting-room book detailing all the bodies that had passed through his theater (the book must have been a recent addition; it never put in an appearance during the Fanny Pigburn inquiry). The magistrates wondered if Bishop knew anything about Eliza Ross and Edward Cook, her common-law husband. The result of the interview is not known.

A Mr. Evans, the owner of a toy shop in Newgate Street, called to ask governor John Wontner to find out if Bishop knew anything about the disappearance of his nephew. The boy had gone for a walk in Hampstead in July and had not been seen again. Bishop told Wontner the boy's disappearance had nothing to do with him.

At nine o'clock on Saturday evening, the statements of all three prisoners, and May's list and poem, were taken to the London home of Sir Nicholas Conyngham Tindal by Wontner, Cotton, Dr. Williams (whose presence was now being tolerated), James Corder of St. Paul's, Covent Garden, and two City of London undersheriffs. The meeting was to establish whether May had a good case to present to the home secretary, Lord Melbourne, for a pardon or at least a "mitigation" while the possibility of a new trial was considered, with the charge reduced to being an accessory after the fact of murder, not a principal. The other two trial judges, Sir John Vaughan and Sir Joseph Littledale, were summoned too, to give their opinion.

There was no court of appeal (that was seventy-six years away) and pardons were obtained by personal intervention to the home secretary's department in Downing Street—one reason the judges' support would have been helpful. The more prestigious the pleader, the more likely a reprieve. "All their proceedings are conducted in the dark," wrote one law reformer of the Home Office and the Privy Council. "[They] now affect to take every pain in coming to a right decision; but what they do is of an occult nature, and unsatisfactory."[10] Historian Albany Fontblanque thought so too: "In this mysterious supreme court no parties appear for or against the prisoner; no witnesses are called; the convicts have no opportunity of protecting themselves against malicious or erroneous representations."[11]

There were four hours of discussion about May's case—none of which will ever be known since it was "in the dark." But while Sir Nicholas and Sir John were in favor of granting May a reprieve, Sir Joseph was not so minded. The warrants for three executions on Monday morning were written out in Downing Street.

Sunday arrived. May was still protesting his innocence; and Bishop and Williams told Dr. Williams, Dr. Cotton, John Wontner, and anyone else who asked them that May had had nothing to do with any killings—that they were not a gang, that Thomas Williams had barely known May, and that when May had come on Friday, 4 November, to extract the dead boy's teeth, it was the first time he had ever been to Nova Scotia Gardens.

The Reverend Dr. Theodore Williams convened a meeting of Tindal, Vaughan, and Littledale in the private apartments above the Old Bailey Sessions House; Wontner, Cotton, and various sheriffs and undersheriffs were present too. Though Littledale would still not budge, a new request, with copies of the further statements that had been made by Bishop and Williams, was forwarded to Lord Melbourne, at his private residence. At half past four in the afternoon, the home secretary returned his final decision.

Cotton and Wontner went without delay to the press room, where all three prisoners were found with their warders. Cotton opened the dispatches from the home secretary and read first to Bishop, then to Williams, the official decision that they would be hanged by the neck on Monday morning. He addressed May next, telling him "that the execution of the sentence upon James May shall be respited during His Majesty's most gracious pleasure." May dropped to the floor as though he had been shot; then his body began to twist and jerk, his arms flailing. Four officers attempted to sit him up and bring him to his senses, but it took a quarter of an hour before May was able to speak. (Bishop and Williams looked on unconcerned, as though the room were empty.) At first he spoke meaningless syllables, then he laughed, then he cried, then he tried to pray but he was shaking too much. Wontner and Cotton had never seen anything like it in all their Newgate years; they told him to calm down, they knew what he meant to say, it was all right. Everything would be all right. May gibbered out his thanks to God, to Wontner, to Cotton, to Dr. Williams. When he calmed down further he said that when Cotton had turned to him to read out his warrant, he had been so earnestly expecting to hear the same words that had been delivered to Bishop and Williams that when he heard the word "respite," despair had suddenly changed to elation—so suddenly that he lost consciousness. He described it as feeling like his heart had burst in his chest. He had never killed anyone, he said; he knew he had not been a good man, but he had never killed anyone.

At some point after the final pronouncements had been made, Bishop and Williams were allowed to say farewell to Sarah and Rhoda. No report of the meeting has emerged; but the newspapers pointed out that none of Bishop's children had been permitted to visit Newgate.

Later that night, another squabble erupted in the jail. While Dr. Williams appears to have been allowed to stay on at the prison to be with Bishop, Thomas Williams had requested the presence of one of his former confidantes, the Reverend Dr. Whitworth Russell, chaplain of Millbank Penitentiary. Dr. Russell had already established a reputation as a dogmatic campaigner for prison reform, and an intense, one-to-one relationship with his charges—in which he urged rehabilitation through repentance and religiosity—was one of his radical measures. Whitworth Russell would soon become Britain's joint first inspector of prisons and would seek to create a uniform, systematic approach to penal care. Yet Thomas Williams had gone into Millbank a petty thief and emerged a killer.

Thomas Williams had several private conversations with the Reverend Dr. Whitworth Russell in his cell, despite the objections of Dr. Cotton, who was supposed to be the only shepherd of Church of England souls at the jail. Catholics, Jews, and Dissenters could do as they pleased and import their own holy men into Newgate; but Anglicans were to be given succor only by the ordinary. Cotton thought Whitworth Russell's and Theodore Williams's approaches to religion were unorthodox and not "useful" to condemned men (though Cotton himself had been criticized for his "condemned" sermons, preached with a coffin placed at the center of Newgate's chapel, which were said to unduly frighten those who were to be executed). Yet it seemed that only Whitworth Russell had any rapport with Thomas Williams; he had the killer praying fervently at times. Bishop, by contrast, had sunk back into his unresponsive stupor: in Cotton's words, "he seems to be of a reserved and sullen temper. It was difficult to lead him into conversation, so as to learn anything of his state of mind."[12] One of the guards asked Bishop if he wanted to be read to from the tracts that Cotton had left in the cell, and Bishop said, "Don't bother me— I was teazed quite enough by the parsons with religious talk during the day and I'll have none of it tonight. I can say no more than I have said."

"*I shall now go to bed* for the last time," said Thomas Williams to his warders at half past midnight on Sunday. He knelt and prayed aloud, then undressed, and took to his mat and horse rugs. Nevertheless, he stayed up talking with the guards for a further hour and wrote the following note for the chaplain of Millbank: "Mr Russell, If you will be kind enough to let my brother prisoners know the awful death which I shall have suffered when you read this, it will, through your expostulations, prevent them from increasing their crimes when they may be liberated; and tell them bad company and drinking and blasphemy is the foundation of all evil. Give my brotherly love to them, and tell them never to deviate from the paths of religion, and have a firm belief in the blessed Saviour. Give my love to John Edwards, John Justin and John Dingle, and receive the prayers of the unfortunate and guilty Thomas Head."

....

THIRTEEN

I, John Bishop...

... do hereby declare and confess that the boy supposed to be the Italian boy was a Lincolnshire boy. I and Williams took him to my house about half-past ten o'clock on the Thursday night, the 3rd of November, from the Bell, in Smithfield. He walked home with us. Williams promised to give him some work. Williams went with him from the Bell to the Old Bailey watering-house, whilst I went to the Fortune of War. Williams came from the Old Bailey watering-house to the Fortune of War for me, leaving the boy standing at the corner of the court by the watering-house in the Old Bailey. I went directly with Williams to the boy, and we walked then all three to Nova Scotia Gardens, taking a pint of stout at a public house near Holywell Lane, Shoreditch, on our way, of which we gave the boy a part; we only stayed just to drink it, and walked on to my house, where we arrived at about eleven o'clock. My wife and children and Mrs Williams were not gone to bed, so we put him in the privy, and told him to wait there for us. Williams went in and told them to go to bed, and I stayed in the garden. Williams came out directly, and we both walked out of the garden a little way to give time for the family getting to bed; we returned in about ten minutes or a quarter of an hour, and listened outside at the window to ascertain whether the family were gone to bed. All was quiet, and we then went to the boy in the privy, and took him into the house; we lighted a candle, and gave the boy some bread and cheese, and after he had eaten, we gave him a cup full of rum, with about half a small phial of laudanum in it. I had bought the rum the same evening at the Three Tuns, in Smithfield, and the laudanum also in small quantities at different shops. There was no water or other liquid put in the cup with the rum and laudanum. The boy drank the contents of the cup directly in two draughts, and afterwards a little beer. In about ten minutes he fell asleep on the chair on which he sat, and I removed him from the chair to the floor, and laid him on his side. We then went out and left him there. We had a quartern of gin and a pint of beer at the Feathers, near Shoreditch Church, and then went home again, having been away from the boy about twenty minutes. We found him asleep as we had left him. We took him directly, asleep and insensible, into the garden, and tied a cord to his feet to enable us to pull him up by, and I then took him in my arms, and let him slide from them headlong into the well in the garden, whilst Williams held the cord to prevent the body going altogether too low in the well. He was nearly wholly in the water of the well—his feet just above the surface. Williams fastened the other end of the cord round the paling, to prevent the body getting beyond our reach. The boy struggled a little with his arms and legs in the water, and the water bubbled for a minute. We waited till these symptoms were past, and then went in doors, and afterwards I think we went out, and walked down Shoreditch to occupy the time, and in about three-quarters of an hour we returned and took him out of the well by pulling him by the cord attached to his feet; we undressed him in the paved yard, rolled his clothes up, and buried them where they were found by the witness who produced them. We carried the boy into the wash-house, laid him on the floor, and covered him over with a bag. We left him there, and went and had some coffee in Old Street Road, and then (a little before two in the morning of Friday) went back to my house. We immediately doubled the body up, and put it into a box, which we corded, so that nobody might open it to see what was in it, and then went again, and had some more coffee in the same place in Old Street Road, where we stayed a little while, and then went home to bed—both in the same house, and to our own beds, as usual.

"I declare that this statement is all true, and contains all the facts as far as I can recollect. May knew nothing of the murder, and I do not believe he suspected that I had got the body except in the usual way, and after the death of it. I always told him that I got it from the ground, and he never knew to the contrary until I confessed since the trial. I have known May as a body-snatcher four or five years, but I do not believe he ever obtained a body except in the common course of men in that calling, by stealing from the graves.

"I also confess that I and Williams were concerned in the murder of a female, whom I believe to have been since discovered to be Fanny Pigburn, on or about the 9th of October last. I and Williams saw her sitting, about eleven or twelve o'clock at night, on the step of a door in Shoreditch, near the church. She had a child, four or five years old, with her, on her lap. I asked why she was sitting there. She said she had no home to go to, for her landlord had turned her out into the street. I told her that she might go home with us, and she walked with us to my house, in Nova Scotia Gardens, carrying her child with her. When we got there, we found the family abed, and we took the woman in and lighted a fire, by which we all sat down together. I went out for beer, and we all partook of beer and rum (I had brought the rum from Smithfield in my pocket); the woman and her child lay down on some dirty linen on the floor, and I and Williams went to bed; about six o'clock next morning I and Williams told her to go away, and to meet us at the London Apprentice, in Old Street Road, at one o'clock; this was before our families were up; she met us again at one o'clock at the London Apprentice, without her child; we gave her some halfpence and beer, and desired her to meet us again at ten o'clock at night at the same place; after this we bought rum and laudanum at different places, and at ten o'clock we met the woman again at the London Apprentice; she had no child with her; we drank three pints of beer between us there, and stayed there about an hour. We should have stayed there longer, but an old man came in, whom the woman said she knew, and she said she did not like him to see her there with anybody; we therefore all went out; it rained hard, and we took shelter under a door-way in the Hackney Road for about half an hour. We then walked to Nova Scotia Gardens, and Williams and I led her into No 2, an empty house, adjoining my house. We had no light. Williams stepped out into the garden with the rum and laudanum, which I had handed to him; he there mixed them together in a half-pint bottle, and came into the house to me and the woman, and gave her the bottle to drink; she drank the whole at two or three draughts; there was a quartern of rum, and about half a phial of laudanum; she sat down on the step between two rooms in the house, and went off to sleep in about ten minutes. She was falling back; I caught her to save her fall, and she lay back on the floor. Then Williams and I went to a public-house, got something to drink, and in about half an hour came back to the woman; we took her cloak off, tied a cord to her feet, carried her to the well in the garden and thrust her into it headlong; she struggled very little afterwards, and the water bubbled a little at the top; we fastened the cord to the palings to prevent her going down beyond our reach, and left her and took a walk to Shoreditch and back in about half an hour; we left the woman in the well for this length of time that the rum and laudanum might run out of the body at the mouth; on our return we took her out of the well, cut her clothes off, put them down the privy of the empty house, carried the body into the wash-house of my own house, where we doubled it up and put it in to a hair-box, which we corded, and left it there.

"We did not go to bed, but went to Shields' house in Eagle Street, Red Lion Square, and called him up; this was between four and five o'clock in the morning; we then went with Shields to a public-house near the Sessions House, Clerkenwell, and had some gin, and from thence to my house, where we went in and stayed a little while to wait the change of the police. I told Shields he was to carry that trunk to St Thomas's Hospital. He asked if there was a woman in the house who could walk alongside of him, so that people might not take any notice. Williams called his wife up, and asked her to walk with Shields, and to carry the hat-box, which he gave her to carry. There was nothing in it, but it was tied up as if there were. We then put the box with the body on Shields' head, and went to the hospital, Shields and Mrs Williams walking on one side the street, and I and Williams on the other. At St Thomas's Hospital I saw Mr South's footman, and sent him upstairs to Mr South to ask if he wanted a subject. The footman brought me word that his master wanted one, but could not give an answer till the next day, as he had not time to look at it. During the interview, Shields, Williams, and his wife were waiting at a public-house. I then went alone to Mr Appleton, at Mr Grainger's, and agreed to sell it to him for eight guineas, and afterwards I fetched it from St Thomas's Hospital and took it to Mr Appleton, who paid me five pounds then, and the rest on the following Monday. After receiving the five pounds I went to Shields and Williams and his wife at the public-house where I paid Shields ten shillings for his trouble, and we then all went to the Flower Pot in Bishopsgate, where we had something to drink and went home.

"I never saw the woman's child after the first time before mentioned. She said she had left the child with the person she had taken some of her things to, before her landlord took her goods. The woman murdered did not tell us her name; she said her age was 35, I think, and that her husband, before he died, was a cabinet-maker. She was thin, rather tall, and very much marked with the small-pox.

"I also confess the murder of a boy who told us his name was Cunningham. It was a fortnight after the murder of the woman. I and Williams found him sleeping about eleven or twelve o'clock at night, on Friday 21st October, as I think, under the pig-boards in the pig-market at Smithfield. Williams woke him, and asked him to come along with him (Williams), and the boy walked with Williams and me to my house in Nova Scotia Gardens. We took him into my house, and gave him some warm beer, sweetened with sugar, with rum and laudanum in it. He drank two or three cups full and then fell asleep in a little chair belonging to one of my children. We laid him on the floor, and went out for a little while and got something to drink, and then returned, carried the boy to the well, and threw him into it, in the same way as we had served the other boy and the woman. He died instantly in the well and we left him there a little while, to give time for the mixtures we had given him to run out of the body. We then took the body from the well, took off the clothes in the garden, and buried them there. The body we carried into the wash-house, and put it into the same box, and left it there until the next evening, when we got a porter to carry it with us to St Bartholomew's Hospital, where I sold it to Mr Smith for eight guineas. This boy was about ten or eleven years old, said his mother lived in Kent Street, and that he had not been home for a twelve-month and better.

"I solemnly declare that these are all the murders in which I have been concerned, or that I know any thing of; that I and Williams were alone concerned in these, and that no other person whatever knew any thing about either of them; and that I do not know whether there are others who practise the same mode of obtaining bodies for sale. I know nothing of any Italian boy, and was never concerned in, or knew of, the murder of such a boy. There have been no white mice about my house for the last six months. My son, about eight months ago, bought two mice, and I made a cage for them. It was flat, with wires at the top. They lived about two months, and were killed, I think, by a cat in the garden, where they got out of the cage. They were frequently seen running in the garden, and used to hide in a hole under the privy. I and my wife and children saw one of them killed by a cat in the garden whilst we were at tea.

"Until the transactions before set forth I never was concerned in obtaining a subject by destruction of the living. I have followed the course of obtaining a livelihood as a body-snatcher for 12 years, and have obtained and sold, I think, from 500 to 1,000 bodies; but I declare, before God, that they were all obtained after death, and that, with the above exceptions, I am ignorant of any murder for that or any other purpose."

John Bishop
Witness: Robert Ellis, Under-sheriff
Newgate, December 4th, 1831

"I, Thomas Head, alias Williams, now under sentence of death in Newgate, do solemnly confess and declare the foregoing statement and confession of John Bishop, which has been made in my presence, and since read over to me distinctly, is altogether true, so far as the same relates to me. I declare that I was never concerned in or privy to any other transaction of the like nature—that I never knew any thing of the murder of any other person whatever—that I was never a body-snatcher or concerned in the sale of any other body than the three murdered by Bishop and myself—that May was a stranger to me, and I had never seen him more than once or twice before Friday, the 4th of November last—and that May was wholly innocent and ignorant of any of those murders in which I was concerned, and for one of which I am about to suffer death."

Thomas Head
Witness: R Ellis
Newgate, December 4th, 1831.
"The above confessions taken literally,
from the prisoners, in our presence,"
T Wood, R Ellis, Under-sheriffs

FOURTEEN

Day of Dissolution

John Bishop and Thomas Williams wake before dawn on Monday, 5 December. Williams says, "Now for it," and seems to become more afraid by the minute. He is attempting to pray when Rev. Whitworth Russell enters his cell; Russell watches as Williams mutters the start of various prayers but proves too agitated to finish any and breaks off, appearing to be in despair.

In his cell, Bishop is listless and appears not to notice anything around him. He has slept soundly but woke in the night with a start on seeing someone in the room with him; when asked by his warder if he wanted anything, he replied no and fell back to sleep. At half past five he stands up, scratches his head, and says, "The time is coming very fast." He is offered and accepts some toast and coffee. He tells his warder, "I deserve what is to come."

While they have been sleeping, a crowd of between thirty and forty thousand has amassed in Old Bailey and Giltspur Street. The scaffold has been in place outside Newgate's Debtors Door since half past midnight, and workmen have completed the final adjustments by torchlight. Large wooden barriers are installed at all entrances to the Old Bailey, to prevent a surge when the men are brought out; no one can recall such a desperate, anxious crowd at an execution, and it is believed the people will want to take their own revenge. Their pain and anger seem personal. By five in the morning, the entire Old Bailey is packed. Sill-side seats are being sold for upward of ten guineas; a guinea buys you a spot farther back from the window. "Will you take a window to see the execution, sir?" is chirruped to every well-dressed man in the vicinity. The publican of the King of Denmark watering house—right opposite Debtors Door—has made a small fortune by cramming spectators in. A nearby shop owner has removed his entire frontage to accommodate as many seats as possible. Many people have climbed up lampposts or found their way onto rooftops; every window is crammed with sightseers. It's a very foggy day, and the scaffold cannot be seen from Ludgate Hill, just two hundred yards to the south.[1] At ground level, people are starting to faint, clothes become torn in the jostling; those who pass out are relayed over the heads of the throng to a less crowded spot. The pickpockets are hard at work, scarcely seeming to care if they are seen. Some eager male spectators are attempting to pass themselves off as constables in order to get right up to the gallows, from which hang three ropes. At around seven o'clock the error is noticed, and the rope that would have dispatched James May is removed. The "last dying speech" man has had a good morning, and many in the crowd have purchased one of a number of hastily cobbled together broadsheets purporting to quote "the dying words of Bishop and Williams," some featuring woodcuts that show May dangling alongside them. Nevertheless, the crowd doesn't seem very surprised by the removal of the third rope; some cheering is even heard at the news that May is not to hang.

It's half past seven and time for the prisoners to be formally handed over to the sheriffs and undersheriffs of the City of London for execution. It's an ancient tradition. The men are escorted downstairs to the press room, where many reporters and around thirty paying visitors (including the two sons of Earl Grey who so enjoyed the trial and John Philips Bean, assistant master at St. Paul's School, who felt "a very urgent desire to watch the workings of such atrocious minds towards the last") are waiting to view Bishop and Williams and the ceremony through which they are about to pass.[2] The guests are told that they may speak only in whispers.

Bishop enters the room gazing at the ground, though he appears to be in such a stupor he may not even be seeing it. He gives no indication that he realizes where he is or what is happening to him. But halfway across the room, he looks up, sees all the eyes upon him, and groans and gasps. Then he sinks back into his trancelike state, continues to move slowly, almost mechanically, across the room, and, approaching a prison officer, holds out his arms, wrists together, for them to be bound. When this is done, and his collar unfastened and folded back and his black neckerchief removed, he sits down on a bench and gazes again at the ground. His demeanor impresses the visitors, who see it as a sign of firmness and resolve. An undersheriff sits down next to him and asks him softly if there is any further confession he would like to make. "No, sir," says Bishop. "I have told all."

Now Williams enters the room, moving with a nervous, jerky walk—he is shaking so badly that he needs to be supported as he crosses the room. As his arms are pinioned, one officer must hold them steady as another ties the cord. His face is flushed, there are tears in his eyes, and he is muttering, "I deserve all this. I deserve all this and more. I deserve what I'm about to suffer." He looks younger than ever. He is sat down on the bench alongside Bishop, and the undersheriff asks him if he has anything more to say, and Williams says, "Oh no, sir, I have told all—I hope I am now at peace with God—What I have told is the truth." He is also heard to say, "Remember me to . . . ," but the final word is not clearly audible because he is crying.

Dr. Cotton says that he understands the men wish to receive the sacraments, but Dr. Williams tells him that this won't be necessary—the prisoners have changed their minds. Dr. Cotton says that he hopes that they have spent the night asking for God's mercy. "Now gentlemen," says Cotton to the interloping churchmen, "you'd better take your man, and retire to different parts of the room, where you can talk without interrupting each other." Dr. Whitworth Russell takes Thomas Williams to the farthest end of the room, where they are seen speaking earnestly; Dr. Theodore Williams sits with Bishop close to the blazing fire. Cotton doesn't like the approach to Christianity that these two churchmen are displaying and he approaches each of the two-man huddles and says, "Now gentlemen, time is hastening.

Suppose you let them go and pray to God. You go there," he says to Bishop, pointing to a bench near the window of the press room, "and you kneel down there," he tells Thomas Williams, indicating a spot near the sink where crockery can be rinsed, "and pray heartily to God to forgive you your sins and have mercy on your souls through your Redeemer." They do as they are told, and as they are praying Cotton is heard to remark, "Now this is a blessed sight."

When they return to the bench near the fireside, Cotton asks them if they would like a little wine. They say yes, and Bishop downs one teacupful, but Williams is shaking and crying so much he is given a little more. Drs. Williams and Whitworth Russell have rejoined them and have started to discuss the crimes once again, and then they begin to advise them on how they should approach their imminent death, at which point Cotton says, "I will give those directions, if you please. All matters of that kind had better be left to me."

St. Paul's can be heard striking eight. Bishop stands and says, "I am ready" and Cotton starts reciting the funeral service as Bishop and Williams, the sheriffs, undersheriffs, clergymen, and visitors rise and begin the walk to the scaffold. They descend into the subterranean Dead Man's Walk, as Cotton reads, with the remains of the executed lying under the slabs they walk on, and then up into the small entrance hall behind Debtors Door, up a flight of stairs and through the prison's bread room and the soup room, from which rise the stairs that lead directly to the gallows. They are opposite the King of Denmark. Bishop walks steadily, slowly, to the foot of the steps, but Williams becomes even more frenzied in appearance and begs to see Whitworth Russell once again. As Bishop moves out onto the platform, the chaplain of Millbank Penitentiary comes alongside Williams, sitting on a bench in the soup room, and their conversation is at first inaudible, but now, with Williams clasping Whitworth Russell's hand as he moves onto the stairs to the scaffold, the condemned man is heard saying: "I hope God will have mercy upon me." Whitworth Russell says that since Williams seems genuinely penitent, God is likely to be merciful. "Then I am ready to die. I know I deserve it, for other crimes I have done." Whitworth Russell says, "You have just another moment between this and death, and as a dying man I implore you, in God's name, to tell the truth. Have you told me the whole truth?"

Deadman's Walk, the subterranean passage that led from the prison to the scaffold at Debtors Door

"All I have told you is true." He won't let go of the chaplain's hands.

"But have you told me all?"

Williams hesitates, then says, "All I have told you is quite true."

The crowd has spotted the executioner, William Calcraft, and his assistant on the scaffold and a cry of "Hats off!" is shouted among the thousands there: you get a better view with hats off. Silence falls. But the moment Bishop appears, there is a roar. He does not seem to notice the shouting, yelling, hooting, screaming, cursing, and he moves obediently as Calcraft places him beneath the beam, which faces south to Ludgate Hill; his last glimpse will be of thick fog, as Calcraft pulls a cloth sack over his head and puts the noose around his neck. The crowd is pleased with the preparation and begins to cheer. It is likely that Bishop knows of Calcraft's reputation for ineptitude— choosing too short a drop, he has had to hang on the backs of the condemned to ensure their necks break—and he often stinks of brandy at his public appearances. Williams's conversation with Whitworth Russell at the foot of the stairs has delayed him by two minutes, so Bishop stands alone, not moving a muscle or making a sound.

Williams appears, totters to the edge of the scaffold, and bows to the crowd. Why is he doing this? Why? Does he think he's a performer on a stage? Is it a gesture he has seen the condemned make at executions? Is he trying to show remorse to the Mob he preyed on? The crowd screams and jeers and curses him. Shaking violently, he is led to the beam, hooded, and noosed. Cotton encourages both men to pray, and Williams does this eagerly, calling out the words along with the churchman, who, midsentence, gives Calcraft the signal for the drop, and both men fall.

Bishop dies instantly. But Williams is seen drawing his legs upward several times, with immense effort, while his neck and chest muscles throb; it is five minutes until his legs stop twitching. By which time, Cotton, the sheriff, the undersheriffs, and the paying visitors are on their way back through the prison to enjoy the breakfast that ancient tradition specifies on the occasion of executions at Newgate.

The excitement of the burkers being "turned off" has led to a catastrophe at the southern end of Giltspur Street. The wooden barrier there has collapsed and many people are crushed in the panic. By a quarter to nine, an entire ward at St. Bartholomew's is filled with injured spectators. Ribs are crushed, limbs are broken, flesh torn, but surprisingly, no one has been killed. Robert Mortimer, the Nova Scotia Gardens tailor who cut his throat rather than give evidence, is in Bart's too, sitting up chatting and expected to make a full recovery.

....

It is nine o'clock, and time for the bodies to be cut down, although this is scarcely the right term, since modern executions involve the rope's being connected to a chain, which is attached to the beam by a hook kept in place by a screw and bolt. This arrangement is seen as a great advance. Calcraft simply turns the bolt and Bishop and Williams fall into the cart waiting below the scaffold. The crowd loves this. The bodies are covered by two sacks and then the cart is driven by the city marshall, wearing full ceremonial regalia, to 33 Hosier Lane, the house rented by the Royal College of Surgeons for the official reception of the bodies of executed murderers. It's only a short distance—really just behind the Fortune of War. The cart moves in a slow, stately manner, and the crowd appears to enjoy the ritual and the costume of this traditional journey. They'd love to get their hands on the corpses, and the police have their job cut out for them keeping people back as Bishop and Williams are carried into No. 33.

It's quite a reception they get: Sir William Blizard himself, eighty-eight-year-old president of the Royal College of Surgeons, has come to Hosier Lane in his college robes. He's there, along with the entire court of the college, to officiate as William Clift, conservator of the college library and museum, draws his knife—ceremonially—across the chests

The true likenesses of Thomas Head and John Bishop sketched by William Clift of the Royal College of Surgeons

and stomachs of Bishop and Williams, creating large cruciform wounds on each man.[3] Then the two are—ceremonially—stitched back up again before presentation to the anatomists. Having witnessed the opening and closing of the bodies, the city marshall leaves. Calcraft, having been given the men's clothes and their nooses, beats a retreat too—these are his perks, and he will make money exhibiting the trophies. (Calcraft isn't particularly interested in his job, preferring gardening, breeding prize rabbits, and caring for his pet pony; he is also said to be good with children.)[4] William Clift sketches the dead men and will later work these drawings up into likenesses that, many will say, are undoubtedly the faces of monsters.

Now Bishop and Williams take their leave of each other for the last time (though to be fair, they have known each other only for five months). Bishop is heading for King's College, as a reward for Richard Partridge and Herbert Mayo, while Williams is off to the Great Windmill Street School, where George Guthrie and Edward Tuson are waiting for him.

FIFTEEN

The Use of the Dead to the Living

And once the scalpels are set to work, it becomes clear what manner of men these were, and how and why these murders came to be committed. At King's College, Bishop had a lecture on medical jurisprudence read over him as he lay on the slab before once again being sliced from throat to abdomen, and across the chest, this time by Richard Partridge as Herbert Mayo stood by. Bishop, it was discovered, had an extraordinarily good physique, proving far more useful as a specimen than the produce he used to deliver. "A more healthy or muscular Subject has not been seen in any of the schools of anatomy for a long time," cooed the *Morning Advertiser*. "The body presented a remarkably fine appearance across the chest. The deltoides were splendidly developed, and the pectorals, major and minor, were particularly displayed."[1] Bishop was five feet seven inches tall and had an inordinate amount of body hair; at some point in his life he had broken both his legs, and he had two scars on his chin—perhaps an inexpertly scaled graveyard wall had left its imprint. The rope had bitten deep into the flesh on the left side of his neck. It was also discovered that Calcraft had made yet another hash of his job: Bishop's spinal cord was intact. With the top of the skull carved off, Bishop's brain was reported to look as though it was in an "unhealthy" state; the observers deduced that this was visual evidence of the mental anguish he had been suffering in the days before his death.

Later, but before he began to smell, Bishop was set up as an exhibit in a room next to the anatomical theater at King's College; a huge crowd came to see the London Burker, who had been disemboweled and had had all his various cuts sewn up with thick twine. Later still, when he ceased to be a moneymaker, Bishop was gradually stripped down to the bone by the students and lecturers of King's.

The clothes that Bishop had died in, alongside Williams's, were exhibited by Calcraft in a private house in Sun Street, Shoreditch, for "only a penny," according to the advertisements.

The dissection of Williams's body caused a minor riot. For a fee,

Head/Williams was dissected at the Great Windmill Street School of Anatomy, founded by William Hunter in 1768; the building still stands, as part of the Lyric Theatre, Shaftesbury Avenue.

the curious were allowed into the dissecting room, where Edward
Tuson and George Guthrie were at work. (Guthrie had put his request
in early, writing to the secretary of the Royal College of Surgeons on 4
December: "If May is not executed, pray do me the favour to beg Mr
Clift to send to Windmill Street the best of the two remaining, for a
natural skeleton." But he was shortchanged, since King's College was
given "the best.")[2] People gathered outside the school to wait for admittance, and a number of medical students decided to police the
crowd—although there were Metropolitan officers on the spot—
arming themselves with staves and chair legs, with which they threatened those on line. Inside, students helped themselves to locks of
Williams's hair. Two students were seen brawling close by the corpse
(which had its eyes wide open); they had become drunk on pots of beer
hauled up on ropes over the heads of the crowd and in through the
school windows. The police informed Tuson that the "exhibition" must
end immediately since the noise from inside and around the school was
disturbing residents.[3] Those who did gain admittance would have seen
Williams's tattooed forearms—which should have settled the issue of
his true identity once and for all. But the tattoos just led to more confusion. In 1827, when his "distinguishing marks" had been so carefully
sketched into a prison ledger, the authorities had noted tattoos of two
intertwined love hearts shot through with arrows on his right forearm,
and four letters on his left forearm. The latter now also featured a number of crudely drawn flowerpots, an anchor, and a scroll surrounding
the four letters. In 1827, these had been transcribed as "T.H.N.A," the
"N.A." assumed to be a sweetheart and related to the hearts and arrows
on his right forearm. But William Clift, conservator of the Royal College of Surgeons museum, sketched the letters into his diary as "JOHN
HEAD," while a newspaper reporter transcribed them as "J. HEAD."
Pierce Egan, author of *Life in London*, also saw "JOHN HEAD" when
he viewed the body, written above the letters "C.E" (never explained),
and Egan wrote to the *Times* expressing his view that the truth of
the killer's confession was to be doubted, since he had signed the
document "Thomas Head," not "John."[4] But Head had consistently
described himself as "Thomas" in all the documentation that mattered:
his wedding certificate, at his Old Bailey trial for theft, his entries in
prison ledgers. Did Thomas decide to inscribe himself "John" at some

point in Millbank or upon his release? Or were Clift and Egan mistaken in what they saw on the forearm?

It was with some confidence that phrenologist Dr. John Elliotson stated, on examining plaster casts of Bishop's and Williams's skulls, that "Bishop had got ideality, and no reflection," while with Williams "the portion devoted to the animal propensities—the lower posterior and the lower lateral parts, especially destructiveness, acquisitiveness, secretiveness—is immense." Williams's head was "by far the worse," claimed Elliotson: it was clear that Williams's Combativeness was Very Large and his Veneration Very Small, while his Esteem was Full and his Love of Approbation Large. No wonder his life had been low and villainous, since he had been deficient in the "sense of what is refined and exquisite in nature and art."[5]

The early 1830s were the high noon of phrenology, and celebrated murderers such as Bishop and Williams were the most sought-after theory-proving material there was. What relation did the shape and size of the skull have to the mind that it contained? Were morality and intellect revealed in human tissue such as the scalp or the brain? What functions could be deduced from the way an organ looked? Sadism knew no social class, according to Dr. Joseph Gall (1757–1828), one of phrenology's pioneers; Gall took pains to demonstrate—anecdotally—that the propensity for murder was as likely to be found in the wealthy lover of the arts as in the poorest peasant. He cited Nero, Henry VIII, a senior member of the Dutch clergy, and a count at the court of Louis XV as particularly depraved (though he never did see their heads).[6] It would be interesting to know what phrenologists would have made of the plaster casts of Bishop's and Williams's heads if these had turned up with no history attached; as it was, the craniometrists knew in great detail the deeds of the men whose skulls they were measuring. Elliotson's report interweaves his analysis of Williams's head shape with regurgitated background details about Williams's life that were taken straight from the newspapers. Alas, Elliotson's favored plaster-cast maker, a Cockney called Deville, had omitted to shave the entire scalps, which rather compromised Elliotson's assessment of Bishop's moral faculties, since matted hair had rendered this particular bump bigger than it really was.

Bishop's head was smaller than Williams's, which, deduced

Elliotson, "agrees with the fact" that it was Williams who had first suggested the burkings (that was what had been reported, at least); and Bishop's enlarged organ of Acquisitiveness tallied with his history as a paid informer and perjurer—more details gleaned from the papers. What we were to learn from these casts, said Elliotson, was that we should be grateful not to possess such terrible "organisation" of faculties and that it was our duty to encourage virtue and to ensure a steady supply of legally obtained corpses to anatomists, thereby removing the cause of Bishop and Williams's crimes. These two men might even, he said, have made decent, if disagreeable, Christians, if murder hadn't come so easily into their lives.

Elliotson tabulated his findings, just to make matters entirely clear:

	BISHOP	WILLIAMS
Amativeness [sex drive]	Very Large	Large
Philoprogenitiveness [Fertility; will to reproduce]	Moderate	Large
Inhabitiveness [Urge to settle in one place]	Moderate	Moderate
Adhesiveness [Tenacity]	Large	Moderate
Combativeness	Very Large	Small
Constructiveness	Small	Moderate
Acquisitiveness	Very Large	Very Large
Destructiveness	Very Large	Large
Secretiveness	Very Large	Large
Self-esteem	Full	Large
Love of approbation	Large	Full
Cautiousness	Very Large	Moderate
Benevolence	Very Small	Small
Veneration	Very Small	Moderate
Hope	Very Small	Small
Conscientiousness	Very Small	Very Small
Ideality	Small	Small
Firmness	Small	Small
Knowing faculties	Large	Large
Intellectual faculties	Small	Very Small

The opponents of "bumpology," as they called it, claimed that there was no relation between cranium and brain and that misshapen skulls were the result of a number of perfectly mundane factors, such as a blow to the head or tight-fitting headwear for children. Much muck was raked in the battle of phrenology, with one often-repeated anecdote (never sourced) about a trainee of Gall's who had disinterred his own mother to prove a point.[7] Phrenology, though, was not a phenomenon that could be proved or disproved by advances in anatomy. Looking at dead matter, however brilliantly dissected, would not reveal how a brain, or brain faculties, worked. The soul, or spirit, could not be located, nor did there seem to be a way of demonstrating that it was merely the product of the nervous system. Discovering the essence of humankind—of life—was eluding those who wielded the scalpel.

While phrenology would decline into a parlor game by the 1860s, physiognomy—the observation and categorization of facial rather than cranial features—emerged into greater respectability as the nineteenth century wore on. It appeared to gain validity from the pioneering work of physiologists such as Herbert Mayo, Charles Bell, and vivisectionist François Magendie, who all helped to reveal the mysteries of facial muscle movement. Physiognomy had formerly been an illegal practice in England, undertaken by itinerant showmen who, in addition to reading "character" and future prospects from the faces of the credulous, might offer palm reading and the divination of omens, activities also outlawed by Puritans in the sixteenth and seventeenth centuries—and still illegal under the 1824 Vagrancy Act; but physiognomy was proving irresistible to the new society that was busy segregating itself into mutually exclusive groups. Anxiety about social flux could be allayed by typologizing and categorizing, and the need to feel certain about the "types" one was living among is likely to have been the driving force that made physiognomy increasingly prescriptive rather than merely descriptive, and nowhere more so than in the analysis of criminality. Thieves and prostitutes were said to know how to wear a "mask of decorum" by the late 1820s, where less than twenty years before, they had made little attempt to disguise who they were or what they did.[8] Beggars could be as adept as Drury Lane actors in striking poses, adopting airs, drumming up pathos. The city dweller was becoming his or her own work of art; self-consciousness and self-presentation were becoming key.

But like phrenology, physiognomy was not innocent of eye; visual data were used to prove points already decided by other types of evidence. So Thomas Williams was described, after his death, as having a "coarse and vulgar physiognomy, . . . a low, designing brow, a harsh severity of features."[9] But before the guilty verdict, it was the very ordinariness of the prisoners' appearance that had been commented on. At that point, the worst that had been said of any of the three was that Williams looked "cunning" (*Times*), though the same newspaper had also claimed that he looked "inoffensive— simple even," while Bishop had never appeared worse than "sullen." Yet a week after the executions, having viewed the sketches of the Bow Street and Old Bailey hearings published by printer Charles Tilt, the *Times* decided: "May looks more stupid, perhaps, than vicious, and yet his countenance is extremely revolting. The face of Williams exhibits the same attempt at disguise as is apparent in his costume, and an equal failure attends both: the metropolitan black-guard is not concealed by the countryman's smock frock, and the brutality of his nature breaks through the affected sheepishness which he put on for the occasion. Bishop is rather more like a hog than a human being, and there is no attempt on his part to soften the harsh character with which Nature has branded him."[10] Except that it was Bishop who wore the smock frock, not Williams—the picture had been wrongly labeled by Tilt.

But as late as 1883, plaster casts of Bishop's and Williams's heads were being advertised as "suitable for public or private museums, lit-erary or scientific institutions," along with the heads of Oliver Cromwell, "the Idiot of Amsterdam," Coleridge, Sir Isaac Newton, William Palmer the Poisoner, and the five idiot progeny of one Mrs. Hillings; they cost a mere five shillings each, or forty shillings for a dozen.[11]

No death portrait had ever been circulated of the dead child of King's College, and so the publishers of broadsheets and ballads were free to make up their own minds about how the victim of the Bethnal Green Tragedy might have looked. London was in love with its Poor Italian Boy, and he was memorialized in many catchpenny prints—

often as a corpulent little chap with an insipid grin beneath a hugely exaggerated furry cap—while doggerel poured from hack poets' pens. "The Italian Savoyard Boy," for example, by one F. W. N. Bayly, appeared in the *Weekly Dispatch:*

> *Poor child of Venice! He had left*
> *A land of love and sun for this;*
> *In one brief day of tears bereft,*
> *Of father's care and mother's kiss!*
> *The valleys of his native home,*
> *The mountain paths of light and flow'rs;*
> *The Savoyard forsook, to roam*
> *For wealth and happiness in ours.*
>
> *And pitying thousands saw the boy,*
> *Feeding the tortoise on his knee;*
> *And beauty bright, and childhood coy,*
> *Oft flung their mite of charity.*
> *And as he rested on the stone,*
> *His organ tun'd to some old air!*
> *Men paus'd at its familiar tone,*
> *And left their little tokens there.*

Et cetera.

In a similar way, *The Trial and Execution of the Burkers for Murdering a Poor Italian Boy,* a broadsheet produced by the most successful of cheap publishers, James Catnach (and so shoddily cobbled together that it reports James May being executed), contains this verse:

> *'Tis of a poor Italian Boy, whose fate we now deplore,*
> *Who wandered from his native land unto old England's shore;*
> *White mice within his box confin'd he slung across his breast,*
> *And friendless, for his daily bread, through London streets he prest.*

From the cheapest broadsheet to the *Times* and the Houses of Parliament, it was decided that the Italian Boy case had revealed

Inexpensive broadsheets, plagiarizing the official accounts, meant that the poor could enjoy reading about trials and executions. Some printers were so keen not to spend money that they reused dated stock scenes from past murders.

London, the world's wealthiest city, failing in the duties of care that its superiority forced upon it. That a nation as great as Britain had let down a young stranger from another land provoked much striking of attitudes. A *Times* editorial on 10 November fulminated against the "wretches" who had "picked up from our streets an unprotected foreign child, and prepared him for the dissecting knife by assassination." For the anonymous writer of *The History of the London Burkers,* a sense of national disgrace was invoked: "Can this be England—the most enlightened, the most civilised country of the globe? Alas! that England should now stand indelibly stained by guilt of so foul, so unnatural a blackness."

Poor homeless Fanny Pigburn—kicked out by her landlord; afraid to return to her relations (for reasons unknown), unwilling to inflict herself on any other friend or family member, and so lacking in self-worth that she had dyed a new white bonnet black because she felt a white one was too smart for her to wear—was never sentimentalized. Carlo had been given the role of Daft Jamie (James Wilson), the eighteen-year-old murdered by Burke and Hare, whose sixteen known victims also included Mary Paterson, eighteen, who was so fine looking that her corpse was sketched and painted at Dr. Knox's school and preserved in spirits.[12] But Fanny—pockmarked, skinny, fond of a drink, unmarried mother of two children she could not afford to care for—was not considered worthy of commemoration. Similarly, young Cunningham of Bishop's confession was dully British, a London street boy, a runaway quite possibly surviving on the fringes of Smithfield's criminal culture, having none of the Latin glamour of Carlo or the pathos of Daft Jamie. In five years' time, Charles Dickens would give a character and dialogue to boys like Cunningham, bringing them into focus with the creation of the Artful Dodger and Charley Bates in *Oliver Twist,* but until then, London urchins appear in writing as a disreputable composite—dirty, dishonest, and barely human. "Your true London boy of the streets [has a] mingled look of cunning and insolence," wrote journalist Charles Knight; while the author of the 1832 penal-reform volume *Old Bailey Experience* decided "they have a peculiar look of the eye . . . and the development of their features is strongly marked with the animal propensities. . . . They may be known almost by their very gait in the streets from other persons. Some of the boys have an approximation to the face of a monkey, so strikingly are they distinguished by this peculiarity. They form a distinct class of men by themselves."[13]

A better-quality representation of Carlo sold as a print after the trial; engraving by J. Thomson after J. Hayes

Meanwhile, *trade* *was* *as* *brisk* *as* *ever* in Nova Scotia Gardens. Broadsheet sellers were crying out their titles and opening lines, and various religious tract societies were cashing in with fire-and-brimstone pamphlets on the wages of sin, with particular reference to the Late Murders. Even during a long downpour, the atmosphere was that of a village fair. The tours of No. 3 were still attracting hundreds of people. An elegantly dressed woman was seen to stoop down and scoop up water from the fatal well in order to taste it, while outside the front of the cottage, a lollipop peddler had set up a stall to sell sugar figurines of three burkers dangling from a miniature sugar gallows (a passerby was heard noting May's reprieve and suggesting the confectionery be adapted accordingly). The talk of local women was about how Bishop and Williams's punishment should have been longer and more painful. Inside the house, a self-appointed master of ceremonies was pointing out to visitors the relevant parts of No. 3, using a large stick. "This here was the wery bed wot he and his woman slept on," he announced in the Bishops' bedroom, though it is surprising that the bed had survived the first waves of visitors—perhaps a replacement had been installed in order not to disappoint.[14]

A contemporary account reveals the more typical entertainment available for high days and holidays in the vicinity during those years, and puts the House of Murder hubbub into perspective. The anonymous essayist who contributed the article "Four Views of London" to the *New Monthly Magazine* described a Whitsuntide holiday trip he had made to Spitalfields, just south of Bethnal Green, his first visit to the area in thirty years and his chance to note its shocking decline since the collapse of the silk trade. For the poor, a holiday treat was tea in a tea garden, where two pennies was the price of hot water and crockery, but the tea leaves were not supplied. The writer watched as families sat on a blackened lawn, the entertainment consisting of one improvised swing for the children, a tiny, covered skittle ground, and a soaped pole to climb. For spectacle, the publican compelled an ill-looking boy to pick up a hundred pebbles within a set time. The eyewitness noted "an entire absence of all mirth and enjoyment."[15]

In *Radical circles,* Bishop and Williams were providing material for satirical entertainment. *Figaro in London* was a scurrilous, antiestablishment weekly newspaper (price one penny) that took its name from the famous French daily and throughout its short life campaigned vigorously for electoral reform. In its Christmas Eve edition, 1831, the details of the Italian Boy case were used to lampoon the bishop of London—Charles Blomfield—and the duke of Wellington, who had been prominent among parliamentarians who had killed off the Reform Bill in October 1831: "I, Bishop, of London, do hereby declare and confess that I took a prominent part in the Burking of the Bill which has caused so great a sensation in the country. My principal accomplice was the person known as the Head of the Tories who endeavoured to cover his notoriously bad character by boasting of being of William's family. We both got the Bill into our power in a house in the neighbourhood of Westminster, and commenced our operations by plying it with a quantity of half and half, and in a very moderate measure, with which we had intended to stupefy it at once, but it did not take sufficient effect."[16]

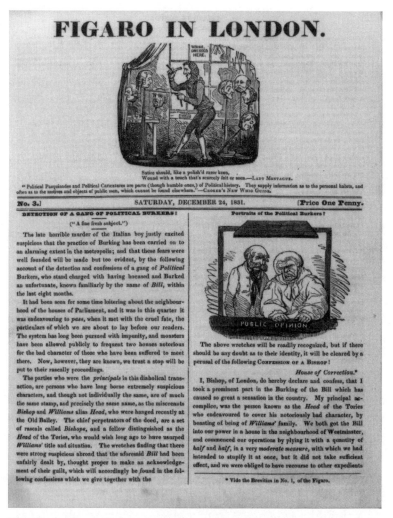

This Radical, pro-Reform journal, edited by Henry Mayhew, used the Italian Boy trial to lampoon the anti-Reform duke of Wellington and bishop of London, shown wearing a smock frock.

But thrills, pathos, and laughter were not Bishop and Williams's principal legacy. Twelve days after their execution, Henry Warburton, MP, introduced his second Anatomy Bill to the Commons; by 20 December, it was having its second reading. In 1829, Warburton's original bill—to make the unclaimed bodies of paupers who died in workhouses and hospitals available to teachers of anatomy for dissection—had been passed by the Commons but thrown out by the Lords. As with the Reform Bill, the upper house rejected attempts to tinker with God's natural order—the aristocracy had ordained rights and privileges but also had a duty of care toward its inferiors, including their corpses. No upstart doctors should be allowed to interrupt this beautiful, natural, sacred hierarchical design for society.

As with the original bill, the opponents of Warburton's second attempt at legislation comprised a broad coalition of, on the one hand, Tories who believed the traditional social order was under attack and foresaw the potential for further civil unrest if such a socially divisive act were to be passed and, on the other, Radicals who believed the poor should never become fodder for middle-class self-betterment.

Sir Frederick Trench, Tory member for Cambridge, told the Commons that Warburton's measure should be renamed "a Bill to Encourage Burking," claiming that legalizing the supply in no way removed the premium for hastening a relative's death. All that was needed to prevent another Bishop and Williams was for surgeons to examine far more carefully the Subjects that were offered to them, said Trench.[17]

Similarly, Cresset Pelham, the member for Shropshire, recognized that Warburton's bill treated the human body as an item of trade, while merely bringing down the price of such a commodity. "The bill would give a legal encouragement to the traffic in human blood," said Pelham, who suggested that the best way to put an end to burking would be to inflict stronger punishment on the "receivers." Alexander Perceval, Tory member for Sligo, also wanted the onus to be placed on the surgeons and said that, in his view, possession of a Subject should be upgraded from a misdemeanor to a felony.

The bill's most vociferous opponent, Henry "Orator" Hunt, capitalized on the unsavory reputation of anatomy schools and spoke of the lack of respect that was shown to corpses by teachers and students, claiming that "the cutting up and mangling of the bodies of human beings was done with as little concern in those human shambles as the bodies of beasts were cut up in Newgate, Smithfield or any other market." Hunt professed to have it on the best authority that "the conduct of the young students in the dissecting-room was too often perfectly disgusting—too disgusting to be described even in an assembly like that, composed as it was entirely of men."[18] (Surgeon George Guthrie had given the game away when he wrote, in 1829, an open letter in which he urged anatomists to end the pretense that dissected corpses had a decent burial once they were finished with. Since the flesh was removed at a slow rate, he wrote, it could not be stored until the skeleton had been revealed; the flesh simply ended up with all the other refuse produced by the schools.)[19]

Orator Hunt told the Commons that in the schools of Paris and Dublin, wax models of the human anatomy had proved quite adequate for teaching purposes, while London "required human carcasses to be sold like pigs or sheep." Henry Warburton's withering reply was that only "the ingenious foreigner" who made and marketed wax anatomical figures would claim that they were good enough to use to teach medical students.[20]

No matter how trenchant and perceptive the arguments made by opponents of the bill, references to Bishop and Williams were reiterated by its supporters to induce a sense of panic, a sense that these imitators of Burke and Hare were likely themselves to have spawned imitators.[21] The supporters of the bill were also able to argue convincingly, if insincerely in many instances, that it was the poor who had most to benefit from the act: no longer would the impoverished need to fear the body snatcher or the burker. Whig member for Calne, in Wiltshire, Thomas Babington Macaulay, told the Commons on 27 February 1832, "That a man has property, that he has connections, that he is likely to be missed and sought for, are circumstances which secure him against the burker. It is curious to observe the difference between murders of this kind and other murders. An ordinary murderer hides the body and disposes of the property. Bishop and Williams dig holes and bury the property, and expose the body to sale. The more wretched, the more lonely the human being may be, the more desirable prey he is to these wretches. It is the man, the mere naked man, that they pursue."

The bill was passed by forty-three votes to five in the Commons on 11 May 1832, and two months later the Lords passed the measure, with the bill's sponsor in the Lords, the Whig-leaning earl of Minto, still harping on one particular rumor concerning Bishop and Williams that had failed to be dispelled, despite months of official denials.

SIXTEEN

How Many?

Orator Hunt had first brought up the rumor. Addressing the House of Commons on Monday, 12 December, he said that according to a statement in the newspapers, the men recently executed for burking, instead of confessing to three or four murders, had confessed to sixty but were stopped in the middle of their confessions by Dr. Cotton, the ordinary of Newgate. Hunt said that "it had greatly agitated the public mind, and was, he believed, at present the source of much excitement." Did the government know whether the tale of the interrupted confession was true or not?

George Lamb, the right honorable secretary for the Home Department (and Lord Melbourne's youngest brother), said he did not know on what authority the statement in the newspapers had been put forth, but he was not aware of any other confession than that officially published.

Alderman Waithman, member for the City of London, replied to Hunt that he himself had spoken to the sheriffs and undersheriffs at Newgate, and the undersheriffs had declared that Bishop and Williams had told everything they knew in the "official" confession.

Waithman claimed to have been astonished to read the allegations that there had been sixty victims.[1]

The official confessions—the "I, John Bishop" and "I, Thomas Head" statements—had been taken down by undersheriffs Robert Ellis and Thomas Wood and authenticated and approved for publication by Dr. Cotton. But strange, unsourced additions to the official confessions had been appearing in the national newspapers. The *Observer,* then as now a Sunday paper, had been among the first to publish an unauthorized alternative account (it was reprinted in full by the *Times,* with acknowledgment, on Monday, 5 December). Twenty-four hours before the executions took place, the *Observer* reported: "Yesterday morning, the Rev. Mr Theodore Williams, vicar of Hendon, according to a promise he made to Bishop, visited him in his cell. . . . After some hesitation, Bishop admitted that he had been concerned in the commission of three murders, viz., that of the Italian boy, the murder of Frances Pigburn, and of a drover—a boy who had come to London with cattle from Lincolnshire, which boy the witnesses on his trial had sworn was the Italian boy, to the best of their belief, though he had disposed of that body before. Bishop entered into a minute description, most horrible in its details, of the mode by which he had perpetrated the inhuman murders. He did not deny that Williams was an actor in the murder of the Italian boy, which had been committed in the cottage in Nova Scotia Gardens. Williams also made a confession which was consistent with the facts stated in that of Bishop; but he declared that he had been involved in the horrid transactions by Bishop's persuasion, whose daughter he had married only three months ago. He also exonerated May from all participation in the murder."

Cunningham of Kent Street does not appear in this report. Instead, there is the admission to killing an Italian boy. Was this admission to a (backdated) murder of an Italian boy a change of heart by Bishop, or sloppy journalism, or wishful thinking by the reporter? And who was the reporter? Who had smuggled out an advance confession—an exclusive—presumably for a good sum of money?

The *Observer* continued: "On further interrogation, both Bishop and Williams declared that the corpse offered for sale at the King's

College, and sworn to as the Italian boy, Carlo Ferrari, was not the body of that ill-fated lad, but they again asserted that it was the corpse of a boy who had come from Lincolnshire to Smithfield with a drove of cattle. They, however, did not deny that the Italian boy was murdered by Bishop." But nor did they state it; which was odd, in light of Bishop's comment that "he had disposed of that body before."[2]

"A veil of secrecy has been thrown over the circumstances which have transpired in Newgate," insisted the *Observer*, "and if there be any inaccuracies, they are [more] attributable to the want of unreserved communication on the part of those who are possessed of the 'secrets of the prison house,' than to the want of zeal on our part to gratify the curiosity of our readers." This seems to be an attack on Cotton and the sheriffs, and it is tempting to suppose that Dr. Theodore Williams had not surrendered his version of the confessions at the sheriff's office, as he had been requested to do, but had smuggled them out and delivered them to the *Observer* on Saturday evening. (The *Observer* offices were at 169 Strand, around fifteen to twenty minutes' walk from the jail.)

There are other suspects, though. It is quite possible that reformist prison chaplain Dr. Whitworth Russell, pamphleteering solicitor James Harmer (a personal friend of Cotton's), or any of the sheriffs, undersheriffs, or warders (Bishop and Williams each had two guards) were rushing out different versions of confessions, or the gist of conversations overheard, in order to raise a guinea or two. In addition to the hunger for newspaper reports about murderers, the "last dying speeches" produced by broadsheet manufacturers could realize a small fortune if prepared in advance to be sold at a "popular" execution. Even Pierce Egan, famous, well established, and celebrated for his *Life in London* books of the mid-1820s, had got in on the act, quite probably using his friendship with Cotton to publish his slightly more expensive version of events, *The Murder of the Italian Boy* ("price only 1s and 6d").[3]

The penal-reform-minded author of *Old Bailey Experience* would, the following year, complain bitterly about rival confessions being sent to newspaper offices by "interlopers" in the jail. He reminded readers of the time a "Dr R" was caught out: he had gone home and penned "the final moments" of a condemned man who was granted a reprieve at the last minute the next morning. (It is possible that "Dr R" was Dr. Whitworth Russell.)[4] *Old Bailey Experience* also claimed that the splits within the Church of England were reflected within the prison and that each "side" enjoyed the complicity of various aldermen in gaining access to noteworthy criminals; rival factions within Anglicanism wanted to be seen to be offering the best form of religious instruction and spiritual comfort to those about to die. Those of an evangelical tendency placed importance on a thrusting, practical, personalized Christianity; the state of mind of the condemned was paramount. Evangelicals were aghast at the seemingly supine approach of some High Church Anglicans, who appeared content to rely on ritual and liturgy, without tailoring pastoral care to the individual receiving it.

But a vigorous, reformist approach to religion had its pitfalls. Though Hendon's Rev. Theodore Williams was a High Church Anglican, words that certain of his parishioners used to describe him included "overbearing," "dictatorial," "hasty," and "irritable." While many considered him a fine preacher (attendance at his sermons was high), the local Methodists dubbed him "the cockfighting parson" because he refused to support a ban on that sport in his parish, and they accused him of inciting local youths to pelt the Methodist minister in Hendon with eggs and old vegetables.[5] In 1823, following a dispute over burial fees, Williams had wrecked the new tomb of one Mrs. Warren with his bare hands, scattering debris across the road outside the church. He had served time in a debtors' prison and would do so again in his old age. In 1836, he would be involved in an infamous brawl in the vestry of St. Mary's, Hendon, and, three years after that, would clash with *Lancet* founder Thomas Wakely, refusing to sanction the disinterment of a body for a coroner's hearing. (A seventy-nine-year-old pauper, Thomas Austin, had fallen into a copper of boiling water at the Hendon workhouse.)[6] Williams's family had made their money from plantations in the West Indies worked by slaves, and the vicar vociferously opposed the antislavery movement. His own personal expenditure was compared unfavorably by some of his parishioners with his parsimony in administering the New Poor Law in Hendon, from 1834. It would be quite in keeping with what is known of the vicar of Hendon that he should have had some hand in making money from newspapers and, in doing so, stirring up controversy.

The *Sunday Times* and the *Atlas* newspapers also ran additional New-gate confessions, and these too were reprinted in full by the *Times* and the *Globe and Traveller* on Monday the fifth. Someone had smuggled out the story that on Saturday night, alone in his cell except for his warder, Thomas Williams had become "anxious and uneasy towards midnight. His agitation increased, and the vigilance of his keeper became more marked. Williams observed it and said, 'Don't be frightened, sir, I am not going to do anything wrong, but I wish to ease my mind. Let me see the governor.' Mr Wontner was then called from his bed and the Reverend Mr Cotton, the Ordinary, was also in atten-dance in a few minutes. When these gentlemen came into the cell, Williams, looking at them steadfastly for a moment or two, burst into tears and said, 'Gentlemen, I wish to unburden my mind. I know I am guilty, and ought to suffer the utmost punishment of the law. I am a murderer, I confess it; but the witnesses were all mistaken as to its being the Italian boy.'"

The report went on: "On Thursday 3rd November, he [Williams] was in the neighbourhood of Smithfield when he saw a boy, whom he had often observed before, assisting in driving cattle to the market. This boy was about fourteen or fifteen years of age, and exactly cor-responded with the description given of the Italian boy. He enticed him from the cattle, and took him to the Fortune of War public house, and sent for Bishop, who was waiting at another pub in the neighbourhood for the purpose of receiving communications from Williams. Bishop came, and they took the boy home to Nova Scotia Gardens, giving him some soup and potatoes by the way. When they got him there, they set him to play with Bishop's children until near dusk, when they gave him some rum and he became stupefied. Bishop and Williams then took him into the garden, and on the way threw him down, and, pushing his head into the water barrel sunk into the ground, held him until he was suffocated. They then conveyed the body back to the house, kept it snug until the next day, when May was applied to, to assist in disposing of it. 'May had nothing to do with the murder of that boy.'"

The *Observer,* however, reported that during the night, Williams had revealed to his warder that it was Bishop who had picked up the drover's boy in the pigpens, had promised him work, and had taken him to the Fortune of War to meet Williams and to drink some beer; this boy had been the first victim, according to Williams in the *Observer,* and Cunningham of Kent Street had been the second boy to die. Williams also admitted, here, to attempting to burke two aged workhouse paupers whom he and Bishop had tempted back to Nova Scotia Gardens with promises of drink but who did not succumb fully to the laudanum. Bishop reportedly said to Williams that "it was no go—they were old drinkers and were not to be so easily done. . . . We shall be grabbed for poisoning them."

The *Atlas* newspaper claimed that on another occasion, Theodore Williams had been told by both Bishop and Williams that they had killed three people—the Lincolnshire drover boy, Fanny Pigburn, and, quite a while before, *an* Italian boy—and that all the clothes found in the garden and privy had indeed belonged to the three victims. In this version, more violence was used in the killings, with the victims having their mouths held shut as they were marched to the well. The *Morning Advertiser* stated that both men vehemently denied that any Italian boy had ever been killed.

In the *Sun,* an evening newspaper, it was claimed that "Bishop several times endeavoured to inveigle to his residence the sister of the young woman who was some time ago missed from the neighbourhood of Bethnal Green; and whose scalp and hair, it is believed, were those found in the privy, but fortunately the young woman resisted his importunity. He also prevailed on a young woman to leave her place, under a promise to take her into keeping; but she felt compunctious, and declined his overtures just in sufficient time to save her life."[7] Yet the ownership of the scalp and hair had never been established.

The papers vied with one another to provide motivations for the murderers. The *Times* of Tuesday, 6 December, stated that Williams had told his warder that he had never, until his marriage, been a resurrection man and had not even known that this was how Bishop made his living. Rhoda had told him on his wedding night and asked him to promise not to join the "snatchers." But when Williams had had his glassmaking apparatus seized, Bishop had asked his neighbor to become a partner, and Williams had agreed. However (Williams is said to have told the warder), after just three graveyard forays, Williams had found it a difficult and dangerous job, so, thinking of the Edinburgh Horrors, he had proposed murder.

Williams was highly likely to have been aware of how his neighbor made a living before his wedding night of 26 September; in any case, Customs and Excise had made their raid on 6 August—seven weeks before Rhoda supposedly told Williams of Bishop's profession. If this account of a conversation between Williams and his warder has been reported accurately, the most probable explanation for its contents is that Williams was attempting to depict Rhoda as a voice of innocence and reason, to try to save her from public hatred. By getting this version of events into the newspapers, Williams could die knowing that he had at least attempted to redeem Rhoda in the eyes of her fellow citizens.

The *Times* report continues with Williams telling the warder that the day after the murder of "the woman Pigburn," he and Bishop had tried to burke a man whom they had lured to Nova Scotia Gardens. The laudanum failed, and the man was not completely unconscious, just dozing, and (in the manner of Lady Macbeth) Bishop froze as he was poised to attack because the sleeping man so resembled his father; the next morning, the man awoke and let himself out of No. 3. On the following Tuesday (presumably 11 October), claimed Williams, the laudanum failed again, and this intended victim also left the cottage none the wiser. These may or may not have been the two old workhouse paupers mentioned by Williams to his warder.

The *Globe and Traveller* and the *Morning Advertiser* added into their reports the story of Cotton's interruption of the confessions, stating that it had happened just as Bishop was talking about a fourth murder, of a black vagrant, and appeared to be implicating other people in this crime. The *Globe and Traveller* and the *Observer* had put a name to the Lincolnshire drover's boy—White—and reported a claim by Thomas Williams that William Woodcock could not possibly have heard anything in the early hours of Friday, 4 November, since the killers had taken their shoes off; and besides, by that time the drover's boy was "as dead as a log." The *Globe and Traveller* also included the information that Cunningham of Kent Street used to help out around Smithfield and had put up a fight on the night of his killing, surprising Bishop and Williams with his strength. The former had uttered "a horrible oath" as he held the boy's legs upright in the well while Williams pushed his head below the surface of the water, waiting until he finally stopped struggling.

The *Sun* further claimed, "Among the murders which they have confessed to, we understand, is one of a little child, whom they found in a destitute condition in the street and covered with filth and vermin. This poor child they inveigled to Bishop's house and destroyed in a similar manner to that of the other unfortunate victims." Was this an inaccurate description of White or Cunningham (hardly "little" children)? Or was this the "large small" bought from Bishop by the anatomical school "near Golden Square" in the first week of November? Or was this the fate of Fanny Pigburn's child, who had been sitting on her lap when Bishop and Williams found Fanny crying on a doorstep in Church Street, Shoreditch, but who disappears from the story soon afterward?

Many of the unofficial accounts of confessions contain internal evidence that they are not accurate eyewitness reports; in some instances, words are quite plainly being put into the killers' mouths. The "I, John Bishop" confession, which runs to twenty-five hundred words, is a lucid, linear tale, told in plain but vivid language. Certain touches give it a compelling, phantasmagoric feel; all too real, mundane phenomena interweave with the nightmarish narrative of relentless, pitiless slaughter. It's a tale of coffee stalls, child-sized chairs, gin, privies, pouring rain, mean-minded landlords, piles of dirty clothes. There are points at which a bizarre tenderness pokes its way into the act of killing: "I then took him in my arms, and let him slide from them headlong into the well"; "She . . . went off to sleep in about ten minutes. She was falling back; I caught her to save her fall"; "We gave him some warm beer, sweetened with sugar. . . . He . . . fell asleep in a little chair belonging to one of my children." The insistent voice of Bishop, the cadence of his unreflective, phlegmatic outlook, is strikingly different from the add-on accounts in the newspapers, where a melodramatic note often appears. So, in the *Globe and Traveller* we have Bishop saying to Rev. Theodore Williams: "Surely, sir, there is a hope of mercy for a repentant sinner. Was not the thief on the cross pardoned?"[8] And we learn that "after having partaken of the Sacrament, Thomas Williams complained of thirst, and said his mouth was so parched that he was quite sure it was a foretaste of hell." The version of this incident that appears in the *Sun* is even more florid: "'I thirst, I thirst—I feel the burning drought of hell in my breast and I know it is ready for me.'"[9] The *Weekly Dispatch* of 11 December reported that on the morning of the execution, when the sacrament of the Lord's Supper was offered to them, Bishop said derisively that he had no understanding of it, but Thomas Williams is reported as clamoring to be taught to understand it and asking Whitworth Russell to explain the meaning of the ritual to him. And Cotton would write in his journal that Thomas Williams cried out to him that he hoped God "would hear his prayers and forgive him, notwithstanding he had been one of the greatest sinners in his time."[10]

There are clearly other hands writing their way into these final scenes. Bishop was an intelligent man; Williams's attainments are harder to discern. Both were literate, at least. Bishop's straightforward, fluent account and the fragments of his speech that have survived indicate some level of education. He may well have brought up the subject of the thief on the cross, and Williams may have mentioned the fires of hell; but the phrasing here is altogether too purple. Similarly, the letter addressed to Dr. Whitworth Russell by Thomas Williams on his final night sounds like the gist of an honestly felt response onto which has been grafted a sermon: "If you will be kind enough to let my brother prisoners know the awful death which I shall have suffered when you read this, it will, *through your expostulations, prevent them from increasing their crimes when they may be liberated;* and tell them bad company and drinking and blasphemy *is the foundation of all evil. Give my brotherly love to them, and tell them never to deviate from the paths of religion, and have a firm belief in the blessed Saviour.* Give my love to John Edwards, John Justin and John Dingle, and receive the prayers of the unfortunate and guilty Thomas Head."

....

On 10 December the most controversial of the discrepancies came to light. In that day's edition of the *Times,* a letter was published from Sir John Sewell, a magistrate at Marylebone police office. Sewell claimed that "one of his brother magistrates" had told him of a confession made by Bishop on the Sunday "which comprehended a catalogue of about 60 murders" until Dr. Cotton had intervened to put a stop to it. Now, the interruption of the conversation between Bishop and Rev. Theodore Williams in the chamber of Brown the turnkey had happened on the Saturday morning—all parties agreed to that. So had Sewell got his dates wrong, or had Cotton made other interruptions? And who had told Sewell in any case?

Sewell's letter provoked a stern response from undersheriff Thomas Wood, friend and supporter of Cotton and cotranscriber of the official confessions: "I have in vain endeavoured to ascertain from Sir John Sewell what authority he had for his assertions, and am favoured with no other answer than that of an after-dinner conversation with some magistrate, whose name he withholds. From the inquiries made in other quarters, as well as from the circumstances of having been with the prisoners, on the Sunday alluded to, from 10 o'clock in the morning till about 4 o'clock in the afternoon, I believe the assertions contained in Sir John Sewell's letter to be totally destitute of foundation. The confession was taken in detail from the prisoners, written down as they gave it, and published in the newspapers from the original documents, signed by them and authenticated by my colleague and myself, and I do not believe that during their imprisonment they ever gave a catalogue of 60 murders or of any other number committed by them than those contained in the statement before the public. I am also bound in justice to the Rev, the Ordinary, whom I attended on some of his visits to the culprits, to say, that so far from his having interfered to prevent or even to check a confession, he used every means in his power to induce them to make a full statement of their crimes, with an earnestness befitting his sacred office."[11]

Sewell replied to Wood in a private letter of 13 December, refusing to name his source but saying that he heard the "sixty" story at a magistrates' dinner on 8 December from "a Middlesex justice of the peace" and that the allegation was heard by at least four other magistrates present. In January 1832, during an official inquiry held into Cotton's conduct, the Reverend Theodore Williams, who was also a Middlesex justice of the peace, owned up to being Sewell's source. The vicar of Hendon claimed, however, that what he had said to Sewell at the magistrates' dinner was "six," not "sixty."[12] Six "cases" is how Williams put it, which is not six murders and could include the two failed druggings along with the actual killings of Fanny Pigburn, the black vagrant, Cunningham of Kent Street, and White the drover's boy/Carlo Ferrari. Or it could have meant the killings of Pigburn, Cunningham, White, the black vagrant, the small verminous child, and an Italian boy.

Whatever the case, the damage had been done by Sewell's letter and the ensuing furor: the notion that Bishop had been a mass burker easily gained a foothold in the popular imagination and was probably accepted as fact within poor communities, which were the most vulnerable to burkers. It was certainly accepted in the House of Lords. As late as 28 June 1832, the earl of Minto, speaking to promote the Second Anatomy Bill, would still be hammering home the notion that Bishop was a mass killer, claiming that he had been on the point of augmenting his official confession "when he was interrupted in his recital."[13] Radical journalist and reformer William Cobbett, meanwhile, made use of the higher estimate to attack surgeons (he called them the "cutters-up") and to show that the poor were merely considered fodder for their scalpels, much as they were fodder for the capitalist and the industrialist. Cobbett claimed that sixty was likely a conservative estimate and that the true total of poor London citizens killed had been "probably hundreds."[14]

No matter how many people really had been slaughtered at Nova Scotia Gardens, no peace of mind was obtainable. To make matters worse, many of the newspapers published a claim allegedly made by Bishop in Newgate that most London resurrectionists committed murder when graveyard or bone-house security tightened or when demand simply exceeded supply. A full-blown media panic had arrived.

A private letter from James Corder, vestry clerk of St. Paul's,

Covent Garden, to Home Secretary Lord Melbourne stated that the crimes "engage to a considerable degree the public mind and I have reason to believe from the many communications which Mr Thomas and myself daily receive on the subject that the public do look for some answer to, or notice of, the Confessions, which have appeared in all the public journals."[15] The alarm and confusion were not helped by the floundering of the authorities on the identity of the dead child delivered to King's College. Richard Partridge, James Corder, and Superintendent Thomas would vainly attempt to prove that the body had been Carlo Ferrari's. First off the mark was Richard Partridge, who wrote to the *Times* on Sunday, 4 December (probably having read that morning's "confessions"):

> I received an anonymous note yesterday evening which contained some pertinent queries respecting the identity of Carlo Ferrari and the body taken to King's College by Bishop and his companions. They were to the following effect: 1. Was Paragalli or Augustus Brin [*sic*] asked whether the ears of Carlo Ferrari were bored [pierced], and if so, what was their reply? 2. Were the ears bored of the body which was offered for sale at the King's College? In reply to these inquiries, I beg to state that when the body was opened at the police station in Covent Garden, I particularly remarked that the ears were not bored. The circumstance struck me at the time as worthy of notice, and as Paragalli, who had recognised the body as that of an Italian boy, was standing at the other end of the room, in a situation where he could not see the head of the corpse, I asked him whether the boy he had known wore ear-rings—he replied, "No." I next inquired if his ears were bored, to which he replied in the negative.
>
> This morning I have put the questions separately to Brin and to Mrs Paragalli and their answers agree with those of Paragalli himself. Moreover, their description of the colour of Carlo Ferrari's eyes and hair and of his general complexion corresponds in every particular with those of the body which was examined at the police station.
>
> I regret that it did not occur to my mind at the Old Bailey

to mention this fact, touching the ears, and I shall, therefore, feel much obliged if you will insert this statement of it now in the columns of the *Times*.

"A Lincolnshire boy! Where are his friends or relations?" an indignant James Corder wrote in the *Times* on 16 December. "It is now nearly six weeks since the murder, and no inquiries are made for him. On the contrary, where is Charles Ferrier? Why does he not appear?" The Paragallis and Andrew Colla had gone as a deputation to Bow Street on 8 December to refute before the magistrates Bishop and Williams's claim that the body had not been Carlo's, and Corder had promised them that he would put the record straight in the newspapers. As he pointed out, the doubt about the victim's identity reflected badly on his parish and on the prosecution it had mounted. Corder's letter stated that "several witnesses of unimpeachable character and integrity" had sworn that the body had been Carlo, having seen the corpse within three days of death. Corder claimed that one of them, Andrew Colla, had in fact made the cage in which Carlo carried about his white mice. Two of the Italians had seen him alive and well in the week of his death, and one had accurately described the trousers worn by the deceased without having seen the pair dug up in Bishop's garden. In addition to this, wrote Corder, "we have it in evidence that an Italian boy with a cage and white mice was seen close to Bishop's house on the day of the murder, wearing a cap similar to the one found on the premises, and which Bishop endeavoured in vain to account for. We then find the white mice and cage at Bishop's house, in the possession of his children on Friday the 4th instant, the day after the murder, as proved by the very young witness, but who gave his evidence with all the simplicity characteristic of truth. And lastly, we find the clothes of the deceased in Bishop's garden; the lower buttons being cut off the jacket apparently to admit the revolution of his cage; the tapes also stitched to the lower part of the same garment for the passage of the strap or riband by which the cage was confined to his body. And against this body of evidence, what is set up? The unsupported assertion of the wretched culprits, who to the latest hour of existence evinced no penitent or religious feeling. Were there any appearances to indicate that the deceased was a Lincolnshire drover boy? None; his hands were smooth and soft, and no horny substance upon them as though he had been used to manual labour."

As with Partridge, Corder here brings up matters that never came up during the coroner's inquest, or the trial, or the weeks between. It is possible that these matters did arise, but it seems highly unlikely that they would so completely have escaped the attention of all the newspaper reporters and the official Old Bailey account. So this is the first we have heard of Carlo's apparently specially adapted clothing— and that the jacket was damaged in this particular way; it's the first time anyone has mentioned the skin quality of the corpse (apart from the question of Carlo's warts, never resolved); and Colla had never before been referred to as the maker of the boy's cage, nor was it ever reported that Colla had seen the body. There had never been any accurate description given of the boy's clothing until *after* the garments were unearthed in Bishop's garden, at which point many people began to recall with great clarity how the Italian boy had been dressed. And no reports indicate that Colla had described the boy's clothing before the items were placed in front of him in the Old Bailey courtroom. Similarly, no cap was mentioned until one was found at No. 3; then, suddenly, many people could recall it in detail. Colla had told Minshull and Corder at Bow Street that Carlo Ferrier had always had a smiling face—he always looked as though he were about to burst into laughter—and the corpse had looked serene and happy, said Colla. Even Minshull himself, the *Sun* reported on 9 December, could now fondly remember many a time seeing a smiling Italian boy around Oxford Street; the magistrate had always wanted to give him a few halfpence but never did, since he worried about encouraging vagrancy, he said. Why had Minshull never mentioned this before?

But the oddest matter of all was that the Italian witnesses, who had known the boy "intimately" (Corder's word), did not come up with a likely name for him until days after the arrests. No Italian of the many who had viewed the body had been able to put a name, or even a nickname, to the boy. In his letter, James Corder was either forgetting or willfully confusing the sequence of events in the case.

Corder also challenged Bishop's statement on the cause of death. Where the killer claimed that the victims had been drowned, Corder noted peevishly that "it is for professional and other scientific men to judge whether the appearances described are compatible with the supposition of death having been produced by drowning, hanging, strangulation or any other mode of suffocation." Corder had assembled from Partridge and George Beaman lengthy reiterations, printed in full by the *Times,* of their findings at the coroner's inquest and again at the trial. But new matters had crept into these postmortem reports, with Partridge claiming to have noted down "general appearance that of a foreigner" and "palms of the hands quite soft."

The icing on Corder's cake came with the verdict of Frederick Tyrrell, lecturer in physiology at St. Thomas's, to whom Corder had sent these post-postmortem reports: "It is my opinion," wrote Tyrrell, "that the death of the boy could not have been caused by any mode of suffocation, as drowning, smothering, &c. I have no doubt that injury to the upper part of the spine, which created the effusion of blood into the spinal canal, was the immediate cause of death." But Bishop and Williams had both stated that the injury to the back of the neck had happened when they had put the body into the trunk in the wash house and that this always happened when a corpse was "doubled up while it is warm."[16] As professional murderers, they had been in a position to observe phenomena the surgeons never saw. Indeed, on Christmas Eve 1831, an article by John Gordon Smith, a professor of medical jurisprudence, appeared in the *Lancet* attacking the official postmortem findings and backing up Bishop and Williams's claim that the injury to the back of the boy's neck had happened when the still-warm corpse was doubled up and placed in the trunk. Smith also found Beaman's, Mayo's, and Partridge's claim that all four chambers of the boy's heart had been "empty," indicating a sudden death, "inconceivable. . . . I am fearless in calling upon every medical jurist in the world to corroborate the assertion that emptiness—even total emptiness of the heart—is a sign of a lingering death from disease, rather than indicative of sudden death from violence in the healthy state."

The editorial writers quashed their own sense of unease about the mystery of the dead boy by plumping heavily and clumsily in favor of the view that Bishop and Williams had lied in their official confessions. Their reasoning was that, as criminals, the two had

gone to their graves attempting to unsettle society, trying to undermine trust in lawyers, policemen, doctors, vicars. Such rogues knew
no other way of behaving. But that explanation posited Bishop and
Williams as men with an organized political purpose rather than as
psychopathic opportunists with drinking problems and uncertain
employment prospects.

The *Times*'s editorial of 16 December 1831 stated that "the last
words with which Bishop and Williams went out of the world were
false. There has nothing ever been heard of any Lincolnshire boy
missing—it is most likely none such was murdered; but at all events
it is certain, beyond doubt, that the murder for which the wretches
suffered was that charged upon them at the trial, namely, the murder
of the poor Italian boy."

The *Globe and Traveller* claimed Bishop and Williams had merely
been seeking a reprieve on the grounds of a legal quibble over the
identity of the dead child. That was the sort of thing criminals did all
the time, the newspaper said.[17] However, the wording of the indictment had made provision for them to be found guilty and hanged for
the killing of Boy Unknown. Bishop and Williams had nothing to gain
for themselves by lying in their official confessions about the identity
of the people they killed.

And in any case, the *Globe and Traveller* was overlooking a short
report that had already appeared in its own pages: on 3 December the
newspaper had reported that Carlo Ferrari was alive, residing in "a
distant part of England."

Time has never revealed the extent of the killings at Nova Scotia
Gardens or the identity of the dead boy delivered to King's College.
The story was a puzzle of sometimes garbled, often contradictory
statements. But whoever really had been drowned in the well, this
was the Italian Boy murder, an easy-to-recount tale, full of pathos,
which sought a strange kind of comfort from giving a name and per-
sona to its victim. The official version is that Carlo Ferrari, the Italian
Boy, was killed by Bishop and Williams on Thursday, 3 November
1831, and that it was eventually discovered that at least two more
destitute people, another boy and Fanny Pigburn, had also died at

their hands. Within weeks of the Old Bailey trial, the series of killings had been contracted into one, with a stage version, *The Italian Boy,* playing at the Shakespeare, an unlicensed theater in Curtain Road, just behind Shoreditch High Street.

The constituent fragments of the London Burkers' story can be arranged and rearranged to create a variety of plausible narratives, but some factors not explored at the time (not, at least, by anyone capable of committing them to print) can help suggest the more likely solutions to the puzzle.

One such factor is "blood money." In 1826, Robert Peel, then home secretary, attempted to modernize the traditional "blood money" common-informer system by giving the courts the power to remunerate, at their own discretion, those who had "been active in the apprehension of certain offenders," including murderers. These "conviction moneys" were paid by the prosecutor, who in turn claimed the money from the Treasury. The archives of the vestry of St. Paul's, Covent Garden, detail the sums that changed hands in the Bishop and Williams case. First off the mark was dentist Thomas Mills, who was impatient for his share of the conviction money. James Corder wrote to him on 5 December: "I beg to acquaint you that none of the witnesses in the late prosecution have yet been paid, nor was it thought so well to take any steps towards obtaining some allowance from the county for that purpose until after the day on which the solemn sentence of the law was carried into effect. I will mention your request relative to the teeth to Mr Thomas."[18] (Mills was also seeking the return of the set of teeth sold to him by May. The dentist did indeed get the grinders back, and they went on display in his shop window, with a label attached, reading "The teeth of Carlo Ferrier—the murdered Italian Boy.")[19] For his part, Joseph Paragalli wrote directly to the Home Office to ask for his share of the reward money on 6 January and was directed to apply instead to the solicitor to the Treasury.[20]

Although the original £200 reward offered by the home secretary went unpaid, since no individual was able to deliver the crucial proof of guilt, the forty-two witnesses for the prosecution were paid £45 12s and 6d, "and they have severally received at the Treasurer's Office the amounts respectively awarded them by the order of the court," wrote Corder to the Home Office on 9 February 1832, though the account book does not specify how much money individual witnesses received. "The sundry incidental expenses incurred in the course of the prosecution were innumerable—an exact account of which it was impossible to keep," continued Corder. "These expenses, many of which were incurred in the course of inquiries made in the neighbourhood of the murder with a view to compleat and duftail the evidence, could only have been avoided by risking the attainment of Justice in the case. . . . There was no moral doubt of the guilt of the parties charged and the great object to be accomplished was to establish that guilt by legal evidence—and that evidence too of a circumstantial nature. Under these circumstances, more than ordinary exertion was necessary to be made—no fair or allowable exertion towards preventing a failure of justice was unmade—and I think it will not be said that one shilling in the enclosed account was improperly incurred."[21] Could sums have been offered to the Kings, Rebecca Baylis, and John Randall to change by a day, or by a week, or by a month, their sighting of an Italian boy close by Bishop's cottage? The frustration of knowing that the right killers were in custody, but for a killing with an unidentified victim and no timetable, could have led to bribery. S. M. Phillips at the Home Office wrote to Corder on 20 February to say that the home secretary and G. Maule, treasury solicitor, had approved the accounts and the reimbursement to St. Paul's, which totaled £112 10s (a sum that, the ledger states, included payments to witnesses). Melbourne considered the payments "fair and reasonable." Did that sum include even more money paid to witnesses, on top of the £45 12s and 6d already, separately, specified for that purpose? The accounts do not provide clarification, but it is possible a great deal of money (for working people) was changing hands.

Some of the witnesses may have had something more than simply cash to gain from cooperating with the police and magistrates. While Joseph and Mary Paragalli may not have had any direct involvement in child trafficking, it is clear that they mixed with padroni, socializing with Elliott, at whose house they claimed to have seen Carlo Ferrari bound over to his new padrone. As it was, the Paragallis were now firmly in favor with Superintendent Thomas—very handy for a family that made its living from street activities that were on the cusp of legality under the Vagrancy Act. Their prevarication about supplying Carlo's name and Joseph's claim that he knew of no other Italian boys who made their living by exhibiting animals in the street are both highly suspect.

Payment and favors aside, a solution to the enigma of the official confessions may be found by entertaining the notion that a monster can be capable of kindness, loyalty, and love—that a killer's final act could be altruistic. Commentators were wrong to assume that Bishop and Williams had anything to gain for themselves by misleading the authorities after their conviction; no privy council in the world would have mitigated their death sentences, even if they were to be hanged for the wrong killing. And, as mentioned before, these were not the sort of men to care about stirring up working-class distrust of policemen, magistrates, courts, and the government. Rather, it seems that what John Bishop was doing in his confession was adapting an essentially true story in order to present a strong impression that his wife and family had no knowledge of the murders committed within their small home. Bishop well knew that anyone tainted by association with the resurrection trade—let alone burking—could be subject to physical attack. So Sarah, Rhoda, and his children simply disappear from the narrative, forced off stage by often highly artificial means. Bishop states that having walked all the way from Smithfield on the night of Thursday, 3 November, Bishop and Williams told the boy to hide in the privy in the garden, since Sarah and Rhoda had not yet gone to bed: "Williams went in and told them to go to bed, and I stayed in the garden. Williams came out directly, and we both walked out of the garden a little way to give time for the family getting to bed . . . and listened outside at the window to ascertain whether the family were gone to bed." The silence of the killing is also emphasized by Bishop ("We found him asleep as we had left him. We took him directly, asleep and insensible, into the garden"), as is the hiding of the corpse ("We immediately doubled the body up, and put it into a box, which we corded, so that nobody might open it to see what was in it").

With the killing of Fanny Pigburn, again "we found the family abed." "This was before our families were up," Bishop says of her departure the next morning, suggesting the unlikely scenario that he got up at six to hustle her out of the house before the family awoke and discovered her asleep on the pile of dirty clothes in the parlor of No. 3 (when all along she could have slept in the empty No. 2).

The message from Bishop is clear: the wives and family saw and heard nothing. They had nothing to atone for.

Williams's official confession is merely a short, uninformative corroboration of Bishop's statement. The only other time Williams expressed himself at any length was in the story given to Wontner and Cotton on Saturday night in his cell and reprinted in the *Atlas* and the *Times*. Here, Williams appears to be telling the same story as Bishop about the events of Thursday, 3 November—the luring of a fourteen- or fifteen-year-old boy from Smithfield. But there is one crucial deviation from the script: "They took the boy home to Nova Scotia Gardens, giving him some soup and potatoes by the way. When they got him there, they set him to play with Bishop's children until near dusk." (Potatoes, along with rum, were found in the boy's stomach at the postmortem.) Bishop, though, claimed that they had arrived home with this boy "at about eleven o'clock" at night; similarly, Fanny and Cunningham were described as late-night/early-hours killings.

A possible timeline for Williams's narrative could be: the killers start their workday in Smithfield at around 10 A.M.; they lure the boy and set him on his journey east at around noon, reaching Nova Scotia Gardens at around one to two o'clock in the afternoon; the boy and Bishop's children play together until around five (dusk set in at around a quarter past five). The boy would have been further put off his guard by this apparently friendly inclusion in the family, and after bedtime, the killing could have happened just as Bishop described it.

Margaret King and her children variously placed their Italian boy at Nova Scotia Gardens between ten o'clock in the morning and one o'clock in the afternoon of Thursday the third; Rebecca Baylis saw him a quarter of an hour before midday, then again slightly after noon; laborer John Randall, however, saw the boy "between nine and ten o'clock" in the morning. It is possible, though very unlikely, that

Bishop and Williams got up, walked to Smithfield, executed the abduction, and walked back to Shoreditch (stopping on the way to eat) before ten in the morning. If these sightings of an Italian boy by the neighbors were truthful and accurate, the more likely explanation is that there was indeed an itinerant Italian beggar doing the rounds of Nova Scotia Gardens/Crabtree Row over a three- to four-hour period on Thursday, 3 November, but that this was not the boy lured from Smithfield. Margaret King told the magistrates that "she had often seen the same boy in the environs of Nova Scotia Gardens." Her son John said: "He used to carry a doll with two heads in a glass case. I saw him about a month ago. He looked like the same boy." Which raises the possibility that the neighbors had become confused about the date on which they saw the beggar boy. Or they could have been asked to become confused.

Alternatively, the neighbors' tales could all have been true—and Bishop's confession a complete fabrication. Perhaps there was no trip to Smithfield on Thursday the third; perhaps an Italian boy, Carlo Ferrari, had lingered too long near the Gardens, had been invited in by Bishop and Williams—with the wives and children present in or around the cottage—and been murdered late that night, just as the prosecution claimed. And Bishop had simply been distancing his family from the crime by claiming that the inveigling had happened in Smithfield. Interestingly, the only other discrepancy between Bishop's official confession and Williams's confession to Wontner and Cotton is the order of the Smithfield/Old Bailey pubs visited. According to Bishop, Williams picked the boy up in the Bell (an old coaching tavern) and brought him to the King of Denmark (the Old Bailey watering house, opposite Newgate); Bishop, meanwhile, was drinking in the Fortune of War, to where Williams came to collect Bishop and bring him to meet the boy, whom he had left standing outside the King of Denmark. But Williams presents a different sequence of pub visits, which is perhaps understandable if this abduction was one of two, or even one of many, and is even more understandable if the killers had been drinking all day. Williams says he "enticed" the boy from his cattle at Smithfield, took him to the Fortune of War, and sent for Bishop, who was waiting at another pub—presumably the King of

Denmark. This confusion may be of little note, or it could indicate that the two men had failed to agree on the minor details in a jointly narrated fallacious story.

Perhaps their tale was intended not only to protect their families but also to preserve resurrection honor. Bishop and Williams never chose to turn king's evidence and betray each other; nor did they implicate anyone else. The figures who hover in the background of this story (the stranger who accompanied Bishop and May to buy secondhand clothing in Field Lane on 4 November; the person who waved goodbye from the gallery of the Old Bailey; the six men on James May's list of potential killers) may have had their necks saved by Bishop and Williams twisting the narrative of their crimes.

Epilogue

On Sunday, 18 December 1831, a man and a woman stood sobbing at the dockside in Woolwich. The estranged wife of James May had come, with their young daughter, to say goodbye—May was about to board the hulk *Justitia,* bound for Botany Bay, where he was to spend the rest of his life. But May never made it to Australia. Despite being described as "healthy" by the compiler of the hulk registers, he died aboard the prison hospital ship *Grampus,* moored off Greenwich, to which he was transferred from the *Justitia* on 20 January 1832 when his health on the outbound ship declined dramatically.[1] No cause of death was given, but his fit at Newgate on hearing of his reprieve may well have been a contributing factor. The newspapers claimed that he had been roughly treated by other inmates on the *Justitia,* who were outraged at having to share a ship with a snatcher.

In the same week as the Mays' farewell, Michael Shields turned up at Covent Garden market at ten o'clock one morning, hoping that one of the salesmen who had formerly employed him as a porter would hire him again. The salesman loudly, indignantly refused to have anything to do with Shields. A crowd gathered and began to jostle Shields, pushing him from one to another, chanting, "I don't want him, I won't have him." Shields made a run for it, grabbing a wrench and brandishing it at those who came close. He fled up Bow Street, screaming for the police officers to help him, as the pursuing crowd yelled, "That's Shields the Burker" and "There he goes, knock his brains out." The officers hauled him into the police office and used their truncheons on any of the crowd who tried to reach the front door. "Turn him out!" they screamed. "Let us have him—we'll dispose of him." Inside, the officers who had known Shields could scarcely recognize him: he had lost so much weight he looked like an animated skeleton. Five hours later, believing it was safe, officers smuggled Shields out of the office, disguised in a voluminous great coat; they took him across the road to the Grapes public house and stayed with him until darkness fell, when they felt it was all right for him to leave the pub alone. Within yards he was spotted and a mob assembled; he ran down into the Strand, then into a small courtyard on the north side, opposite King's College, and into the warren of alleys beyond, where we lose sight of him for good.

On the evening of Saturday, 17 December, Andrew Colla was walking home on Great Saffron Hill when three men surrounded him. One was masked, but Colla nevertheless recognized him as the

The Grampus hospital hulk, moored off Greenwich

person to whom Thomas Williams had waved goodbye at the Old Bai-
ley. Though Colla did not know it, all three men had been on James
May's list of resurrectionists capable of burking: John Shearing, the
masked man; his brother Thomas; and Robert Tighe/Tye, also called
James Cattle/Kettle, lover of Bridget Culkin. Just two weeks earlier,
Tighe had been released from custody on suspicion of having been
Culkin's accomplice in the supposed burking of five-year-old Margaret Duffey in Golden Lane. "This is the bloody bastard!" shouted
John Shearing. "Let's serve him out!" And all three set upon Colla,
kicking him to the ground. Passersby rushed to help, and, outnum-
bered, the Shearings and Tighe fled. But when a police officer
arrived, he refused to go after them, even though some in the crowd
knew that the Shearings lived in nearby Rosoman Street; nor would
the officer raise the alarm, claiming that as he himself had not witnessed the assault, there was nothing he could do to help.

A month later, John Shearing, "a very powerful-looking young
man," according to the *Morning Advertiser,* was arrested and taken
before the magistrates at Bow Street, accused of sending a threatening letter to Colla. Shearing admitted to the JPs, "I deal in the stiff
line, but I'm no Burker," and denied having written the note, which
read, "You bloody murdering bugger, do you expect you'll be suffered
to live, after the evidence you gave at the Old Bailey? No, you bloody
thief, you and Hill shall share the fate of those you have assisted in
sending to the other world. Prepare yourself, for in a very short time
you will be a dead one." A former associate of Shearing's, a snatcher
called Stringall, claimed that the note was in Shearing's handwriting.
Shearing was remanded.

On Boxing Day, a letter was received, by two-penny post, by
William Hill, dissecting-room porter at King's College. It read: "You
bloody murdering bugger, you think you are all right to get tip, but
only loke out, for you will have your bloody guts out before many days
his over, for blow my eyes if there shan't be another tucked up for you,
you gallus life-selling warmint. You think you've done the trick up,
master Billy, but I will put a spoke in your weal, damn my eyes if I
don't, you noing kovy, Yours affectionately, The Gost of Bishop and
Williams."

Doubtless another Shearing effort.

Hill took the letter to George Rowland Minshull, telling the magistrate that Mrs. Hill was sick with worry about the family's safety and
asking if he could be licensed to carry a small pistol for protection.
Best not, said Minshull, who told Hill that the threats were probably
nothing to worry about—Superintendent Thomas and he himself
would see that no harm came to Hill.

Within a year, Hill was sacked by King's College, without character references. The rumor reported (or was it started?) by the *Lancet*
was that the college anatomy department's entire supply of corpses
had ceased because the London resurrectionists refused to do business with the porter who had alerted the authorities to Bishop and
Williams's boy cadaver. The point that the *Lancet* writer was making
was that, despite the passing of the Anatomy Act in the summer of
1832, the resurrection trade continued to thrive, since the machinery
of the act had yet to bring about a large enough supply of friendless,
unclaimed paupers, and arguments about unfair distribution between
the medical schools rumbled on, with resurrectionists helping to
make up the corpse shortfalls at many schools. Thus it was stated in
the *Lancet* of 17 November 1832 that "practices which would disgrace a nation of cannibals" remained common in the capital a year
after the Italian Boy case. (In fact, snatching was being referred to in
official documents as late as 1838; in that year the Poor Law commissioners reported that two resurrectionists had died from fever caught
from a putrid corpse disinterred in a Somers Town graveyard.)[2] An
anonymous letter in the following week's *Lancet* contradicted the earlier issue, claiming that King's had used "secret and undue" influence
to obtain a higher number of workhouse corpses than other London
medical schools. According to the correspondent, King's now had
access to so many bodies it was burying them without bothering to
dissect them first. Another rumor was that King's was using its fine
portland stone water gates to dispose of its unwanted corpses and
body parts by flushing them into the Thames.

Late one night in December, dentist Thomas Mills was awoken by
someone hammering at his door. When he looked from his window, a
man below claimed to have a bad toothache—would Mills treat him?

Despite the darkness, Mills could make out two other men lurking behind the first and saw that all three were in smock frocks and carried bludgeons. Mills refused to open his shop, and the three walked off, shouting threats of future violence.

Before Christmas, Sarah Bishop took lodgings in Paradise Row, Battle Bridge, and Rhoda in nearby Edmund Street. Three miles west of Bethnal Green and a mile and a half northeast of Covent Garden, Paradise Row was mocked at the time for being distinctly unheavenly: lying behind a smallpox hospital, it was a half-built, half-tumbledown, undrained, unlit street whose piles of manure (human, horse, donkey, and dog) left it reeking and dangerous to health. But the living condition that most disturbed the residents was the presence among them of the kin of burkers. Newspaper reports stated that local women were refusing to let their children play outside so long as Sarah and Rhoda were known to be residing in the area.

Nothing more appears in the newspapers about Bishop's and Williams's widows and children, though four young Bishops—Thomas William, twelve, Frederick Henry, ten (actually twelve), Thomas, seven, and Emma, two—were admitted together to the Shoreditch workhouse on 5 March 1832, staying for three weeks. These seem likely to be the killer's children, along with one older boy. Perhaps Thomas William was a cousin, since, when the three boys—without Emma—turned up at the workhouse again two and a half years later for a one-night stay, they were discharged to Thomas William's father, described in the workhouse register as living in Norwood, south London. Frederick and Thomas Bishop were admitted once again, for two days, in April 1835.[3] After that, the children's whereabouts and fates—how they felt about their parentage, whether they were shunned or were shown sympathy—are unknown.

Joseph Sadler Thomas was never able to capitalize on the recognition he gained from his role in the Bishop and Williams investigation. Despite the eulogies that appeared in all the newspapers praising the

New Police as a body, and Thomas as an individual officer, for securing the conviction of the London Burkers, his enemies never ceased
to pillory him, and he was singled out for criticism for "high-
handedness" during the Coldbath Fields Riot of 13 May 1833. This
meeting of three hundred members of the National Union of the
Working Class and their supporters took place on a large stretch of
open ground just behind Coldbath Fields Prison and was broken up
by an equal number of badly organized and belligerent Metropolitan
Police officers, who managed to turn a good-humored gathering into a
general brawl, with one fatality—a police officer's.

But it was a more petty row that sealed Thomas's fate. Just after
the Coldbath Fields Riot, he was accused of victimizing a publican
called Williams who had applied for a pub license in Seven Dials,
Covent Garden. Thomas opposed the license, saying that there were
already thirty pubs within 150 yards of Williams's proposed venue, and
Thomas was one of fifty local residents who signed a petition to limit
the number of pubs in the area. Two magistrates (one of whom, Rotch,
loathed the New Police, and Thomas in particular) complained to the
Home Office about Thomas's antipathy to Williams's license application, and at the justices' behest, Thomas was suspended from the Metropolitan Police for five weeks until the commissioners themselves
intervened and apologized to Thomas for this overreaction.

Thomas felt that he had been humiliated once too often "in a
neighbourhood where I had been for 20 years with an unpolluted
character"; he would, he said, "as well have met my death" than
endure the disgrace of suspension.[4] On 22 July 1833, he resigned
from the Metropolitan Police and with his wife and three children
moved north, becoming deputy constable of Manchester's "old
police" and among the first of Manchester's "new" Borough Police
Force, when this Met-style organization was set up in 1839. His
salary—six hundred pounds per annum—was three times his Covent
Garden pay.

He did not stay long with the new force, however; his health dete-
riorated, and for the last two years of his life he was unable to work
and was supported by a public subscription—a vote of thanks from
many in Manchester who had appreciated his work as a constable.
He died in October 1841.

....

Herbert Mayo was fired by King's College in 1836 for his poor teaching skills, though he went on to cofound the successful Middlesex Hospital anatomy school. By 1842 he was crippled by osteoarthritis and moved to the German spa town of Bad Weilbach, where he became increasingly mystical, publishing such works as *On the Truths Contained in Popular Superstitions* (1849). He was also intrigued by phrenology and physiognomy, and his medical writing now appeared to have more in common with the Tudor theory of the humors than with the brave new world of anatomy and physiology, in which latter field he had once been such a brilliant pioneer. Typical observations from Mayo's later years were that sanguine people tend to have red hair and to respond well to being bled, that Italians are bilious or melancholic and have olive complexions, and that cards, angling, and chess are excellent defenses against insanity (from *The Philosophy of Living*, 1837). He died in a German hydropathic hotel in 1852.

Richard Partridge failed to fulfill his potential. Though he succeeded Mayo as King's College's professor of anatomy in 1836, he never ceased to be nervous as a surgeon and maintained a stolid, unremarkable role as teacher and anatomical draftsman. In 1862, he had the honor to inspect, before a number of onlookers, the injured foot of Italian patriot and freedom fighter Giuseppe Garibaldi. He failed to spot a bullet lodged in Garibaldi's ankle; another surgeon approached and located and removed the bullet straightaway. Partridge's reputation never recovered, and he died in poverty eleven years later.

While lecturing at King's College, Partridge would tell his students the Bishop and Williams story, embellishing it with the fiction that the convictions had been secured when the New Police had placed cheese on the floor of 3 Nova Scotia Gardens and a number of little white mice had crept out of hiding to nibble it, thereby proving that the Italian boy had been killed in the house.

Thomas Williams was pledged to St. Bartholomew's Hospital museum, though he does not appear in the nineteenth-century catalogs of that institution, and his whereabouts are unknown. The remains of John Bishop maintained a moderate profile for much of the century: his skeleton and the skin of his arms had pride of place

*Richard Partridge's disastrous examination of
Garibaldi in 1862; the anatomist's career did
not recover.*

in King's College's pathological museum for decades. In 1871, however, he was spotted in a private moneymaking concern, Dr. Kahn's
Anatomical Museum, near Leicester Square in the West End; either
King's had decided to sell their once-famous prize or Dr. Kahn was
deceiving the public with an imitation John Bishop among his display
of Siamese twin fetuses, harelips, hemorrhoids, hernias, "the dreadful
effects of lacing stays too tightly," plus plenty of oddly formed genitals, displayed "for medical gentlemen only."[5]

But the London Burker has not taken up his rightful place in a
glass cabinet alongside 1820s boxing promoter turned killer John
Thurtell, the "Red Barn murderer" William Corder, and other long-
forgotten villains in the Hunterian Museum in the Royal College of

Surgeons, though it is possible that he was once there and that his remains perished in the same Luftwaffe direct hit that destroyed many items in the museum in May 1941, including the skeleton of Chunee the elephant and the (alleged) intestine of Napoleon Bonaparte.

So much for the actors; as for the location, Nova Scotia Gardens acquired a new sobriquet, Burkers Hole, by which it would be known for the next twenty-five years. A myth arose that the cottages communicated with one another via a warren of cellars and subterranean passages—a vivid image of how London's criminal fraternity were felt to be able to move around unseen along secret pathways of their own making. In the 1840s Nova Scotia Gardens was one of the slums traversed by such sanitary reformers as George Godwin, Henry Austin (Charles Dickens's brother-in-law), and Dr. Hector Gavin. Godwin, in 1859, decided that "an artistic traveller, looking at the huge mountain of refuse which had been collected, might have fancied that Arthur's Seat at Edinburgh, or some other monster picturesque crag, had suddenly come into view, and the dense smell which hung over the 'gardens' would have aided in bringing 'auld reekie' strongly to the memory. At the time of our visit, the summit of the mount was thronged with various figures, which were seen in strong relief against the sky; and boys and girls were amusing themselves by running down and toiling up the least precipitous side of it. Near the base, a number of women were arranged in a row, sifting and sorting the various materials placed before them. The tenements were in a miserable condition. Typhus fever, we learnt from a medical officer, was a frequent visitor all round the spot." "Refuse" was Godwin's euphemism for human feces; Gavin described the same scene as "a table mountain of manure," which towered over "a lake of more liquid dung."[6] A refuse collector was using Nova Scotia Gardens as his official tip, accumulating this vast mound from which the still-destitute residents of that part of Bethnal Green came to salvage some sort of living. So much for the New Poor Law: people chose to live off, and play on, noxious rubbish tips rather than enter the workhouse.

Half a century later a nostalgia column, "Chapters of Old Shoreditch," in the local newspaper, the *Hackney Express and Shoreditch*

Observer, featured an aged local resident's eyewitness memory of "the fearful hovels . . . once so famous in the days of Burking, . . . a row of dilapidated old houses standing back from the line of frontage and in a hollow, with a strip of waste land in front, on which was laid out for sale flowers, greengrocery and old rubbish of all kinds"; the following week another contributor recalled "the antiquated property known as The Hackney Road Hollow."[7]

Royalty, too, came to gawk at the natives; Princess Mary Adelaide, duchess of Teck—granddaughter of George III and mother-in-law to the future George V—recalled of the Gardens: "There was a large piece of waste ground covered in places with foul, slimy-looking pools, amid which crowds of half-naked, barefooted, ragged children

Architectural/sanitary campaigner George Godwin discovered a mountain of rubbish and sewage when he visited Nova Scotia Gardens in 1859; this sketch appeared in his campaigning book Town Swamps and Social Bridges.

chased one another. From the centre arose a great black mound. . . . The stench continually issuing from the enormous mass of decaying matter was unendurable."[8] But the most important visitor to these fetid regions was Angela Burdett-Coutts (1814–1906), heiress, philanthropist, baroness (from 1871), and, for two decades, close friend of Charles Dickens. Together, she and the novelist would take long night walks to some of the "vilest dens of London" during the 1840s and 1850s; and from time to time Nova Scotia Gardens, "the resort of murderers, thieves, the disreputable and abandoned," featured on their East End itinerary, according to Mary Spencer-Warren, author of the only press interview that Burdett-Coutts ever gave.[9]

No documentary evidence survives to reveal whether it was Dickens or Burdett-Coutts who first suggested Nova Scotia Gardens as a destination. But Burdett-Coutts's link to Burkers Hole was striking indeed. Her grandfather Thomas Coutts, founder of the bank Coutts & Co., had died in 1822, leaving his £900,000 fortune to his second wife, actress Harriot Mellon, who, in 1827, married the duke of St. Albans and became even richer. Her mother dead, and with no close female relative, Angela spent weeks, even months, with her adored stepgrandmother in Harriot's Highgate villa, Holly Lodge. Harriot, who was spoken of fondly by, among others, William Wordsworth, Sir Walter Scott, and poet laureate Robert Southey, had a quick wit, a deep purse, and a very kind heart, perhaps too kind. "Her charities were abused and misapplied by too many of the thankless wretches who had partaken of her bounty," according to one who knew her.[10] One of the many local people whom Harriot tried to help out, in 1816, was the pregnant young Highgate widow Sarah Bishop. It is known that at the time of the Bishop and Williams case, Angela, then seventeen, was living with Harriot; had she perhaps heard background details of the case from her sprightly hostess?

Harriot died in August 1837 and left her fortune to twenty-three-year-old Angela. (She had intended to leave it to Lord Dudley Stuart, who, in 1834, had been so indignant when two Italian boys were arrested outside his home, but Harriot had cut him out of her will when he went against her advice and married the niece of Napoleon Bonaparte.) Possibly inspired by Harriot's kindness, but determined to be more discriminating in her giving, Angela set out upon a lifetime of philanthropy, which she conducted according to both her religious principles and the dominant social ideals of the midcentury. Dickens, while their friendship endured, from 1839 to 1859, was to be one of her mentors as she struggled to transcend the limits of her outlook and experience.

In 1852, Angela bought Nova Scotia Gardens for £8,700. She intended to raze the cottages and in their place build salubrious homes that would lead to the moral, spiritual, and physical improvement of the dwellers of Burkers Hole. But she had not been informed that the refuse collector was legally entitled to stay on the land, no matter who owned it, and to use it as he saw fit until 1859. It was only in that year that she was able to set about her grand project. She employed architect Henry Darbishire to create Columbia Square, a magnificent five-story block of one-, two-, and three-room apartments, housing 180 families who paid the affordable sum of between 2s 6d and 5s a week in rent; there were shared washing facilities and WCs on each floor, and a library, club room, and play areas. Before long, there was a waiting list of families keen to move into the apartments.

Columbia Square was an odd amalgam of industrial-style tenements onto which were grafted Gothic Revival pinnacles and pointed arches; plain yellow stock bricks were dressed with portland stone and terra-cotta moldings. What followed next was even more exotic: Columbia Market, built just to the west of the square between 1863 and 1869, was a Castle Perilous extravaganza that included thirty-six shops and four hundred market stalls for local traders and produce sellers. It looked like a miniature cathedral and came complete with pieties painted on the walls, such as "Speak everyman truth unto his neighbour," and orders forbidding swearing, drunkenness, and Sunday trading. It went bust within six months.

The baroness's housing continued to be popular for nearly a hundred years, but Columbia Square was finally condemned as unfit for human habitation in the 1950s; the market died alongside it when Henry Darbishire's masterpieces fell to the demolition ball in 1960. A local authority housing estate, still in use, was built on the site. The Birdcage pub opposite has watched all this, unscathed.

Philanthropist Angela Burdett-Coutts built Columbia Market (top) and Columbia Square on the site of Nova Scotia Gardens in the 1860s.

....

The Bishop and Williams case itself began a slow decline into
obscurity, a number of factors combining to push the London Burkers
into the shadows. The "Asiatic cholera" had entered the country at
Sunderland in August 1831; it reached London in February 1832 and
by the summer had killed an estimated thirty-two thousand people in
Britain, fifty-five hundred of them Londoners. The fear of urban
miasma—the exhalations of graveyards and the stinking, sluggish air
in courts, alleys, and warrens that were (mistakenly) blamed for the
outbreak—quickly pushed "Burkiphoby" from its top billing. The
bacillus cholera vibrio could kill within hours of being ingested in
food or, more frequently, in drinking water, where it could live for up
to a fortnight—all of which would remain unknown until the 1850s
and not fully accepted by the medical community until the 1880s. A
typhus epidemic struck London in 1837–38, while cholera revisited
London in 1848–49 (killing fifteen thousand), 1853–54, and 1866–67.
It was the air of London—its smells, mists, fogs, smoke—rather than
its criminal element that held a mysterious terror for the city's inhabitants and visitors in the 1830s.

Besides, Burke and Hare were continuing to do perfectly good duty
as archetypal murderers for dissection. The story of the Edinburgh
Horrors had charming, voluble Burke, hideous, cretinous Hare; sinister, proud Dr. Knox, pathetic Daft Jamie, and alluring Mary Paterson.
And from the mid-1830s, a new era of complex and exciting murders
was ushered in, reported by an increasingly sophisticated newspaper
and periodical press that could now reproduce high-quality illustrations
of scenes of crime and dramatis personae. An ever more literate population wanted to read about people of quality (professionals, many of
them) murdering one another in drawing rooms, boudoirs, hotel
rooms; they preferred their killers and victims to be able to express
themselves at great length in letters; they wanted—and got—swindlers
and frauds, adulterers and adulteresses; bigamists, usurped heirs, jeal-
ous spouses, all pursued, from August 1842, by the specialist Detective
Branch of Scotland Yard, the first permanent plainclothes squad.

Bishop and Williams crop up toward the end of the century in

George Eliot's *Middlemarch* (1871–72), chapter 50, when the rector's gossipy wife, Mrs. Cadwallader, says snobbishly of the book's heroine, Dorothea Brooke, that she "might as well marry an Italian with white mice" as marry Will Ladislaw, and thereby lose her fortune. *Middlemarch* is set in 1829–32, and partly concerns the efforts of the idealistic young doctor Tertius Lydgate to found a new hospital in the town. Mrs. Cadwallader's remark is a wholly contemporary reference to the London Burkers and to the scandal that doctors could find themselves linked to.

Before that, though, the killers had provided inspiration for one of the midcentury's biggest-selling works of fiction. In 1844, journalist George William MacArthur Reynolds (1814–79), a bankrupt Radical and teetotaler, read an English translation of the French popular literary sensation *Les Mystères de Paris* (1842), written by Eugène Sue, and immediately hit on the idea of a British imitation. Reynolds's *The Mysteries of London* was published between October 1844 and 1856 in weekly issues, at the low price of one pence to attract the working-class reader.[11] Those who were unable to afford a penny a week for fiction or who were illiterate could nevertheless enjoy the stories since literate members of the community would read aloud to groups of twelve or so in a tavern or some other public space. Reynolds's tales are said to have outsold every other rival serial and novel, with thirty to forty thousand copies a week printed at the height of their popularity; in 1846, three different stage adaptations could be seen in London.

The Mysteries of London is a vast, rambling series of interconnecting episodes in which two brothers, Richard Markham, the hero, and his dissolute brother, Eugene, the villain, endure various adventures. In the course of the plot, the misdeeds of a corrupt, enervated aristocratic elite are juxtaposed with the depredations of London's underworld characters, and the most important of the latter, occupying the dark heart of the book, is the Resurrection Man.

The Resurrection Man lives in Bethnal Green, in a squalid, damp house that has an eight-room dungeon beneath it, accessed by the pull of a lever near the hearth. A small alley runs alongside the house, and late one night the Resurrection Man is observed with another man in the alley—they are dragging between them a blindfolded woman, who never emerges alive from the Resurrection Man's cellar. His favorite drinking places are the Dark House at the northern end of Brick Lane (not far from Nova Scotia Gardens) and the Boozing Ken on Saffron Hill; he serves time in Coldbath Fields; he disinters a girl's body from beneath the flagstones of Shoreditch Church. *The Mysteries* opens in July 1831—a very specific time, though its significance is not explained to the reader; perhaps it is coincidence, but this is the month in which Bishop and Williams first met. In the series' opening scene, a youth becomes lost in the maze of alleys near the Fleet Ditch, then, trapped in a rotting hovel called "The Old House in Smithfield," he is flung by two men through a trapdoor into a well that empties into the Fleet.

Though the Anatomy Act had finally killed off the trade by 1844, resurrection, it seems, remained a potent folk memory, a fact that Reynolds was keen to play on in his choice of bogeyman, who in the course of *The Mysteries* is stabbed, blown up, imprisoned, and left for dead on a plague ship but who nevertheless returns to stalk the hero of the book.

Reynolds's story also cleverly capitalized on the deeper physical strata of London that were being unearthed in the mid-1840s, with the so-called Metropolitan Improvements—new roads, railway lines, bridges, tunnels, and the laying of drains. The discoveries made during these works revealed some uncanny facts about the old fabric of the city and fed into a particularly urban paranoia about subterranean spaces—the sort of anxiety that created the legend that Nova Scotia Gardens was sitting atop a warren of passages connecting the cottages. In 1837, a Parliamentary Select Committee convened to examine the feasibility of bricking over the Fleet River and converting it into a sewer revealed that the neighborhood of Saffron Hill, close to Smithfield, featured a great many manholes leading to shafts twenty to thirty feet deep into which a person could descend below the level of the street. These had never been properly mapped or charted before, and, along with the Fleet and its fetid tributaries, were being investigated as possible miasmatic sources of the cholera and typhus outbreaks.[12] In 1844, as part of these same belated improvements, Farringdon Road was built through the slums around the Fleet, and to the thrilling horror of nonlocals, the Old Red Lion Tavern at 3 West Street, Smith-

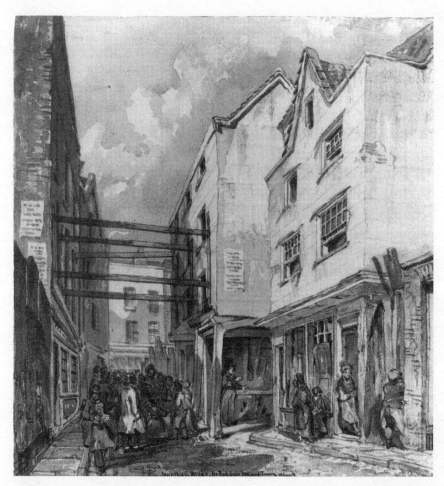

In 1844, sightseers lined up to visit the soon to be demolished Old Red Lion Tavern in Smithfield (above) and its warren of passages and hidden chambers. It had been built on the banks of the filthy Fleet, from which people scavenged a living (overleaf, top) and above which were cheap lodging houses for the poor (overleaf, bottom).

field, was discovered to have been a warrenlike house, hollowed out and customized to hide booty and prisoners on the run; it featured secret passages, trapdoors, subterranean rooms, sliding panels, and escape routes into other houses or onto the slimy banks of the Fleet. The building dated back to 1683 and was also known locally as the Old House in West Street and Jonathan Wild's House, after the notorious magistrate-cum-thief hanged in 1725. Sightseers paid to be taken

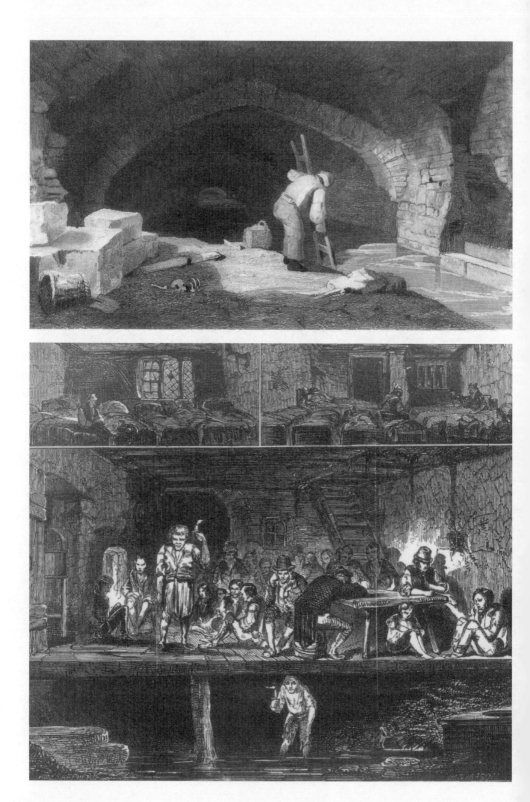

on tours of the house and the remains of the semidemolished streets around Saffron Hill, Field Lane/West Street, Turnmill Street, Cowcross. A similarly uncanny honeycomb of rotting old houses and convoluted streets was discovered in the same year when St. Giles, near Covent Garden, was razed for the building of New Oxford Street and, in the following year, when Victoria Street was constructed through the Devil's Acre slums in Westminster.

The Metropolitan Improvements revealed that some of the worst imaginings by "respectable" Londoners about criminal enclaves and about how their topography assisted wrongdoers to evade justice had been accurate in substance as well as in spirit. But by then, the moves to sweep away the rottenness of previous ages had gathered unstoppable momentum, and the recent past was feeling as ancient as biblical times.

Notes

I have based the narrative of the case on the *Times's* reports of the inquest, committal proceedings, and trial of Bishop, May, and Williams, supplemented by reports from the other main national newspapers whenever these give additional information or direct quotations; the printed Old Bailey Sessions Papers of 1831 filled in gaps in the newspapers' reports of the murder trial.

Few original records exist of proceedings at London's magistrates courts in the late 1820s and early 1830s, and I have had to rely heavily on newspaper accounts of summary justice.

The reports of Parliamentary Select Committees have proved a rich source of evidence about street life in London in the 1820s and 1830s, though doubtless these are somewhat bowdlerized accounts, and they do not, generally, encompass the views of the poor themselves; nevertheless, fascinating snippets creep into much of the witnesses' testimony.

Chapter One: Suspiciously Fresh

1. *Times*, 9 November 1831.
2. The *Morning Advertiser* reports the boy's name as Giacomo Montrato; but its cloth-eared reporter also calls Shields "Sheen" until quite late in the case; Shiel is a variant the *Globe and Traveller* and the *Morning Herald* used. The name Paragalli went through many transcriptions, as

did all the Italian names mentioned in the case; even the *Times* and the Old Bailey trial reports contain wild variations on the Italian witnesses' names.

Liquorpond Street now lies under the line of Clerkenwell Road, running east from Gray's Inn Road.

3. West Street was also called Chick Lane and led into Smithfield. Torn down in 1844, it followed roughly the line that Charterhouse Street traces today.

4. This phrase puzzled lawyers and reporters covering the case and was widely transcribed as "to locus or burke me." To "burke" is to kill by the method used by William Burke. "Hocus" was contemporary slang for alcohol to which a drug—usually opium in its liquid form, laudanum—had been added, and to hocus was to stupefy someone with such a concoction before robbing him or her. To "locus" was slang for spiriting someone away after getting him drunk. "Locust," meanwhile, was a slang term for laudanum; and "locus-ale," beer containing laudanum, is referred to as early as 1693, according to *A Dictionary of Slang and Unconventional English* by Eric Partridge (1937).

5. For example, "to topper his smellers" was Regency slang, meaning to land a punch on an opponent's nose. From Partridge's *Dictionary of Slang*.

6. Rum-hot was a variant of "egg-hot"—strong ale brought to the boil with sugar, cinnamon, and a little lemon juice, to which was added a glass of cold ale; this mixture was then poured over beaten egg yolks, with nutmeg and more sugar added to taste. Some preferred to heat it by thrusting a hot poker into the mixture and making it bubble (*The Curiosities of Ale and Beer* by John Bickerdyke [1886]).

7. The *Globe and Traveller* of Saturday, 26 November, reported this conversation as: "What do you think of our new one now? Isn't he a staunch one? Didn't he go up to him well? You stick to me old fellow and I'll be true to you. I know the other one is all right—he is a good 'un. I told you he was a staunch one." The *Globe and Traveller* reported May's reply to Bishop as: "I don't know what you mean by 'It's all right.'"

8. *The 1824 Hackney Coach Directory* by James Quaife.

9. In the *Morning Advertiser* of 9 November 1831, May's reply to Hill is reported as: "That is nothing to you or us. Here it is, and that's all about it."

10. St. Giles-in-the-Fields is Henry Flitcroft's 1731 church in St. Giles High Street, beneath today's Centrepoint. St. Mary's Moorfields stood on the north corner of Blomfield Street and Finsbury Circus between 1820 and 1899; it had a small cemetery as well as burial vaults beneath the church, and it is possible Shields was stealing more than silverware.

11. Public Record Office, Petitions and Pardons 1830–31, HO64/2.

Chapter Two: Persons Unknown

1. The bishop of London's figures as given in the pamphlet *Evidence of the Reverend William Stone, Rector of Christ Church Spitalfields, and Others as to the Operation of Voluntary Charities* (1833).
2. This is the number given for private schools in 1832 by historian M. J. Durey in the essay "Bodysnatchers and Benthamites" (1976). However, this figure is unlikely to include many far smaller enterprises, such as those private courses given by hospital surgeons from their own homes; Dr. C. Walker, for example, gave classes in midwifery at his lodgings at 93 Bartholomew Close, and Dr. Ryan gave lectures on medical jurisprudence at his rooms in Hatton Garden. Source: advertisements in the *Lancet* in the late 1820s.
3. *Morning Advertiser*, 16 October 1827.
4. A variety of views on the number of corpses required for teaching purposes were given by surgeons in their evidence to the Select Committee on Anatomy in 1828, and three per student is the average that was settled on by the Select Committee Report's authors (*Report*, p. 4).
5. Over two hundred offenses were punishable by death in 1800; by 1837, the figure had dropped to eight. Still capital in 1831 were treason, murder, attempted murder causing injury, rape, sodomy, forgery, several forms of counterfeiting, horse stealing, housebreaking with larceny, returning from a sentence of transportation, sacrilege, stealing letters, stealing goods worth five shillings or more from a shop and five pounds or more from a private house.
6. *Report and Evidence of the Select Committee into the State of the Police of the Metropolis*, 1828, pp. 284–85, and the same committee's report of 1833.
7. *Times*, 9 April 1830.
8. *Globe and Traveller*, 19 October 1831. Williams gave his name as William Jones—which was the name of a noted east London snatcher (see n. 12 below).
9. *Morning Advertiser*, 30 December 1828.
10. *Quaint Signs of Olde Inns* by G. J. Monson-Fitzjohn (1926). But William West in his *Tavern Anecdotes* (1825)—a compendium of London inns and pubs—guesses that the Fortune of War was named after a prizefighter who retired with his winnings to open a pub.

    The *Lancet* points out that there was a small theater of anatomy— a private medical school—at 18 Giltspur Street, though, perhaps surprisingly, this does not feature in our story. Nor does the Giltspur Street Compter, a small jail at the southern end of the street, opposite Newgate, that held many convicted under the Vagrancy Act.

    A version of the Golden Boy still dangles from the office block that stands on the site today.

11. Evidence of retired parish constable James Glennon given to the 1828 Select Committee on Anatomy (*Report*, p. 105).
12. In January 1830, at Lambeth Street police office in Whitechapel, Cornelius Fitzgerald, George Gibson, and George and William Kent were discharged when they appeared on a charge of attempting to rob the burial ground at Globe Lane, Bethnal Green, since they had been arrested on suspicion only and no other evidence was offered.

In April 1830, at Union Hall police office, Southwark, resurrectionists complained of increased police vigilance at graveyards during the hearing of a pair named Williams and Edwards, who were arrested at St. John's, West Lane, Walworth; it is possible they were members of the gang so determined to get their hands on Miss Christy.

In August 1830, George Robins and William Jones, two well-known body snatchers, were charged at Lambeth Street with attempting to steal the body of a Mrs. Brown from the rear of a chapel in Cannon Street Road, off Ratcliffe Highway, in the East End. A Metropolitan Police officer had spotted them around midnight and saw that Mrs. Brown's grave was half open, with tools lying around it. Robins and Jones were sentenced to three months in jail.

In March 1831, James Bailey, John Chapman, and Daniel Baker were charged at Union Hall with stealing two dead bodies, which had been found when police officers stopped the men's cart in Brixton Road. The magistrate granted them bail.

M.J. Durey's "Bodysnatchers and Benthamites" alerted me to these references in the *Times* editions of 25 January, 9 April, and 24 August 1830 and 21 March 1831, respectively.
13. *Report*, pp. 93–101.
14. Partridge's £50 allowance noted in King's College archives file KA/C/M2; Bell quotation from *Sir Charles Bell: His Life and Times* by Sir Gordon Gordon-Taylor (1958), p. 30.
15. According to Ruth Richardson, in her 1988 book *Death, Dissection and the Destitute* (reissued in 2001), "CD" was likely to have been Joshua Naples (p. 115). Naples is also strongly believed to be the author of the other major contemporary source of knowledge about resurrection in London; his *Diary of a Resurrectionist*, a diary-cum-logbook, dated 1811, is housed in the library of the Royal College of Surgeons of England in Lincoln's Inn Fields. CD told the committee that although he was virtually the sole supplier of corpses to the London schools between 1809 and 1811, he gave up the trade in 1820 because it had become too dangerous, with guards at graveyards increasingly likely to be armed and ready to fire (*Report*, p. 118).
16. This was how anatomist Joshua Brookes (1761–1833) described them to the Select Committee (*Report*, p. 82).
17. "Old Stories Re-Told" in *All The Year Round*, 16 March 1867.
18. *Weekly Dispatch*, 27 November 1831.

19. The Bishops lived near the Red Lion inn, which was at 90 North Hill (demolished in 1900), and the Wrestlers inn, which dates back to 1547 and today still holds the medieval Swearing on the Horns of Highgate drinking ritual. John Bishop the younger's pub of choice, the Green Dragon (which dated back to at least 1730), was at 10 North Road, the southern end of North Hill; it was demolished in 1898 and Highgate School is now on the site.

20. Their marriage license is in the St. Leonard's, Shoreditch, marriage registers at Guildhall Library and it reveals that Sarah was illiterate, as she signed with an X. St. Leonard's, by architect George Dance the Elder (1695–1768), was completed in 1740 and still stands, at the busy junction of Shoreditch High Street, Old Street, Kingsland Road, and Hackney Road.

21. *Morning Advertiser*, 25 November 1831.

22. London Metropolitan Archives, Clerkenwell New Prison Committals Lists, MJ/CC/V/003.

23. *Revelations of Prison Life*, pp. 28–30. Coldbath Fields, rebuilt in 1794, stood on the site of today's Royal Mail depot at Mount Pleasant.

24. Old Bailey Sessions Papers, First Session, 1827, p. 31.

25. *Times*, 2 April 1831; *Morning Herald*, 2 April 1831.

26. The *Globe and Traveller* of 5 December 1831 described the ground beneath the Gardens as "former waste—slag and rubbish," which would indicate that it had once been a brickyard.

27. *The Victoria History of the Counties of England: A History of the County of Middlesex*. Vol. II: *Early Stepney with Bethnal Green* (1998), p. 114.

28. Figures given in the pamphlet *Evidence of the Reverend William Stone* (1833).

29. "Four Views of London," an anonymous essay in the June 1833 issue of the *New Monthly Magazine*.

30. *Morning Advertiser*, 7 November and 12 November 1831.

31. The Heads' baptisms and burials took place at St. Leonard's Church, Bridgnorth; the registers are held in the Shropshire Records and Research Centre in Shrewsbury, at P40/68 to P40/71 (1803–08). In a number of accounts, including those published by the Crown and by the *Times*, his names are used interchangeably, and James Williams and James Head are also thrown into the mix.

32. As the anonymous writer of the penal-reform book *Old Bailey Experience* (James Harmer?) put it: "No man goes into Newgate twice with the same name, trade, or place of nativity" (p. 112).

33. Old Bailey Sessions Papers, Fourth Session, 1827, p. 323. Pontifex's had been in business since 1780 and by 1831 stretched almost halfway down Shoe Lane on the east side; its main building survived until 1894 (*The Parish of St Andrew Holborn* by Caroline M. Barron [1979], pp. 107–08).

34. Public Record Office, The Newgate List, 1826–28, PCOM 2/199.

35. The riots are referred to in Michael Ignatieff's *A Just Measure of Pain: The Penitentiary in the Industrial Revolution, 1750–1850* (1978), p. 172.

36. *Weekly Dispatch*, 11 December 1831. If found guilty, Williams would have faced a fine of a hundred pounds.

37. St. Leonard's, Shoreditch, marriage register at Guildhall Library; Rhoda was illiterate and signed with an X. Thomas Head, "bachelor of this parish," could read and write. The records of St. Leonard's, Shoreditch, also show that one Mary Ann Bishop died aged five months in the workhouse on 2 March 1828; it is possible she was a daughter of John and Sarah.

38. Dorset Street was a short road running east-west, just north of Rockingham Street. Today, the Rockingham Estate, postwar London County Council flats, covers the site, approximately where Rennie House stands.

39. Clare Market opened in 1657. Until 1900, it stood where the northeastern section of Aldwych is today. Both New Inn and Clare Market disappeared during the construction of Aldwych and Kingsway, though a small section of street bearing the name Clare Market remains.

40. Figures given by journalist Charles Knight in his *London*, vol. 1 (1841), p. 164, a collection of essays on the capital previously published as newspaper columns.

Chapter Three: The Thickest Part

1. *Oliver Twist*, ch. 54.

2. Public Record Office, Bow Street Magistrates Outgoing Correspondence, MEPO 1/49 and 1/50.

3. Public Record Office, Home Office Letters, HO 59/2.

4. King also called it "Thursday the 4th"—Thursday was in fact the third; the *Morning Advertiser* quotes her as giving the time as "between ten and eleven o'clock" in the morning.

5. Report of the hearing in the *Times*, 22 November 1831.

6. Public Record Office, Petitions and Pardons 1830–31, HO 64/2.

7. Public Record Office, Home Office Domestic Letter Book, vol. 67, letter dated 15 November 1831, HO 43/41.

8. Middle Row stood at the bottom of Gray's Inn Road in front of Staple Inn and comprised a small cluster of Tudor buildings forming an island in the middle of High Holborn. It was pulled down in 1866 to widen the road.

9. *Times*, 19 November 1831.

10. *Globe and Traveller*, 12 November 1831.

11. The outer walls and basement cells of the Clerkenwell New Prison

(also called the Clerkenwell House of Detention) still stand, at Clerkenwell Close.

12. Exchange reported in the *Sun*, 14 November 1831.

13. "A Detective Police Party," *Household Words*, 27 July 1850; reprinted in *Dickens' Journalism: The Amusements of the People*, ed. Michael Slater (1996), vol. II of the Dent Uniform Edition of Dickens's Journalism. In *Oliver Twist*, Dickens had shown his contempt for the Runners' acumen by naming the two Runners called on to investigate a burglary Blathers and Duff.

14. In a stimulating essay, historian Ruth Paley disputes the stereotype of the Charley, claiming that he was no older, more decrepit, or badly paid than most New Police officers in the early years of the Metropolitan Police ("An Imperfect, Inadequate and Wretched System? Policing London Before Peel," *Criminal Justice History* 10 [1989]: 95–130). Certainly, a look through papers in the Public Record Office (at MEPO 1/44) shows a high turnover of recruits in the early years of the Met, with dismissals given largely on grounds of lack of physical fitness, absenteeism, and drunkenness. The first Metropolitan Police officer to be sworn in, PC William Atkinson, was sacked within an hour for drunkenness, as was the second, PC William Alcock. Some 1,790 of the first 2,800 men enlisted were sacked for being drunk on duty.

15. *Morning Chronicle*, 26 September 1828.

16. *Times*, 31 March 1832.

17. Papers at the Public Record Office (at MEPO 1/44) include what amounts to an apology from Commissioner Rowan to the editor of the *Times* for the number of reprimands and dismissals of Metropolitan Police officers, dated 11 November 1830; while on 16 December 1830 the chief clerk of Bow Street wrote to the editors of the *Times*, the *Morning Chronicle*, and the *Morning Herald* to deny reports that there were plans to enlarge the force.

18. *Memoirs of a Bow Street Runner* by Henry Goddard; written in 1856 but not published until 1956.

19. The most recent literary sensation before Vidocq's *Mémoires*—similarly reaching all classes of Londoner—had been Pierce Egan's *Life in London* books, published (and much plagiarized) between 1821 and 1828. The appeal of Egan's comic series lay in its evocation of high life and low life, with its heroes crossing social boundaries in a way that real Londoners could not.

20. *Report of the 1828 Police Select Committee*, p. 73.

21. Ibid., p. 76.

22. Ibid., p. 80. The Marquis of Anglesey is still there; the Brown Bear is no more.

23. *Report from the Select Committee on Allegations Relative to the Conduct of Certain Magistrates in the Holborn Division of Middlesex in Granting Licences for Victual Houses*, 1833, p. 261.

24. Public Record Office, Letter from Richard Mayne, 19 May 1830, MEPO 1/44 3.
25. Among Minshull's judgments to cause merriment and alarm in equal measure was his decision in December 1831 to jail four boys—itinerant peddlers of broadsheets—for selling prints of a picture of a child playing with a kitten that was dressed in a petticoat; Minshull took it into his head that this picture was somehow indecent, and, according to the *Sun* of 26 December 1831, his aim "was to stop the circulation of such an infamous publication." The article goes on to sneer that if Minshull was right, the reporter would never let his grandmother visit the British Museum again, in case any of the antiquities should inflame her passions.
26. *The First Detectives* by Belton Cobb (1957), p. 59.
27. *British Police and the Democratic Ideal* by Charles Reith (1943), pp. 90–93.
28. The Place Papers, British Museum Add Mss 27,789, vol. 1, ff184–86.
29. *Report of the 1828 Police Select Committee*, p. 81.

Chapter Four: Houseless Wretches

1. *Lord Melbourne* by L. G. Mitchell (1997), p. 152. William Lamb, second Viscount Melbourne (1779–1848), became home secretary in November 1830 in the Whig government led by Earl Grey; his undersecretary was his brother, George.
2. Public Record Office, Petitions and Pardons 1830–31, HO 64/2.
3. *Morning Advertiser*, 9 November 1831.
4. Dickens worked at Warren's blacking factory at 30 Hungerford Stairs, just off the Strand, near to where Charing Cross station stands today, and then in Chandos Street, when the factory moved premises. The work involved pasting labels onto pots of blacking—used to keep fire grates, stoves, boots, and metalwork freshly black. In Camden his landlady was Mrs. Roylance, "a reduced old lady," as he later described her, whose house was in Little College Street. (*The Life of Charles Dickens* by John Forster, vol. 1 [1872], pp. 31–38.)
5. John Wontner's evidence in the *Report of the Select Committee Appointed to Inquire into the Cause of the Increase in the Number of Commitments and Convictions in London and Middlesex*, 1828, p. 54.
6. *Times*, 21 March 1826.
7. *The Sixth Report of the London Society for the Suppression of Mendicity* (1824).
8. The *Morning Chronicle* of 27 September 1829 reported 120 vagrants being repeatedly cleared from a brickyard in Ratcliff, east London, where they were accustomed to spending the night; they included children as young as eleven years old.

9. *Morning Post*, 29 September 1828.
10. *Report of the 1828 Police Select Committee*, appendix D, p. 317. An attempt to assess each child's educational level is made in this table; Elizabeth Butler could make out a few words but was unable to write; her only schooling had been at a Sunday school in Whitechapel. Most of the children who passed through London's judicial and penal systems in the 1820s seemed to have acquired at least a small degree of literacy.
11. The Corn Laws, introduced in 1804, set high import tariffs to prevent foreign corn from coming into the country until British corn had attained a certain price, whereupon the tariff dropped. This protectionism kept bread prices high until the repeal of the laws in 1846. By contrast, "free trade" had ensured the collapse of the English silk industry.
12. Brenton's open letter to the bishop of London was published in 1832 in pamphlet form as part of a series of addresses to the great and good entitled *On Population, Agriculture, Poor Laws and Juvenile Vagrancy*. On retiring from the navy, Brenton (1774–1839) founded the Society for the Relief of Shipwrecked Mariners and the Children's Friend Society and set up the Brenton Juvenile Asylum at East Ham. He was also on the board of management of the Society for the Suppression of Juvenile Vagrancy.
13. London would not get a unitary authority until 1888—decades after Britain's other cities—with the creation of the London County Council. Until then, London's local government was administered by its parish vestries—of medieval origin—and boards for lighting, paving and "works" (construction), and so on.
14. For example, of 3,035 committals for vagrancy between February 1827 and April 1828, only 73 convictions were properly documented by London magistrates, which meant that almost 3,000 people were being detained in prison with no written proof of their guilt or of the evidence that had been used to convict them (evidence given by Serjeant Pell, a Middlesex magistrate, to the 1828 Police Select Committee, *Report of the 1828 Police Select Committee*, p. 236).
15. *Morning Post*, 24 November 1831.

    Similarly, police officers are on record as showing kindness to vagrants. In 1831 officers took a sick and homeless man to St. Giles workhouse in order to find him a meal and a bed for the night but were told by the doorkeeper that since it was after nine o'clock at night there could be no new admission, and that they could take the man "to hell." Instead, the officers formally arrested the beggar to give him shelter in a tiny cell in Covent Garden's Dyott Street station. In the morning they found him dead. Source: *Lancet*, 13 August 1831.
16. 5 Geo IV c 83.
17. *Report of the 1828 Police Select Committee*, p. 81.

18. A total of nineteen men were executed for taking part in Swing disturbances.

19. Conway lived at 52 North Road, close to the Bishop family home (*Report from the Select Committee on the Existing Laws Relating to Vagrants*, 1821, p. 39).

20. *The Twelfth Report of the Society for the Suppression of Mendicity* (1830). One of the Dicity's founders was William Henry Bodkin, who crops up later in our story as a prosecuting counsel at the Old Bailey. Bodkin had also been chairman of the Houseless Poor Association charity and had a place on the 1828 Police Select Committee.

21. *The Eleventh Report of the Society for the Suppression of Mendicity* (1829).

22. *Morning Chronicle*, 22 September 1829. Laing would be satirized by Charles Dickens as the arrogant and vicious magistrate Fang in *Oliver Twist* (ch. 11), while the satirical newspaper *Figaro in London* would claim of Laing "his inhumanity is as proverbial as his ignorance" (24 December 1831).

23. *The Twelfth Report of the Society for the Suppression of Mendicity* (1830).

     The year before, the following people had arrived at Red Lion Square:

     "MS," 17, a female pilferer, keeps running from home;

     "EB," 21, a Bristol girl, persistently begs in London;

     "AG," 30, deserted by husband and has a child, no legal settlement given since she is Irish, though has spent 19 years in London;

     "CF," 12, a girl sent out to beg by her mother;

     "JR," 14, a Scot, his father's vessel sailed and he was abandoned in London, taken in by a woman, sent to the Society and thence to Scotland;

     "TL" and "WL," two strong, lazy, idle fellows arrested for infesting the Kent Road and given three months in Guildford jail;

     "RG," borrowed a wife and three children to beg at the office;

     "PC," 16, "Swiss," an impostor with a wealthy brother;

     "WM," queued at the dock gates for fourteen days applying to get shifts;

     "MC," 29, Irish with four children, found in a doorway in Chancery Lane with three women standing by looking worried, all were fakes, even the children—whatever money is procured by the deception is equally divided, and the night spent most jovially in the purlieus of St. Giles (*The Eleventh Report of the Society for the Suppression of Mendicity* [1829]).

24. *The Twelfth Report of the Society for the Suppression of Mendicity* (1830).

25. *Times*, 2 April 1834.

26. Young Charles Dickens amused himself by looking at the pineapples during his lunch hour (*The Life of Charles Dickens* by John Forster, vol. 1, p. 36).

27. *The Cries of London* by J. T. Smith (1839).

28. *Eighth Report of the London Society for the Suppression of Mendicity* (1826).

29. *Globe and Traveller*, 12 November 1831.

30. Two books contain fascinating background on the trade in Italian children: *The Little Slaves of the Harp* by John E. Zucchi (1992) and *Italian Immigrants in 19th-Century Britain: Realities and Images* by Lucio Sponza (1988).

31. Giuseppe Leonardi, fifteen, died of lung disease—thought to have been brought on by neglect—in St. Giles workhouse in 1845; his padrone, Rabbiotti, was charged with manslaughter but acquitted. In 1861, five-year-old Carminello Ada died in St. Pancras workhouse after having been found suspended by his arms and legs from a ceiling and covered in bite marks (*The Little Slaves of the Harp*).

32. *Times*, 2 April 1834. I have been unable to find any such petition in the surviving Home Office records in the Public Record Office. Stuart (1803–54) was the grandson of Thomas Coutts, banking tycoon. His cousin was the philanthropist Angela Burdett-Coutts, who in 1837 would inherit the Coutts fortune.

33. Charles MacFarlane, *Popular Customs, Sports and Recollections of the South of Italy* (1846), p. 135; Charles Knight, *London*, vol. 1 (1841), p. 423.

Chapter Five: Systematic Slaughter

1. *The Registers of St Paul's Church, Covent Garden*, ed. the Reverend William H. Hunt, vol. 5: *Burials, 1752–1853* (1909). The entry says, "supposed to be about 14." Although the graveyard, in Cleveland Street, has been cleared, the workhouse building, dating from 1778, remains as the outpatients' department of the Middlesex Hospital.

2. *Globe and Traveller*, 14 November 1831.

3. Method described in *The Sack 'Em Up Men* by Richard L. Hewer (1928), p. 152.

4. *The Life of Sir Astley Cooper* by Bransby Cooper (1843), p. 395.

5. Quotation from *Weekly Dispatch*, 20 November 1831; *Observer*, 20 November 1831.

6. *Times*, 21 November 1831.

7. *Morning Advertiser*, 12 November 1831.

Chapter Six: Houseless Wretches Again

1. Horsey, Johnson, Dancing Doll Man, and Blind Charles Wood feature in J. T. Smith's *Vagabondiana* (1817). In vol. 1 of journalist Charles Knight's *London* (1841), Samuel Horsey is also fondly remembered as "half a Hercules" (p. 424).

2. Tim Buc Too was also known as Brutus Billy; he lived in White Horse Yard, off Stanhope Street, Drury Lane, dying in 1854 at the age of eighty-seven (*Some Account of the Parish of Saint Clement Danes Past and Present* by John Diprose [1868], p. 164). "TL" is mentioned in *The Thirteenth Report of the Society for the Suppression of Mendicity* (1831). Work on Marc Isambard Brunel's tunnel from Wapping to Rotherhithe started in 1825 but was not to be completed until 1840, by which time ten men had died during construction and the project was over budget. The *Times* dubbed it the Great Bore.

3. *London*, vol. 1, p. 424.

4. *Report of the 1828 Police Select Committee*, p. 83.

5. *Suggestions for the Architectural Improvement of the Western Part of London* by Sydney Smirke (1834).

6. De Quincey, "The Nation of London" (1834), in *The Selected Writings of Thomas De Quincey*, ed. Philip Van Doren Stern (1939), p. 173; Poe, "The Man of the Crowd" (1840), in *Selected Tales*, ed. Julian Symons (1980); and John Hogg, *London as It Is* (1837). Hogg diagnosed even the upper-class London male as haggard, glassy-eyed, and emaciated: "Everything is getting later and later, due to the pressure of commerce and business," he said (p. 342).

7. George Boulton Mainwaring, a JP at the Worship Street magistrates office, one of the offices that dealt with the East End of London (*Report from the Select Committee on the Existing Laws Relating to Vagrants*, 1821, p. 61).

8. Williams Burke and Hare and their wives spent a large portion of the proceeds of murder on ostentatious clothing; their new glamour was noted by neighbors, who did not suspect how they had come into the money.

9. *Report of the 1828 Police Select Committee*, p. 128.

10. *A Treatise on the Police and Crimes of the Metropolis* (1829), p. 135.

11. There were others engaged in the trade of London typologizing: Francis Grose published his *Lexicon Balatronicum: A Dictionary of Buckish Slang, University Wit, and Pickpocket Eloquence* in 1823; *The Strangers Guide: or, Frauds of London Detected* was published in 1808 by George Smeeton, who also wrote *Doings in London* in 1828.

12. Ann Taylor story from the *Morning Chronicle*, 29 September 1829; Taylor was sentenced by magistrates to three months in the Bridewell prison for attempting to obtain charity under false pretenses. Jane

Weston case reported in *Hue and Cry*, 27 January 1826. James Prior case in *Hue and Cry*, 7 February 1827.

13. *The Cries of London* (1839).

14. *Report of the 1828 Police Select Committee*, p. 128.

15. The alderman's comment was reported in the *Morning Chronicle*, 6 October 1829; the attraction of the Temple Bar shenanigans is mentioned in *British Police and the Democratic Ideal* by Charles Reith (1943), p. 73.

16. To what extent the police took advantage of these powers has been discussed by Steven Inwood in his essay "Policing London's Morals: The Metropolitan Police and Popular Culture, 1829–1850," *London Journal* 15, no. 2 (1990): 129–46. Inwood points out that although the following activities were banned in 1839, accounts from the 1840s and later show that they nevertheless proliferated: causing public obstruction or danger with animals or vehicles; rolling tubs, hoops, and wheels unnecessarily; posting bills; writing on walls; using threatening or abusive words or behavior; using noisy instruments in the process of begging, selling, or entertaining in the street; throwing stones; lighting fires or fireworks; ringing or knocking at doors; putting out lamps; soliciting or loitering; selling indecent pictures; singing indecent songs; using profane language; flying kites; and using a dogcart.

17. The 1662 Act of Settlement was modified over the course of the eighteenth century and places of settlement could be changed in a number of other ways: paying ten pounds or more in rent in a new parish automatically granted resettlement, as did the payment of local taxes for a specified period, the completion of a year's service in a parish office, or the fulfillment of an indentured apprenticeship—all of which actions tended to favor those who were either reasonably wealthy or educated or in a fairly secure trade. However, some parishes were "closed," forbidding any kind of settlement to newcomers in order to keep the poor rates down. James Stephen Taylor's excellent book *Poverty, Migration and Settlement in the Industrial Revolution* (1989) gives many examples of settlement disputes within the City of London's St. Martin Vintry ward.

18. A Select Committee of 1828 claimed that parish poor relief was uncoordinated across the country and that while some people received help without having to perform any parochial tasks, others had to do a great deal of work. The level of financial support given was supposed to reflect the number of people the head of the family maintained. Some parishes refused to give any outdoor relief, insisting that the workhouse was the only option, even for the sick or elderly; the committee estimated that nine out of ten impoverished people were refusing to go into the workhouse—even if that was the only source of aid (*Report of the Select Committee on That Part of the Poor Laws Relating to the Employment or Relief of Able-Bodied Persons from the Poor Rate*, 1828, p. 169).

19. Richard Burn's five-volume *Justice of the Peace and Parish Officer*—a manual of legal rules and precedents for JPs, published in various editions beginning in 1818—dedicates one whole volume, volume 4, at 1,286 pages, to the "relief and ordering of the poor," with advice on settlements and removal orders.

20. J. Wade, *A Treatise on the Police and Crimes of the Metropolis* (1829), pp. 137–40.

    Wade's life's work was to expose in print the idiocies and inequities of a nation ruled by a backward-looking aristocracy. A workingman made good (he had been a woolsorter), he was a Benthamite Radical, whose *Extraordinary Black Book* (1831) was colloquially known as "the Reformer's Bible," as it listed the abuses of the undemocratic, unaccountable bodies that controlled British public life.

21. *Morning Chronicle*, 9 October 1829.

22. Wade, *Treatise*, p. 6; *The Selected Writings of Thomas De Quincey*, pp. 173–74; James Grant, *The Great Metropolis,* vol. 1 (1837), p. 6.

23. Smith, *Vagabondiana*. The Select Committee that investigated vagrancy in 1821 included evidence from Yorkshire that members of the working class never refused money to a blind beggar and would even borrow in order to be able to give alms; those in receipt of parish relief had also been spotted helping beggars (*Report from the Select Committee on the Existing Laws Relating to Vagrants*, 1821).

24. Quoted by Edward Gibbon Wakefield in *Facts Relating to the Punishment of Death in the Metropolis* (1831), p. 210.

25. *Lord Melbourne, 1779–1848* by L. G. Mitchell, p. 127.

26. *Weekly Dispatch*, 20 November 1831.

Chapter Seven: Neighbors

1. Grant, *The Great Metropolis*, vol. 1, p. 10; Wade, *Treatise*, p. 6.

2. Dodd had been appointed to his position in June 1831 at a wage of twenty-five shillings a week; his predecessor had been sacked for sexually assaulting a woman in custody (Public Record Office, Letters from the Public Office, Bow Street, MEPO 1/49 and 1/50).

Chapter Eight: Meat—An Interlude

1. Evidence given to the Select Committee on the State of Smithfield Market, 1828, p. 72; hereafter referred to as *1828 Report on Smithfield Market*.

2. An anonymous pamphlet of 1847 entitled *Smithfield and the Slaughterhouses*.

3. *Report of the 1828 Police Select Committee*, p. 292.

4. Evidence of John Bumpas, local bookseller, *1828 Report on Smithfield Market*, p. 72.
5. Ibid., p. 16. Later in the century, Charles Dickens would recount the tale of another victim of Smithfield's droving practices, whom he discovered while visiting the vast St. Luke's insane asylum, which stood in Old Street from 1782 to 1966, to the northwest of the present Underground station: "I had been told of a patient in St Luke's—a woman of great strength and energy, who had been driven mad by an infuriated ox in the streets—an inconvenience not in itself worth mentioning, for which the inhabitants of London are frequently indebted to their inestimable Corporation. She seized the creature literally by the horns, and so, as long as life and limb were in peril, vigorously held him; but the danger over, she lost her senses." ("A Curious Dance Round a Curious Tree," *Household Words*, 17 January 1852.)
6. *1828 Report on Smithfield Market*, pp. 144–45.
7. Public Record Office, HO 62/8.
8. It is likely that the publication of this pamphlet was timed to coincide with the attempt, in 1823, to pass a parliamentary act banning animal fights and baiting (the measure was defeated in the Commons by 29 votes to 18), and with parliamentary debate on the forthcoming Vagrancy Bill.
9. *1828 Report on Smithfield Market*, p. 15; evidence of William Hickson, shoe warehouse owner.
10. *Hue and Cry/Police Gazette*, 1 October 1825.
11. *1828 Report on Smithfield Market*, p. 148; evidence of William Collins, salesman.
12. *Times*, 25 February 1832. *Wives for Sale* by S. P. Menefee (1981) explores the British phenomenon of wife selling in detail.
13. *Great Expectations*, ch. 20 (though written in 1860–61, the novel is set in the 1820s and early 1830s); *Oliver Twist*, ch. 21 (1837–38).
14. *1828 Report on Smithfield Market* contains horrifying eyewitness accounts of slaughter, though many of these are comments on the (even more appalling) conditions in the slaughterhouses of Whitechapel and Shoreditch. Though it is true that many of the accusations were made by reformers keen to provoke change, the substance of their reports was not challenged by any of the slaughtermen or butchers who also gave evidence to the committee.
15. John Hogg, *London as It Is* (1837); Hogg estimated that around ten thousand cows were kept for milk in London yards and cellars.
16. Evidence on horse slaughter in Smithfield was given to the 1828 Police Select Committee (*Report of the 1828 Police Select Committee*, p. 186) by one Charles Starbuck, the stockbroker who mistakenly identified an Italian boy to the coroner's court of St. Paul's, Covent Garden. Starbuck was a Quaker and involved in a number of reform campaigns— the Friends were renowned for their political lobbying skills. Although

he claimed not to be a member of an anticruelty league, Starbuck was most keen to tell the 1828 Police Select Committee that he had himself inspected abattoirs in Cow Cross, Smithfield, and found half-starved horses awaiting slaughter, many of them stolen, in his opinion. It is puzzling that Starbuck was co-opted onto the list of witnesses, since he had no obvious expertise or involvement in the trade; it may be that he enjoyed some kind of personal rapport with whoever convened the witnesses—perhaps using whatever networks Quakers had at their disposal—and thus found a channel for his views.

17.   The hospital treated, and learned from, market injuries. *Histories of Specimens in the Museum*, a logbook compiled by surgeons Edward Stanley and James Paget between 1832 and 1845, describes a typical case of "a drover, 25, brought into the hospital for a wound in the back part of the right leg which had bled profusely. His boot was full of arterial blood and his steps could be traced for some way across the square of the hospital and in Smithfield in large spots of blood. The wound had been inflicted by a large pointed instrument and had passed about two inches deep." Three days after his admission, delirium tremens set in, and the drover died not long after (Manuscript vol. MU3 in St. Bartholomew's Hospital Archives, p. 139).

18.   The phrase is that of 1828 Smithfield Select Committee witness Michael Scales (*Report of the 1828 Select Committee on the State of Smithfield Market*, p. 129).

19.   Quoted in *Old and New London*, ed. Walter Thornbury (1879–85), vol. 2, p. 350. Aleph's original column appeared in the *City Press* newspaper.

The city fog of those years—the True London Particular—had a taste and smell, too, according to the writer of "The Mirror of the Months" in 1831: "There is something tangible in a London fog. . . . You can feel what you breathe and see it too. . . . The taste of it, when dashed with a due seasoning of sea-coal smoke, is far from insipid. It is also meat and drink at the same time, something between an egg flip and omelette soufflé, but much more digestible than either" (reprinted in the *Weekly Dispatch*, 13 November 1831).

20.   After the Act of Union of 1801, Irish MPs sat in Westminster. Main sources of information on Richard Martin: *Humanity Dick* by Shevawn Lynam (1975), *Richard Martin* by Wellesley Pain (1925), *Valiant Crusade* by A. W. Moss (1961), and *A Century of Work for Animals* by E. Fairholme and Wellesley Pain (1924).

21.   After losing all his spare change at cockfighting at Hockley-in-the-Hole, Saffron Hill, George IV turned up at the Castle inn, on the corner of Cowcross Street and Turnmill Street, and pledged his watch and chain to pay off his gaming debts. As a favor to the obliging landlord, the pub was granted a license to receive pledges as well as sell alcohol, a unique honor. Today, the Castle still has its pawnbroker status, plus a

highly flattering portrait of George IV standing at the bar, to commemorate his visit.

22. Today, Portcullis House is near the spot. Dickens describes the gloomy decrepitude of Manchester Buildings in *Nicholas Nickleby*, ch. 16.

23. Pain, *Richard Martin*, p. 91.

24. Reported in *François Magendie* by J. M. D. Olmsted (1944), p. 140.

25. Bell and Magendie quotations, ibid., pp. 93, 117–18.

26. From the *Lancet;* quoted in Isobel Rae's *Knox: The Anatomist* (1964), p. 17.

27. Fairholme and Pain, *A Century of Work for Animals,* pp. 35–36.

28. The name has nothing to do with killing; the inn's first landlord, in 1692, was Thomas Slaughter. Slaughter's stood on the southwest corner of the junction with Cranbourn Street—today a coffee/sandwich chain has the site.

29. *1828 Report on Smithfield Market*, p. 48.

30. Richard Martin, however, was the son of a Roman Catholic but had been brought up in the Protestant faith so that he might go to Cambridge and then enter Parliament; Catholics were not allowed to sit as MPs until 1829.

31. *Cursory Remarks on the Evil Tendency of Unrestrained Cruelty, Particularly on That Practised at Smithfield Market*, pp. 7–12.

32. Recalled by Percy Fitzgerald in his *Chronicles of a Bow Street Police Officer* (1888).

33. The phrase is from the anonymous pamphlet *Smithfield and the Slaughterhouses* (1847), p. 6.

34. The wiping out of slums was not to be the main thrust of nineteenth-century metropolitan improvements, but it was viewed as a highly desirable side effect. Rundown districts were almost always the location for new roads and railway lines, since low-grade housing stock was the cheapest to buy up for demolition.

35. George Godwin, *Town Swamps and Social Bridges* (1859), p. 13. Frying Pan Alley disappeared during the construction of Clerkenwell Road in 1878.

36. Old Bailey Sessions Papers, Fourth Session, 1827, p. 323; evidence of James Spoor.

37. It is, though, impossible now: it lies approximately where the Underground runs alongside Farringdon Road, on a latitude with Benjamin Street.

Chapter Nine: Whatever Has Happened to Fanny?

1. "The Diseased Appetite for Horrors," *Examiner*, 11 December 1831, p. 787; reprinted in Fontblanque's *England Under Seven Administrations* (1837).

2. Harmer (1777–1853) was the orphan of a Spitalfields weaver and rose to become a wealthy attorney. He would be elected alderman of the City ward of Farringdon Without in 1833 and became a sheriff of London and Middlesex and proprietor of the campaigning newspaper the *Weekly Dispatch*. He was a prolific pamphleteer on the subject of criminal-law reform and is the most likely candidate for author of the anonymous 1832 account of the Bishop and Williams case, *The History of the London Burkers*, which relies heavily on the *Times*'s account of the investigation. Harmer had already published a number of reformist pamphlets arising from his intimate knowledge of some of London's most notable trials of the day, including those of John Holloway and Owen Haggerty, hanged for murder in 1807, though they may have been innocent. Harmer knew personally the Reverend Dr. Cotton, the vicar—or "ordinary"—of Newgate, and this may have given him greater access to the accused and the condemned.

    I also believe Harmer to be the author of the anonymous book *Old Bailey Experience: Criminal Jurisprudence and the Actual Working of Our Penal Code of Laws* (1833), which has variously been attributed to John Wontner (governor of Newgate Prison) and Edward Gibbon Wakefield (who worked as a schoolmaster in Newgate during his three-year sentence for eloping with an heiress and who wrote the influential *Facts Relating to the Punishment of Death in the Metropolis*, published in 1831). Close reading shows that both Wontner and Wakefield were robustly criticized for their views on penal matters in *Old Bailey Experience*. The author of *Old Bailey Experience* also mentions that he met James May at Newgate, which suggests the likelihood of his being the author of *The History of the London Burkers* as well.

3. Two days later, James Gardener, a cart driver, of Caroline Place, Lambeth, was charged with assaulting White and of attacking another boy, fourteen-year-old Thomas Hammond, in Webber Street, Waterloo, at eleven o'clock at night. Gardener denied the pitch-plaster attack on White but admitted grabbing Hammond by the wrists, saying he had been so drunk he could remember nothing about the incident (*Globe and Traveller*, 25 November 1831).

4. Henry Edward case, *Morning Advertiser*, 22 November 1831; Martha Allenby and Henry Fore cases, *Morning Advertiser*, 2 December 1831; Elizabeth Turner case, *Globe and Traveller*, 15 November 1831.

5. *Globe and Traveller*, 1 December 1831.

6. *Weekly Dispatch*, 11 December 1831. Details of the Culkin case are taken from the Old Bailey Sessions Papers, Second Session, 1832, pp. 178–84. Hartshorn Court is no more; Broad Arrow Court is today's Milton Court.

7. The *Morning Advertiser* of 12 December 1831 carried a news story that is fairly typical of the style in which such cases were reported: "J Moore,

an old and deformed pauper, who walks on crutches, and who has been frequently before the magistrates for various outrages and assaults, was charged with committing a series of the most indecent attacks on several little girls in Shadwell workhouse. The evidence against the prisoner was wholly unfit for publication." An "outrage" was one of the contemporary euphemisms for rape.

Sexual assaults within the family were openly reported too. The *Morning Chronicle* of 11 October 1829 published the case of Alexander Barry, in his fifties, who was taken to court by his nineteen-year-old daughter, Elizabeth, on a charge of attempted rape; she said that he had been "repeatedly taking liberties with [her] person" since she was six years old. Joseph Woodhouse, meanwhile, "a fiend in human shape," was executed at Chester for raping his eleven-year-old daughter (*Morning Chronicle*, 29 September 1829).

8. *Times*, 28 November 1831; *Morning Advertiser*, 28 November 1831.
9. These tiny streets are largely given over to the auto trade now, with garages, repair shops, and a large parking lot.
10. Bransby Cooper in *The Life of Sir Astley Cooper*, pp. 374–76.
11. John Flint South (1797–1882) had succeeded Sir Astley Cooper as demonstrator of anatomy on the baronet's retirement in 1825. Apparently "deeply religious" (according to his entry in *Plarr's Lives of the Fellows of the Royal College of Physicians of England*), South retired early, in 1841, "due to neurosis." South's professional reminiscences, *Memorials of the Craft of Surgery* (1886), contain little on his dealings with resurrectionists.
12. This large coaching inn stood on the northern corner with Camomile Street and was demolished in 1863 for architect John Gibson's stunning National Provincial Bank, which still stands today, as Gibson Hall.
13. Pilcher (1801–55) was a practicing surgeon and an ear specialist.

Chapter Ten: A Horrid System

1. The Great Windmill Street School was founded in 1737 and closed in 1835; in 1878 the building was reconstructed as part of the Lyric Theatre, Shaftesbury Avenue. Interestingly, the rear of Joseph Carpue's anatomy school at 72 Dean Street, Soho, was also incorporated into a theater, when, in 1840, a Miss Kelly built the Royalty next door. (Carpue had vacated his school in 1833.) In 1845, Charles Dickens performed at Miss Kelly's theater in Ben Jonson's *Every Man in His Humour*. It is likely that Dickens knew of the building's history, since as a child he had been a regular visitor to the house, at 10 Gerrard Street, Soho, of his maternal uncle Thomas Culliford Barrow, when Barrow was laid up with a broken thigh during the winter of 1822–23.

Eventually, the leg had to be amputated, and it was taken off by Carpue in the Dean Street school. Barrow fainted during the operation, and Dickens's family lore had it that when he came round, he asked, "Where's my leg?" and was told by Carpue, "Under the table" ("The Barber of Dean Street" by William J. Carlton in *Dickensian* 48, part 1, no. 301 [1952]: 8).

2. *King's and Some King's Men* by H. Willoughby Lyle (1935), p. 7.

3. *Lancet*, 14 September 1833.

4. *The Centenary History of King's College London* by F. J. C. Hearnshaw (1928), p. 22.

5. *Lancet*, 16 October 1831.

6. *Lancet*, 29 September 1832.

7. *Report of the Select Committee on Medical Education,* part 2 (1834), Q6714, p. 203.

8. Sir Astley's price list is according to *Lancet*, 3 November 1832.

9. The Brookesian building survived until the early 1920s, having served as offices to a publisher and then an architectural practice. Blenheim Steps is today Ramillies Street, and the school was near the eastern corner with Great Marlborough Street. In his back garden, Brookes had constructed his Vivarium, a grottolike folly built of rock to which were chained live birds and animals, including an eagle, a hawk, an owl, pheasants, foxes, racoons, and a tortoise. The site of the garden is now 1 and 2 Ramillies Street ("Joshua Brookes's Vivarium" by Tim Knox, in *London Gardener; or, The Gardener's Intelligencer* 3 [1997–98]).

10. Joseph Constantin Carpue (1764–1846) was of Spanish descent, born in Brook Green, Hammersmith, and had been a priest, a bookseller, a barrister, and an actor before entering the medical profession; later he became a Liberal member of Parliament. A tall, ungainly, gray-haired man, he always dressed in black with a huge white neckerchief. He was said to be among the best anatomical draftsmen in London but nevertheless was one of a number of anatomists/surgeons ostracized by the medical establishment. A pioneer of plastic surgery, he published his *Account of Two Successful Operations for Restoring a Lost Nose from the Integuements of the Forehead* (1816). Carpue's other specialty was galvanism and he was present at the attempt, on 18 January 1803, to pass an electrical current through the body of the executed George Foster, hanged at Newgate for murdering his wife. Foster opened one eye, wiggled his legs, and clenched his right hand but failed to be revived (*The Newgate Calendar*, ed. George Theodore Wilkinson, vol. 2 [1962], pp. 80–82).

In 1800, painters Benjamin West, Richard Costway, and Thomas Banks asked Carpue to nail up a just-executed criminal (a murderer called Legg), who was still warm, so that they could take a plaster cast of how the body hung, in order to produce more realistic Crucifixion scenes; a cast of the crucified Legg is in the Royal Academy, London.

Edward William Tuson (1802–65) trained at Carpue's school and at the age of twenty-two became a surgeon at the Middlesex Hospital—close to the Little Windmill Street School, where he gave private lectures in anatomy. (Little Windmill Street is plain Windmill Street today, running between Tottenham Court Road and Charlotte Street; Tuson's school was at Nos. 8–10, now demolished.) While still in his twenties, Tuson published his celebrated work *Myology*, which revealed the various layers of muscles; he was said to have gone through a great many Subjects in his research for *Myology*.

11. Exeter 'Change, built in Tudor times, was pulled down in 1829; Exeter Street is near the spot today. Joshua Brookes was involved in the notorious Chunee incident in 1826, when an enraged elephant of that name burst out of another menagerie, owned by one Edward Cross, close to that of Brookes's brother. After Chunee had finally been destroyed by armed troops, and when his corpse had lain stinking in the Strand for days, Brookes publicly dissected the beast and later angrily denied newspaper reports that he had grilled and eaten a slice of Chunee as part of his investigations (*Memoirs of a Bow Street Runner* by Henry Goddard). Chunee had been brought from India in the ship *Lady Astell* and had worked at Astley's Theatre in Lambeth; Astley's sold him to menagerie owner Stephen Polito (sale negotiated by Mr. Norman, the clown); on Polito's death, Chunee passed to Edward Cross, who succeeded Polito at the menagerie (Manuscript diaries of William Clift, housed in the Library of the Royal College of Surgeons).

12. Sir Astley Cooper himself was the proud owner of a chunk of intestine, featuring a fungal growth, that he claimed was a section of Napoleon's gut. Its authenticity was uncertain at the time and will always remain so since it was destroyed when the Royal College of Surgeons was hit during an air raid in May 1941, in which Chunee's skeleton also perished.

13. *Lancet*, 24 November 1832.

14. Reported in *The Memoirs of John Abernethy* by George MacIlwain (1853), p. 305.

15. *Lancet*, 23 July 1833.

16. Ibid., 1 October 1831.

17. Sir Benjamin Brodie—a member of the Royal College council and, later, RCS president—was the son of a rural clergyman and became a baronet on the strength of his being made surgeon to William IV; Sir William Blizard, president of the Royal College in 1831, was the son of an auctioneer and had no formal education until his late adolescence; Sir Charles Bell had been excluded from the Edinburgh medical elite and subsequently suffered seven years of being overlooked in London before gaining respect for his work on nerve function; George Guthrie had been a child prodigy, becoming an RCS member at the

age of fifteen before going off to the wars as a surgeon, his skills coming to the notice of the duke of Wellington (Guthrie turned down a knighthood).

18. The *Lancet* gives a slightly different version of the story, claiming that the Anatomical Society pushed the price of bodies *up* so as to destroy Grainger and that, when the resurrectionists heard this, they decided to supply Grainger for free in order to make Webb Street flourish and so force the prices paid by hospitals even higher (*Lancet*, 24 November 1831).

19. *Report of the Select Committee on Medical Education*, vol. 13, part 2, Q6602, p. 192. The 1828 Select Committee on Anatomy put the number of medical students in London at one thousand in 1823 and eight hundred in 1828 (*Report of the 1828 Select Committee on Anatomy*, p. 4).

20. Richardson, *Death, Dissection and the Destitute* (1988), p. 163.

21. Ruth Richardson discusses attacks on medical schools in Paisley, Sheffield, Inveresk (near Edinburgh), and—most dramatically—in Aberdeen, where the school of anatomy was burned to the ground upon the discovery of discarded dissected human remains.

22. This anecdote is told in *Westminster Hospital, 1716–1966* by J. G. Humble and Peter Hansell (1966) and in *Things for the Surgeon* by Hubert Cole (1964).

23. *Morning Chronicle*, 2 October 1829; I have been unable to find any further reports of this case. In October 1831, Superintendent Joseph Sadler Thomas told George Rowland Minshull that "young medical students had repeatedly annoyed the neighbourhood"; Minshull had just remanded a student for assaulting Thomas in Brydges Street, Covent Garden (*Globe and Traveller*, 20 October 1831).

24. *Report and Evidence of the Select Committee on Anatomy*, p. 81.

25. Isobel Rae's biography *Knox: The Anatomist* is a moving account of Knox's life, while Owen Dudley Edwards, in *Burke & Hare* (1980), presents an equally compelling, though more hostile, portrait of him.

26. "Mary's Ghost," *Hood's Whims and Oddities* (1826), a volume of verse on the topics of the day.

27. Edward Cook was named as "a known resurrectionist" by "a publican who 12 years ago kept a house in West Smithfield," according to the *Sun*, 14 November, 1831; this house may well have been the Fortune of War. Eliza Ross ostensibly made her money from selling old clothes, reputedly stripped from bodies snatched by Cook; the dealers she sold to, at Rag Fair, near the Tower of London, were able to name a number of articles that tallied with Walsh's belongings that had been sold to them by Ross at the end of August. Ross's neighbors in Goodman's Yard also alleged that she was a notorious cat skinner, stealing and killing local cats and selling the furs at Rag Fair (reports in *Sun, Globe and Traveller*, and *Times*, November and December 1831, January 1832).

28. *John Clare's Autobiographical Writings*, ed. Eric Robinson (1983), p. 132. It is ironic that when Clare died, insane, in 1864, his friends in the Northamptonshire village of Helpston held a wake for his body, as it had been rumored that a London anatomist intended to get hold of Clare's brain in order to dissect it and discover how it was that a madman had been able to write poetry (*A Right to Song: The Life of John Clare* by Edward Storey [1982], p. 297).

29. Ruth Richardson tells this story in *Death, Dissection and the Destitute*, p. 221.

30. *Report and Evidence of the Select Committee on Anatomy*, p. 47.

31. Knox's letter to the *Caledonian Mercury*, written two months after William Burke's execution, and Knox's only public pronouncement on the affair; quoted in Isobel Rae's *Knox: The Anatomist*, pp. 98–99.

32. *Report and Evidence of the Select Committee on Anatomy*, p. 18.

33. *The Life of Astley Cooper* by Bransby Cooper (1843), p. 334. An example of one of these experiments is on show in the Gordon Museum at Guy's Hospital. According to R. C. Brock in *The Life and Work of Sir Astley Cooper* (1952), Cooper kept human corpses in his attic from time to time and had obtained permission to do so from the lord mayor of London, who assured Cooper that he would not be troubled by constables and magistrates.

34. *Lancet*, 16 October 1831.

35. *A Letter to the Right Honourable the Secretary of State for the Home Department Containing Remarks on the Report of the Select Committee of the House of Commons on Anatomy* (1829).

36. *Morning Advertiser*, 11 October 1831.

37. *British Police and the Democratic Ideal* by Charles Reith, p. 94.

38. George Douchez, who had also been present at the 6 November postmortem in St. Paul's watch house, lived—and may have had a theater of sorts—in Golden Square itself; Thomas Copland, surgeon, lived at 4 Golden Square, on its east side; while John Joberns, surgeon, lived at 9 Upper John Street, which led into the square. Joseph Carpue's school in Dean Street, the Brookesian, and the Great Windmill Street School could have been described as near to Golden Square. But the most likely candidate is George Darby Dermott's practice; Dermott was working from a theater actually on the square before taking his anatomy academy to Gerrard Street in 1833. The great John Hunter (brother of William of the Great Windmill Street School) lived and lectured at 31 Golden Square (where he had built a dissecting room) between 1763 and 1769, and it is possible that Dermott, or even Douchez, was using Hunter's former premises.

39. John Hilton (1805–78) was demonstrator of anatomy at Guy's from 1828 on. He had a brilliant reputation as an anatomist and later in life became surgeon to Queen Victoria and president of the RCS; he had the honor of performing the postmortem on Sir Astley Cooper when

the baronet died in 1841. Hilton was the first surgeon to give a clear account of cerebrospinal fluid; and his book *Rest and Pain*, on the importance of recuperation, was the first to explore in an empirical way the benefits of rest. He himself shunned the notion of empiricism and the "scientific" community and found Charles Darwin's ideas ludicrous. Hilton believed that life, death, and the spirit could never be understood in chemical or physical terms: "All is darkness to the human understanding," he said (*A Biographical History of Guy's Hospital* by Samuel Wilks and G. T. Bettany [1892]). Hilton gave waxwork-maker Joseph Towne detailed anatomical information when Towne was producing his celebrated wax anatomical figures, which are still in the Gordon Museum at Guy's. Towne habitually worked alone in a locked room with corpses and wax, and his methods died with him.

40. *Morning Advertiser*, 5 December 1831.
41. The quotation is from *The Centenary History of King's College London* by F. J. C. Hearnshaw, p. 293.
42. *King's and Some King's Men* by H. Willoughby Lyle, p. 301.

Chapter Eleven: At the Bailey

1. Serjeant Ballantine, *Some Experiences of a Barrister's Life* (1882). No one seems to have recorded how lawyers smelled.

     As a child, Ballantine was taken by his father to see the trial of Bishop, Williams, and May.
2. Reports from the *Times, Morning Advertiser,* and *Globe and Traveller* are from editions dated 3 December 1831, the *Weekly Dispatch* from 4 December 1831. The basic narrative of the trial is taken from Old Bailey Sessions Papers for 1831. It is supposed to be a comprehensive report of proceedings but is nothing of the sort: much is left out, and the newspaper accounts are an invaluable backup. The staccato, elliptical nature of the Sessions Papers are evidence that much was jettisoned in publishing a formal report of trials of the day.
3. Bodkin's copy of *Arabiniana* is in the British Library.
4. The disparaging contemporary was Serjeant Ballantine.
5. See n. 12, below.
6. The indictment can be found in the London Metropolitan Archives, Old Bailey Sessions Roll, OB/SR609/10.
7. In *Old Bailey Experience: Criminal Jurisprudence and the Actual Working of Our Penal Code of Laws* (1833), some judges were said to boast of their capacity to get through sixty to seventy criminal cases a day (p. 60).
8. "Mr Adolphus and His Contemporaries," *Law Magazine* 4 (1846): 60. Drunkenness among lawyers and judges is also noted in Ballantine's *Experiences*, p. 54.

9. Roderick Floud's book *Height, Health and History, 1750–1980* (1990) contains tables of the heights of adolescent recruits to the Marine Society—a charity that "rescued" street boys and trained them to be sailors—and to the Sandhurst Military Academy; Floud's data for the 1820s and 1830s suggests the class basis for height differentials.

10. In the late 1820s, a five-year-old who could not see over the bar of the prisoners' dock was put on trial at the Old Bailey; he had taken a watch from the counter of a baker's shop in Ealing, thinking that his mother would like to see how pretty it was ("The Schoolmaster's Experience of Newgate," *Fraser's Magazine*, June 1832).

11. William Street is today's Rockingham Street; the Alfred's Head is no more.

12. There is a striking similarity between this passage and the paragraphs in Chapter 52 of *Oliver Twist* that describe Fagin's trial at the Old Bailey.

> The court was paved, from floor to roof, with human faces. Inquisitive and eager eyes peered from every inch of space. From the rail before the dock, away into the sharpest angle of the smallest corner in the galleries, all looks were fixed upon one man—the Jew. Before him and behind: above, below, on the right and on the left: he seemed to stand surrounded by a firmament, all bright with gleaming eyes.
>
> He stood there in all this glare of living light, with one hand resting on the wooden slab before him, the other held to his ear, and his head thrust forward to enable him to catch with greater distinctness every word that fell from the presiding judge, who was delivering his charge to the jury. At times, he turned his eyes sharply upon them to observe the effect of the slightest feather-weight in his favour; and when the points against him were stated with terrible distinctness, looked towards his counsel, in mute appeal that he would, even then, urge something in his behalf. Beyond these manifestations of anxiety, he stirred not hand or foot. He had scarcely moved since the trial began; and now that the judge ceased to speak, he still remained in the same strained atti-tude of close attention, with his gaze bent on him, as though he lis-tened still.
>
> A slight bustle in the court recalled him to himself. Looking round, he saw that the jurymen had turned together, to consider of their verdict. As his eyes wandered to the gallery, he could see the people rising above each other to see his face: some hastily applying their glasses to their eyes: and others whispering to their neighbours with looks expressive of abhorrence. A few there were, who seemed unmindful of him, and looked only to the jury, in impatient wonder how they could delay. But in no one face—not even among the women, of whom there were many there—could he read the

faintest sympathy with himself, or any feeling but one of all absorb-
ing interest that he should be condemned.

As he saw all this in one bewildered glance, the death-like stillness came again, and looking back, he saw that the jurymen had
turned towards the judge. Hush!

They only sought permission to retire.

He looked, wistfully, into their faces, one by one, when they
passed out, as though to see which way the greater number leant;
but that was fruitless. The jailer touched him on the shoulder. He
followed mechanically to the end of the dock, and sat down on a
chair. The man pointed it out, or he would not have seen it. . . .

At length there was a cry of silence, and a breathless look from
all towards the door. The jury returned, and passed him close. He
could glean nothing from their faces; they might as well have been
of stone. Perfect stillness ensued—not a rustle—not a breath—
Guilty.

The building rang with a tremendous shout, and another, and
another, and then it echoed deep loud groans, that gathered
strength as they swelled out, like angry thunder. It was a peal of joy
from the populace outside, greeting the news that he would die on
Monday.

The noise subsided, and he was asked if he had anything to say
why sentence of death should not be passed upon him. He had
resumed his listening attitude, and looked intently at his questioner
while the demand was made; but it was twice repeated before he
seemed to hear it, and then he only muttered that he was an old
man—an old man—an old man—and so, dropping into a whisper,
was silent again.

The judge assumed the black cap, and the prisoner still stood
with the same air and gesture. A woman in the gallery uttered some
exclamation, called forth by this dread solemnity; he looked hastily
up as if angry at the interruption, and bent forward yet more atten-
tively. The address was solemn and impressive; the sentence fearful
to hear. But he stood, like a marble figure, without the motion of a
nerve. His haggard face was still thrust forward, his under-jaw hanging down, and his eyes staring out before him, when the jailer put
his hand upon his arm, and beckoned him away. He gazed stupidly
about him for an instant, and obeyed.

In the Bishop, Williams, and May passage, an attempt is made to
"read" the accused by examining their movements and appearance,
though the writer has the humility to show that this exercise is doomed
to failure: we cannot know what is passing through their minds. And the
portrait of the three accused is not hostile, even though they were

standing trial for appallingly brutal crimes. This humility, this sensitivity and empathy, is more novelistic than journalistic. With Fagin in the dock in *Oliver Twist*, Dickens sees a similar scene from the inside: Fagin cannot confront his own thoughts, and as soon as the full horror of his situation rises in his mind, his consciousness takes flight by alighting on the various phenomena in front of him in the courtroom. In both quoted passages, what is about to happen is so dreadful that surface details rush in to fill the vacuum of the unthinkable.

Not long into researching this book, I learned that two others had also suspected that the passage from the Bishop, Williams, and May trial that begins "The Most Deathlike Silence" was the unacknowledged early work of Charles Dickens, a nineteen-year-old shorthand reporter at the time of the trial. A cutting, "Dickens and the *Times*: Traces of His Hand," is one of many smaller items collated by Dickensiana collector John F. Dexter and presented to the British Museum (and now held in the British Library). Dexter's cutting from the *Times* dates from 1933 and discusses the similarity between Dickens's fiction and a number of police-court cases—at Great Marlborough Street and Hatton Garden—that had appeared in the *Times* one century earlier. In a handwritten note, Dexter prefaces a copy of the 1831 broadsheet *Burking the Italian Boy! Fairburn's Edition of the Trial of Bishop and Williams, Tried at the Old Bailey. Taken in Shorthand* (which reprints "The Most Deathlike Silence" paragraphs in full) with the words: "FW Pailthorpe gave me this pamphlet stating that it was 'reported' by Charles Dickens and that he had this information from an authoritative source. The description of the prisoners on pages 21–22 bears evidence of Charles Dickens's hand." Frederick William Pailthorpe (1838–1914) was an illustrator of Dickens's fiction in editions that appeared after Dickens's death in 1870; I have been unable to establish that Pailthorpe ever met Dickens. Pailthorpe's "authoritative source" is unknown, but artist, satirist, and illustrator George Cruikshank (1792–1878), who provided illustrations for *Sketches by Boz*, *Oliver Twist*, and other Dickens works and who often sketched prisoners in the dock at the Old Bailey, is a strong candidate.

Dickens's biographer Peter Ackroyd briefly mentions this find of John F. Dexter's in his 1990 book *Dickens* (p. 134).

There is only anecdotal evidence that Dickens's reporting career before the spring of 1832 consisted of anything other than stints in the reporters' gallery of the Houses of Parliament and at the ecclesiastical and naval court of Doctors Commons, which stood just to the south of St. Paul's Cathedral, in Knightrider Street. Furthermore, while Dickens's maternal uncle John Henry Barrow had links with the *Times* (and is said to have helped Dickens learn shorthand), there is no evidence that his nephew was connected to that paper at any point in the earliest stage of his career; and none whatever that Dickens had anything to do with Fairburn, purveyor of inexpensive woodcut-illustrated broadsheets.

It is reasonable to assume that if such a lucky—and lucrative—break as reporting one of the crimes of the century had come Dickens's way in 1831, he would have referred to it at the time (in letters or in conversation) or in later years. In fact, direct references to the Bishop and Williams case are scarce in Dickens's journalism and nonexistent in his correspondence that has survived. Though body snatchers appear in *Barnaby Rudge* and *A Tale of Two Cities*, these novels are set in the 1780s; resurrection and burking were, it seems, of comparatively little interest to Dickens in his tales of urban lowlife of the 1820s and 1830s.

In November 1835, Dickens was given an entrance pass to Newgate so that he could tour the jail, with a view to writing a profile of it. In his sketch "A Visit to Newgate," which Dickens wrote soon after, he notes the death masks of "the two notorious murderers" Bishop and Williams (which were almost the only objects furnishing a small anteroom), "the former, in particular, exhibiting a style of head and set of features which might have afforded sufficient moral grounds for his instant execution at any time, even had there been no other evidence against him." Is it just the facetious tone here that gives the impression that Dickens knew not a great deal about Bishop? Certainly, he makes no attempt to add any background information, as he would surely have been tempted to if he had once had the good fortune to sit just yards from the killers and observe them in minute detail.

These arguments notwithstanding, it is possible to piece together a plausible explanation for what instinct urges: that the author of Fagin's trial scene had reported the trial of Bishop, Williams, and May. Firstly, there is no need to search for evidence that Dickens had any official connection with the *Times* or with any other publication, for that matter: it is perfectly conceivable that "The Most Deathlike Silence" paragraphs were the work of a "penny-a-line" freelancer syndicating his work to more than one newspaper. "The Most Deathlike Silence" appeared first in the *Times* of Saturday (morning), 3 December, and then made its way into the *Globe and Traveller* of Saturday evening, 3 December, then the *Sunday Times*, the *Observer*, and the *Weekly Dispatch*, all of Sunday the fourth, and it then filtered down to the broadsheet by Fairburn and another published by one J. Kiernan, called *The Execution of Bishop and Williams for the Horrid and Inhuman Murder of the Italian Boy*. Pierce Egan's own pamphlet, which went on sale on Tuesday, 6 December, also reproduced the passages; Egan's effort simply grafted onto a foreword and afterword some underworld slang ("flash") words—his literary party trick.

There is anecdotal evidence that as early as the age of fourteen,

Charles Dickens was attempting to sell penny-a-line journalism that he had produced on a speculative basis. Samuel Carter Hall, in his 1883 memoirs, *Retrospect of a Long Life*, recalls the boy calling at the office of the newspaper the *British Press*, where Hall worked alongside Dickens's father, John. Charles would drop off his own reports of news that, claimed Hall, had escaped the attention of the regular reporters of the *British Press*.

John Dickens had embarked on his journalistic career in the mid-1820s. He was working as a shorthand writer and reporter when the *British Press* ceased publication in the autumn of 1826; he subsequently appears to have joined the parliamentary staff of the *Morning Herald* and then the *Mirror of Parliament*, a rival to *Hansard* (the official published record of the proceedings in the Houses of Parliament), set up in 1828 by John Dickens's brother-in-law, John Henry Barrow, the man with the *Times* connections. Another maternal uncle, Edward Barrow, was a newspaper reporter and may also have offered a helping hand to the impecunious John Dickens. Charles Dickens, meanwhile, left school in 1827, aged fifteen, and worked as a lawyer's clerk for about two years and at seventeen or eighteen began work as a freelance shorthand reporter, renting an office at 5 Bell Yard, close by the court of Doctors Commons, where he obtained most but not all his work; he did not relinquish this office until April 1832. By some point in 1831, Charles was also working for the *Mirror of Parliament*, alongside his uncle and father. (I have followed W. J. Carlton's attempted chronology of Dickens's early career in *Charles Dickens: Shorthand Writer* [1926].)

Precise dates and employers (and knowledge of which stints of moonlighting overlapped with which bouts of more established, regular employment) are maddeningly hard to come by for Charles Dickens's very early career, and even W. J. Carlton found himself flummoxed when attempting a definitive chronology—a likely result of Dickens's own attempts to make murky his early years. Dickens rarely spoke or wrote about his pre-1834 career—1834 being the year in which he gained a full-time staff position (as parliamentary reporter) on a noteworthy publication (the *Morning Chronicle*), at a salary of five guineas a week. Presumably in reply to a specific inquiry from novelist and friend Wilkie Collins, Dickens wrote, on 6 June 1856, an uncharacteristically imprecise and unmistakably disdainful summary of his early working life: "I was put in the office of a solicitor, a friend of my father's, and didn't much like it; and after a couple of years (as well as I can remember) applied myself with a celestial or diabolical energy to the study of such things as would qualify me to be a first-rate parliamentary reporter. . . . I made my debut in the Gallery (at about 18, I suppose) engaged on a voluminous publication no longer in existence called *The Mirror of Parliament*. When the *Morning Chronicle* was purchased by Sir John Easthope and acquired a large circulation, I was

engaged there, and I remained there until I found myself in a condition
to relinquish that part of my labours. I left the reputation behind me of
being the best and most rapid reporter ever known, and could do anything in that way under any sort of circumstances, and often did"
(quoted in Carlton's *Charles Dickens: Shorthand Writer*).

"[He] was extremely sensitive as to the possibility of any rubbish
being given to the public in the form of 'early writings' . . ." wrote Dickens's sister-in-law Georgina Hogarth to H. G. Kitton, who was compil-
ing a memorial volume of tributes to Dickens, *Charles Dickens by Pen
and Pencil*. Hogarth recalled an incident when a female friend from
Dickens's late adolescence proudly presented the now famous novelist
with the manuscript of a play he had written in 1833. "He made a bargain with her," Hogarth told Kitton, "by making her a present of a
Christmas Book just completed, on condition that she gave up the boy-
ish production to him, which he had the satisfaction of putting into the
fire with his own hands." Dickens wrought a campaign of ruthless
destruction on his personal archive: for all the volumes of Dickens's
letters that have been found and published, an even greater number
were destroyed at his hands or by friends at his request. On 3 September 1860, he was observed building a bonfire in his garden and committing to the flames caches of letters and papers.

Furthermore, Dickens came to disapprove strongly of newspaper
accounts of murderers in the dock, execution scenes, last words, and
official confessions. It is difficult to date with precision this change of
heart, the point at which the author of such Grand Guignol passages
as the death of Bill Sikes, the murder of Nancy, and Fagin's last night
alive decided that criminals' final hours should not be committed to
print; but the conviction was certainly strongly felt by 1849. On 17
November of that year Dickens wrote to the *Times* to express his dis-
gust at public executions. (He had recently gone to Horsemonger Lane
Gaol, Newington, and reported on the dreadful public scenes at the
hanging of husband and wife Charles and Maria Manning, condemned to death for killing a former lodger.) "I would place every
obstacle in the way of his sayings and doings being served up in print
on Sunday mornings for the perusal of families," wrote Dickens of the
executed murderer. Seven years later he expanded on this theme—
claiming that the way in which the press reported the final days of
murderers made killers appear noteworthy, even admirable—in two
articles in his magazine, *Household Words*, "The Demeanour of Murderers" (published 14 June 1856) and "The Murdered Person" (published 11 October 1856).

A genuine change of heart, doubtless, but was it also informed by
the wish to shake off his past career? The epitome of the nineteenth-
century self-made man, Dickens was never generous in acknowledging

sources, influences, and helping hands. He wished to appear as though he had sprung from nowhere. Hence his slightly sniffy denials in response to queries about inspirations, role models, his early years. If he had indeed been part of the tribe of shabby, opportunistic penny-a-liners who made a living, and received useful introductions, at court-houses and inquests, he is very likely to have made every effort to suppress any reminders of that past. Unless a letter by, or addressed to, Dickens comes to light or a manuscript memoir from a contemporary of his early reporting years turns up, the authorship of "The Most Deathlike Silence" must remain, like so much else in this case, a mystery.

Chapter Twelve: A Newgate Stink

1. Reprinted in [Harmer?], *The History of the London Burkers* (1832).
2. "A Visit to Newgate," *Sketches by Boz* (1836).
3. *Facts Relating to the Punishment of Death in the Metropolis* by Edward Gibbon Wakefield (1831); [Harmer?], *Old Bailey Experience* (1833); *The Hangmen of England* by Horace Bleackley (1929). The condemned cells stood near to where the Old Bailey's current service road abuts Newgate Street.
4. Quoted in *The Life and Work of Astley Cooper* by R. C. Brock, p. 15.
5. Forty-eight-year-old Wontner had only one leg, after a fall from a horse in 1821; he would die in 1833 and his successor, William Cope, would prove incompetent.
6. *Report and Evidence of the Select Committee Appointed to Inquire into the Cause of the Increase in the Number of Commitments and Convictions in London and Middlesex* (1828), p. 307.
7. [Harmer?], *Old Bailey Experience*, p. 339.
8. Corporation of London Records Office, *Report Delivered to the Court of Aldermen by the City Gaols Committee, on the Conduct of the Reverend the Ordinary Cotton*, Key Rep 1831/32, p. 163.
9. If these sheets should ever come to light they would help fill the many vast gaps in what is known of the London resurrection community.
10. [Harmer?], *Old Bailey Experience*, p. 105. In extraordinary circumstances, a "writ of error" could overturn a verdict, but only by challenging a point of law. The author of *Old Bailey Experience* could recall only one instance in which a writ of error had overturned a death sentence.
11. Fontblanque, *England under Seven Administrations*, p. 161.
12. Extract from *Cotton's Book of Reports and Occurrences*, copied into the *Report Delivered to the Court of Aldermen by the City Goals Committee*, p. 163.

Chapter Fourteen: Day of Dissolution

1. This is where the *Morning Advertiser*'s reporter was stationed; he only knew the execution had happened by the reaction of the crowd.
2. Bean's evidence to the Court of Aldermen, 28 December 1831; Corporation of London Records Office, Key Rep 1831/32, p. 175.
3. Edward Pearson, porter to the Royal College of Surgeons, had bought refreshments for the twelve policemen on duty at Hosier Lane and along the route: four half-quartern loaves, 1s and 6d; one and a quarter pound of cheese, 11d; six pints of porter, 2s (manuscript diaries of William Clift, Royal College of Surgeons Library, 5 December 1831).
4. Calcraft (1800–79) had been in the job only two years. He was originally a cobbler.

Chapter Fifteen: The Use of the Dead to the Living

1. *Morning Advertiser*, 7 December 1831.
2. Guthrie's letter quoted by Jessie Dobson in her essay "The Anatomising of Criminals," *Annals of the Royal College of Surgeons of England* 9, no. 2 (August 1951): 112.
3. Letter forwarded to Tuson from the police, Public Record Office, Metropolitan Police Outgoing Correspondence, 3 December 1831–16 March 1832, MEPO 1/8/10163-12032.
4. *Times*, 29 December 1831. Superintendent Thomas had presented, or perhaps sold, Bishop's apprentice indentures to Egan too, which Egan claimed were signed "Thomas" Bishop; however, the killer had an elder brother called Thomas (born on 5 January 1794), and it is likely Superintendent Thomas had acquired the wrong document—or had perhaps been sold a fake memento. Needless to say, Superintendent Thomas had no right to sell these objects.

     Clift's drawing of Williams's tattoo is to be found in his diaries, housed in the library of the Royal College of Surgeons; entry dated 5 December.
5. *Lancet*, 14 January 1832.
6. Gall, quoted by Elliotson in *Lancet*, 14 January 1832, as part of the report of Elliotson's London Phrenological Society lecture on Bishop and Williams. Elliotson (1791–1868) was University College London's first professor of the principles and practice of medicine, in 1832. He became a personal friend of Charles Dickens, and the two men shared an interest in mesmerism, the field that Elliotson moved on to when he had tired of phrenology.
7. Repeated by John Wade in his *Treatise on the Police and Crimes of the Metropolis*, p. 204.

8. "Mask of decorum" is borrowed from Sir Walter Scott by John Wade in his *Treatise*, p. 149.
9. *Bell's Weekly Messenger*, 11 December 1831.
10. *Times*, 12 December 1831.
11. Advertisement for phrenological casts in *The Phrenological Record* by A. L. Vago (1883).
12. According to H. Lonsdale's *Sketch of the Life and Writings of Robert Knox* (1870), quoted in Ruth Richardson's *Death, Dissection and the Destitute*, p. 96.
13. Knight, *London*, vol. 1, p. 424; [Harmer?], *Old Bailey Experience*, p. 40.
14. *Globe and Traveller*, 5 December 1831.
15. *New Monthly Magazine*, June 1833.
16. *Figaro in London* ran from November 1831 until December 1834, and its first editor was Henry Mayhew, future compiler of the influential volumes *London Labour and the London Poor*. George Rowland Minshull found himself one of its targets when it reported his bad-tempered decision to jail a vagrant mother who refused to name her child's father, even though he had deserted her; *Figaro in London* stated that Minshull himself was probably the father. But the newspaper subsequently decided that it liked the magistrate when he released a boy who had been arrested for selling *Figaro* in Leicester Square— Minshull was seen chuckling in court over the newspaper's cartoons.
17. *Hansard Parliamentary Debates*, 27 February 1832, p. 836.
18. Pelham, Perceval, and Hunt were speaking on 17 January 1832 (*Hansard*, pp. 578–83).
19. Guthrie, *Letter to the Right Honourable the Secretary of State for the Home Department Containing Remarks on the Report of the Select Committee of the House of Commons on Anatomy* (1829).
20. *Hansard*, 6 February 1832, pp. 1276–78.
21. As Ruth Richardson points out in her meticulous account of the passage of the Anatomy Act: "At several crucial moments in the parliamentary progress of the [second Anatomy] Bill, when the opposition had argued persuasively, or when general discussion threatened to delay its passage, the Bill's supporters did not scruple to remind all present of the late 'enormities.' The reminder served as a way of curtailing debate by the introduction of a note of urgency, and decoyed parliamentary attention from important issues arising from the Bill" (*Death, Dissection and the Destitute*, p. 198).

Chapter Sixteen: How Many?

1. *Hansard*, 12 December 1831, pp. 154–55.
2. The earliest reports to escape Newgate also stated that Bishop and

Williams vigorously denied that pitch plasters were used in killing their victims—surely one of the least important aspects of the case, but one that was given prominence in the Sunday papers. Perhaps it was in response to the rash of alleged burking attacks across London, which, victims claimed, had involved pitch plasters being sealed across the mouth and nose for suffocation.

3. J. C. Reid's book *Bucks and Bruisers* (1971) and Serjeant Ballantine's *Some Experiences of a Barrister's Life* (1882) are the sources for the interesting connection between Cotton and Egan. Cotton was, according to Ballantine, fond of a joke, "well-fed," rubicund, and a keen book and curiosity collector. He is said to have invited Egan to a number of banquets at Newgate/Old Bailey.

4. If, as I suspect, *Old Bailey Experience* was written by James Harmer, then it would make sense for Cotton (Harmer's friend) to be so warmly defended and for an evangelical "interloper" such as Dr. Whitworth Russell to be criticized.

5. Sources for Theodore Williams's misdemeanors: *Report of the Evidence, with Bill of Costs, in a Suit Promoted in the Consistory Court by the Reverend Theodore Williams, Vicar of Hendon, against James Hall, a Resident of That Parish, for Brawling at a Vestry Meeting, Held for the Purpose of Making a Church Rate* (1838), a pamphlet in the British Library; *The Victoria History of the Counties of England: A History of the County of Middlesex*, vol. 5 (1976); and *The History and Topography of the Parish of Hendon, Middlesex* by Edward T. Evans (1890). Evans points out that Williams had a library of thousands of volumes at his vicarage in Parson Street and an unusual collection of potted conifers in the garden there. Williams died in 1875, aged ninety-one, and is buried in the graveyard of his church, St. Mary's, on Greyhound Hill, Hendon.

6. *Times*, 2 October 1839.

7. *Sun*, 5 December 1831 reprinted in *Times*, 6 December 1831.

8. *Globe and Traveller*, 5 December 1831. The authorship of this report becomes clear when we read Theodore Williams's reply to Bishop's inquiry about the thief on the cross: "Yes, but he had no knowledge of our blessed Redeemer till that moment, but you have from your earliest days been taught to know Christ and have rejected his precepts. Besides, yours cannot be called a true repentance, it is incomplete. Yours is more the fear of human punishment, in consequence of your offence having been discovered, than the repentance of a true Christian. The first step towards a true repentance is a full and open confession of your crimes. Still, I exhort you to pray with all the sincerity and fervour you are capable of. And as the mercy of God is unbounded, your prayers may obtain favour in his sight." In this way, not only would Theodore Williams save a soul, he would get the full confession to publish, too.

9. *Sun*, 12 December 1831.
10. Extracts from Cotton's journal relating to the events of 3–5 December 1831 copied into *Report Delivered to the Court of Aldermen by the City Gaols Committee*, p. 163.
11. *Times*, 24 December 1831.
12. *Report Delivered to the Court of Aldermen*, p. 163.
13. *Hansard*, 28 June 1832, p. 1086.
14. *Cobbett's Weekly Political Register*, 28 January 1832, pp. 258–59.
15. Letter dated 5 December 1831, in the Westminster Archives at the Westminster Reference Library, St. Paul's, Covent Garden, Parish Records Letter Book, H864.
16. *Globe and Traveller*, 3 December 1831.
17. Ibid., 15 December 1831.
18. Westminster Archives, St. Paul's, Covent Garden, Parish Records, Annual Accounts, 1829–54, H872.
19. *Morning Advertiser*, 22 December 1831.
20. Public Record Office, Home Office Domestic Letter Book, vol. 67, letter from the Home Office to Joseph Paragalli, 10 January 1832, HO 43/41.
21. Westminster Archives, Parish Records Letter Book, H865. In addition, "The sum of £2 was contributed by a lady, per Mr Minshull, towards these expenses whilst the proceedings were pending. . . . As the contribution was anonymous, no opportunity has been offered of thanking the donor" (H872).

Epilogue

1. Public Record Office, Hulk Returns, HO 8/31.
2. Appendix A of the *Fourth Annual Report of the Poor Law Commissioners for England and Wales* (1838), p. 106; evidence of Dr. Arnott.
3. Hackney Archives at the Hackney Local Studies Library, Admission and Discharge Registers of Shoreditch Workhouse, 1832–36, XP507; this is one of the few east London workhouses from which registers of inmates exist for the 1820s and early 1830s.
4. *Report of the Select Committee on Allegations Relative to the Conduct of Certain Magistrates in the Holborn Division of Middlesex in Granting Licences for Victual Houses*, 1833, p. 15.
5. *The Catalogue of Dr Kahn's Celebrated Anatomical Museum* is in the British Library. Kahn, a German showman, moved his museum several times in the middle of the century, and its venues included Regent Street, Oxford Street, and Coventry Street.
6. George Godwin, *Town Swamps and Social Bridges* (1859), p. 23; Hector Gavin, *Sanitary Ramblings, Being Sketches and Illustrations of Bethnal Green* (1848), pp. 9–10.

7. *Hackney Express and Shoreditch Observer*, 1 and 8 January 1898.

8. *Baroness Burdett-Coutts: A Sketch of Her Public Life and Work* by HRH Princess Mary Adelaide, duchess of Teck (1893).

9. "The Baroness Burdett-Coutts" by Mary Spencer-Warren, part of the *Illustrated Interviews* series in *Strand Magazine* 7 (1894): 248.

10. *Authentic Memoirs of the Lives of Mr and Mrs Coutts, Communicated by a Person of the First Respectability* (1819).

11. The complete twelve-volume bound set of *The Mysteries of London* is extremely rare. However, in 1996 an abridged, annotated copy, with an introduction containing biographical material on Reynolds and reproducing some of the original wood engravings, was published by Trefor Thomas (in the Keele University Press imprint).

12. Evidence given in the *Second Report from the Select Committee on Metropolis Improvements*, 1837–38, p. 82.

Bibliography

Papers and Publications

GOVERNMENT PAPERS
AT THE PUBLIC RECORD OFFICE, KEW

HO	8/31	Hulk Returns
HO	43/41	Home Office Letters
HO	59/2	Home Office Letters
HO	62/8	Daily Police Reports
HO	64/2	Petitions and Pardons
MEPO	1/8/10163–12032	Metropolitan Police Outgoing Correspondence
MEPO	1/44	Commissioners of Police Outgoing Correspondence
MEPO	1/49 and 1/50	Bow Street Magistrates Outgoing Correspondence
PCOM	1/23	Old Bailey Sessions Papers, First and Fourth Sessions, 1827
PCOM	1/28	Old Bailey Sessions Papers, First Session, 1831, and Second Session, 1832
PCOM	2/199	The Newgate List, 1826–28

LONDON METROPOLITAN ARCHIVES
OB/SR609/10   Old Bailey Sessions Roll
MJ/CC/V/003   Clerkenwell New Prison Committals Lists

CORPORATION OF LONDON RECORDS OFFICE
Key Rep 1831/32   *Report Delivered to the Court of Aldermen by the*
                     City Gaols Committee on the Conduct of the Rev-
                     erend the Ordinary Cotton

KING'S COLLEGE ARCHIVES
KA/C/M2   Minutes of King's College Council Meetings

ST. BARTHOLOMEW'S HOSPITAL ARCHIVES
MU3   *Histories of Specimens in the Museum*

ROYAL COLLEGE OF SURGEONS OF ENGLAND LIBRARY
Manuscript diaries of William Clift

GUILDHALL LIBRARY MANUSCRIPTS ROOM
MS   7498/30   St. Leonard's, Shoreditch, Marriage Registers

BRITISH MUSEUM MANUSCRIPTS
The Place Papers, BM Add Mss 27,789, Vol. 1, ff184–186.

SHROPSHIRE RECORDS AND RESEARCH CENTRE
P40/68 to P40/71   Registers of St. Leonard's Church, Bridgnorth,
                     1803–08

CITY OF WESTMINSTER ARCHIVES
H864 and H865   St. Paul's, Covent Garden, Parish Records, Let-
                     ter Books
H872   St. Paul's, Covent Garden, Parish Records,
                     Annual Accounts, 1829–54

HACKNEY ARCHIVES
XP507   Shoreditch workhouse admission and discharge
                     registers, 1832–36

Reports of Parliamentary Select Committees

Report from the Select Committee on the Existing Laws Relating to Vagrants, 1821
Report and Evidence of the Select Committee on Anatomy, 1828
Report and Evidence of the Select Committee into the State of the Police of the
  Metropolis and of the Districts Adjoining Thereto, 1828

Report and Evidence of the Select Committee Appointed to Inquire into the Cause of the Increase in the Number of Commitments and Convictions in London and Middlesex, 1828

Report of the Select Committee on That Part of the Poor Laws Relating to the Employment or Relief of Able-Bodied Persons from the Poor Rate, 1828

Report and Evidence of the Select Committee on the State of Smithfield Market, 1828

Report and Evidence of the Select Committee into the State of the Police of the Metropolis, 1833

Report from the Select Committee on Allegations Relative to the Conduct of Certain Magistrates in the Holborn Division of Middlesex in Granting Licences for Victual Houses, 1833

Report and Evidence of the Select Committee on Medical Education, 1834

Second Report from the Select Committee on Metropolis Improvements, 1837–38

Fourth Annual Report of the Poor Law Commissioners for England and Wales, 1838

Hansard Parliamentary Debates

Acts

5 Geo IV c 83 An Act for the Punishment of Idle and Disorderly Persons, and Rogues and Vagabonds, in That Part of Great Britain Called England, 1824

Newspapers and Journals

All the Year Round
Atlas
Bell's Weekly Messenger
City Press
Cobbett's Weekly Political Register
The Examiner
Figaro in London
Fraser's Magazine
Globe and Traveller
Hackney Express and Shoreditch Observer
Household Words
Hue and Cry (from 1828 *Police Gazette*)
Lancet
Morning Advertiser
Morning Chronicle
Morning Herald
Morning Post
New Monthly Magazine

Observer
Strand Magazine
Sun
Sunday Times
Times
Weekly Dispatch

Contemporary Books, Articles, and Pamphlets

Anonymous. *An Exposure of the Various Impostures Daily Practised by Vagrants of Every Description*. London, [1842?].

————. *Authentic Memoirs of the Lives of Mr and Mrs Coutts, Communicated by a Person of the First Respectability*. London, 1819.

————. *Cursory Remarks on the Evil Tendency of Unrestrained Cruelty, Particularly on That Practised at Smithfield Market*. London, 1823.

————. "Four Views of London." *New Monthly Magazine* (London), June 1833.

————. "Mr Adolphus and His Contemporaries." *Law Magazine* 4 (London), 1846.

————. "Old Stories Re-Told: Resurrection Men." *All the Year Round* (London), 16 March 1867.

————. *Report of the Evidence, with Bill of Costs in a Suit Promoted in the Consistory Court by the Reverend Theodore Williams, Vicar of Hendon, against James Hall, a Resident of That Parish, for Brawling at a Vestry Meeting, Held for the Purpose of Making a Church Rate*. London, 1838.

————. "The Schoolmaster's Experience of Newgate." *Fraser's Magazine*, June 1832.

————. *Smithfield and the Slaughterhouses*. London, 1847.

Ballantine, Serjeant William. *Some Experiences of a Barrister's Life*. London, 1882.

Brenton, Edward Pelham. *Letters to His Majesty, to Earl Grey, the Duke of Richmond, the Bishop of London, Lord Melbourne, Lord Kenyon and Capt the Hon George Elliot on Population, Agriculture, Poor Laws and Juvenile Vagrancy*. London, 1832.

Burking the Italian Boy! Fairburn's Edition of the Trial of Bishop and Williams. London, 1831.

Burn, Richard. *Justice of the Peace and Parish Officer*. 5 vols. 22nd ed. London, 1830.

Catalogue of Dr Kahn's Celebrated Anatomical Museum. London, 1871.

Catnach, James, publisher. *The Trial and Execution of the Burkers for Murdering a Poor Italian Boy*. London, 1831.

Chesterton, George Laval. *Revelations of Prison Life*. London, 1856.

Churchill, Henry Blencowe. *Arabiniana; or, The Remains of Mr Serjeant Arabin*. London, 1843.

Cooper, Bransby. *The Life of Sir Astley Cooper*. London, 1843.

De Quincey, Thomas. "The Nation of London" (1834) in *The Selected Writings of Thomas De Quincey*, ed. Philip Van Doren Stern. New York, 1939.

Dickens, Charles. "A Curious Dance round a Curious Tree." *Household Words*, 17 January 1852.

————. "The Demeanour of Murderers." *Household Words*, 14 June 1856.

————. "A Detective Police Party." *Household Words*, 27 July 1850.

————. *Great Expectations*. London, 1860–61.

————. "The Murdered Person." *Household Words*, 11 October 1856.

————. *Nicholas Nickleby*. London, 1838–39.

————. *Oliver Twist*. London, 1837–38.

————. *A Tale of Two Cities*. London, 1859.

————. "A Visit to Newgate." *Sketches by Boz*. London, 1836.

Diprose, John. *Some Account of the Parish of Saint Clement Danes Past and Present*. London, 1868.

Egan, Pierce. *Life in London*. London, 1821–28. Reissued as volume 2 of *Unknown London: Early Modernist Visions of the Metropolis, 1815–1845*, ed. John Marriott. 6 vols. London, 2000.

Evidence of the Reverend William Stone, Rector of Christ Church Spitalfields, and Others as to the Operation of Voluntary Charities. London, 1833.

Fontblanque, Albany. "The Diseased Appetite for Horrors." *Examiner*, 11 December 1831; reprinted in his *England under Seven Administrations*. London, 1837.

Gavin, Hector. *Sanitary Ramblings, Being Sketches and Illustrations of Bethnal Green*. London, 1848; reprinted Leicester, 1971.

Goddard, Henry. *Memoirs of a Bow Street Runner* (1856). London, 1956.

Godwin, George. *Town Swamps and Social Bridges*. London, 1859.

Grant, James. *The Great Metropolis*. London, 1837.

Grose, Francis. *Lexicon Balatronicum: A Dictionary of Buckish Slang, University Wit, and Pickpocket Eloquence*. London, 1823.

Guthrie, George. *A Letter to the Right Honourable the Secretary of State for the Home Department Containing Remarks on the Report of the Select Committee of the House of Commons on Anatomy*. London, 1829.

Hall, Samuel Carter. *Retrospect of a Long Life*. London, 1883.

[Harmer, James?]. *The History of the London Burkers*. London, 1832.

————. *Old Bailey Experience: Criminal Jurisprudence and the Actual Working of Our Penal Code of Laws*. London, 1833.

Hogg, John. *London as It Is*. London, 1837.

Hood, Thomas. "Mary's Ghost." *Hood's Whims and Oddities*. London, 1826.

Hunt, William H., ed. *The Registers of St Paul's Church, Covent Garden*. Volume 5: *Burials, 1752–1853*. London, 1909.

Kiernan, J., publisher. *The Execution of Bishop and Williams for the Horrid and Inhuman Murder of the Italian Boy*. London, 1831.

Knight, Charles. *London*. 6 vols. London, 1841.

MacFarlane, Charles. *Popular Customs, Sports and Recollections of the South of Italy*. London, 1846.

MacIlwain, George. *The Memoirs of John Abernethy*. London, 1853.

[Naples, Joshua?] *The Diary of a Resurrectionist,* ed. J. B. Bailey. London, 1896.

Poe, Edgar Allan. "The Man of the Crowd" (1840) in *Selected Tales,* ed. Julian Symons. Oxford, 1980.

Quaife, James. *The 1824 Hackney Coach Directory*. London.

Reports of the London Society for the Suppression of Mendicity, 1824, 1826, 1829, 1830, 1831.

Reynolds, G. W. M. *The Mysteries of London* (1844–56); selections edited by Trefor Thomas into single volume, *The Mysteries of London*, Keele, 1996.

Smeeton, George, publisher. *Doings in London*. London, 1828.

———. *The Strangers Guide; or, Frauds of London Detected*. London, 1808.

Smirke, Sydney. *Suggestions for the Architectural Improvement of the Western Part of London*. London, 1834.

Smith, J. T. *The Cries of London*. London, 1839.

———. *Etchings of Remarkable Beggars*. London, 1815.

———. *Vagabondiana*. London, 1817.

South, John Flint. *Memorials of the Craft of Surgery*. London, 1886.

Stow, John. *Survey of London*. London, 1603.

Vago, A. L. *The Phrenological Record*. London, 1883.

Vaux, James Hardy. *New and Comprehensive Vocabulary of the Flash Language*. London, 1819.

Vidocq, Eugène-François. *Mémoires*. Paris, 1828–29.

Wade, John. *A Treatise on the Police and Crimes of the Metropolis*. London, 1829.

———. *Extraordinary Black Book*. London, 1831.

Wakefield, Edward Gibbon. *Facts Relating to the Punishment of Death in the Metropolis*. London, 1831.

West, William. *Tavern Anecdotes*. London, 1825.

Secondary Sources

Ackroyd, Peter. *Dickens*. London, 1990.

Barron, Caroline M. *The Parish of St Andrew Holborn*. London, 1979.

Bickerdyke, John [Charles Henry Cook]. *The Curiosities of Ale and Beer*. London, 1886.

Bleackley, Horace. *The Hangmen of England*. London, 1929.

Brock, R. C. *The Life and Work of Astley Cooper*. London, 1952.

Carlton, William J. "The Barber of Dean Street." *Dickensian* 48, part 1, no. 301.

———. *Charles Dickens: Shorthand Writer*. London, 1926.

Cobb, Belton. *The First Detectives*. London, 1957.

Cole, Hubert. *Things for the Surgeon*. London, 1964.

Dexter, Walter, ed. *The Letters of Charles Dickens*. Nonesuch edition. London, 1938.

Dobson, Jessie. "The Anatomising of Criminals." *Annals of the Royal College of Surgeons of England 9,* no. 2 (August 1951).

Durey, M. J. "Bodysnatchers and Benthamites." *London Journal* 2, no. 2 (1976).

Edwards, Owen Dudley. *Burke & Hare*. Edinburgh, 1980.

Evans, Edward T. *The History and Topography of the Parish of Hendon, Middlesex*. London, 1890.

Fairholme, E., and Wellesley Pain. *A Century of Work for Animals*. London, 1924.

Fitzgerald, Percy. *Chronicles of a Bow Street Police Officer*. London, 1888.

Floud, Roderick. *Height, Health and History, 1750–1980*. Cambridge, 1990.

Forster, John. *The Life of Charles Dickens*. 3 vols. London, 1872.

Gordon-Taylor, Gordon. *Sir Charles Bell: His Life and Times*. London, 1958.

Hearnshaw, F. J. C. *The Centenary History of King's College London*. London, 1928.

Hewer, Richard L. *The Sack 'Em Up Men*. London, 1928.

Humble, J. G., and Peter Hansell. *Westminster Hospital, 1716–1966*. London, 1966.

Ignatieff, Michael. *A Just Measure of Pain: The Penitentiary in the Industrial Revolution, 1750–1850*. New York, 1978.

Inwood, Steven. "Policing London's Morals: The Metropolitan Police and Popular Culture, 1829–1850." *London Journal* 15, no. 2 (1990).

Kitton, H. G. *Charles Dickens by Pen and Pencil*. London, 1889.

Knox, Tim. "Joshua Brookes's Vivarium" in *London Gardener; or, The Gardener's Intelligencer* 3 (1997–98).

Lyle, H. Willoughby. *King's and Some King's Men*. London, 1935.

Lynam, Shevawn. *Humanity Dick*. London, 1975.

Menefee, S. P. *Wives for Sale*. Oxford, 1981.

Mitchell, L. G. *Lord Melbourne, 1779–1848*. Oxford, 1997.

Monson-Fitzjohn, G. J. *Quaint Signs of Olde Inns*. London, 1926.

Moss, A. W. *Valiant Crusade*. London, 1961.

Olmsted, J. M. D. *François Magendie*. New York, 1944.

Pain, Wellesley. *Richard Martin*. London, 1925.

Paley, Ruth. "An Imperfect, Inadequate and Wretched System? Policing London before Peel" in *Criminal Justice History* 10 (1989).

Partridge, Eric. *A Dictionary of Slang and Unconventional English*. London, 1937.

Plarr's Lives of the Fellows of the Royal College of Physicians of England. Bristol, 1930.

Rae, Isobel. *Knox: The Anatomist*. Edinburgh, 1964.

Reid, J. C. *Bucks and Bruisers*. London, 1971.

Reith, Charles. *British Police and the Democratic Ideal*. London, 1943.

Richardson, Ruth. *Death, Dissection and the Destitute*. London, 1988 (reissued 2001).

Robinson, Eric, ed. *John Clare's Autobiographical Writings*. Oxford, 1983.

Slater, Michael, ed. *Dickens' Journalism*. 4 vols. Dent Uniform Edition. London, 1996–2000.

Spencer-Warren, Mary. "The Baroness Burdett-Coutts." *Strand Magazine* 7 (1894).

Sponza, Lucio. *Italian Immigrants in 19th-Century Britain: Realities and Images*. Leicester, 1988.

Storey, Edward. *A Right to Song: The Life of John Clare*. London, 1982.

Taylor, James Stephen. *Poverty, Migration and Settlement in the Industrial Revolution*. London, 1989.

Teck, duchess of. *Baroness Burdett-Coutts: A Sketch of Her Public Life and Work*. London, 1893.

Thornbury, Walter, ed. *Old and New London*. 6 vols. London, 1879–85.

The Victoria History of the Counties of England: A History of the County of Middlesex, vol. 5 (1976); and vol. 11: *Early Stepney with Bethnal Green* (1998), both published Oxford.

Wilks, Samuel, and G. T. Bettany. *A Biographical History of Guy's Hospital*. London, 1892.

Wilkinson, George Theodore, ed. *The Newgate Calendar*. London, 1962.

Zucchi, John E. *The Little Slaves of the Harp*. Montreal, 1992.

Illustration Credits

Acknowledgments

This book would probably not have been written had I not enrolled on the Victorian Studies postgraduate degree course at London University's Birkbeck College in 1994. There, I had the immense good fortune to be taught by three inspirational tutors: Dr. David Feldman, of Birkbeck's History Department, Professor Michael Slater of the English Faculty, and Professor Clive Emsley, co-opted from the Open University to teach Birkbeck's Nineteenth-Century Crime course.

Ever the best of friends, Debbie Millett and Wanda Opalinska read an early draft of the book and gave me detailed feedback that was both wise and kind; they, along with Anne-Marie Collins, Prue Jeffreys, Liz Tames, Katie Matthews, and Helen Woolston, cheered me up whenever my spirits or energy flagged.

I am grateful to Phil Daoust and Caroline Roux, both of the *Guardian*, and to Dominic Lutyens, for giving me stimulating and enjoyable commissions that helped to keep my writing life from being exclusively devoted to early-nineteenth-century slum life.

The staffs of the following libraries and archives were never less than friendly and knowledgeable: the British Library at St. Pancras;

the British Library's Newspaper Library at Colindale; the Public Record Office at Kew; the library of the Wellcome Institute for the History of Medicine; the Guildhall Library; the Corporation of London Records Office; the London Metropolitan Archives; the City of Westminster Archives Centre; and the Shropshire Records and Research Centre in Shrewsbury.

My thanks also to Malcolm Barr-Hamilton, David Rich, and Chris Lloyd at the Tower Hamlets Local History Library and Archives; Mark Annand, author of the Greenwood's Map Web site, hosted by Bath Spa University College; the staff of the Hackney Archives; Jeff Gerhardt of the Haringey Museum and Archive Service; and Hugh Petrie, Heritage Officer at Barnet Archives. Marion Rea at St. Bartholomew's Hospital allowed me to riffle through that institution's archives, while Tina Craig of the Royal College of Surgeons Library allowed me to consult items in the college's manuscript collection, and Chris Reed of the RSPCA supplied me with suggestions for further reading on the life of animal-cruelty campaigner Richard Martin. Duncan Broady of the Greater Manchester Police Museum helped me track the later life of Joseph Sadler Thomas, while Ray Seal and Steve Earle at the Metropolitan Police Museum and Roger Appleby of the City Police Museum allowed me access to documents and exhibits, which, sadly, remain inaccessible to the general public. John Ross, curator of Scotland Yard's Black Museum, allowed me to visit his gruesome archive in the hope that I would find Bishop and Williams on his shelves of nameless, dateless phrenological casts of criminals; they weren't there, but the visit was unforgettable nevertheless.

Many thanks to my wonderful editor at Metropolitan Books, Sara Bershtel; to her assistant, Shara Kay; and to my copy editor, Roslyn Schloss.

Last but foremost, Peter Neish has read—and proofread—various early versions of this story and put up with hours of talk about long-dead strangers; our life together has been peopled by a cast of pretty unpleasant characters for longer than I care to remember. For this and for much more, many thanks.

Index

About the Author

SARAH WISE is a historian of Victorian England, with a special focus on poverty and class, criminal justice, urban architecture, and the city in literature. Also a journalist, she has written for *The Guardian, The Observer,* and *The Independent on Sunday,* as well as *Marie Claire* and other magazines. *The Italian Boy* is her first book. She lives in London.